FEAR OF A QUEER PLANET

CULTURAL ⚓ POLITICS

A series from the Social Text Collective

Aimed at a broad interdisciplinary audience, these volumes seek to intervene in debates about the political direction of current theory and practice by combining contemporary analysis with a more traditional sense of historical and socioeconomic evaluation.

Cultural Politics, Volume 6

FEAR

OF A

QUEER

PLANET

Queer Politics and Social Theory

MICHAEL WARNER, EDITOR

(for the Social Text Collective)

University of Minnesota Press
Minneapolis
London

Chapter 1, Jonathan Goldberg, "Sodomy in the New World: Anthropologies Old and New," adapted by the author from *Sodometries* by Jonathan Goldberg, with the permission of the publishers, Stanford University Press; copyright 1992 by the Board of Trustees of the Leland Stanford Junior University.

Chapter 3, Diana Fuss, "Freud's Fallen Women: Identification, Desire, and 'A Case of Homosexuality in a Woman,'" used with permission of *The Yale Journal of Criticism* 6.1, Spring 1993.

Chapter 8, Cathy Griggers, "Lesbian Bodies in the Age of (Post)mechanical Reproduction," from Laura Doan (editor), *The Lesbian Postmodern,* copyright 1994 (forthcoming) by Columbia University Press, New York; reprinted with the permission of the publisher.

Chapter 10, "The Black Man's Burden," copyright 1993 by Henry Louis Gates, Jr.

Chapter 11, Phillip Brian Harper, "Eloquence and Epitaph: Black Nationalism and the Homophobic Impulse in Responses to the Death of Max Robinson," from Suzanne Poirier and Timothy Murphy (editors), *Writing AIDS,* copyright 1993 by Columbia University Press, New York; reprinted with the permission of the publisher.

Published by the University of Minnesota Press
111 Third Avenue South, Suite 290, Minneapolis MN 55401-2520
Printed in the United States of America on acid-free paper
Second Printing, 1995

Library of Congress Cataloging-in-Publication Data

Fear of a queer planet : queer politics and social theory / Michael
    Warner, editor, for the Social Text Collective.
      p. cm. — (Cultural politics ; v. 6)
    Includes bibliographical references and index.
    ISBN 0-8166-2333-3 (alk. paper). — ISBN 0-8166-2334-1 (pbk. : alk. paper)
    1. Homosexuality—Political aspects—United States.
    2. Homosexuality—United States—Philosophy. 3. Gays—United
    States—Political activity. I. Warner, Michael, 1958–
    II. Social Text Collective. III. Series: Cultural politics
    (Minneapolis, Minn.) ; v. 6.
    HQ76.3.U5F43   1994
    306.76'6—dc20   93-28703

Contents

Introduction
Michael Warner

What do queers want? This volume takes for granted that the answer is not just sex. Sexual desires themselves can imply other wants, ideals, and conditions. And queers live as queers, as lesbians, as gays, as homosexuals, in contexts other than sex. In different ways queer politics might therefore have implications for any area of social life. Following Marx's definition of critical theory as "the self-clarification of the struggles and wishes of the age," we might think of queer theory as the project of elaborating, in ways that cannot be predicted in advance, this question: What do queers want?

For the most part, left traditions of social and political theory have been unwilling to ask the question. They have posited and naturalized a heterosexual society. For left social theorists this book suggests how queer experience and politics might be taken as starting points rather than as footnotes. At the same time, this book urges lesbian and gay intellectuals to find a new engagement with various traditions of social theory. These twin purposes can to some extent be found in each essay, though the volume is divided into two parts. The first, "Get Over It: Heterotheory," takes issue with traditions of theory, especially anthropology, Marxism, psychoanalysis, psychology, and legal theory. The second, "Get Used to It: The New Queer Politics," describes current issues in queer culture: shifting styles of identity politics; intersections of nationality, race, and gender; conflicts over the state and the media; and the building of new cultures.

It might seem reductive to suggest that social theory has always

ignored such issues. Many of the leading figures of social thought
for the past century have in varying degrees thought about sexuality as a field of power, as a historical mode of personality, and as
the carrier of utopian imagination. Some major branches of social
theory have made the connection between sexuality and politics an
important or even paradigmatic concern: French social thought from
Bataille to Deleuze; radical psychoanalysis, elaborated from Freud
by Reich and others; the Frankfurt School, especially the strand that
resulted in Marcuse's *Eros and Civilization;* comparative anthropological theory beginning with Malinowski's *Sex and Repression in
Savage Society;* even the critical liberalism of Bentham (or Sade).
Liberationist sexual movements from as early as Whitman, Carpen-
ter, and Wilde involved reflections on democracy and socialism; and
radical gay social theory revived after 1969 in France, England, and
Italy, in the work of Guy Hocquenghem, Jeffrey Weeks, the Gay
Left Collective, Mario Mieli, and others. To these traditions Foucault
brought such a reinvigorating transformation that his *History of Sexuality* has become an inescapable text for intellectuals otherwise
oblivious to its subject. Meanwhile feminism has made gender a
primary category of the social in a way that makes queer social theory newly imaginable. And in recent years feminists have returned
powerfully to the topics of sexuality and lesbian/gay politics in the
work of Gayle Rubin, Adrienne Rich, Eve Kosofsky Sedgwick, Judith Butler, Iris Marion Young, and many others. These writers have
argued that a nonoppressive gender order can only come about
through a radical change in sexuality, even while they have also
begun to argue that sexuality is a partially separate field of inquiry
and activism.[1]

    With such an illustrious history, with a literature so massive
that it can be sketched this broadly, it might seem that queer left
social/sexual theory stands at a convergence point for many of the
most important intellectual movements of our time. What could be
needed to create this convergence when so many paths of modern
thought already lead there?

    Yet it remains depressingly easy to speak of "social theory" and
have in mind whole debates and paraprofessional networks in
which sexuality figures only peripherally or not at all — to say
nothing of manifestly homophobic work.[2] Often the omission paradoxically seems to result from the desire for a general picture of

what is called social reproduction; thus Jürgen Habermas, Anthony Giddens, and others have been able to write ambitiously comprehensive works (with titles like *The Constitution of Society*) in which sexuality plays no role.[3] In most such cases the politics of marginal sexualities seems not so much neglected as blocked from view. In other writers, especially those such as Niklas Luhmann who share a structural or system-theoretical bent, sexuality features more importantly but only as a rather unqueer institution — not only heterosexual but normalized and functional.[4]

Perhaps more surprising is the absence of a more than fleeting consideration of sexuality in Laclau and Mouffe, in Bourdieu, or in the current theory of post-Fordism. Marcuse has fallen from view, while Foucault's history increasingly tends to be summarized as a treatise on power or on an abstraction called "the body."[5] Lacanian-Althusserian cultural studies, trying to bring politics and sexuality onto comparable conceptual levels, has relied on categories that make the two equivalent ("phallus") or evacuated into structural effects ("subjectivity").[6] Social theory as a quasi-institution for the past century has returned continually to the question of sexuality, but almost without recognizing why it has done so, and with an endless capacity to marginalize queer sexuality in its descriptions of the social world.

Even the literature on the so-called new social movements, where theorists might have been expected to take lesbian and gay politics as a model, continues to treat it as an afterthought, and then often with significant homophobia. Alberto Melucci, for example, refers to the gay movement only twice in a book designed to argue that new forms of democratic social movements are transforming the political landscape. The first instance is in a section called "Reproduction as a Choice." As a heading for sexual politics, this title already inclines toward hetero and voluntarist assumptions, assimilating sexuality to the subject of reproduction and treating dissident sexuality only as a parallel choice: "In addition to the model of the heterosexual and monogamous couple, who are the foundation of the family institution and guarantee of the continuity of the reproductive process, new choices become possible. These parallel models, which are capable of coexisting with the heterosexual model and even of becoming institutionalized, include homosexuality, singles, and a range of mobile and temporary couples living outside a stable matrimonial friendship."[7] Melucci's commitments to "the family in-stitution" and reproductive continuity run so deep that he doesn't seem to have imagined that lesbians and gays might be critical of them. Thus he imagines "homosexuality" only as an additional choice, one that entails no challenge to the heterosexual order and seems to have nothing to do with power. Even this gesture turns out to be too generous for Melucci, who a few pages later takes it back by remarking that gay culture, "depriving sex of its erotic content, reduces it to a gymnastics of orgasm. . . . [I]t hastened the reduction of sex to the genital level and revealed the poverty of an exclusively male sexuality without eros."[8] This is the kind of stuff that often passes as left social theory of gay politics; that it can do so indicates how little people like Melucci imagine participating in exchange with lesbian or gay intellectuals.

At the same time it remains possible to speak of "gay studies" and have in mind a booming field dominated by literary criticism, film criticism, and cultural history. But despite powerful work on AIDS and in feminist social theory, the energies of queer studies have come more from rethinking the subjective meaning of sexu-ality than from rethinking the social.[9] The major theoretical debate over constructionism seems exhausted. Partly because that debate resulted in a more historicized and localized view of gay interests, and partly because the disciplines of literature and film studies have afforded a relatively free space for lesbian and gay critics, there has been a turn in gay studies toward the production of impressive new readings of particular cultural texts, usually with a psychoanalytic emphasis.[10] The effect of this new "queer theory" wave has been to show in ever more telling detail how pervasive the issues of lesbian and gay struggles have been in modern culture, and how various they have been over time. But the success of that work now makes some other kinds of thinking necessary.

The essays in this volume suggest that the new wave of lesbian and gay studies is at the point of having to force a thorough revi-sion within social-theoretical traditions, of the kind being won by feminism. There are a number of distinct reasons why that engage-ment has become necessary: (1) from the most everyday and vulgar moments of gay politics to its most developed theoretical language, the sexual order blends with a wide range of institutions and so-cial ideology, so that to challenge the sexual order is sooner or later to encounter those other institutions as problems; (2) many of the specific environments in which lesbian and gay politics arises have not been adequately theorized and continue to act as unrecognized constraints; (3) concepts and themes of social theory that might be pressed to this purpose are in fact useless or worse because they embed a heteronormative understanding of society; and (4) in many areas a new style of politics has been pioneered by lesbians and gays, little understood outside of queer circles. Let me briefly clarify each of these.

Sexual Politics and the Social Order

There are many people, gay and straight, who think that sexual orientation is a fairly clear and simple political matter, that discrimination should be eliminated but that gay people have no further political interest as a group. Those who hold this view have certain obvious political facts to rely on, not least of which is that gay men and lesbians can be found on both sides of any political issue. The argument can be made in an old-fashioned conservative-libertarian way (sex is a private matter that should be left to choice and kept out of public politics altogether), or with a postmodern, post-identitarian emphasis (liberationist agendas have required utopian metanarratives that obscure differences among gays and lesbians, who might in fact have nothing in common). Either way, it can be shown that broad visions of social change do not follow from sexuality in any way that seems obvious and necessary to all those affected by sexual politics.

And why should they? If social vision were dictated in such an inevitable way, it wouldn't be politics. But there remains a question whether or in what context queers have political interests, *as queers,* that connect them to broader demands for justice and freedom.

Theories of sexuality to date have tended to verge in two directions — psychoanalytic and historicist — neither of which has fully answered this question. Because the most rigorous and sophisticated language about sexuality is that of psychoanalysis, queer critics from the heady days of gay liberation onward have developed varieties of psychoanalytic radicalism. They have traced the demands of lesbian and gay liberation to fundamental psychic structures: the preoedipal, innate bisexuality, the exchange of women, reverse oedipalization, the instability of identification.[11] For all their strengths, none of these arguments has proven to be very subtle in recognizing historical or cultural differences.

Theories oriented to differences do, however, abound. The 1980s saw a massive literature of social constructionism, designed to localize all concepts of sexuality, sexual identity, and political interests relating to sex.[12] This literature raises skepticism about rights discourse and other forms of universalism in gay politics. Some extreme versions would seem to recognize gay politics only in cultures with a functioning sexological lexicon. But constructionist accounts have not replaced the universalizing discourse of identity and rights with new theories of political interest and sexual identity. Many of the insights of social constructionism have simply been ignored in political contexts — even by politically active constructionist scholars themselves.

The tension between globalizing and localizing arguments is different from the universalizing/minoritizing tension analyzed by Eve Sedgwick;[13] there are globalizing arguments about minority interests, just as there are localizing arguments about quasi-universal interests (i.e., everyone in the context of modern sexual discourse, gay or straight, is equally affected by its oppressiveness). But the problem seems just as irreducible. In the middle ground between the localism of "discourse" and the generality of "the subject" is the problem of international — or otherwise translocal — sexual politics. As gay activists from non-Western contexts become more and more involved in setting political agendas, and as the rights discourse of internationalism is extended to more and more cultural contexts, Anglo-American queer theorists will have to be more alert to the globalizing — and localizing — tendencies of our theoretical languages.[14]

Nowhere has the need for transnational comparative thinking been clearer than on the subject of AIDS. AIDS activists have had to insist over and over on the cultural construction of the discourses about AIDS, including those of science, and on the global dimensions of the problems posed by AIDS. These twin emphases have led theorists to think comparatively about political environments of sexuality, some local and others translocal.[15]

The essays in this volume suggest that political struggles over sexuality ramify in an unimaginably large number of directions. In the everyday political terrain, contests over sexuality and its regulation are generally linked to views of social institutions and norms of the most basic sort. Every person who comes to a queer self-understanding knows in one way or another that her stigmatization is connected with gender, the family, notions of individual freedom, the state, public speech, consumption and desire, nature and culture, maturation, reproductive politics, racial and national fantasy, class identity, truth and trust, censorship, intimate life and social display, terror and violence, health care, and deep cultural norms about the bearing of the body. Being queer means fighting about these issues all the time, locally and piecemeal but always with consequences. It means being able, more or less articulately, to challenge the common understanding of what gender difference means, or what the state is for, or what "health" entails, or what would define fairness, or what a good relation to the planet's environment would be. Queers do a kind of practical social reflection just in finding ways of being queer.[16] (Alternatively many people invest the better parts of their lives to avoid such a self-understanding and the social reflection it would imply.)

Social reflection carried out in such a manner tends to be reactive, fragmentary, and defensive, and leaves us perpetually at a disadvantage. And it is easy to be misled by the utopian claims advanced in support of particular tactics.[17] But the range and seriousness of the problems that are continually raised by queer practice indicate how much work remains to be done. Because the logic of the sexual order is so deeply embedded by now in an indescribably wide range of social institutions, and is embedded in the most standard accounts of the world, queer struggles aim not just at toleration or equal status but at challenging those institutions and accounts. The dawning realization that themes of homophobia and heterosexism may be read in almost any document of our culture means that we are only beginning to have an idea of how widespread those institutions and accounts are.

Large-scale social questions tend to be backgrounded in all local struggles, and bringing them into view can often transform those struggles. As Cindy Patton has shown in *Inventing AIDS*, for example, the local requirements of AIDS organizing have newly brought into focus problems of welfare-state–client relations, health-care professionalism, relations between the first and third worlds, civil-society structures of voluntary association, the privatized production of health services and goods, and disparities of position between gays and other affected populations or between lesbians and gay men.[18] The more lesbians and gay men elaborate our positions in this political environment, the more we are called upon to consider our resistance to normalized sexuality in terms that are not always initially evident as sex-specific. Care of the elderly, to take yet another example, does not initially seem to be an issue of sexuality. But a society that relegates care systematically to offspring and spouses leaves elderly lesbians and gays with a disproportionately high likelihood of neglect.

Two arguments by Eve Kosofsky Sedgwick, in *Between Men* (1985) and *Epistemology of the Closet* (1990), more forcefully suggest the necessity for such reconceptualizations, where gay politics would be the starting point rather than the exception, and where it would not be limited to manifestly sex-specific problems. One of Sedgwick's best-known theses is that "homosocial" forms of domination are constituted in part by the repudiation of erotic bonds among men. According to Sedgwick, the ability to project those erotic bonds onto a marginal figure — the stigmatized body of the homosexual — has been crucial to the creation of modern homosociality, which in turn has inflected class identity and male domination. A more recent addition to this view is her argument that the strategic separation of mutually implied knowledges — secret knowledge, superior insight, disavowal, science, coded knowledge, open secrets, amnesia, the unsayable — is a medium of domination not reducible to other forms of domination, and one that finds its paradigmatic case in the homosexual and the closet.

In effect, Sedgwick's work has shown that there are specifically modern forms of association and of power that can be seen properly only from the vantage of antihomophobic inquiry. Both arguments therefore point the way toward significant social-theoretical problems. In the face of such questions, queer theory is opening up in the way that feminism did when feminists began treating gender more and more as a primary category for understanding problems that did not initially look gender-specific. The prospect is that queer theory may require the same kinds of revision on the part of social-theoretical discourse that feminism did, though we do not know yet what it would be like to make sexuality a primary category for social analysis — if indeed "sexuality" is an adequate grounding concept for queer theory. As more work develops on these lines, it will become more and more plausible to assert, as Sedgwick does in the first paragraph of *Epistemology,* that "an understanding of virtually any aspect of modern Western culture must be, not merely incomplete, but damaged in its central substance to the degree that it does not incorporate a critical analysis of modern homo/heterosexual definition."[19]

All five of the essays in the first part of this volume show that contested issues of sexuality involve problems not captured by the languages designed to name them. Jonathan Goldberg, for example, shows that an apparent conflict between sexual identities in the early colonial period cannot be understood as the difference between heterosexual Europeans and Indian sodomites — as has been thought both in colonial accounts and in contemporary anthropology. He shows that the interpretation of sexuality was itself part of the conflict, and was overdetermined by other conflicts, including conflicts of class and gender among Europeans and among Indians.

Indeed, all of the essays in this section show that attempts to fix or name sexual identities tend to be overdetermined by other conflicts. Thus Freud's anxieties about women, according to Diana Fuss, systematically distort his view of sexuality between women; so do his anxieties about class and about the professional status of psychoanalysis. His language remains incapable of capturing the social or contested dimensions of sexuality, as he responds to these problems by exaggerating an etiological account that traces sexuality to ever earlier moments, approximating as closely as possible a fantasy source in biological reproduction from (and to) which lesbian sexuality can be interpreted as a fall. For Andrew Parker, Marx's and Engels's keen interest in sexual inversion has to do not only with their relation to each other but also with unacknowledged problems in their thinking about the political sources of identity. And Janet Halley shows that modern legal theory and practice not only remain trapped in homophobia, but even at their most gay-affirmative moments struggle with the limits of liberal languages about identity and practice.

In each case, the authors do not simply call for the inclusion of lesbians and gays into a theory that would remain otherwise unaltered. They suggest, indeed, that the theoretical languages in question can specify sexual identities only in ways that produce the ideology of heterosexual society. Even when coupled with a toleration of minority sexualities, heteronormativity can be overcome only by actively imagining a necessarily and desirably queer world. As Sedgwick shows in her contribution to this volume, any imagination of desirable queerness is conspicuously absent in the psychoanalytic and psychiatric literature about child-rearing, which has allowed itself to imagine only tolerating adult gays (lesbians rarely figure there). The idea that the emergence of more queers might be a desirable outcome remains unthinkable. Heterosexual ideology, in combination with a potent ideology about gender and identity in maturation, therefore bears down in the heaviest and often deadliest way on those with the least resources to combat it: queer children and teens. In a culture dominated by talk of "family values," the outlook is grim for any hope that child-rearing institutions of home and state can become less oppressive.

The Social Environment of Queer Politics

Theoretical writing has come to recognize more and more what activists have been learning for years — that queer politics brings very differently sexualized and differently politicized people into a movement that, despite its heterogeneity, must address broad questions and common identifications. Much depends on how the common ground is defined, and in recent years an important multicultural critique has shown, as Steven Seidman makes clear in this volume, that too often the common ground has been assumed to be that of relatively dominant positions: whites, males, and middle-class activists of the United States. In order to continue this self-clarification of the movement, queer social theory must also reflect on the conditions that make the current practices of queer politics possible.

The predominance of white, middle-class men in gay organizing, after all, is not simply the result of evil intent, personal discrimination, or willed exclusion. In the lesbian and gay movement, to a much greater degree than in any comparable movement, the institutions of culture-building have been market-mediated: bars, discos,

special services, newspapers, magazines, phone lines, resorts, urban commercial districts. Nonmarket forms of association that have
been central to other movements — churches, kinship, traditional
residence — have been less available for queers. This structural environment has meant that the institutions of queer culture have been
dominated by those with capital: typically, middle-class white men.
Alliance politics have only begun to correct for that structural dis-
tortion in queer politics. But such conditions mean that strategic
requirements may differ even where people act in the best faith.

What we may be less prepared to recognize is that the frame of
identity politics itself belongs to Anglo-American traditions and has
some distorting influences. It seems impossible in this context to
raise the possibility of sexual conflict or diversity except by appealing for the homosexual minority and by making comparisons to
other minority movements. In the United States, the default model
for all minority movements is racial or ethnic. Thus the language
of multiculturalism almost always presupposes an ethnic organization of identity, rooted in family, language, and cultural tradition.
Despite its language of postmodernism, multiculturalism tends to
rely on very modern notions of authenticity, of culture as shared
meaning and the source of identity.[20]

Queer culture will not fit this bill. Whatever else it might be, it
is not autochthonous. It cannot even be in diaspora, having no
locale from which to wander. Thus, while notions of alternative
traditions or canons have been very useful for African-American
and feminist scholars, because queer politics does not obey the
member/nonmember logics of race and gender, alternative canons
and traditions cannot always be opposed to the dominant ones in
the same way.[21] Indeed, the emphasis on reproductive continuity
in such models can produce an extreme homophobia, and the tension resulting from such unrecognized disparities can make alliance
politics difficult.

People tend not to encounter queerness in the same way as ethnic
identity. Often the disparity between racial and sexual imperatives
can be registered as an unresolved dissonance. One correspondent
writes me on this point: "As a gay man of color I find certain aspects
of my identity empowered and fortified within the space of the ethnic family while other aspects of my identity are negated in that very
same space. I fall in between what seems to me a split between the

racially marked family and the white queer."[22] Familial language deployed to describe sociability in race- or gender-based movements (sisterhood, brotherhood, fatherland, mother tongue, etc.) can either be a language of exile for queers or a resource of irony (in voguing houses, for example, one queen acts as "Mother"). Given such realities, theory has to understand that different identity environments are neither parallel — so that the tactics and values of one might be assumed to be appropriate for another — nor separable. Queer struggles and those of other identity movements, or alternatively of other new social movements, often differ in important ways — even when they are intermingled in experience.

There are many unavoidable structural relations between the different fields of identity politics, if only because of the intrication of genetic and erotic logics in both race and gender. Is race, is gender, a mode of desire or of reproduction? Reproduction usually implies eros; but when identity is apprehended as desire, as in same-sex or cross-race relations, its reproductive telos disappears. This very incommensurability between genetic and erotic logics suggests that queerness, race, and gender can never be brought into parallel alignment. Sedgwick has gone so far as to suggest that

> a damaging bias toward heterosocial or heterosexist assumptions
> inheres unavoidably in the very concept of gender....Although
> many gender-based forms of analysis do involve accounts, sometimes
> fairly rich ones, of intragender behaviors and relations, the ultimate
> definitional appeal in any gender-based analysis must necessarily
> be to the diacritical frontier between different genders. This gives
> heterosocial and heterosexual relations a conceptual privilege of
> incalculable consequence.[23]

This sort of speculation about queer problematics, their irreducibility to and/or definitional conflict with other problematics, is still only emergent. Much remains to be said about the unique relation of queer politics to histories of all sorts. Unlike other identity movements, for example, queerness has always been defined centrally by discourses of morality. There have always been moral prescriptions about how to be a woman or a worker or an Anglo-Saxon; but not about whether to be one. Queerness therefore bears a different relation to liberal logics of choice and will, as well as to moral languages of leadership and community, in ways that continually pose problems both in everyday life and in contexts of civil rights. A particularly striking example can be found in Phillip Brian Harper's essay, which interprets the death of Max Robinson as a cultural event condensing strains among white mass-mediated nationalism, African-American identity, gay men, and the discourse of AIDS.

The language of multiculturalism and alliance politics has encouraged us to recognize such strains and differences, as in the slogan "race, class, and gender." The slogan, however, often implies not alliance or intersection — much less structural relations of incommensurability — but rather a fantasized space where all embodied identities could be visibly represented as parallel forms of identity. This ethnicizing political desire has exerted a formative influence on Anglo-American cultural studies in the form of an expressivist pluralism that might be called Rainbow Theory. It aspires to a representational politics of inclusion and a drama of authentic embodiment. There are many worse things in the world than Rainbow Theory, but its standard of expressivist pluralism results in several dangers, especially a reification of identity. Already people speak as though "difference" were in itself a term of value. (It isn't.) They also speak of inclusion as though it were synonymous with equality and freedom. Exclusion plays exactly the same role for expressive pluralism that discrimination played for high liberalism; it reduces power to a formalism of membership. Marginal styles of embodiment, even while they appear more in a public arena, therefore continue to do so in hyper-allegorized form: that is, as representing "race" or "gender" or "sexuality," now interpreted as signs of inclusion and authenticity.

A popular button sold in gay bookstores says, "Racism, Sexism, Homophobia: Grasp the Connections." Whatever the connections might be locally, they are not necessary or definitive for any of these antagonisms. Any one can do without the others and might have more connection with political conflicts less organized by identity. "Race, class, and gender" stand for different and overlapping ways of organizing people in response to different kinds of power. As styles of politics they have to be disarticulated from the national-representational space often fantasized in the very act of listing them. Historically we might say that queer sexuality is like gender or race in being a political form of embodiment that is defined as noise or interference in the disembodying frame of citizenship.[24] This is to point to the common ground of "identity politics," itself insufficiently theorized as yet, and to the close relation between identity politics and a national imagination. Within this liberal-national frame of citizenship there is an important common ground to be grasped among identity movements. But it will be necessary to break this frame if we are to see the potential alliances with movements that do not thematize identity in the same way.

Several of the essays in the second half of this volume show that national frames of reference have been an unrecognized constraint on sexual politics. Lauren Berlant and Elizabeth Freeman describe the tactics and aims of Queer Nation and the new queer activism as in part a response to alienating conditions of citizenship and national membership. Queer activism, in their account, tries to reimagine public space of all kinds. Robert Schwartzwald argues that a homoerotic imaginary plays a very different role in Québécois nationalism than in the United States — much to the consternation of some francophone theorists of Québécois identity. Henry Louis Gates similarly picks up on the theme of nationalism, arguing that "national identity became sexualized in the sixties, in such a way as to engender a curious subterraneous connection between homophobia and nationalism." Like Harper, Gates has in mind black nationalism in particular, and thus he regards a black gay tradition — represented here by Isaac Julien — as both radicalizing and transcending identity politics.

The tension between queerness and the ethnic assumptions of multiculturalism may be one reason why so many queer theorists have protested against the very notion of identity. In her essay here, for example, Cathy Griggers associates current lesbian practice with postmodern mass-media contexts, showing that lesbian identity has been mediated by conceptions of the body and sexuality that have made liberal languages of identity archaic. All of the essays in the second part of this volume speak, at some level, to the issue of identity politics. Steven Seidman narrates the shifts from post-Stonewall identitarianism to current queer multiculturalism. Cindy Patton argues that the common frame of identity politics mutually defines queers and their new-right opponents. And Douglas Crimp shows how various transformations in gay politics — from shifting conditions of AIDS activism to the more aggressive style of queer protest — have put new pressure on political identity and cross-identifications. These essays, taken together, point the way toward new comparative thinking about the social environment of queer politics.

Heteronormativity in Social Theory

The essays in this volume go beyond calling for tolerance of lesbians and gays. They assert the necessarily and desirably queer nature of the world. This extra step has become necessary, if only because so much privilege lies in heterosexual culture's exclusive ability to interpret itself as society. Het culture thinks of itself as the elemental form of human association, as the very model of inter-gender relations, as the indivisible basis of all community, and as the means of reproduction without which society wouldn't exist. Materialist thinking about society has in many cases reinforced these tendencies, inherent in heterosexual ideology, toward a totalized view of the social. I think this is what Monique Wittig has in mind when she writes that the social contract is heterosexuality: "[T]o live in society is to live in heterosexuality. . . . Heterosexuality is always already there within all mental categories. It has sneaked into dialectical thought (or thought of differences) as its main category."[25] Wittig notes that Aristotle grounds *The Politics* in the necessity of male-female union (42), and it is certainly true that Western political thought has taken the heterosexual couple to represent the principle of social union itself. In social thought this principle is typically mediated through such concepts as dependence and reproduction, and is thus naturalized in otherwise sophisticated work.

The core idea remains the same as the (literally) cartoon image of human society devised by Carl Sagan (and drawn, appropriately enough, by his wife, Linda) for use on NASA's *Pioneer 10* spacecraft (see figure 1). NASA's official explanation of this design reads: "The *Pioneer 10* spacecraft, the first man-made object to escape from the solar system, carries this pictorial plaque. It is designed to show scientifically educated inhabitants of some other star system — who might intercept it millions of years from now — when *Pioneer* was launched, from where, and by what kind of beings. . . . The man's hand is raised in a gesture of good will."[26]

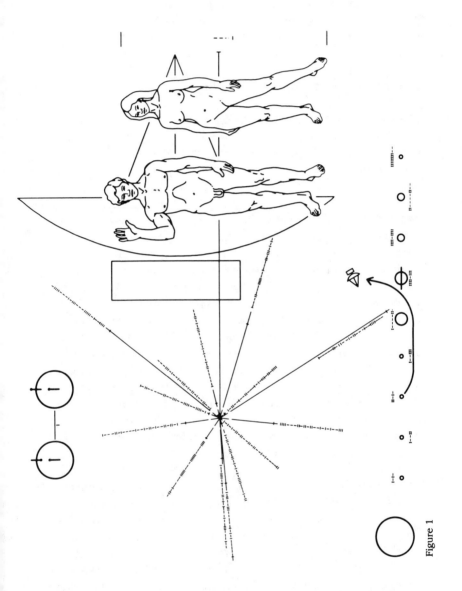

Figure 1

Although Sagan claims great care was taken to make a "panracial" image, the cartoon betrays several kinds of foolishness typical of bureaucrats, technicians, and Americans. (The designers, I would like to be able to say, weren't exactly rocket scientists.) It assumes that its space-alien, junk-dealer audience will be visually oriented, conceptually equipped with the conventions of outline drawing, and disposed to interpret the outlines not as individual objects but as generic persons, images for something like "humanity." There are other, more damaging assumptions here as well, for the NASA plates do not carry just any images of persons in their attempt to genericize humankind. They depict — if you share the imaging conventions of postwar U.S. culture — a man and a woman. They are not just sexually different; they are sexual difference itself. They are nude but have no body hair; the woman has no genitals; their heads are neatly coiffed according to the gender norms of middle-class young adults. The man stands square, while the woman leans one hip slightly forward. To a native of the culture that produced it, this bizarre fantasy-image is immediately recognizable not just as two gendered individuals, but as a heterosexual couple (monogamous, one supposes, given the absence of competition), a technological but benign Adam and Eve. It testifies to the depth of the culture's assurance (read: insistence) that humanity and heterosexuality are synonymous. This reminder speeds to the ends of the universe, announcing to passing stars that earth is not, regardless of what anyone says, a queer planet.

Heteronormative thinking about society is seldom so cartoonish. Like androcentrism, it clothes itself in goodwill and intelligence. Much of the work of feminist social theory has consisted of showing that basic conceptualizations — ways of opposing home and economy, the political and personal, or system and lifeworld — presuppose and reinforce a paradigmatically male position.[27] Queer theory is beginning to be in a position to make similar criticisms, sometimes with reference to the same oppositions (political and personal, intimate and public, market and lifeworld), but also with others — ways of distinguishing group members from nonmembers and the sexual from the nonsexual, ways of opposing the given and the chosen, and ways of identifying the intimate with the familial. Even the concept of oppression has to be reevaluated here, because in queer politics the oppression of a class of persons is only sometimes distinguishable from the repression of sexuality, and that in turn is a concept that has become difficult to contain since Foucault.

It is too early to say how many conceptualizations of this sort may have to be challenged, but many of them have been central to left social theory. I have already suggested that conceptions of culture as shared identity should be criticized in this way. Class may be another example. Andrew Parker suggests that at a fundamental level Marx's thought is especially bound up with a reproductivist conception of the social, falsely ontologized. Parker suggests that the language of theatricality in *The Eighteenth Brumaire* marks a crisis in the relation between production and interests, on one side, and politics and representation, on the other. Metropolitan sexuality appears unruly if not untheorizable given Marx's general productivist and economist commitments. Theatricality and metropolitan sexuality, in Parker's reading, are therefore related and indicative problems in Marx's thought because the othering of each helps to constitute the Marxian paradigm of production and reproduction.

This othering and the need to install it are not merely theoretical lapses but historical pressures that have conditioned Marxist thought from the moment the two writing bodies of Marx and Engels began to collaborate. By calling our attention to the homosocial dynamics of that collaboration, Parker suggests that Marxist thought is embedded in a history of sexuality, reproductivism, and homosociality in a way that prevents it from grasping these problems as conditioning its own project. Similar objections could be made against other traditions of social thought, of course, and Marxism has important countercurrents. But core elements of the Marxist paradigm may have to be seen as properly ideological moments in the history of reproductivist heterosexuality.[28]

Feminists and others have long objected to the general subordination of status conflict to class conflict in Marxist thought. It is instructive to consider, however, that at present there is no comparable category of social analysis to describe the kind of group or nongroup that queer people constitute. "Class" is conspicuously useless: feminism could at least have a debate whether women constituted a specific economic class; in queer theory the question is unintelligible. "Status," the classical alternative in social theory, is somewhat better but does not account for the way the ascribed trait of a sexually defined group is itself a mode of sociability; nor does it describe the terror and atomization by which its members become "members" before their presence in any codefined group; nor does it express the definitive pressure exerted by the assumption that this group, far from constituting one status among many, does not or should not exist. A lesbian and gay population, moreover, is defined by multiple boundaries that make the question who is and is not "one of them" not merely ambiguous but rather a perpetually and necessarily contested issue. Identity as lesbian or gay is ambiguously given and chosen, in some ways ascribed and in other ways the product of the performative act of coming out — itself a political strategy without precedent or parallel. In these ways sexuality defines — for most modern societies — a political interest-constituency unlike even those of gender or race. Queer people are a kind of social group fundamentally unlike others, a status group only insofar as they are not a class.

Queer Politics

The problem of finding an adequate description is a far from idle question, since the way a group is defined has consequences for how it will be mobilized, represented, legislated for, and addressed. Attempts have been made to use "nation," "community," even "ethnicity," just as "sexual orientation" has often been used as though it were parallel to "race" or "sex." But in each case the results have been partly unhappy, for the same reasons.[29] Among these alternatives the dominant concept has been that of a "gay and lesbian community," a notion generated in the tactics of Anglo-American identity politics and its liberal-national environment, where the buried model is racial and ethnic politics. Although it has had importance in organizational efforts (where in circular fashion it receives concretization), the notion of a community has remained problematic if only because nearly every lesbian or gay remembers being such before entering a collectively identified space, because much of lesbian and gay history has to do with noncommunity, and because dispersal rather than localization continues to be definitive of queer self-understanding ("We Are Everywhere"). Community also falsely suggests an ideological and nostalgic contrast with the atomization of modern capitalist society.[30] And in the liberal-pluralist frame it predisposes that political demands will be treated as demands for the toleration and representation of a minority constituency.

It is partly to avoid this reduction of the issues that so many people in the last two or three years — including many of the authors in this volume — have shifted their self-identification from "gay" to "queer."[31] The preference for "queer" represents, among other things, an aggressive impulse of generalization; it rejects a minoritizing logic of toleration or simple political interest-representation in favor of a more thorough resistance to regimes of the normal. For academics, being interested in queer theory is a way to mess up the desexualized spaces of the academy, exude some rut, reimagine the publics from and for which academic intellectuals write, dress, and perform. Nervous over the prospect of a well-sanctioned and compartmentalized academic version of "lesbian and gay studies," people want to make theory queer, not just to have a theory about queers. For both academics and activists, "queer" gets a critical edge by defining itself against the normal rather than the heterosexual, and normal includes normal business in the academy. The universalizing utopianism of queer theory does not entirely replace more minority-based versions of lesbian and gay theory — nor could it, since normal sexuality and the machinery of enforcing it do not bear down equally on everyone, as we are constantly reminded by pervasive forms of terror, coercion, violence, and devastation. The insistence on "queer" — a term initially generated in the context of terror — has the effect of pointing out a wide field of normalization, rather than simple intolerance, as the site of violence. Its brilliance as a naming strategy lies in combining resistance on that broad social terrain with more specific resistance on the terrains of phobia and queer-bashing, on one hand, or of pleasure, on the other. "Queer" therefore also suggests the difficulty in defining the population whose interests are at stake in queer politics.

"Queer" is also a way of cutting against mandatory gender divisions, though gender continues to be a dividing line. Men in queer theory, as well as women who write about gay men or AIDS, tend to be strongly influenced by Foucault and constructionist theory in general. They infuse queerness into their work through a mixture of tempered rage and carnivalesque display. Women who write about women, by contrast, typically refer to French feminisms (Monique

Wittig, Luce Irigaray, Julia Kristeva) and Anglo-American psycho-analytic feminism, especially in film theory (Teresa de Lauretis, Judith Mayne, Sue-Ellen Case, Judith Roof, but also Judith Butler and Diana Fuss). As Diana Fuss points out in her influential book *Essentially Speaking*, this tradition of lesbian feminism has made lesbian theorists more preoccupied with the theme of *identity* — the attempt to define (or, more recently, ironize) the common core of lesbian or female subjects. "A certain pressure is applied to the lesbian subject," Fuss points out, "either to 'claim' or to 'discover' her true identity before she can elaborate a 'personal politics.'"[32] For lesbian theorists, queer theory offers a way of basing politics in the personal *without* acceding to this pressure to clean up personal identity.[33]

Organizing a movement around queerness also allows it to draw on dissatisfaction with the regime of the normal in general. Following Hannah Arendt, we might even say that queer politics opposes society itself. Arendt describes the social as a specifically modern phenomenon: "[T]he emergence of the social realm, which is neither private nor public, strictly speaking, is a relatively new phenomenon whose origin coincided with the emergence of the modern age and which found its political form in the nation-state."[34] She identifies society in this sense with "conformism, the assumption that men behave and do not act with respect to each other" — an assumption embedded in economics and other knowledges of the social that "could achieve a scientific character only when men had become social beings and unanimously followed certain patterns of behavior, so that those who did not keep the rules could be considered to be asocial or abnormal."[35] The social realm, in short, is a cultural form, interwoven with the political form of the administrative state and with the normalizing methodologies of modern social knowledge. Can we not hear in the resonances of queer protest an objection to the normalization of behavior in this broad sense, and thus to the cultural phenomenon of societalization? If queers, incessantly told to alter their "behavior," can be understood as protesting not just the normal behavior of the social but the *idea* of normal behavior, they will bring skepticism to the methodologies founded on that idea. The essays in this volume, all at some level informed by a skepticism about knowledges of the social, may be regarded in that respect as reflecting the modern conditions of queerness.

It would be a daredevil act of understatement to say that not all gays and lesbians share this view of the new queer politics. It will continue to be debated for some time. I have made my own sympathies clear because the shape of any engagement between queer theory and other social-theoretical traditions will be determined largely by the political practice in which it comes about. In fact, however, no term — even "queer" — works equally well in all the contexts that have to be considered by what I am nevertheless calling queer theory. Queer activists are also lesbians and gays in other contexts — as for example where leverage can be gained through bourgeois propriety, or through minority-rights discourse, or through more gender-marked language (it probably won't replace lesbian feminism). Queer politics has not just replaced older modes of lesbian and gay identity; it has come to exist alongside those older modes, opening up new possibilities and problems whose relation to more familiar problems is not always clear. Queer theory, in short, has much work to do just in keeping up with queer political culture. If it contributes to the self-clarification of the struggles and wishes of the age, it may make the world queerer than ever.

NOTES

1. This paragraph gestures toward a bibliography so enormous that it could not be given here, and need not since most of it is well known. Texts that might not otherwise be familiar or readily accessible include Gayle Rubin, "Thinking Sex: Notes for a Radical Theory of the Politics of Sexuality," in Carole Vance, ed., *Pleasure and Danger: Exploring Female Sexuality* (Boston: Routledge and Kegan Paul, 1984), 267–319; Guy Hocquenghem, *Homosexual Desire,* trans. Daniella Dangoor (London: Allison and Busby, 1978); Mario Mieli, *Homosexuality and Liberation: Elements of a Gay Critique,* trans. David Fernbach (London: Gay Men's Press, 1980); the Gay Left Collective, *Homosexuality: Power and Politics* (London: Allison and Busby, 1980); Jeffrey Weeks, *Sexuality and Its Discontents* (Boston: Routledge and Kegan Paul, 1985); and Dennis Altman, *The Homosexualization of America* (New York: St. Martin's Press, 1982). For an extended discussion of Bentham's interest in homosexuality as a test case for the liberal paradigm of privacy, choice, and individual expression, see Louis Crompton, *Byron and Greek Love* (Berkeley: University of California Press, 1985).

2. Sometimes the blindness to queer issues seems truly inexplicable. An earlier volume that served as the model for this same series, *The 60s without Apology,* dealt with the social movements and cultural politics of the 1960s, broadly defined. Yet there is no reference to the gay liberation movement, and although the volume has an extensive chronology of events, no gay- or lesbian-related event is listed — not even the famous Stonewall riots of 1969, from which the modern gay liberation movement

is often dated. That the volume was produced by the relatively gay-friendly Social Text Collective shows that heterosexism is far from obsolete or unusual on the left.

3. Anthony Giddens, *The Constitution of Society* (Berkeley: University of California Press, 1984).

4. Niklas Luhmann, *Love as Passion: The Codification of Intimacy*, trans. Jeremy Gaines and Doris L. Jones (Cambridge: Harvard University Press, 1986).

5. The English translation of Habermas's *The Philosophical Discourse of Modernity* (Cambridge: MIT Press, 1988) makes a revealing slip on p. 270; it refers to Foucault's text as *The History of Subjectivity*. The situation is not always better within gay studies. Because of the dominance of the textual model of literary or film criticism, Foucault's work is often interpreted in the new gay studies as arguing, almost in an echo of Whorf, for the efficacy of lexical shifts — as though discourse theory required us only to date the coinage of the term "homosexuality."

6. Eve Kosofsky Sedgwick has put this point in a striking way: "In spite of every promise to the contrary[,] every single theoretically or politically interesting project of postwar thought has finally had the effect of delegitimating our space for asking in detail about the multiple, unstable ways in which people may be like or different from each other. This project is not rendered otiose by any demonstration of how fully people may differ also from themselves. Deconstruction, founded as a very science of *différ(e/a)nce,* has both so fetishized the idea of difference and so vaporized its possible embodiments that its most thoroughgoing practitioners are the last people to whom one would now look for help in thinking about particular differences. The same thing seems likely to prove true of theorists of postmodernism. Psychoanalytic theory, if only through the almost astrologically lush plurality of its overlapping taxonomies of physical zones, developmental stages, representational mechanisms, and levels of consciousness, seemed to promise to introduce a certain becoming amplitude into discussions of what different people are like — only to turn, in its streamlined trajectory across so many institutional boundaries, into the sveltest of metatheoretical disciplines, sleeked down to such elegant operational entities as *the* mother, *the* father, *the* preoedipal, *the* oedipal, *the* other or Other" (*Epistemology of the Closet* [Berkeley: University of California Press, 1990], 23–24).

7. Alberto Melucci, *Nomads of the Present* (Philadelphia: Temple University Press, 1989), 152.

8. Ibid., 159.

9. There are, of course, exceptions, especially work produced by the *Socialist Review,* such as Lisa Duggan's recent essay "Making It Perfectly Queer," *SR* 22, no. 1 (1992): 11–31; or Jeffrey Escoffier's "Sexual Revolution and the Politics of Gay Identity," *SR* 15 (1985): 119–53. The very breadth and tentativeness of Escoffier's article, however, shows to what degree it is exceptional in the new gay studies. A similar example is Barry Adam's "Structural Foundations of the Gay World," *Comparative Studies in Society and History* 27 (1985): 658–71. Both essays make gestures toward continental social theory, but remain primarily interested in defining a minority constituency for American identity politics.

10. Readers not familiar with this large and rapidly growing body of work might consult the following essay collections: Ronald Butters, John Clum, and Michael Moon, eds., *Displacing Homophobia* (Durham, N.C.: Duke University Press, 1989); Joseph Boone and Michael Cadden, eds., *Engendering Men* (New York: Routledge, 1990); Diana Fuss, ed., *Inside/Out* (New York: Routledge, 1991); Bad Object-Choices

Collective, *How Do I Look? Queer Film and Video* (Seattle: Bay Press, 1991); Andrew Parker et al., eds., *Nationalisms and Sexualities* (New York: Routledge, 1992); Teresa de Lauretis, ed., *Queer Theory,* special issue of *Differences* 3, no. 2 (summer 1991); and Sally Munt, ed., *New Lesbian Criticism* (New York: Columbia University Press, 1992).

11. For influential examples, see Herbert Marcuse, *Eros and Civilization* (Boston: Beacon Press, 1974); Gayle Rubin, "The Traffic in Women," in Rayna Reiter, ed., *Toward an Anthropology of Women* (New York: Monthly Review Press, 1975), 157–210; Kaja Silverman, *Male Sexuality on the Margins* (New York: Routledge, 1992); and Judith Butler, *Gender Trouble* (New York: Routledge, 1990).

12. The most comprehensive work in this area is David Greenberg, *The Construction of Homosexuality* (Chicago: University of Chicago Press, 1988). A theoretically rigorous exposition can be found in David Halperin, *One Hundred Years of Homosexuality* (New York: Routledge, 1990); Celia Kitzinger corrects for the constructionist emphasis on men in her *Social Construction of Lesbianism* (London: Sage, 1987), which also stresses a critique of social science.

13. See Sedgwick, *Epistemology,* chap. 1.

14. The fact of international gay discourse has been neatly documented in Stephan Likosky, ed., *Coming Out: An Anthology of International Gay and Lesbian Writing* (New York: Pantheon, 1992).

15. "Translocal," of course, does not necessarily mean universal. In this paragraph I have in mind such exemplary work as Cindy Patton's *Inventing AIDS* (New York: Routledge, 1990); Gilbert Herdt and Shirley Lindenbaum, eds., *The Time of AIDS: Social Analysis, Theory, and Method* (London: Sage, 1992); and Douglas Crimp, ed., *AIDS: Cultural Analysis, Cultural Activism* (Cambridge: MIT Press, 1990).

16. The common ground between social reflection and everyday practice here is similar to that described by Harold Garfinkel's 1967 essay "Passing and the Managed Achievement of Sex Status in an Intersexed Person," in his *Studies in Ethnomethodology* (Cambridge: Polity Press, 1984), 116–85. In a section called "Agnes, the Practical Ethnomethodologist," for example, Garfinkel writes: "Agnes' methodological practices [Agnes is his name for the transsexual in his study] are our sources of authority for the finding, and recommended study policy, that normally sexed persons are cultural events in societies whose character as visible orders of practical activities consists of members' recognition and production practices. We learned from Agnes, who treated sexed persons as cultural events that members make happen, that members' practices alone produce the observable-tellable normal sexuality of persons, and do so only, entirely, exclusively in actual, singular, particular occasions through actual witnessed displays of common talk and conduct" (181).

17. For a critique of utopian interpretations of gay cultural tactics see Leo Bersani, "Is the Rectum a Grave?" *October* 43 (Winter 1987): 197–222.

18. Patton, *Inventing AIDS.*

19. Sedgwick, *Epistemology,* 1.

20. For a critique of the notion of culture as shared meaning, see Greg Urban, *Toward a Discourse-Centered Approach to Culture* (Austin: University of Texas Press, 1992).

21. See Sedgwick, *Epistemology,* 48–59.

22. José Muñoz, personal correspondence, March 1992.

23. Sedgwick, *Epistemology,* 31.

24. Lauren Berlant, *The Anatomy of National Fantasy* (Chicago: University of Chicago Press, 1991); and Michael Warner, "The Mass Public and the Mass Subject," in Craig Calhoun, ed., *Habermas and the Public Sphere* (Cambridge: MIT Press, 1991), 377–401.

25. Monique Wittig, *The Straight Mind* (Boston: Beacon Press, 1992), 40, 43.

26. I want to thank Max Cavitch for alerting me to this public release from NASA's Ames Research Center. Carl Sagan has commented on the controversy surrounding the design in his *The Cosmic Connection* (New York: Anchor, 1973), as has his collaborator F. D. Drake, in Drake and Sagan, *Murmurs of Earth* (New York: Ballantine, 1978).

27. I have in mind here especially Nancy Fraser, "What's Critical about Critical Theory? The Case of Habermas and Gender," *New German Critique* 35 (Spring/Summer 1985): 97–131; reprinted in her *Unruly Practices* (Minneapolis: University of Minnesota Press, 1989), 113–43.

28. Another blockage against sexual politics in the Marxist tradition, noticeable in the Melucci passage I quoted earlier, is the close connection between consumer culture and the most visible spaces of gay culture: bars, discos, advertising, fashion, brand-name identification, mass-cultural camp, "promiscuity." Gay culture in this most visible mode is anything but external to advanced capitalism and to precisely those features of advanced capitalism that many on the left are most eager to disavow. Post-Stonewall urban gay men reek of the commodity. We give off the smell of capitalism in rut, and therefore demand of theory a more dialectical view of capitalism than many people have imagination for.

29. For an explicit elaboration of this model, see Steven Epstein, "Gay Politics, Ethnic Identity: The Limits of Social Constructionism," *Socialist Review* 93, no. 94 (1987): 9–54.

30. On this problem see Iris Marion Young, *Justice and the Politics of Difference* (Princeton, N.J.: Princeton University Press, 1990), 226–56.

31. On the logic of the term, see Lisa Duggan, "Making It Perfectly Queer"; Arlene Stein, "Sisters and Queers: The Decentering of Lesbian Feminism," *Socialist Review* 22, no. 1 (1992): 33–55; Jeffrey Escoffier and Allan Bérubé, "Queer/Nation," *Out/Look* 11 (Winter 1991): 14–16; and the essays in this volume by Seidman, Berlant and Freeman, and Griggers.

32. Diana Fuss, *Essentially Speaking: Feminism, Nature, and Difference* (New York: Routledge, Chapman, and Hall, 1989), 99–101.

33. I have said more on the subject in a review essay on queer theory by lesbians in *VLS* (June 1992), from which the preceding paragraph is derived.

34. Hannah Arendt, *The Human Condition* (Chicago: University of Chicago Press, 1958), 28.

35. Ibid., 41–42.

Part I

Get Over It: Heterotheory

Sodomy in the New World:
Anthropologies Old and New
Jonathan Goldberg

Jonathan Katz's groundbreaking *Gay American History* or Walter Williams's more recent *The Spirit and the Flesh* points my way here to the systematic persecution of so-called sodomitical Indians in the new world "discovered" by Europe in the Renaissance, the transportation to the Americas of habits of thought and prejudice endemic in Europe.[1] After the deplorable 1986 decision of the U.S. Supreme Court in *Bowers v. Hardwick* (478 U.S. 186), with its appeals to sodomy laws enrolled in English statute books in the sixteenth century and to a time-out-of-mind hatred of homosexuality, the recovery of the history of sodomy in the New World is of signal importance as one way of resisting modes of thinking that, every day, seem to be growing more widespread, and that the decision of the Supreme Court can be said to have licensed. This history needs to be retold in as unpresuming and discriminating a fashion as possible in order to uncover the density of the concept of sodomy and to understand the work it is put to do, but also to recognize that sodomy, "that utterly confused category," as Foucault memorably put it, identifies neither persons nor acts with any coherence or specificity.[2] This is one reason why the term can be mobilized — precisely because it is incapable of exact definition; but this is also how the bankruptcy of the term, and what has been done in its name, can be uncovered. It is that double reading that governs the inquiry that follows, situating and desituating colonialist texts — of more than one era — and their accusations.

In the pages that follow I take as an originary moment in the

3

history of the making of America what happened two days before
Balboa first laid eyes on the Pacific Ocean. In a Panamanian village,
after killing the leader of the Indians of Quarequa and six hundred
of his warriors, Balboa fed to his dogs forty more Indians accused
of sodomitical practices. The earliest account of these events of
October 1513 that I know of appears in Peter Martyr's *Decades,* first
published in 1516. I will be citing from the 1555 English translation
as one way of immediately suggesting that these events cannot be
thought of solely as episodes in Spanish-American history; I have no
interest in perpetuating the "black legend" that seeks to exculpate
northern Europeans from the atrocities of the Spanish and that is
fuelled with proto-nationalist and racist energies.[3] Richard Eden,
the translator, not only makes Peter Martyr's text English; he also
cannot resist endorsing Balboa's final act of carnage. His is not a
unique response: the habits of mind inscribed in these Renaissance
texts find their way into the menacing decision of the U.S. Supreme
Court;[4] moreover, as we will see, they can be found as well in
the supposedly more enlightened domains of the academy. What
Balboa saw continues to haunt the anthropological literature.

Here is the scene in Peter Martyr:

> [Balboa] founde the house of this kynge infected with most abhom-
> inable and unnaturall lechery. For he founde the kynges brother and
> many other younge men in womens apparell, smoth & effeminately
> decked, which by the report of such as dwelte abowte hym, he
> abused with preposterous venus. Of these abowte the number of
> fortie, he commaunded to bee gyven for a pray to his dogges. (89v)

A number of elements in this description make it clear that sodomy
is its subject even though the term is never used. The reference to
the crime of "preposterous venus" says this in a highly condensed
way. "Preposterous" means a confusion of before and behind; here
the cross-dressed Indians have confused gender and the supposed
"natural" procreative sexuality that follows from it. What they do is
thus termed unnatural and abominable, an infection in danger of
spreading. All this is familiar enough in the discourse of sodomy,
but simply to identify that as its topic fails to take stock of the excessiveness of this representation of sodomy.[5] In simple narrative
terms, Balboa has already established his power by the act of carnage that precedes this one. If he seeks to remove the king's brother

in order to make his position absolutely secure, it's more than a bit odd that the king's brother is depicted as a cross-dresser. But what this does — it is not something that can be found in the description of the battle scene — is to infuse Balboa's acts with moral purpose. It's as if he's righting a wrong against the prerogatives of gender. (In this context, it's worth noting that many sixteenth-century narratives describe native women as offended by the sodomites in their midst.)[6] But if the elimination of the king's brother and his minions is done for the sake of women and for the sake of the proprieties and prerogatives of gender, it is also obviously fuelled with misogyny, as the disgust at effeminacy implies. Yet that disgust is displaced upon the cross-dressed/sodomitical body and its making preposterous the act of Venus.

Moreover, one must notice that what Balboa knows about the king's brother he has learned thanks to native informants. If the king's brother's manliness is discredited — no warrior, he stays at home with his cross-dressed minions — his political abilities also are impugned. And this seems to be an opinion about him shared by the native informants. Balboa is thus represented as serving the interests of those he has conquered. This is, in fact, registered in the aftermath of the slaughter of the forty Panamanians, as the Indians accommodate Balboa by handing over more sexual offenders, delivering up "al such as they knewe to bee infected with that pestilence" in order to be rid of such "contagious beastes" (90r). "This stinkynge abhomination," Peter Martyr explains, "hadde not yet entered among the people, but was exercised onely by the noble men and gentelmen. But the people lyftinge up theyr handes and eyes toward heaven, gave tokens that god was grevously offended with such vyle deedes" (90v). It is at this point that Richard Eden cannot resist his comment; in the margin of the text beside these lines, he writes: "I wolde all men were of this opinion." The slaughter of sodomites is thus mobilized as a kind of quasi-democratic device; this is, of course, a ruse of power: Balboa eliminates and supplants the Indian rulers but appears to be acting as the liberator of the oppressed. Political oppression has been translated into sexual oppression, the abuse of preposterous Venus. The Indians who decry sodomy are "good" Indians, not merely in their accommodating behavior, but also in providing a belief that Eden endorses. They have been made the site upon which European values can be foisted, but also an exemplary mirror in which Europeans might find themselves.

In the battle that precedes the slaughter of the forty Panamanian sodomites, all Indians are described as animals, and their slaughter is explicitly an act of butchery; they were, Martyr writes, with perfect equanimity, "hewed . . . in pieces as the butchers doo fleshe . . . , from one an arme, from an other a legge, from hym a buttocke, from an other a shulder, and from sume the necke from the bodye at one stroke" (89v). After the forty sodomites are fed to the dogs, two kinds of Indians appear in the text, sodomitical ones and noble savages. As the latter lift their hands to heaven, it's as if they're proto-Christians, at the very least testifying to the universality of the Judeo-Christian condemnation of "unnatural" sexuality. Serving as a mirror of European belief, this split representation of Indians permits the covering over of divisions within the invading troops. For Balboa himself is no noble or gentleman, although that is the position he strives to achieve in his conquests. The representation of the Indians (which, of course, starts with believing that they are ruled by a king, and that their society is divided along European class lines) serves to dissimulate Balboa's power grab within Spanish society. In this post-facto rewriting, Balboa is not only the righter of sexual wrongs, he's also the universal liberator of the under classes.

The slaughter of sodomites, from such a vantage point, serves only as a spectacle for Europe and its ruses of power. Such mirror effects are quite complicated, however. Balboa's elevation is predicated on his replacing the native powers: yet when natives are made to voice European beliefs about corrupt sexuality, the truth they utter is one about the corruptions of those in power — about nobles and gentlemen, about the very courtier Balboa seeks to become. The mirror that the natives hold up suggests, in the doubleness of native construction, divisions within the Europeans. Moreover, although the natives give Balboa the knowledge he requires, this does not necessarily reveal anything about their attitudes toward sexual practices; it certainly suggests, however, that the natives themselves also are divided. This moment of accommodation is not at all untypical of native responses to invasion, for the history of native peoples in the New World is not one of simple pastoral contentment, and one mode of resistance developed in the face of a history of warfare and invasions has been to seem to go along with the demands of the conquerors.[7] Nothing in Peter Martyr will tell us why the natives at this moment accede to the Spanish, but there is no reason simply to write the episode off as one of co-option and victimage, or to assume that the natives shared European beliefs about sodomy. But there is no reason either to assume that they simply and uncomplicatedly embraced it. Sexuality is never simply a set of acts unconnected to questions of power. The Indians can be imagined to be using European beliefs as a way to work their way into the European system, or represented as if that is what they are doing, but this also is a way to accomplish what they conceivably want — the elimination of certain members of their own society.

To read the episode this way makes more visible that two non-homogeneous forces meet here, and that the situation is unduly simplified if Spaniards and Indians are thought of each as self-identical or as entirely oppositional (the usual paradigm of self and other, oppressor and oppressed). Rather, one can see that the account of sexuality that seems to exceed the requirements of the narrative nonetheless supplies ideological justifications that are elsewhere lacking in the account of the conquest of Quarequa. But while it provides them, it does so — perhaps in part because of the very excessiveness of the representation — in ways that cannot be stabilized. These cross-dressed bodies are the locus of identity and difference, a site for crossings between Spaniards and Indians, and for divisions between and among them. The differentials involve class, race, and gender, all in uneasy relation to each other, sites capable of ideological mobilization, but also of resistance. (One must think through what effects of identification the narrative attempts, and how the unities supposed may be broken.) What the scene offers is not the truth of a naked body but a site the text well names as preposterous. After the fact of massive slaughter, the additional slaughter of forty more Indians retrospectively justifies it. Post-facto, the body of the sodomite takes on an originary status, as the cause for what was done to the Indians in the first place, but its originary status is troubled not merely by being presented as an after-effect but also because, cross-dressed, it is a double body, and the only truth it testifies to is the preposterous nature of colonial accounts.[8]

These complicities between colonial representations and the sodomitical body can be illustrated, too, by turning briefly to a story about the origins of sodomy that circulated widely in the period;

I cite from the version offered by Pedro de Cieza in 1553 as it is quoted in Garcilaso de la Vega's *Royal Commentaries of the Incas* (1609), Cieza's version being the fullest of the several accounts to which Garcilaso alludes.[9] The story, presented as one "which the natives have received as a tradition" (561), is set in Peru and involves the arrival of giants who ravage the countryside, indulging in cannibalism on a wide scale, but who find themselves sexually frustrated in their attempts on native women:

> After some years the giants were still in this region, and as they had no women of their own and the Indian women were too small for them, or else because the vice was habitual to them and inspired by the demon, they practiced the unspeakable and horrible sin of sodomy, committing it openly and in public without fear of God or personal shame. (562–63)

The truth of the account is credited: Cieza reports the finding of the bones of the giants.

Cieza, and Garcilaso after him, offer accounts of sexual practices in Peru that divide the native body. The Incas are said to have suppressed sodomy — they are like the "good" Indians of the Balboa account whom the Spaniards replaced. But, in offering this story about the native origins of sodomy, sodomy is something that comes from the outside, and is not native at all. While this could be a story about the Incan invasions of Peru (they bring sodomy to Peru as the act that needs to be discovered and extirpated), in many respects it seems more like a story about the Spanish invasion, and not merely because these Incan beliefs may be Spanish ones — these giants come from over seas, and they arrive without any women in their company. Moreover, while it is certainly possible that native mythologies included a belief in ancient giants, the story seems fetched from Genesis. And, of course, as it is told, the supposed native tradition is inflected with Christian values, so much so that the end of the giants is their burning at the hands of an avenging angel sent by God (the very punishment ordered for sodomites in many European legal codes). Is this story about native tradition one that the natives tell about the Spaniards, whose concepts have forever altered the native understanding of their own myths and practices? Or is it a story that the Spaniards tell as if it were a native account, in order to produce "good" Indians who "properly" abominate sodomy? Or is it a story that the natives tell to the Spaniards as if it were traditional, accommodating their beliefs to Spanish ones, but keeping in reserve their own story under the cover of this acceptable one? By the time this story is told, can one separate native and Christian beliefs?

Clearly not, but what can be recognized is that this story of the origins of sodomy depends upon the complicities that these questions raise. This story, repeatedly told and elaborated, retrospectively — preposterously — locates an origin that is a divided and doubled one. Yet, for all the ways in which the story doubly articulates native and Spanish beliefs, what it also bespeaks is the unassimilable nature of sodomy. Its origins lie neither with the Spaniards nor with the Indians, but with a race of giants. The sexual practices of male with male are seen as a response to the impossibility of male-female intercourse (an explanation that could justify such practices *among the Spanish,* and that obscures the fact that in European culture of the time men found boys as well as women possible sexual objects). The excessiveness of the story is registered in its giant form, as much as in the ways in which whatever there is of native belief occupies the same discursive space as Christian belief (but, by the time the story is told to the Spaniards, these two belief systems can no longer be thought of as sealed off from each other). Precisely because the story is about what cannot be assimilated, about something that cannot be stabilized, it is capable of being told in the double register of "native" tradition and Spanish-Christian belief. Yet, however extravagant the story, it is also down to earth, its truth testified to by the empirical evidence of the bones that remain to be seen. And another fact about Puerto Viejo that Garcilaso quotes from Cieza: the wells of pitch found in the region that could be used " 'to tar all the ships one wished with it.' . . . Thus far Pedro de Cieza, whose history we have followed to show the Indian tradition about the giants, and the well of pitch at the same place, for it too is remarkable" (563). Remarkable and, it seems, natural — the coincidence of the tar pits and the giants is clinching evidence, a naturalization that serves the Spanish conquerors.

A similar coincidence, the slippages around sodomy that write colonial accounts, can also be found in two accounts of origin that frame Peter Martyr's telling of the slaughter of the Panamanian sodomites. As the Spaniards advance with their guns, the

Indians flee in panic, certain that the Spaniards are one with the violent forces of nature: "[A]s soone as they harde the noyse of the hargabusies, they beleved that owre menne caryed thunder and lyghtenynge with them" (89v). After they deliver up the sodomites, the accommodating Indians report themselves relieved, convinced that the practices of the Indians they have handed over were the source of natural violence, "affirmynge this to bee the cause of theyr soo many thunderinges, lyghtnynge, and tempestes wherwith they are soo often troubeled" (90r). Spaniards and native sodomites are identified here as originary forces. The account serves the narrative, of course, both the desire to represent the forces of civilization as one with the providential control of nature (the Indians are made to voice a naive belief that it is in the interest of the Spaniards to believe they believe), as well as the aim of the narrative to represent the bodies of sodomites as the subversion of everything that retrospectively can be called nature. Within the space of a page in Peter Martyr's account, these two origins — this ignorance and knowledge — come to coincide.

Sodomy punctuates the scene of discovery, October 7, 1513, Balboa's first sight of the Pacific, two days after the episode in Quarequa with which we began:

[H]e behelde with woonderinge eyes the toppes of the hygh
mountaynes shewed unto hym by the guydes of *Quarequa,* from
the whiche he myght see the other sea soo longe looked for,
and never seene before of any man commynge owte of owre
worlde. Approchinge therefore to the toppes of the mountaynes, he
commaunded his armye to stey, and went him selfe alone to the
toppe, as it were to take the fyrst possession therof. (90v)

The scene is staged through the familiar ideological structures that have written such events: an individual, a hero, a great man, fulfills everyone's dream. "Fyrst possession" is a spiritual event — a matter simply of seeing, and, as the narrative continues, Balboa falls to his knees in prayer, performing a "spirituall sacrifice," humbling himself in thanks for what his God has given him.

How staged this scene of possession is, how euphemized its presentation of self-conquest and humiliation, is suggested even in Peter Martyr's account. Balboa is there alone only because he has refused to allow his soldiers to accompany him. The spirituality, the providential history constructed in Balboa's prayer, the transcendental event — the mountaintop communication with God — are belied (and supported) by the troops and by quite other notions of possession and victory. He is there because he has been led, not by God, but by "the guydes of *Quarequa*," and they are our guides, too, leading us back to the scenes of carnage this arrival seeks to efface, the excessive, supplementary (and for the purposes of Peter Martyr's narrative absolutely necessary) slaughter of sodomitical Indians. Balboa's self-sacrifice euphemizes that scene of slaughter: the forty sacrificed as "pray" there have become here Balboa's prayer. It is on the bodies of those who are equated with animals that this European man can rise up to his spiritual heights. The connection can be brought down a peg when we hear the last thing that Balboa thanks his God for, that so great a victory has been given to "a man but of smaule witte and knowledge, of lyttle experience and base parentage" (90v). The — literal — dividing of the Indian body is requisite for covering over European divisions, for the construction, eminently deconstructable, of the unified European body. Preposterously, the guides of Quarequa lead the narrative back to the (de)foundational scene to which we have been attending, and to the work that the sodomitical body performs in this account.

Similar slippages around sodomy mark Peter Martyr's account. The natives ultimately mouth European beliefs in a mimetology that undermines them even as they produce them. In such ways colonial texts produce the sodomitical body as the body that needs to be effaced. Yet, as these accounts suggest, that body also founds an ineffaceable site of disruption. It does so not least because there is no such thing as *the* sodomitical body. The characterization of the cross-dressed Indians as sodomites has already voided any possibility of reading that body on its own terms. Rather, its crossings, its refusals of gender and class difference, are what is made to tell, and what may be made to speak against the prejudicial designs of the account. But any attempt to read cross-dressing on its own terms would fall prey to — and be enabled by — the same conditions of non–self-identity. For there is no such thing as the singular cross-dressed body; nor does it carry with it a univocal meaning.

This can be seen in the various attempts to consign it, and not merely in the Renaissance texts I have been considering. Contemporary and more sympathetic readings like that offered by Walter

Williams have sought in the special status accorded by some tribes to cross-dressing a transhistorical locus for the affirmation of alternative sexual practices. This interpretation has been resisted in a variety of ways: by a gay-affirmative historian, for instance, whose misogyny leads him to reject cross-gender identification, but who also points to cross-dressing as a native practice of humiliating captured warriors;[10] by a feminist anthropologist whose reading of male cross-dressing as an attempt to encroach upon female powers and prerogatives is fuelled with homophobia but also with a sense that the crossing of gender divisions varies within native cultures and in ways not easily homologized with our own.[11] Without denying the value of affirming solidarity between gay identity and those persecuted for what have been seen as sexual transgressions, and certainly with no desire to endorse the misogyny or homophobia that has marked the refusal of such affirmations, it nonetheless has to be recognized that *all* these accounts offer projections upon native bodies, but that each suggests, too, insofar as it offers historical and anthropological evidence that can be credited, further revelations that cross-dressed bodies are not of themselves singular. Cross-dressing does not mean the same thing from one native situation to another, or even within the same tribe; to believe otherwise is to homogenize all natives into the figure of the Indian, and to once more give in to the ethnocentricity that has invented the category of people without history.[12]

As a most telling instance of the dangers of such readings, I would close this discussion by considering an episode in structuralist anthropology, an essay in Pierre Clastres's *Society against the State* called "The Bow and the Basket," which is available as a glossy Zone book, presented with all the trimmings of the latest thought from Paris.[13] Clastres looks at a small nomadic society, the Guayaki Indians of South America, and writes a prose infused with lyrical identification with a people offered as a model for a sociality that has not yet arrived at the oppressions of state formation. "The Bow and the Basket" takes up their gender organization. Like many other anthropologists, Clastres insists that in this tribe, gender differences are rigidly maintained, here in an extreme form since both hunting and gathering are performed by the men, while the women tend hearth and the temporary homes established as they wander through the forest. The bow and basket emblematize for Clastres this strict separation, since members of one sex cannot touch the object associated with the other sex without disastrous consequences. Clastres's view is, however, a heterosexist fantasy about these people, belied by numerous details in his account that suggest that such crossings do in fact occur: "[W]omen do scarcely any collecting" (103), Clastres admits at one point, thus revealing that women do occasionally gather — at which point gathering is redivided by Clastres to posit the form of that activity that "properly belongs in the category of masculine activities" (103). "Men do the hunting, which is only natural" (103), Clastres writes, voicing and ventriloquizing Guayakan belief. "Natural" and "proper" assume their heterosexist definitions. Yet, the account slips again as Clastres reveals that it is the women, who supposedly never touch the male bows, who make the strings for them (104). Moreover, their "proper" activity, the preparation of food, and the fact that, because of demographic inequalities, they may take more than one husband, belie the division that Clastres sets up in which men are the "producers" and women are, as he calls them, the "consumers." These may be people living before the state, but as Clastres's misogyny writes them they are already proto-bourgeois.

The sole place in which Clastres registers the possibility of the violation of his schema of division (one that he thinks is a model of equality and balance but that is, as he writes it, a hierarchy always affirming the place of men over women) is in the existence within this group of twenty-odd people of two cross-dressed men who carry baskets rather than bows. Tellingly, with their presence, Clastres thinks that all the permutations possible in his mathematical schema have been realized; it never occurs to him that there might be bow-carrying women, or any arrangement for female-female sexual expression, nor to remark their absence among the Guayaki.[14] These two men are the only named figures in Clastres, and although both cross-dress, they are otherwise quite different. One of them is the maladjusted Chachubutawachugi, who refuses to carry his basket as women do, and who refuses to behave as a woman. How he came to be a basket-carrier is not spelled out — bad luck in hunting, or some such event, has led him to be stigmatized and denied male prerogatives. The other basket-carrier, Krembegi, Clastres applauds as a model of social adjustment, and he offers his liberal endorsement of the tribe that has found room for him. Yet who is Krembegi?

14 Jonathan Goldberg

Clastres offers in the space of a paragraph several explanations: "Krembegi was in fact a sodomite" (108), we are first told. He was "an incomprehensible pederast," Clastres continues. "Krembegi was homosexual"; he was "an unconscious invert" (109). He's also naturally artistic. Each peg, of course, names not some singular form of sexual identity, but various behaviors that at historically different times have been available for sexual self-identification or that have served — as they do here — as prejudicial markers. Clastres may think he is telling us who Krembegi is or what his cross-dressing means, but the figure of the well-adjusted male basket-carrier panics him into a proliferation of incoherent explanations and, to echo Foucault, utterly confused categories.

My point, however, is not simply to dismiss Clastres's homophobic and ignorant interpretations, but to suggest that his response to Krembegi is endemic to all readings of cross-dressing. Even as Clastres celebrates how well Krembegi fits into his tribe (his "homosexuality had permitted him to find the topos he was logically consigned to by his unfitness to occupy the space of men" [110]), he also mentions his exclusion; in a footnote, Clastres mentions that unlike both men and women in the tribe, whose singing Clastres examines in highly invidious ways (the men turn out to be proto-poststructuralists whose songs discover that language is not a means of communication but a way of enunciating an I, while the women turn out to sing indistinguishably one from another in songs that Clastres redescribes as howling and wailing — "one can scarcely speak of singing where the women are concerned" [111]), "Krembegi never sang" (113 n. 2).[15] "He was a *krypy-meno* (anus-make-love)" (109), Clastres tells us, giving the native word as a final "true" definition. But what of the men who slept with him? They "would make him their sexual partner," and play their "erotic games" (this form of sex couldn't possibly be serious we are assured) in a spirit of "bawdiness" and not of "perversion" (109); *they* were not anus-make-loves. Before anyone seizes upon Krembegi as a model for the wonders of "Indian" acceptance of sexual diversity, of "tolerance," that "invidious descriptor one finds laced throughout this literature," as Gilbert Herdt puts it,[16] it would be good to see how excluded Krembegi is by the label he is given, by the place he occupies, and by his silence. It might almost be better to seek to identify with the maladjusted Chachubutawachugi, whose behavior at least protests the space to which he has been consigned.

Consigned by whom? It would be hard finally to disentangle the Guayaki from their sympathetic interpreter. As the essay ends, Clastres offers a last idyllic glimpse: "Such is the life of the Guayaki Indians. By day they walk together through the forest, women and men, the bow in front, the basket behind" (127–28). The hierarchy of male and female is thus quietly but unmistakably affirmed. But what is denied is that it is not only cross-dressers who have bows and baskets, a front and a behind. Such a "preposterous" admission would be too threatening to the heterosexism that marks Clastres's reading. For it suggests that, in any clothing, bodies are not singular. Clastres fastens on a male anxiety among the Guayaki — their dislike of having to share their wives with other men. But nowhere does he think that relations between men are a sexual possibility except for cross-dressed men who play the woman's part; nowhere, that is, does he acknowledge the preposterous truth that the bow and the basket is not only a figure for man in opposition to woman but also for a cross-identification that could define men's bodies or women's bodies, and the multiple possibilities for sexual relations of men with men and of women with women.

NOTES

1. See Jonathan Katz, *Gay American History* (New York: Thomas Y. Crowell, 1976), 281–334; Walter L. Williams, *The Spirit and the Flesh* (Boston: Beacon Press, 1986), 131–51. In *Memory of Fire: Genesis* (New York: Pantheon, 1985), 58–59, Eduardo Galeano offers a stunning evocation of the Balboan moment. The fullest anthology of colonial texts on sodomy is found in Francesco Guerra, *The Pre-Columbian Mind* (London: Seminar Press, 1971); Guerra is entirely uncritical of the material that he offers, homophobically believing that the accounts simply offer the truth about "aberrant" native practices. For a much more astute account of the connections between colonialist discourses on sodomy and the Portuguese in Brazil, see João S. Trevisan, *Perverts in Paradise,* trans. Martin Foreman (London: Gay Men's Press, 1986).

2. See Michel Foucault, *The History of Sexuality: An Introduction,* trans. Robert Hurley (New York: Pantheon, 1978), 101.

3. I will be citing Peter Martyr's *The Decades of the Newe Worlde or West India,* March of America Facsimile series, no. 4 (Ann Arbor, Mich.: University Microfilms, 1966). Richard Eden translates the 1533 edition of Pietro Martire d'Anghiera's *De rebus oceanicis et orbe novo decades tres.* For an impassioned rebuttal of the black legend, see Roberto Fernández Retamar, "Against the Black Legend," in *Caliban*

and Other Essays, trans. Edward Baker (Minneapolis: University of Minnesota Press, 1989), 56–73.

4. This is a topic that I took up in "Sodometries," a lecture delivered at the English Institute in August 1991 and incorporated in my book of the same name (Stanford, Calif.: Stanford University Press, 1992).

5. Familiar not only in terms of the discourse of sodomy in the Renaissance, as Alan Bray suggests in *Homosexuality in Renaissance England* (London: Gay Men's Press, 1982), but uncannily familiar also, as Lee Edelman suggests, because the preposterous is a trope for what he terms the "(be)hindsight" with which Freudian *Nachtraglichkeit* arrives at a primal scene of sex *a tergo;* see "Seeing Things, the Scene of Surveillance, and the Spectacle of Gay Male Sex," in Diana Fuss, ed., *Inside/Out: Lesbian Theories, Gay Theories* (New York: Routledge, 1991).

6. For example, in Fernández de Oviedo, the enormously influential first vernacular account of the New World (*Natural Historia de las Indias* [1526]), not least because Las Casas undertook to debunk it; see Guerra, *Pre-Columbian Mind:* "they are hated extremely by the women" (55); "this abominable sin against nature, very much practised among the Indians in this island [Santo Domingo], hateful to women" (56).

7. In work that perhaps makes these processes more benign than is warranted, and that tends to look at acts of intellectual accommodation and their relation to belief systems, Sabine MacCormack nonetheless points to some of the processes I have in mind here; see "From the Sun of the Incas to the Virgin of Copacabana," *Representations* 8 (1984): 30–60; and "*Pachacuti:* Miracles, Punishments, and Last Judgment: Visionary Past and Prophetic Future in Early Colonial Peru," *American Historical Review* 93 (1988): 960–1006.

8. This analysis has been aided by the insights of a number of postcolonial theorists: Peter Hulme, to whose *Colonial Encounters* (London: Methuen, 1986) I am indebted for the phrase "ruses of power" as well as for a model analytic of incommensurable differentials; Benedict Anderson, whose *Imagined Communities* (London: Verso, 1983) brilliantly explores the constructedness of nationalisms; Homi Bhabha, who, in essays like his "The Other Question: Difference, Discrimination and the Discourse of Colonialism," in Francis Barker et al., eds., *Literature, Politics and Theory* (London: Methuen, 1989), has written on colonial ambivalence and mimetology (this work opens spaces within the projection of stereotypes and thereby destabilizes hegemonic discourses, moving analysis beyond the model of opposition and victimage); and Gayatri Spivak, who has done similar work in finding the ways in which a deconstructive analytic can produce subalternity (see, e.g., "Subaltern Studies: Deconstructing Historiography," in Ranajit Guha and Gayatri Chakravorty Spivak, eds., *Selected Subaltern Studies* [Oxford: Oxford University Press, 1988]). Important as this work has been for me, and crucial as it is in its approach to questions of nationality, race, and gender, it has not opened the questions of sexuality that concern me here.

9. Garcilaso de la Vega, *Royal Commentaries of the Incas,* trans. Harold V. Livermore (Austin: University of Texas Press, 1966). He mentions versions of the story by Acosta and Zarate; for these and other versions of the story, see Guerra, *Pre-Columbian Mind:* p. 90 for Cieza; p. 99 for Zarate (1555); p. 131 for Juan López de Velasco (1574); pp. 141–42 for Pedro Gutiérrez de Santa Clara (c. 1580); p. 155 for Antonio de Herrera (1601), who dates the story to 1527.

10. See Ramón A. Gutiérrez, "Must We Deracinate Indians to Find Gay Roots?" *Out/Look* 1 (1989): 61–67. Gutiérrez distorts his evidence (fetched from Guerra, among other sources); the "fact" of cross-dressing as humiliation is not the only "native" practice. As the Balboa account suggests, it may moreover, in some instances, represent a Europeanization of natives. But even where that cannot be supposed, one cannot argue from the practices of some Indians at some times to all Indians. This is Gutiérrez's argument with Katz and Williams, among others, but it can also be mobilized against his own account.

11. See Harriet Whitehead, "The Bow and the Burden Strap," in Sherry B. Ortner and Harriet Whitehead, eds., *Sexual Meanings* (Cambridge: Cambridge University Press, 1981), 80–115. For all Whitehead's attempts to get beyond ethnocentricity and to present the diversity of cases of cross-dressing, one must pause over the anthropological knowledge that leads to this conclusion: "In our own culture, homosexual behavior itself tends to redefine a person to the status of an intermediate (and, except in liberal circles, strongly disapproved) sex type" (110). Not only is it hard to know whether Whitehead locates herself as a "liberal," but her "knowledge" of present-day definitions of homosexuality was a prevailing definition in certain academic/psychoanalytic circles a half-century ago. In this she follows one of the classic articles in the anthropological literature, George Devereux's "Institutionalized Homosexuality among the Mohave Indians," *Human Biology* 9 (1937): 498–527, which, as Gilbert Herdt points out in "Representations of Homosexuality: An Essay on Cultural Ontology and Historical Comparison, Part I," *Journal of the History of Sexuality* 1 (1991): 481–504, reads the Mohave practices through the late Victorian and Freudian lens of inversion. Similarly, it's thanks to that model of the gay man as having a woman trapped inside of him that Whitehead can elide cross-dressing and homosexuality, can view cross-dressing as a male encroachment upon women, and can reduce cross-dressing and homosexuality to "the dominance of heterosexuality" (110) in all forms of sexual behavior. The notion is attributed to Gayle Rubin in a palpable misreading of the relation of homo- and heterosexualities in "The Traffic in Women: Notes on the 'Political Economy' of Sex," in Rayna R. Reiter, ed., *Toward an Anthropology of Women* (New York: Monthly Review Press, 1975), 157–210.

12. For a summary of various accounts of cross-dressing practices that reviews much of the anthropological literature from the first European contacts to the present day, see David E. Greenberg, *The Construction of Homosexuality* (Chicago: University of Chicago Press, 1988), 40–65. Greenberg usefully stresses the range and diversity of practices, although his conclusion that these reflect differences in notions of gender from one society to another too easily effaces the role that sexuality plays in the definitions of gender.

13. Pierre Clastres, *Society against the State,* trans. Robert Hurley and Abe Stein (New York: Zone Books, 1987), 101–28. The book appeared in French in 1974.

14. Clastres refers to "the logic of this closed system, made up of four terms grouped into two opposite pairs" (108) and thinks all the permutations of male and female, bow and basket, are realized when he can produce two male basket-carriers.

15. When Clastres celebrates how well Krembegi fits in, it is to relabel him finally as a woman (110); given the misogyny in Clastres's account, this is hardly a liberatory move across gender. Like other anthropologists, Clastres does not want to

admit the possibility of an indigenous homosexuality. For an example of the ordinary homophobia that circulates as objective anthropological knowledge, see, e.g., Raymond E. Hauser, "The *Berdache* and the Illinois Indian Tribe during the Last Half of the Seventeenth Century," *Ethnohistory* 37 (1990): 45–65.

16. Herdt, "Representations," 489.

Unthinking Sex:
Marx, Engels, and the Scene of Writing
Andrew Parker

— for Robbie and Bruce

*I was also happy in the auditorium itself since I found out that —
contrary to the representation with which my childish imaginings had
for so long provided me — there was only one stage for everyone. I had
thought that one must be prevented from seeing clearly by the other
spectators, as one is in the middle of a crowd; but now I realized that,
on the contrary, thanks to an arrangement which is like the symbol of
all perception, each one feels himself to be the center of the theatre.*

Marcel Proust, *À la recherche du temps perdu*

Dramatizing links between core elements of Marxist theory, moments from nineteenth-century political history, and scenes from Marx's and Engels's "private" lives, this essay suggests that Western Marxism's constitutive dependence on the category of production derives in part from an antitheatricalism, an aversion to certain forms of parody that prevents sexuality from attaining the political significance that class has long monopolized. My title plays on that of an increasingly influential essay published in the 1984 collection *Pleasure and Danger:* Gayle Rubin's "Thinking Sex."[1] Widely noted for its impassioned defense of the rights and practices of a range of sexual minorities, "Thinking Sex" is also a major revision of Rubin's earlier analysis of patriarchy as a system predicated upon gender binarism, obligatory heterosexuality, constraints on female sexuality, and the exchange of women between men "with women being a conduit of a relationship rather than a partner to it." If this conception of the "traffic in women" has proven to be immensely

19

productive for feminist analysis, Rubin's concomitant elaboration of what she termed the "sex/gender system" — "a systematic social apparatus which takes up females as raw materials and fashions domesticated women as products" — has become nothing less than indispensable, forming indeed one of the cornerstones of the field of women's studies.[2]

Yet Rubin's "Thinking Sex" begins to question the adequacy of this very framework. Recognizing that her earlier work "did not distinguish between lust and gender" but lumped the former indiscriminately with the latter, Rubin challenges in her later essay

> the assumption that feminism is or should be the privileged site of a theory of sexuality. Feminism is the theory of gender oppression. To automatically assume that this makes it the theory of sexual oppression is to fail to distinguish between gender, on the one hand, and erotic desire, on the other. (307)

In arguing for the relative autonomy of a new theoretical object — one separate both from chromosomally determined *sex* and from culturally constructed *gender* — Rubin now reserves the term *sexuality* for, in Eve Kosofsky Sedgwick's words, "the array of acts, expectations, narratives, pleasures, identity-formations, and knowledges, in both men and women, that tends to cluster most densely around certain genital sensations but is not adequately defined by them."[3] Rubin acknowledges, of course, that "gender affects the operation of the sexual system, and the sexual system has had gender-specific manifestations" (308) — one need only recall, as I'll do again later in this essay, Karl Heinrich Ulrichs's mid-nineteenth-century account of "sexual inversion" as a confusion between manifest and latent gender identities: *anima muliebris in corpore virile inclusa*. But Rubin's overarching point is that, although historically and structurally imbricated in one another, gender and sexuality "are not the same thing" (308).[4] Indeed, where in most instances the binary codes governing gender difference leave relatively little room for hermeneutic error, sexual orientation — in troubling any simple continuity between outer appearance and inner identity — remains far more capable of generating the most wrenching interpretive anxieties.

If Rubin's essay has helped to place the thinking of sexuality on the contemporary political agenda, this would appear to be a task for which Western Marxism has been and remains underprepared. A case in point would be the 1989 "Marxism Today" conference held at the University of Massachusetts at Amherst: of its fifty-eight assorted panels, many containing the word "gender" or its various cognates in their titles, one session alone was devoted explicitly to questions of sexuality. Given the U.S. government's brutally grudging response to the AIDS crisis and its renewed attacks on the reproductive freedoms of women, such scanty attention seems significant in reflecting what counts *as* political among the varied knowledges and practices comprising "Marxism Today." My intention here is hardly to criticize the conference (as if it simply could have proceeded otherwise), for its reluctance seems continuous with what might be described (with a few important but relatively isolated exceptions like Alexandra Kollontai)[5] as Western Marxism's *tradition* of unthinking sex. When Marxist theorists *have* concerned themselves directly with sexual issues, they've tended to relate the story (impossible to repeat after Foucault) of how a natural or potentially liberatory sexuality has been set upon, repressed, commodified, or otherwise constrained by the institutions of capitalism: as if sexuality were not always already institutional, existing only in its historically sedimented forms and discourses.[6] In addressing, for example, the question "What has sexuality to do with class struggle?" Reimut Reiche seemed to answer *not much* in describing his "personal" interests in "sexual theory" as paling before genuinely "political problems": as if the relationship between the two could in fact be figured simply as a distinction between the public and the private.[7] Recognizing these shortcomings, other theorists have proposed instead to analyze the material conditions of "desire": as if this conception of desire — in tending in practice almost inevitably toward the monolithic, the unmodified, and the hetero — could possibly perform the theoretical work of an unnamed and seemingly unnameable sexuality.[8] Why has thinking sex proven to be so difficult for Western Marxism? Why, if never simply or entirely an absence, does sexuality form an *aporia,* a blockage within the tradition's production-centered paradigm?

What I find remarkable by contrast is that Marxism has experienced no such difficulty in thinking gender — from the nineteenth century onward a range of discourses has existed through which the "woman question" could at least be broached. Gender as a category *registered* even if, for classical Marxism, it was typically classed as an epiphenomenon. The history of Marxist theory has been among other things a history of contesting this secondary and derivative status: not only, for example, has Marx's typical proletarian long since been identified as male (his industrial labors forming the norm against which domestic work appears to be *non*labor), but even the concept of class, as Joan Scott has recently argued, can itself be viewed as masculinist in its implicit assumption of a familial division of labor.[9] In consequence, Marxist feminists have created new forms of analysis in which class and gender are accorded commensurate hermeneutic weight — and such work has enabled the important recognition that class makes its influence felt only in and through its gendered embodiments, and vice versa.[10] Yet Marxist feminism, too, "has typically proceeded in the absence of a theory of sexuality and without much interest in the meaning or experience of sexuality. Or more accurately, it has held implicitly to a view of female sexuality as something that is essentially of a piece with reproduction"[11] — which helps to explain why, even among Marxist feminists, the maternal is often construed as a synecdoche for woman as such, and this despite the rather obvious fact that feminine sexuality is not reducible to what is, after all, only one of its possible components.[12]

I should add, at this point, that Marxism's problems with thinking sex are perhaps not as bleak or as totalizing as I've just made them out to be. More and more historical research — I'm thinking of such work as John D'Emilio's "Capitalism and Gay Identity"[13] — is currently being compiled on the myriad ways that class position affects the formation of sexual practices and identities. And Jeffrey Weeks has even suggested that "the very idea of 'sexuality' itself is an essentially bourgeois one, which developed as an aspect of the self-definition of a class, both against the decadent aristocracy and the rampant immorality of the lower orders in the course of the eighteenth and nineteenth centuries."[14] But both D'Emilio and Weeks proceed from what they assume to be a known and invariant category (production) in order to illuminate what is, from this perspective, unknown and contingent (sexuality). Thus, while we have begun to appreciate how class impinges upon sexual formations, we still have nothing resembling what might be called a sex-inflected analysis of class formations (indeed, this reversal of terms doesn't make any kind of customary sense). Yet if feminist readings have found insistent figurations of gender in Marx's writing even — or especially — when the relation of men to women is not his explicitly thematized concern, this strategy might be borrowed in the interest of performing a *sexual* reading of Marx's texts, a reading that could map the (de)structuring effects of eroticism even — or especially — in works whose subjects seem utterly unsexy. The remainder of this essay takes up this latter possibility: if Marxist theory traditionally hasn't thought sexuality, I want to begin to explore some ways that sexuality — in one of its prominent forms — nevertheless thinks Marx.

My main text will be *The Eighteenth Brumaire of Louis Bonaparte,* that inspired work of political journalism in which Marx, armed "with the weapons of historical research, of criticism, of satire and of wit," explored the causes and consequences of Napoleon III's coup d'état in December 1851.[15] Written in the early months of 1852 for a German emigré newspaper in New York, the *Eighteenth Brumaire* (as Engels described it) "laid bare the whole course of French history" from the workers' uprisings of June 1848, through the defeat of the petit bourgeois *Montagne* in June 1849, to Bonaparte's coup on the anniversary of his uncle's ascension to power — the original Eighteenth Brumaire of Napoleon I. In Engels's view, Marx succeeded in grasping the essence of these events where other commentators failed because "it was precisely Marx who had discovered the great law of motion of history, the law according to which all historical struggles, whether they proceed in the political, religious, philosophical or some other ideological domain, are in fact only the more or less clear expression of struggles of social classes. . . . Consequently, events never took [Marx] by surprise" (14).

Despite the tenor of Engels's remarks, most contemporary readers of the *Brumaire* would probably agree that Marx *was* surprised by recent events in France. For Marx confronted not only a crisis in French history but a crisis in his theory as well, a crisis of representation testing the limits of this claim that politics is "only the more or less clear expression" of class antagonisms. Seeking to confirm an important tenet of his earlier writings — the notion that the state functions as "but a committee for managing the affairs of the whole bourgeoisie"[16] — Marx begins the *Brumaire* by trying to match each parliamentary faction with specific class interests. What frustrates Marx's design, however, is his discovery of "the most motley mixture of crying contradictions" (43), for rather than representing coherently the interests of any one or even of several classes, the state under Bonaparte seems to have "made itself an independent power" (131), not only freeing itself from but even overwhelming its putative ground in production:

> [T]he state enmeshes, controls, regulates, superintends and tutors civil society from its most comprehensive manifestations of life down to its most insignificant stirrings, from its most general modes of being to the private existence of individuals; where through the most extraordinary centralization this parasitic body acquires a ubiquity, an omniscience, a capacity for accelerated mobility and an elasticity which finds a counterpart only in the helpless dependence, in the loose shapelessness, of the actual body politic. (62)

Far from issuing in the revolutionary upheaval that Marx had predicted would erupt, French history under Bonaparte appears instead to have swerved from its dialectical course, generating only what Marx glumly describes as "confusions of cause and effect" (132): "passions without truth, truths without passions; heroes without heroic deeds, history without events; development, whose sole driving force seems to be the calendar, wearying with constant repetition of the same tensions and relaxations" (43). Bonaparte would seem to have thrown "the entire bourgeois economy into confusion" (135), in the process confusing the terms of Marx's own account.

Some of the best recent readings of the *Brumaire* have shown how Marx sought to contain this confusion by treating Bonaparte's rule as merely a temporary aberration, a setback that history "even now" is working to correct. "Let there be no misunderstanding," he writes: the state "is *not* suspended in midair" (123); history is proceeding on its dialectical path; the revolution, despite appearances, "*is* thoroughgoing"; soon "Europe will leap from its feet and exultantly exclaim: Well grubbed, Old Mole!" (121). (We'll shortly see how interesting it is that this voice of authentic revolution should end up citing . . . *Hamlet*.) Struggling desperately to support this optimism by identifying some social class that Bonaparte can be said to represent, Marx turns first to the peasantry, then to a more narrowly defined "conservative peasantry," only to reject each of these groups in turn in favor of a solution that, given his own terms, is hardly a solution at all: a class with no class, a metonymic assemblage rather than a metaphoric unity, the pseudo-class of the lumpen proletariat who formed "the scum, offal and refuse of all [other] classes":

Alongside decayed *roués* with dubious means of subsistence and of dubious origin, alongside ruined and adventurous offshoots of the bourgeoisie, were vagabonds, discharged soldiers, discharged jailbirds, escaped galley slaves, swindlers, mountebanks, *lazzaroni,* pickpockets, tricksters, gamblers, *maquereaus,* brothel keepers, porters, *litterati,* organ-grinders, ragpickers, knife grinders, tinkers, beggars — in short, the whole indefinite, disintegrated mass, thrown hither and thither, which the French term *la bohème.* (75)

A grotesque, serialized mass whose heterogeneity is as fully lexical as it is social, the lumpen in Marx's analysis merely circulate goods but produce no value themselves — Marx's sine qua non for the emergence of an authentically politicized consciousness. His catalog owes much to Adam Smith's inventory in *The Wealth of Nations* of similar kinds of "unproductive" work:

The sovereign, for example, with all the officers both of justice and war who serve under him, the whole army and navy, are unproductive labourers. . . . In the same class must be ranked, some both of the gravest and most important, and some of the most frivolous of professions: churchmen, lawyers, physicians, men of letters of all kinds; players, buffoons, musicians, opera-singers, opera-dancers, &c. . . . Like the declamation of the actor, the harangue of the orator, or the tune of the musician, the work of all of them perishes in the very instant of its production.[17]

Marx might say that all of these activities are mere *parodies* of production; an actor can represent the labor of others, but such a representation is not to be confused with labor strictly defined. Indeed, that the sovereign can be classed with other "theatrical" professions enables Marx to conclude the *Brumaire* on a positive note. For by arguing that Bonaparte is just an actor who belongs as well to a *class* of actors (the "appalling parasitic body" of the lumpen [121]), Marx in effect can salvage the paradigm of representation — of the priority of a productive ground to its secondary and derivative political expression — even as Bonaparte seems to have reduced this paradigm to shambles.[18]

This, at least, would appear to have been Marx's goal. The problem, as he clearly acknowledges, is that this crisis in representation has exceeded the political realm as such in saturating French history and society in a more pervasive confusion of ground and expression. In the famous opening pages of the *Brumaire,* Marx describes this overriding problem as a perverse generalization of the theater, an eruption within civil society of literary relations that have perversely overstepped their textual limits:

> Hegel remarks somewhere that all facts and personages of great importance in world history occur, as it were, twice. He forgot to add: the first time as tragedy, the second as farce. Caussidière for Danton, Louis Blanc for Robespierre, the *Montagne* of 1848 to 1851 for the *Montagne* of 1793 to 1795, the Nephew for the Uncle. And the same caricature occurs in the circumstances attending the second edition of the eighteenth Brumaire! (15)

Marx's point, of course, is not simply that French history repeats itself but that it has done so along a scale of descending literary values. For farce is the most *declassé* of theatrical spectacles: rather than imitating the nobility of a tragic action, farce is a secondary and derivative mode that imitates only the conventions of theater. This is precisely Marx's diagnosis of the course of French history since the era of the Revolution; instead of seizing the moment and acting, the French in the nineteenth century have only, well, *acted:*

> Just when they seem engaged in revolutionizing themselves and things, in creating something that has never yet existed, precisely in such periods of revolutionary crisis they anxiously conjure up the spirits of the past to their service and borrow from them names, battle cries and costumes in order to present the new scene of world history in this time honoured disguise and this borrowed language. (15)

Although Marx recalls that even the great French Revolutionaries dressed themselves up as resurrected Romans, he aims here specifically at later revolutionary movements that "knew nothing better to do than to parody, now 1789, now the revolutionary tradition of 1793 to 1795" (15). These parodies culminate with the rule of Bonaparte, an actor disguised as a statesman (a kind of Ronald Reagan *avant la lettre*) who "conceives the historical life of the nation and their performances as comedy in the most vulgar sense, as a masquerade where the grand costumes, words and postures merely serve to mask the pettiest knavery" (76). Under Bonaparte only "the ghost of the old revolution" walks about; unable to "get rid of the memory of Napoleon," the French continually mistake the nephew for his uncle, the present for the past: "An entire people, which had imagined that by means of a revolution it had imparted to itself an accelerated power of motion, suddenly finds itself set back into a defunct epoch" (17). Marx concludes that only when these ghosts of the past can be busted, when real action replaces mere acting, when all costumes have been returned to the theaters, will revolution once more become possible: "Society seems now to have fallen behind its point of departure; it has in truth first to create for itself the...conditions under which alone modern revolution becomes serious" (19).

Revolution hence is a serious business where seriousness itself is defined as an ability to distinguish the imaginary from the real, representations from what they represent, the theatrical from the authentic. If "men and events appear as inverted *Schlemihls,* as shadows that have lost their substance" (44), Marx seeks to invert this inversion by treating "the spectacle of politics as a farce which, if it is merely exposed as such, will vanish into air like Propsero's masque."[19] Although Jeffrey Mehlman has claimed that Marx *affirms* this becoming-theater of history,[20] my reading has argued just the reverse: that Marx is not celebrating an endless profusion of simulacra but decrying any such mistaking of history for its other. If the *Brumaire* itself adopts a consistent theatrical rhetoric, describing French history as a progression of prologues and scenes, it does so not to endorse this imagery but to reduce it *ad absurdum*. For while Marx's language exuberantly imitates the theater, the text implies throughout not only that he finds this drama wanting but — in keeping with an inherently classical conception of theatrical space — that he is not himself on stage: "[T]he spectacle is represented to a subject who remains outside the drama, outside representation."[21] Indeed, prevented by political events from assuming a leading role, Marx situates himself in the nondramatic space of criticism, an exterior site from which he can parody the parody while still retaining his ironic distance. This is not of course to say that Marx was disinterested in his theatrical criticism (no one could have been less so than he), but that *his* interests would be circumscribed as wholly different from and external to those portrayed on the stage. For if all of France confuses theater with history, insides with outsides, the imaginary with the real, Marx the critic does not, offering the *Brumaire* as testimony to the fact that he, for one, has not been taken in. Although Marx would not perform (in) this scene of writing, his texts quite typically act otherwise. In a longer version of this essay I describe how, in the *Economic and Philosophic Manuscripts* as well as in *Capital,* this exterior space of criticism is ruptured when Marx undertakes "readings" of *Faust* and *Timon of Athens.* I consider as well Marx's highly fraught relationship with Ferdinand Lassalle, a rival for the leadership of the German working class whom Marx pilloried not only for his Jewishness and (what, for Marx, amounted to the same thing) his sexual promiscuity, but for a play Lassalle wrote that Marx pointedly condemned for its "failures of representation."

Here, however, I'd like to take up the thread of the *Brumaire* once more by repeating a question posed by Rousseau in his *Lettre à d'Alembert:* "Who among us is sure enough of himself to bear the performance of such a comedy without halfway taking part in the turns that are played out?...For is being interested in someone anything other than putting oneself in his place?"[22] I raise these questions in connection with the *Brumaire* since its author seems especially to be "interested in someone." For why does Marx hate Bonaparte *so much?* The obvious (if no less true) response is that Bonaparte was the preeminent class enemy who eviscerated the life of a nation. But the more one tries to account for the virulence of Marx's rhetoric — he calls Bonaparte an "indebted adventurer" (68), a foreigner who identified the course of French history "with his own person" (57) — the more one begins to suspect that Marx recognized some uneasy kinship between Bonaparte and another indebted foreigner who similarly tended to identify the course of French history with his own person: Marx himself. Indeed, the only two individuals in the entire *Brumaire* who seem fully aware of what is "really" happening in France are Bonaparte and Marx, both of whom are imputed with the knowledge that essence differs from appearance, insides from outsides, history from theater. The knowledge they share thus remains unique since they alone are unconstrained by class position — "Bonaparte understood" (110), writes Marx, who similarly, almost empathically, understands. But the implications of this secret sharing must have been, at some level, terribly unsettling to Marx, for if Bonaparte detached himself from the class structure, "representing" only a nonrepresentative class, one of Marx's greatest anxieties was that he too did not (simply) represent anyone, that his own writings (even as they traced the effects of the division between intellectual and manual labor) were potentially as unproductive as the lumpen he despised.[23] Perhaps understanding Bonaparte *too* well, finding himself "halfway taking part in the turns that are played out," Marx may have realized, in effect, that it takes one to know one: the very phrase, as Eve Sedgwick has suggested, around which male same-sex desire began to organize itself in the nineteenth century. Lest one takes this possibility of homoeroticism to be extraneous to the *Brumaire,* an imposition of contemporary concerns upon a text that historically resists them, we need only recall that the last page of the text features not only the famous prediction of the fall of the Vendôme Column but also an image of sexual inversion, Madame Girardin's *bon mot* that France has been transformed under Bonaparte from a government of mistresses to a government of "*hommes entretenus* [kept men]" (135) — a transformation Marx must have felt keenly ambivalent about, having already begun to depend upon the regular financial support of one Frederick Engels.[24]

I am not to be sure suggesting, despite the immense amount we know about his life, that Marx was "a homosexual." Of course not, and for several reasons, not the least being that no one could have been more indefatigably heterosexual than he: "Love," he wrote to his wife, Jenny, "not for the being of Feuerbach, not for the transmutation of Molechott, not for the proletariat, but love for the beloved, and particularly for you, makes a man a man."[25] More to the point, the very category of "the homosexual" (as distinct, for example, from "the invert") comes into legal and medical currency only toward the end of the nineteenth century. Yet the phenomenon described by Sedgwick as male homosexual panic was certainly well established by the mid-1800s as men became increasingly "pressed to defend their friendships against imputations of homosexual feelings," feelings that were particularly likely to arise whenever men collaborated closely with each other.[26] In Sedgwick's words: "Because the paths of male entitlement, especially in the nineteenth century, required certain intense male bonds that were not readily distinguishable from the most reprobated bonds, an endemic and ineradicable state of what I am calling male homosexual panic became the normal condition of male heterosexual entitlement." Since, in this reading, the threat of homophobic persecution regulated not only "a nascent minority population of distinctly homosexual men" but "the male homosocial bonds that structure all culture," no man could ever be sure of proving — or be exempt from having to prove — "that he is not (that his bonds are not) homosexual."[27] If one result of this double-bind was a paranoic aversion to self-disclosure, another may have been the nineteenth century's obsessive fantasy of an authentic self immune from the dangers of theatricality, a fantasy that has generated commentary from Lionel Trilling's *Sincerity and Authenticity* to Nina Auerbach's recent *Private Theatricals.* Indeed, that male homosexual panic and antitheatricalism resonate strikingly with one another can be seen in a passage from David Marshall's *The Figure of Theater;* in describing an intense ambivalence of certain writers toward the possibility that theatrical relations may exist "outside the playhouse," Marshall writes: "Theater, for these authors, represents, creates, and responds to uncertainties about how to constitute, maintain, and represent a stable and authentic self; fears about exposing one's character before the world; and epistemological dilemmas about knowing or being known by other people."[28]

That Marx and Engels *were* concerned about knowing or being known by other people seems a safe inference given the evidence of several letters recently translated into English for the first time in full. Dating from 1869 (when Marx was revising the *Brumaire* for its first German edition), these letters are remarkable in that they reveal firsthand knowledge of the writings of Karl Heinrich Ulrichs, the Hanoverian lawyer who, in a series of booklets appearing in the mid-1860s with the collective title *Researches into the Riddle of Love between Men,* developed his theory of sexual inversion postulating the existence of a "Third Sex": the *Urning* or Uranian whose anatomically masculine outside misrepresents a spiritually feminine inside.[29] Ulrichs makes his appearance in the Marx–Engels correspondence in connection with the current political situation in Germany, where Wilhelm Liebknecht's pro-Communist organization seemed to be losing ground to the General Association of German Workers (the ADAV), whose leadership, after the death of Lassalle, passed into the hands of Johann Baptist von Schweitzer. The first Social Democrat to hold legislative office in a European parliament, Schweitzer was a lawyer who authored the four-act comedy *Alcibiades oder Bildung aus Hellas,* a play "with some strikingly realistic references to Greek love.*"* It was only through Lassalle's intervention that Schweitzer could first join and then rise to prominence in the ADAV, for he had been arrested in 1862 when "two elderly ladies enjoying a quiet stroll through the public park of Mannheim came upon Schweitzer and an unidentified young man in a highly compromising situation."[30] Ulrichs had been casually acquainted with Schweitzer, and in response to the arrest composed a legal defense that he sent to Schweitzer in jail. When Schweitzer nonetheless was convicted and barred from the practice of law, Ulrichs began writing his booklets about Uranism in an effort to repeal the antisodomy provisions of the North German Penal Code, thereby laying the groundwork for what would later become the German homosexual movement. Schweitzer, meanwhile, was finally admitted to the ADAV over the protests of some of its members when Lassalle argued that "the abnormality attributed to Dr. von Schweitzer has nothing whatever to do with his political character.... I could understand your not wishing Dr. von Schweitzer to marry your daughter. But why not think, work, and struggle in his company? What has any department of political activity to do with sexual abnormality?"[31]

Engels, for one, seemed to think the two had something to do with one another. Condemning elsewhere the ancient Greeks for their "abominable practice of sodomy [which] degraded alike their gods and themselves with the myth of Ganymede,"[32] Engels writes the following to Marx when Schweitzer succeeded, Liebknecht's efforts notwithstanding, in unifying the two main wings of the ADAV:

Manchester, 22 June 1869

Dear Moor,

I don't know whether you have such fine weather there as we have here, but daylight has been so exhausted that, on the longest day, we had to turn the gas on at 4 o'clock in the afternoon. And it is devilish to read or write when you don't know whether it is day or night.

Tussy [Marx's daughter Eleanor, then visiting the Engels household] is very jolly. This morning the whole family went SHOPPING; tomorrow evening they want to go to the theatre....

So that is Wilhelm [Liebknecht]'s entire success: that the male-female line [Schweitzer's faction of the ADAV] and the all-female line [the group supported by the Countess von Hartzfeld, Lassalle's former patron] have united! He really has achieved something there. Schweitzer will naturally be re-elected [as head of the ADAV] — in view of the precipitancy with which the business has been conducted — and then he will, once again, be the chosen one of general suffrage. Wilhelm is also preserving an obstinate silence about this event.

The *Urning* [identified by the editors of the correspondence as Ulrichs's *Argonauticus,* but this volume wouldn't appear until September of that year] you sent me is a very curious thing. These are extremely unnatural revelations. The paederasts are beginning to count themselves, and discover that they are a power in the state. Only organisation was lacking, but according to this source it apparently already exists in secret. And since they now have such important men in all the old parties and even in the new ones, from [Johannes] Rösing [a Bremen merchant] to Schweitzer, they cannot fail to triumph. *Guerre aux cons, paix aus trus-de cul* [war on the cunts, peace to the assholes] will now be the slogan. It is a bit of luck that we, personally, are too old to have to fear that, when this party wins, we shall have to pay physical tribute to the victors. But the younger generation! Incidentally it is only in Germany that a fellow like this can possibly come forward, convert this smut into a theory, and offer the invitation: *introite* [the title of a section from Ulrichs's earlier book *Memnon*], etc. Unfortunately, he has not yet got up the courage to acknowledge publicly that he is "that way," and must still operate *coram publico* "from the front," if not "going in from the front" as he once said by mistake. But just wait until the new North German Penal Code recognizes the *droits du cul;* then he will operate quite differently. Then things will go badly enough for poor frontside people like us, with our childish penchant for females. If Schweitzer could be made useful for anything, it would be to wheedle out of this peculiar honorable gentleman the particulars of the paederasts in high and top places, which would certainly not be difficult for him as a brother in spirit. . . .

Close of post. Best greetings.

Your

F. E.[33]

Astonishing in the virulence of its misogyny and homophobia, Engels's letter proceeds from anticipating a visit to the theater to reflecting on Schweitzer's recent victory — which then puts him in mind of the book Marx had sent him. Recognizing some resemblance (if only fleeting and parodic) between the pederasts' secret societies and those of the radical left, he fantasizes about what will happen to "poor frontside" men — "like us," he adds, to dispel any doubt — if the pederasts carry the day, a strategy that allows him the freedom to experience vicariously the anal eroticism he seems to condemn. If it's a good thing, on the one hand, that Marx and I are too old and unattractive to have to engage in such acts ourselves, it's even better for me to imagine, on the other, the fulsome erotic surplus that would accrue to us from engaging in homophobic blackmail. The ease with which this scenario occurs to Engels surely indicates his awareness that he could always be so targeted himself. Indeed, described by his biographers as a "semibachelor" who lived unmarried first with Mary Burns, then after her death with her sister Lizzie (whom he would marry on *her* deathbed), and then to the end of his life with a succession of designated housekeepers, Engels must have felt himself acutely vulnerable to the imputation of homoerotic feelings — a vulnerability exacerbated by his identification with and subordination to his closest male friend, of whom he wrote late in life: "I have done what I was cut out for — namely to play second fiddle — and I think that I have done quite well in that capacity. And I have been happy to have had such a wonderful first violin as Marx."[34] The erotic overtones of all this fiddling around could hardly have been lost on Engels, for whom proscribed and prescribed male behavior indeed must have looked remarkably similar. Caught in a viselike double bind that I can never acknowledge directly (with Marx above all), my best policy would be to guard against self-revelation by safely attacking "real" inverts — which will help mitigate my "devilish" fear that I don't really know if it's day or night.

If Marx replied directly to Engels's letter a copy no longer survives. (Elsewhere he called Schweitzer a "shitty cur," urging a friend to "spread" jokes about him in the newspapers.)[35] We do, however, have a subsequent letter demonstrating Marx's own familiarity with Ulrichs's work, a letter that — though far less panicked than Engels's — manages to register a similar ambivalence (43:403):

London, 17 December 1869

Dear Fred,

Best thanks for £100. Yesterday I couldn't acknowledge because of the sudden appearance of [Wilhelm] Strohn [a member of the Communist League]. The poor fellow had his blood relapse again in May. Because of his health, he has had to hang around since then in Switzerland, etc.; looks very poorly and is very peevish. The doctors recommend him to marry. Strohn will be returning from here to Bradford, and desires you to return him the *Urnings* or whatever the pederast's book is called.

As soon as he goes (on Monday) I shall myself buzz around town to raise the [J. P.] *Prendergast* [author of *The Cromwellian Settlement of Ireland*]. I couldn't do it last week because of the filthy weather, which I couldn't risk TO UNDERGO in my not-yet-restored state of health.

Opening with the first of what will become a series of strangely regulated exchanges, Marx acknowledges the receipt of yet another monetary gift from his friend. This circulation of funds, however, immediately gives rise to other kinds: the circulation of their friend Strohn's blood; the circulation of Ulrichs's book,[36] whose title Marx seems to have forgotten but which Strohn now wants Engels to return; the circulation between heterosexual marriage and sexual inversion; and even the circulation of verbal signifiers, the word "paederast" immediately calling up the name Prendergast, whose book Marx can "raise" without "risk" now that the "filthy" weather has abated.

What Engels's and Marx's letters both put into play, of course, is a way of safely raising something filthy between themselves. While many scholars have noted (how could they not?) that their correspondence is smeared liberally with excremental imagery, these same readers never acknowledge that shit can acquire significance only by activating an economy of anal pleasures, desires, and attachments. Others similarly recognize that the lumpen — "a coagulating mass," "the scum, offal, and refuse of all other classes" — both repel and fascinate Marx and Engels, but what predictably escapes analysis is just what — or where — this *lump* may be. When in 1845 Jules Janin called the lumpen "foul rags that have no name in any language,"[37] his description reverberates with the church's condemnation of sodomy as the act *inter Christianos non nominandum*. Indeed, Marx's and Engels's writings on the lumpen echo strikingly the emerging discourse popularly associated with the gay underworld: the lumpen are "a phenomenon that occurs in more or less developed form in all the so far known phases of society" (10:408); they have "their headquarters in big cities" and are "absolutely venal and absolutely brazen" (21:99); they actively "recruit" new members (10:62); they have "unhealthy and dissolute appetites," and their pleasure "becomes *crapuleux*, where money, filth and blood commingle" (10:50–51). If, as we recall from the *Brumaire*, the French state receives from Bonaparte "an *accelerated mobility* and an *elasticity* which finds a counterpart only in the *helpless dependence*, in the *loose shapelessness*, of the actual body politic" (62; my emphases), we now may better understand why the lumpen would be figured repeatedly through a rhetoric of anality.

If Marx remains both horrified and attracted by this tropology, this may be because he finds that it parodies the central categories of his thought. The question of where values come from animates the whole of his evolving critique of political economy, and his dependable answer is labor defined as "life-activity, productive life itself," where production has been modeled on procreation.[38] In Hannah Arendt's words: Marx's work "rests on the equation of productivity with fertility"; "he based his whole theory [of production] on the understanding of laboring and begetting as two modes of the same fertile life process."[39] The heterosexism of this formulation is not to be dismissed as merely figural, for Marx views labor invariably as the "life of the species," as "life-engendering life"; "productive labor" is a fact "imposed by Nature"; labor is the "father" and the earth the "mother" of value.[40] Hence Marx's disgusted fascination with acts (quoting one of Ulrichs's German reviewers) that "*imitate* coitus between male persons," acts that parody production in the "sterile" ways that they eroticize "the final ending of the intestine."[41] Hence, as well, Marx's mordant delight in finding that Bonaparte secured his rule with the sausage — *farce* — his famous gift to the masses of meat extruded into alien intestinal membranes.

Thus to discover farce once more within the body politic is to appreciate why theater and anality can each stand indicatively for the crisis in representation Marx grapples with throughout the *Brumaire*. A sexuality that fails to embody approved gender norms looks, to Marx, nothing so much like Bonaparte's theatricalized France: *both* are travesties in his view, parodies of authentic production relations that systematically confuse proper insides and outsides. Although Marx's normative categories depend for their coherence on the demonization of these parodic others, the *Brumaire* never quite succeeds in expelling them from itself — which may help to account not just for its moment of panic but for the misogyny implicit in its antipathy to theater. Adopting a strategy that, by midcentury, already had been proven tried and true, Marx attempts to manage his ambivalence by recasting it along the axis of gender, the seemingly stable opposition between male and female offering itself as a remedy for sexually charged relations that seem to have lost all such distinction. As Marx will be relieved to discover, it is the *woman* (Dame Quickly from *Henry IV, Part I*) who is "neither fish nor flesh; a man knows not where to have her."[42] This displacement onto gender has been profoundly generative in its effects and continues to influence recent readings of the *Brumaire* — from Daumier's effeminizing sculpture selected for the cover of the International Publishers edition, through Dominick La-Capra's characterization of Bonaparte's voice as "falsetto,"[43] to the following utterly remarkable passage by Terry Eagleton (which I quote here in full):

> It is not just that bourgeois revolution swathes itself in theatrical costume: it *is* theatrical in its essence, a matter of panache and breathless rhetoric, a baroque frenzy whose poetic effusions are in inverse proportion to its meagre substance. It is not just that it manipulates past fictions: it *is* a kind of fiction, an ill-made drama that expends itself in Act Three and totters exhausted to its tawdry conclusion. If bourgeois revolutions trick themselves out in flashy tropes, it is because there is a kind of fictiveness in their very structure, a hidden flaw that disarticulates form and content.[44]

Breathless and tawdry, dissimulating an inner lack with tropes and feather boas, French history in Eagleton's synopsis is depicted as an actress, a sordid floozy whose fate was just what she deserved. Eagleton is altogether faithful here to the spirit of the *Brumaire,* for it was Marx who inaugurated this practice of blaming the victim: "It is not enough to say, as the French do, that their nation was taken unawares. A nation and a woman are not forgiven the unguarded hour in which the first adventurer that came along could violate them" (21). Completing this predictable pattern of imagery, Marx avers that Bonaparte brings "the bride [of France] home at last, but only after she had been prostituted" (37). French history as public woman unfettered: overstepping the bounds of decent decorum, she will be figured unfailingly as the consummate actress who, in leaving the confines of home, in making a public spectacle of herself, infects her society with her sleazy theatrics.

As Joan Scott has recently argued, the category of the domestic sphere tends to operate in political theory "as a double foil: it is the place where a presumably natural sexual division of labor prevails, as compared with the workplace, where relations of production are socially constructed; but it is also the place from which politics cannot emanate because it does not provide the experience of exploitation that contains within it the possibility of the collective identity of interest that is class consciousness."[45] Although Marx has done far more than most to deconstruct the opposition of the private and the public, the *Brumaire* also honors this distinction in ridiculing "the *dames des halles,* the fishwives" (114) who, supposedly notable for their characteristic *odeur,* formed in Marx's imagination one of Bonaparte's constituencies. This engendering of the division between privacy and publicity would be one last attempt to patrol the distinction between insides and outsides, one last resistance to performing the scene of writing. As I've been implying throughout, however, Marx can respect such distinctions only in their breach, finding himself acting when he only would be ... acting, criticizing theater from a position already (up)staged, unthinking sex but performing it instead. I offer as a coda one last theatrical engagement.

"In private life," Marx wrote in the *Brumaire,* "one differentiates between what a man thinks and says of himself and what he really is and does" (47). At home, indeed, Marx was crazy about the theater, reading aloud from *Faust* to his children, playing the part of Mephistopheles in parlor productions, hosting regular meetings of a Shakespeare Club where he was described by a fellow member as "delightful, never criticising, always entering into the spirit of any fun that was going on, laughing when anything struck him as particularly comic, until the tears ran down his cheeks — the oldest in years, but in spirit as young as any of us. And his friend, the faithful Frederic Engels, was equally spontaneous."[46] Marx imparted this enthusiasm to his favorite daughter, Eleanor, the future translator of *Madame Bovary* and coauthor (with Edward Aveling) of *The Woman Question.* When she fell seriously ill at age nineteen with what Marx described as "one of these female complaints, in which the hysterical element plays a part," he fully supported her in her decision to become an actress, to exchange a private for a public audience. She did so, becoming friends not only with Havelock El-

lis but also with G. B. Shaw, to whom she wrote on the subject of
Ibsen's reception in England:

> How odd it is that people complain that his plays "have no end"
> but just leave you where you were, that he gives no *solution* to
> the problem he has set you! As if in life things "ended" off either
> comfortably or uncomfortably. We play through our little dramas, and
> comedies, and tragedies, and farces, and then begin it all over again.

Grateful to Marx for his encouragement, Eleanor disclosed the following in a letter to a friend: "Our natures were exactly alike! Father
was talking of my elder sister and of me, and said: 'Jenny is most
like me, but Tussy... *is* me.' "[47]

NOTES

Versions of this essay were presented as lectures at the "Marxism Now" Conference
(Amherst), the American Comparative Literature Association Conference (San Diego),
and at Rutgers, Cornell, New York, and Duke universities. I thank my hosts and
audiences for their helpful responses, as well as Peter Stallybrass and Michael Warner
for their conversation and suggestions.

1. Gayle Rubin, "Thinking Sex: Notes for a Radical Theory of the Politics of
Sexuality," in Carole S. Vance, ed., *Pleasure and Danger: Exploring Female Sexuality*
(Boston: Routledge and Kegan Paul, 1984), 267–319. All further references to this
work will appear in the text.

2. Gayle Rubin, "The Traffic in Women: Notes on the 'Political Economy' of Sex,"
in Rayna R. Reiter, ed., *Toward an Anthropology of Women* (New York: Monthly
Review Press, 1975), 174, 158.

3. Eve Kosofsky Sedgwick, *Epistemology of the Closet* (Berkeley: University of
California Press, 1990), 29.

4. Cf. David M. Halperin, *One Hundred Years of Homosexuality* (New York:
Routledge, 1990), 25: "Now sexual identity, so conceived, is not to be confused with
gender identity or gender role: indeed, one of the chief conceptual functions of
sexuality is to distinguish, once and for all, sexual identity from matters of gender —
to decouple, as it were, *kinds* of sexual predilection from *degrees* of masculinity and
femininity." As Sedgwick observes, moreover, sexuality extends in dimensions that
may have little if any bearing on the *gender* of the object-choice: human/animal,
adult/child, singular/plural, autoerotic/alloerotic (*Epistemology of the Closet,* 35).

5. See Alexandra Kollontai, *Selected Writings,* trans. Alix Holt (London: Allison
and Busby, 1977).

6. See Jeffrey Weeks, *Sexuality* (London: Tavistock, 1986), 24.

7. Reimut Reiche, *Sexuality and Class Struggle,* trans. Susan Bennett (New York:
Praeger, 1971), 8.

8. See, for example, Richard Lichtman, *The Production of Desire* (New York:
Free Press, 1982).

9. Joan Wallach Scott, *Gender and the Politics of History* (New York: Columbia University Press, 1988), 53–65. See also Donna Haraway's wonderfully succinct overview of this history in *Simians, Cyborgs, and Women: The Reinvention of Nature* (New York: Routledge, 1991), 127–48, esp. 132: "The root difficulty [for Marx] was an inability to historicize sex itself; like nature, sex functioned analytically as a prime matter or raw material for the work of history."

10. This literature is vast even if confined to the United States and the United Kingdom. See, among many others, Michèle Barrett, *Women's Oppression Today: Problems in Marxist Feminist Analysis* (London: Verso, 1980); Rosalind Coward, *Patriarchal Precedents: Sexuality and Social Relations* (London: Routledge and Kegan Paul, 1983); Zillah Eisenstein, ed., *Capitalist Patriarchy and the Case for Socialist Feminism* (New York: Monthly Review Press, 1979); Nancy Fraser, *Unruly Practices: Power, Discourse, and Gender in Contemporary Social Theory* (Minneapolis: University of Minnesota Press, 1989); Nancy Hartsock, *Money, Sex and Power: Toward a Feminist Historical Materialism* (New York: Longman, 1983); Annette Kuhn and AnnMarie Volpe, eds., *Feminism and Materialism: Women and Modes of Production* (London: Routledge and Kegan Paul, 1978); Catherine A. MacKinnon, *Toward a Feminist Theory of the State* (Cambridge: Harvard University Press, 1989); Sheila Rowbotham, *Women, Resistance and Revolution* (New York: Vintage, 1974); Lydia Sargent, ed., *Women and Revolution* (Boston: South End Press, 1981); Lise Vogel, *Marxism and the Oppression of Women: Toward a Unitary Theory* (New Brunswick, N.J.: Rutgers University Press, 1983); Eli Zaretsky, *Capitalism, the Family, and Personal Life* (New York: Harper and Row, 1976).

11. Eve Kosofsky Sedgwick, *Between Men: English Literature and Male Homosocial Desire* (New York: Columbia University Press, 1985), 12.

12. An especially egregious instance would be Christine Di Stefano's *Configurations of Masculinity: A Feminist Perspective on Modern Political Theory* (Ithaca, N.Y.: Cornell University Press, 1991). After noting that "what is missing in Marx's theory is, of course, an explicit reckoning with gender," Di Stefano proceeds at length to castigate Marx solely for his inability to recognize "the laboring mother" (106, 122). As Judith Butler explains, to conflate in this way the feminine with the maternal is "to reinforce precisely the binary, heterosexist framework that carves up genders into masculine and feminine and forecloses an adequate description of the kind of subversive and parodic convergences that characterize gay and lesbian cultures" (*Gender Trouble: Feminism and the Subversion of Identity* [New York: Routledge, 1990], 66).

13. John D'Emilio, "Capitalism and Gay Identity," in Ann Snitow, Christine Stansell, and Sharon Thompson, eds., *Powers of Desire: The Politics of Sexuality* (New York: Monthly Review Press, 1983), 100–13.

14. Weeks, *Sexuality*, 37.

15. Karl Marx, *The Eighteenth Brumaire of Louis Bonaparte* (New York: International Publishers, 1963), 8. All further references to this work will appear in the text.

16. Karl Marx and Friedrich Engels, *The Communist Manifesto*, ed. A. J. P. Taylor (New York: Penguin, 1967), 82.

17. Adam Smith, *The Wealth of Nations*, ed. Edward Cannan (Chicago: University of Chicago Press, 1976), 1:352. My thanks for this reference to Peter Stallybrass.

18. On theater as a generalized "parasite" see Jacques Derrida, *Limited Inc* (Evanston, Ill.: Northwestern University Press, 1988).

19. Peter Stallybrass, "Marx and Heterogeneity: Thinking the Lumpenproletariat," *Representations* 31 (summer 1990): 87–88.

20. Jeffrey Mehlman, *Revolution and Repetition: Marx/Hugo/Balzac* (Berkeley: University of California Press, 1977), 13.

21. Mikkel Borch-Jacobsen, *The Freudian Subject*, trans. Catherine Porter (Stanford, Calif.: Stanford University Press, 1988), 44.

22. Cited in David Marshall, *The Surprising Effects of Sympathy* (Chicago: University of Chicago Press, 1988), 136.

23. See my *Re-Marx: Deconstructive Readings in Marxist Theory and Criticism*, Rhetoric of the Human Sciences series (Madison: University of Wisconsin Press, forthcoming).

24. "In terms of present-day values, Engels subsidized Marx and his family to the extent of over £100,000" (David McLellan, *Friedrich Engels* [New York: Penguin, 1977], 95). Inflation has of course since boosted this figure.

25. Saul K. Padover, ed., *The Letters of Karl Marx* (Englewood Cliffs, N.J.: Prentice-Hall, 1979), 107.

26. Wayne Koestenbaum, *Double Talk: The Erotics of Male Literary Collaboration* (New York: Routledge, 1989), 2. (After Koestenbaum, indeed, it's impossible to read Terrell Carver's *Marx and Engels: The Intellectual Relationship* without finding its title a tad defensive.) Another collaborative project would be the child whose paternity Marx and Engels "shared." Helen (Lenchen) Demuth was given as a "gift" from Jenny's parents to the Marx family, for whom she would work for decades as a servant. Demuth became pregnant almost immediately upon her arrival in June 1851 (the gestation would include the period when Marx wrote the *Brumaire*). The child's father was long presumed to be Engels, but now it is generally accepted that the boy in fact was Marx's. Christened Henry Frederick Demuth, his first name honored Marx's father, his second name Engels. (Cf. the conclusion of Bram Stoker's *Dracula*, where the child's "bundle of names links all our little band of men together.") In Jerrold Seigel's account: "When Engels was near death in 1895, however, and had not mentioned Frederick Demuth in his will, he let his friend and housekeeper Louise Freyberger (Karl Kautsky's ex-wife) know the truth lest he be thought of disowning his own son. Louise Freyberger told Eleanor Marx who, disbelieving, made Engels tell her, too" (*Marx's Fate: The Shape of a Life* [Princeton, N.J.: Princeton University Press, 1978], 275). A tighter fit than this for Gayle Rubin's traffic-in-women template would be difficult to imagine, but it's just as difficult to fathom, in light of this history, why *Marx* would attack Bonaparte in the *Brumaire* for having outlawed research into paternity (124).

27. Sedgwick, *Epistemology of the Closet*, 184–85.

28. David Marshall, *The Figure of Theater: Shaftesbury, Defoe, Adam Smith, and George Eliot* (New York: Columbia University Press, 1986), 1.

29. See Hubert Kennedy, *Ulrichs* (Boston: Alyson Publications, 1988), which explains why, in Ulrichs's view, *any* "love that is directed toward a man is necessarily a woman's love" (50). "That sexual object-choice might be wholly independent of such 'secondary' characteristics as masculinity or femininity never seems to have entered anyone's head" until Havelock Ellis and Freud (Halperin, *One Hundred Years*

of Homosexuality, 16). Freud attacks Ulrichs by name in his *Three Essays on the Theory of Sexuality,* trans. and ed. James Strachey (New York: Basic Books, 1962), 8.

30. See James Steakley, *The Homosexual Emancipation Movement in Germany* (New York: Arno Press, 1975).

31. Cited in David Footman, *Ferdinand Lassalle: Romantic Revolutionary* (New Haven: Yale University Press, 1947), 181–82. For more on Schweitzer see Roger Morgan, *The German Social Democrats and the First International, 1864–1872* (Cambridge: Cambridge University Press, 1965).

32. Frederick Engels, *The Origin of the Family, Private Property and the State,* ed. Eleanor Burke Leacock (New York: International Publishers, 1972), 128.

33. Karl Marx and Frederick Engels, *Collected Works* (New York: International Publishers, 1988), 43:295–96. All further references to this work will be cited by volume and page in the text.

34. Cited in McLellan, *Friedrich Engels,* 92. McLellan describes Engels as a "semi-bachelor" on 94.

35. Cited in Kennedy, *Ulrichs,* 135.

36. That Strohn's "blood relapse" called Ulrichs to mind is another sign that Marx had read his work: "Ulrichs wondered in writing if the transfusion of the blood of an Urning into a Dioning would turn him into an Urning" (Kennedy, *Ulrichs,* 77).

37. Cited in Stallybrass, "Marx and Heterogeneity," 72.

38. Karl Marx, *The Economic and Philosophic Manuscripts of 1844,* ed. Dirk J. Struik (New York: International Publishers, 1964), 113.

39. Hannah Arendt, *The Human Condition* (Chicago: University of Chicago Press, 1958), 106.

40. Marx, *Economic and Philosophic Manuscripts,* 113, and *Capital,* ed. Frederick Engels (New York: International Publishers, 1967), 1:81, 43.

41. Cited in Kennedy, *Ulrichs,* 146, 133.

42. "The reality of the value of commodities differs in this respect from Dame Quickly, that we don't know 'where to have it'" (*Capital* 1:47).

43. Dominick LaCapra, *Re-Thinking Intellectual History* (Ithaca, N.Y.: Cornell University Press, 1983), 287.

44. Terry Eagleton, *Walter Benjamin, or Towards a Revolutionary Criticism* (London: Verso, 1981), 167. Cf. Eagleton's "Nationalism: Irony and Commitment," in Seamus Deane, ed., *Nationalism, Colonialism, and Literature* (Minneapolis: University of Minnesota Press, 1990), 31: "As Oscar Wilde well understood, socialism is essential for genuine individualism; and if Wilde's own outrageous individualism prefigures that in one sense, it also testifies in its very flamboyant artifice to the way in which any individualism of the present is bound to be a strained, fictive, parodic travesty of the real thing."

45. Scott, *Gender and the Politics of History,* 74.

46. Cited in Yvonne Kapp, *Eleanor Marx* (New York: Pantheon, 1972), 1:193. S. S. Prawer further recalls "that the Marx household in London was full of the sound of poetry being declaimed, or novels and plays being read aloud; and that Marx himself loved the sonorities of *Faust* so much that he tended to overdo his declamations" (*Karl Marx and World Literature* [New York: Oxford University Press, 1978], 207).

47. Citations are from Seigel, *Marx's Fate,* 282–84.

Freud's Fallen Women: Identification, Desire, and "A Case of Homosexuality in a Woman"
Diana Fuss

This essay selects for discussion one of the most underdiscussed texts in the psychoanalytic library, Sigmund Freud's case history of 1920, "The Psychogenesis of a Case of Homosexuality in a Woman,"[1] in order to scrutinize the submerged metaphorics that underwrite Freud's theory of female inversion. Postulating that no scientific language can escape the pull of metaphor, I would like to suggest that the cognitive paradigm of "falling" that Freud provides in this case study to "explain" female homosexuality is already a rhetorical figure. The allegory of the fall — upon which Freud's entire theory of inversion hinges — activates in psychoanalysis a certain Newtonian metalogics of force, counterforce, attraction, repulsion, and reversal. These figurative traces of psychodynamics in psychoanalytic theory name more than the subject's fall into (or out of) sexuality; they critically define and delimit the operations of two psychical mechanisms Freud locates as central to the formation of any sexual identity: identification and desire. Specifically for Freud, a gravitational fall back into preoedipality, secured through an identification with the father and a concomitant desire for the mother, accounts for the "psychogenesis of a case of homosexuality in a woman." The case history Freud published under this name represents his most sustained attempt to engage with the subject of female homosexuality; Freud's efforts to trace and to codify the "preoedipalization" of the homosexual subject are largely responsible for establishing the perimeters of a sexology that is founded upon questions of space, time, duration, gravity, and motion, and that continues to set the terms of the psychoanalytic debates on sexuality today.

In the history of psychoanalysis, female homosexuality is theorized almost exclusively in terms of the "pre": the preoedipal, the presymbolic, the prelaw, the premature, even the presexual. The critical presupposition that female homosexuality occupies the space and time of an origin — that it is widely assumed to be, in a word, pretheoretical — could account for its long-term neglect in revisionist theoretical work ordinarily devoted to challenging normative definitions of sexual desire. Part of the general critical disregard for homosexuality in contemporary theories of sexual difference may well be occasioned by a judicious devaluation of false foundationalisms and a healthy suspicion of theories of primacy — those very theories of primacy within which homosexuality has historically been understood. However, such antifoundationalisms, while crucially challenging the dangerous ideology of natural origins, need also both to investigate how a concept like "preoedipality" is itself constituted as an effect of a cultural symbolics and, more particularly, to ask how homosexuality comes to be so routinely situated in the regressive, conservative space of this fictive origin. How and why do psychoanalytic theories of female homosexuality position their subjects *as* foundational, as primeval, as primitive, and indeed as presubjects, presubjects before the normative, heterosexualizing operations of the Oedipus complex, that "legal, legalising coordinate"?[2] This study will attempt to confront the limits and the dangers of preoedipality as an explanatory model for female homosexuality, focusing specifically upon the crucial role identification and desire play in Freud's theorization of sexual identity formation.

Liminal Foundations

Let me begin by posing the following historical and institutional question: Where is female homosexuality to be found in psychoanalysis? The answer is in psychoanalysis's very foundations. Of the six case studies Freud completed, both the first case study, *Fragment of an Analysis of a Case of Hysteria* (1905), and the last, "The Psychogenesis of a Case of Homosexuality in a Woman" (1920) are studies of inversion in women, studies of deviations in respect of a woman's object-choice.[3] Jacques Lacan's dissertation on paranoid psychosis, his 1932 thesis in medicine, betrays a similar fascination for female paranoiacs whose lack of distance from other women and from themselves (attributed by Lacan to their presymbolic, prelinguistic, preseparation relation to the mother) constitutes the very source of their paranoia.[4] So deep is Lacan's early preoccupation with the question of homosexuality in women that one would have to amend Catherine Clément's general observation, "In the beginning Lacan was interested only in women,"[5] to the more precise formulation, "In the beginning Lacan was interested only in *homosexual* women." More recently, Julia Kristeva's work on sexual difference is noteworthy for its relative uninterest in, not to say dismissal of, female homosexuality, work that addresses the question of homosexuality in women only in occasional postscriptural asides. But it is in her earliest books that female homosexuality emerges as "foundational" and as preparatory to her later depreciation of it — especially in *About Chinese Women* (1974), where the first third of the book defers the question of the Orient to elaborate instead a theory of orientation.[6]

From Sigmund Freud to Julia Kristeva, preoedipality defines the fundamental psychical organization of the homosexual subject who never, it seems, fully accedes to the position of subject but who remains in the ambiguous space of the precultural. Beginning with Freud's study of the "sexual aberrations" upon which he bases his entire theory of sexuality, moving through Lacan's thorough subsumption of female homosexuality into a preoedipalized paranoid psychosis, and reaching toward Kristeva's theory of female homosexuality as not a fulfillment of the revolutionary potential of the semiotic but a refusal of it, what we see in psychoanalysis's positioning and repositioning of homosexuality is a critical fall back to the earliest stages of the subject's formation. The progressive movement in psychoanalysis is backward, deep into the subject's prehistory. The most recent work on the question of subjectivity has pushed back the point of sexual identity formation to a time before the preoedipal; the trajectory from Freud to Lacan to Kristeva advances a fast-fall from oedipal to preoedipal to semiotic (or what one might call the pre-preoedipal). The very history of the institution of psychoanalysis enacts a critical temporal inversion: the preoedipal is theorized after the oedipal, suggesting that any "pre" is a construct of the "post."[7] Ironically, psychoanalysis itself performs the very regressive movement that Freud, and Lacan in his famous "return to Freud," describe as constitutive of what might be called homosexuality's "devolutionary" process—that is, a temporal fall back, a return to a time before the beginning of time, before culture, before oedipality, and before history. Inverted in its progression, psychoanalysis uncannily follows a developmental path strikingly similar to the etiology of homosexuality first set out by Freud.

What this essay does not address is the question of female homosexuality's "etiology" (the "cause" or "origin" of inversion) — a question that can only assume in advance what it purports to demonstrate. Rather it seeks to understand how female homosexuality is not only structurally situated in the inaugural moments of psychoanalysis but theoretically located at the site of an origin, the origin of *any* female sexual identity. These latter questions will tell us far more about what Patricia Williams has recently termed "inessentially speaking"[8] than what even Freud recognizes as the pointless resuscitation of debates over etiology (i.e., Is homosexuality innate or acquired?).[9] Inessentiality is a particularly useful figure for describing homosexuality's foundational yet liminal position in psychoanalytic accounts of identity formation. The preposition "in" in "inessential," which here doubles as a prefix, connotes at once a relation of exteriority or nonessentiality (in the sense of incidental, superfluous, peripheral, unimportant, immaterial, lesser, minor, secondary...) and a relation of interiority, of being inside essentiality (in the sense of indispensable, central, important, fundamental, necessary, inherent, vital, primary...). Homosexuality is "inessential" in this double sense, positioned within psychoanalysis as an essential waste ingredient: the child's homosexual desire for the parent of the same sex, essential to the subject's formation as sexed, is nonetheless simultaneously figured as nonessential, a dispensable component of desire that ultimately must be repudiated and repressed. Could repeated emphasis on the essential inessentiality of homosexuality, its status as repressed excess, reflect a secondary reaction-formation against psychoanalysis's own attraction to an economy of the same, its desire for the homo, and indeed its narcissistic fascination with its own origins?

Homosexuality, Law, and Excess

I want to turn now to Freud's "The Psychogenesis of a Case of Homosexuality in a Woman"[10] to begin to work through this question of the essential inessentiality of homosexuality in women. We are faced immediately with a certain ambiguity in the title, where "The Psychogenesis of a Case of Homosexuality in a Woman" can be glossed as either the psychogenesis of an *instance* of homosexuality in a woman or the psychogenesis of Freud's own *study* of homosexuality in a woman. In the first case, Freud characteristically bases an entire theory of female sexual inversion on a single case history: that of an eighteen-year-old girl, "beautiful and clever," from a family of "good standing," who has become infatuated with a woman ten years her senior, a "lady" of "fallen" circumstances known for her "promiscuous" behavior. In the second case, Freud traces, also in characteristic fashion, the genesis of his own work, reminding us that psychoanalysis has always been fascinated with beginnings, especially its own, and preoccupied with its relation to the law, indeed its status *as* law. The case begins: "Homosexuality in women, which is certainly not less common than in men, although much less glaring, has not only been ignored by the law, but has also been neglected by psychoanalytic research" (147). In their specific relation to the question of homosexuality in women, psychoanalysis and the law are analogously related: neither is able to see what is immediately before it. Homosexuality constitutes not an absence, strictly speaking, but an overpresence, an excess, a surplus, or an overabundance; homosexuality may be "less glaring" in women than in men, but it is still "glaring" (*lärmend*). Freud's choice of the word *lärmend* (riotous, noisy, unruly) to describe homosexuality insinuates that the blindness issues from homosexuality itself, its very excess an assault upon the senses, a blinding and deafening spectacle. The law has "ignored" homosexuality in women and psychoanalysis has "neglected" it not because homosexuality is invisible but because, apparently, it is too visible, too audible, too present. The precise characterization of homosexuality as "glaring" permits Freud to deflect psychoanalysis's concentrated "work of elucidation" (171) away from its own powers of definition and concealment, for it is the law of psychoanalysis to establish the frame of reference, the conditions of visibility and audibility, by which sexual identities can be seen and heard in the first place and, in the case of homosexuality, *as* first places, as sites of origin.

Freud continues: "The narration of a single case, not too pronounced in type, in which it was possible to trace its origin and development in the mind with complete certainty and almost without a gap may, therefore, have a certain claim to attention" (147). Although elsewhere, in *Three Essays on the Theory of Sexuality*, Freud theorizes three different kinds of inverts — absolute (inverts whose "sexual objects are exclusively of their own sex"), amphigenic ("psychosexual hermaphrodites" whose "sexual objects may equally well be of their own or of the opposite sex"), and contingent (inverts who "under certain external conditions . . . are capable of taking as their object someone of their own sex")[11] — he prefers to psychoanalyze in his practice only the latter kind, contingent inverts, cases "not too pronounced in type," where libidinal change is possible and a turn away from the same-sex love-object can be effected by the analysis. It is crucial to point out here that there is at least an implied distinction in Freud's work between "homosexual women" and "homosexuality in women." At the end of this particular case study Freud concludes that "a very considerable measure of latent or unconscious homosexuality can be detected in all normal people" (171), that "latent" homosexuality is, in fact, a central precondition of all "manifest" heterosexuality. But whereas homosexuality can be found in all women, not all women are homosexual. For Freud there must be some "special factor" (168), some libidinal remainder or surplus, that converts the contingent homosexuality in women into homosexual women.

Here we need to turn to the case history itself to understand the dynamics of this object conversion. Freud's patient is an adolescent girl, the only daughter in a family with three sons, brought to Freud by a strict and puritanical father in the hopes that analysis might "cure" his daughter of an infatuation with a lady of questionable social standing and loose sexual mores. In the course of the analysis Freud uncovers the girl's "exaggeratedly strong affection" in early puberty for a small boy, not quite three years old, an affection that gradually evolved into an interest in "mature, but still youthful women" (156) who are themselves mothers. The motivation for this curious shift in the girl from a "maternal attitude" (156) (wanting to *be* a mother) to a homosexual one (wanting to *have* a mother) Freud attributes to the unexpected pregnancy of the girl's own mother and the birth of her third brother. The girl is, in short, in love with her own mother and redirects this tabooed desire toward a series of mother-substitutes. Freud immediately disavows, however, this homosexual daughter-mother incest by reading it as a displacement of a preceding heterosexual daughter-father incest. The "origin" of the girl's (preoedipal) mother-love is a prior (oedipal) father-love; she turns away from her father and toward her mother out of disappointment and resentment that it is her "hated rival," her mother, and not herself who can give the father what it is assumed he most desires, a son. The daughter, in Freud's account, to diffuse the identificatory rivalry with her mother, falls back, "retires in favor of" her mother and renounces men, in effect removing the obstacle hitherto responsible for her mother's hatred by taking her mother instead of her father as love-object (159). Freud reads the daughter's desire for the mother as a ruse or a screen to protect the girl against her frustrated oedipal desire for the father. But why is it presumed from the outset that desire for the mother is a displaced articulation of unfulfilled desire for the father, and not the other way around? Why is the daughter's "disappointment" imagined to be provoked by her inability to have the father's baby and not her failure to give her mother one (a possibility Freud later allows for in "Femininity")? Why are the daughter's resentment and bitterness surmised to be directed toward the mother as competitor for the father's affections and not toward the father as interloper into the mother-daughter relation? Why, in short, is the daughter's "rivalry" assumed to be with the mother and not with the father?

Falling

Freud deploys a complicated rhetoric of "turns" in his work to explain these ambiguous shifts in sexual object-choice, theorizing sexual identities and the sexual identifications that produce them in terms of returns, revivals, regressions, retirements, renunciations, and restorations. In the present case history, the analysand's turn toward a same-sex love-object is triggered in adolescence by a change in the family configuration (the mother's pregnancy and the birth of a new brother) and a coinciding "revival" of the girl's infantile Oedipus complex. For Freud a revival is a peculiar kind of return: every revival of the girl's unresolved Oedipus complex is a regression — a fall back into a preoedipal identification with the father and desire for the mother. In "Femininity," Freud explains the turn back toward the mother as a response to an "inevitable disappointment" from the father:

> [F]emale homosexuality is seldom or never a direct continuation of infantile masculinity. Even for a girl of this kind it seems necessary that she should take her father as an object for some time and enter the Oedipus situation. But afterwards, as a result of her inevitable disappointments from her father, she is driven to regress into her early masculinity complex.[12]

Freud was not, of course, the only psychoanalyst to understand female homosexuality as a backward motion, although his theory of regression remains one of the most elaborately developed. Hélène Deutsch, for example, also reads the female homosexual's apparent preoedipal attachment to the mother as a postoedipal regression — "not a question of a simple fixation on the mother as the first love-object, but rather a complicated process of returning." And Otto Fenichel puts the case even more bluntly:

> In women, the turning away from heterosexuality is a regression that revives memory traces of the early relations to the mother. Female homosexuality therefore has a more archaic imprint than male homosexuality. It brings back the behavior patterns, aims, pleasures, but also the fears and conflicts of the earliest years of life.[13]

For the homosexual presubject, every "pre" contains the specter of a "re": female homosexuality is posited as regressive and reactive, primitive and primal, undeveloped and archaic. Moreover, any gesture of "retirement" signals a form of renunciation, a refusal to compete and a retreat from conflict; inability to sustain psychical conflict and desire to ward off "open rivalry" (195) actuate the girl's return to the preoedipal. Turning back in this reading is always read as a turning away, a retrenchment rather than an advance, a retreat *from* the father rather than a move *toward* the mother.

But there is a second and equally important sense of "turning" in Freud's work on homosexuality, namely psychoanalysis's own attempts to effect a conversion in the homosexual patient, a turning of one genital organization into another through the actual work of analysis. In his discussion of the proper conditions for a successful analysis, Freud admits that such conversions of sexual identifications in the subject are futile; the most psychoanalysis can do, he writes, is to "restore" the invert to his or her "full bisexual functions" (151). The earlier the inversion takes hold, the less likely a conversion can be effected: "It is only where the homosexual fixation has not yet become strong enough, or where there are considerable rudiments and vestiges of a heterosexual choice of object, i.e. in a still oscillating or in a definitely bisexual organization, that one may make a more favorable prognosis for psycho-analytic therapy" (151). Just as homosexuality is figured as a return, a fall back, so is its apparent psychoanalytic resolution, but whereas the one is posited as a regression, a retiring in favor of a rival, the other is presented as a restoration, a process of recuperation and reconsolidation. One can legitimately ask here why the return to a homosexual object-choice is seen as "regressive" when the return proffered as the means to "cure" homosexuality is seen as "restorative."[14] What marks the difference between these two types of returns? And how, exactly, is a turn from one sexual object to another produced in the subject?

A third sense of "turning" in psychoanalysis speaks to these questions: the turn as fall. For Freud, a woman's return to desire for the mother enacts a fall — not a prelapsarian fall that was, after all, a fall into heterosexuality, but a postlapsarian fall into homosexuality. The female subject passes through the Symbolic, through the process of oedipalization, but because of a series of "inevitable disappointments from her father" lapses back into the preoedipal. It is hardly insignificant to Freud that the event that immediately precedes the beginning of the analysis, and indeed the crisis that occasions it, is the girl's attempted suicide. Strolling on the street one day in the company of the lady, the girl encounters her father, who passes the couple by with "an angry glance [*zornigen Blick*]" (148); incurring the sudden wrath of both father and beloved, the infatuated girl throws herself over a wall and falls onto a suburban railway track. Freud reads the suicide attempt as the fulfillment of the girl's unconscious wish: "the attainment of the very wish which, when frustrated, had driven her into homosexuality — namely, the wish to have a child by her father, for now she 'fell' through her father's fault" (162). Freud here plays on the double signification of the German word for "fall," *niederkommen,* which means both "to fall" and "to be delivered of a child" (162). The girl's fall back into a homosexual desire for the mother actually constitutes a particular kind of maternity in Freud's reading — a fall equivalent to a deliverance.

Cathy Caruth has suggested that "the history of philosophy after Newton could be thought of as a series of confrontations with the question of how to talk about falling,"[15] a proposition that takes on considerable force in light of Freud's own compulsive returns to the problem of the subject's "fall" into sexual difference. Scenes of falling in Freud's work frame sexuality as an injurious event. While working on "A Case of Homosexuality in a Woman," Freud added a passage to *The Interpretation of Dreams* that recounts one of his earliest childhood memories of an accident that befell him between the ages of two and three: "I had climbed up on to a stool in the store-closet to get something nice that was lying on a cupboard or table. The stool had tipped over and its corner had struck me behind my lower jaw; I might easily, I reflected, have knocked out all my teeth."[16] A lesson of the retribution inflicted upon young boys attempting to reach covertly into their mothers' cupboards, this remembrance of an early fall functions as a parable for the symbolic threat of permanent injury that precipitates Freud's own painful and sudden entry into oedipality. For the already castrated woman, however, falling symbolically registers another kind of injury. In "Dreams and Telepathy" (1922), published shortly after "A Case of Homosexuality in a Woman," Freud recounts a woman patient's recurrent nightmare of falling out of bed, where falling is taken to represent specifically a "fresh representation of childbirth"[17] — for Freud, the very mark of female heterosexual desire. "If a woman dreams of falling," he explains in *The Interpretation of Dreams,* "it almost invariably has a sexual sense: she is imagining herself as a *'fallen woman'* " (202). Or elsewhere, unable to resist summoning an old misogynistic proverb, Freud concludes that "when a girl falls she falls on her back."[18] And in the case history presently under discussion, "A Case of Homosexuality in a Woman," Freud notes with more than a physician's anecdotal detail that his homosexual patient "paid for this undoubtedly serious attempt at suicide with a considerable time on her back in bed" (148). Fear of falling for a woman apparently represents in this thinking both a fear of heterosexuality and a dread of one of its potential consequences, pregnancy, and yet it is precisely the motion of falling that Freud takes as constitutive of female homosexuality. The theoretical problem that insistently poses itself to any reader trying to make sense of Freud's often incoherent writings on female homosexuality is the question of what a woman's *homosexual* identity formation has to do with *maternity,* with "fresh representations of childbirth."

It cannot be a matter of indifference to feminist readers of Freud that "A Case of Homosexuality in a Woman" begins with the word "homosexuality" and concludes with the word "motherhood" — perhaps the most obvious staging of Freud's inability to think homosexuality outside the thematics of maternity. But how do we read the relation between these two poles of sexual identity formation: between homosexuality and motherhood, or between, in Freud's questionable theoretical alignment, same-sex desire and same-sex identification? Freud could be suggesting a symmetrical relation between the two, an irresolvable psychical tension in the young girl's life between wanting to *be* a mother and wanting to *have* her. Or he could be following a more conventional Victorian logic that posits motherhood as a possible antidote to homosexuality, the "answer" to the question that female homosexuality poses for the psychoanalysis that sees itself as a science of restoration. Still another possibility to explain the homosexuality-motherhood alliance in this particular case study could be Freud's attempt to formulate an evolutionary sexual continuum with homosexuality as the originary "before" and motherhood as the developmental "after." Then again, Freud could also be suggesting that homosexuality represents a regressive return *to* the mother — a desire to have the mother by figuratively becoming the mother — a return achieved through a literal fall enacting a symbolic delivery. Details of the case history rule out none of these possibilities; in fact, the analyst's contradictory twists and turns in logic appear to mimic the unfolding drama of the analysand's own infinitely reversible and reactive identifications. The more difficult question for interpreters of Freud is determining precisely how the agencies of identification and desire are invoked to fashion this particular structural relation of dependency between homosexuality and motherhood, and why the first term (homosexuality) must always be read in relation to, and must eventually give way to, the second term (motherhood).

Identification and Desire

The return as fall, as deliverance, marks female homosexuality as not simply the subject's return *to* the mother but the subject's turn *as* mother. But this reading of the homosexual turn suggests that the daughter must *become* the mother in order to *have* her. It undermines one of the fundamental laws of psychoanalysis, preserved from Freud through Kristeva, which holds that desire and identification are structurally independent of one another, the possibility of one always presupposing the repression of the other. A subject's desire for one sex can be secured only through a corresponding identification with the other sex; a simultaneous desire for and identification with the same object would be a logical impossibility for Freud.[19] A year after publication of his "Homosexuality in a Woman" case study, Freud completed *Group Psychology and the Analysis of the Ego* (1921), where he first begins to systematize the complicated dialectical relation between identification and object-choice in the formation of the sexed subject:

> It is easy to state in a formula the distinction between an identification with the father and the choice of the father as an object. In the first case one's father is what one would like to *be,* and in the second he is what one would like to *have.* The distinction, that is, depends upon whether the tie attaches to the subject or to the object of the ego. The former kind of tie is therefore already possible before any sexual object-choice has been made.[20]

To identify with the father is to wish to be him, whereas to desire the father is to wish to have him. The very notion of identification appears to be gendered for Freud, modeled on a masculine oedipality even when Freud is most concerned with theorizing the child's preoedipal (presexual) identification with the mother. Philippe Lacoue-Labarthe's shrewd observation that Freud "cannot help 'identifying' the figure of identification with the father figure"[21] further strengthens the suspicion that it is a postoedipal "secondary" identification that instantiates and organizes the preoedipal "primary" identification in the first place. A woman's desire for a woman, Freud maintains throughout his work, can be thought of only in terms of the subject's fall back into a preoedipal identification with the father. But even Freud comes eventually to recognize, in *The New Introductory Lectures on Psychoanalysis* (1932–33), that the structural "independence" of identification and object-choice is never so neatly symmetrical as this "formula" would suggest and is only ever precariously achieved. It is desire, for Freud, that continually risks turning (back) into identification: "Identification and object-choice are to a large extent independent of each other; it is however possible to identify oneself with someone whom, for instance, one has taken as a sexual object, and to alter one's ego on his model."[22] This turn from object-choice to identification is no simple turn; it operates, in fact, as a *return* and more properly a *regression;* "object-choice has regressed to identification," Freud writes on thinking back to his first case study of homosexuality in a woman, the Dora case.[23]

But Freud still needs to account for what motivates these turns in sexual object-choice, for what provokes the fall of desire into sexual identification. The answer to the problem of the turn in the "Homosexuality in a Woman" case study comes, as so many answers do in Freud, in a footnote:

> It is by no means rare for a love-relation to be broken off through a process of identification on the part of the lover with the loved object, a process equivalent to a kind of regression to narcissism. After this has been accomplished, it is easy in making a fresh choice of object to direct the libido to a member of the sex opposite to that of the earlier choice. (158)[24]

Freud attributes the turn to an excess of desire, a surplus of love, or some other "overcompensation" (158). Why do some subjects have this "overness," this essential inessential psychical component, and not others? Freud is unable to answer the question he himself implicitly poses, but what is perhaps even more significant is that in the very attempt to prove that identification and desire are counterdirectional turns, Freud in fact demonstrates their necessary collusion and collapsibility, the ever-present potential for the one to metamorphose into, or turn back onto, the other. The instability of sexual identity lies in the capacity of its psychical mechanisms *to desire and to identify with each other.*

Identification in Freud's work is typically figured in terms of height: identification works as a displacement *upward;* the ego elevates itself through identification, imagines itself always in relation

to a higher ideal.[25] Situated at the very bottom of Freud's developmental scale, homosexuals are caught in the Sisyphean labor of
pulling themselves up toward the ego-ideal only to be repeatedly
disappointed by the object once attained. Sexuality in this scene
of falling is neither given nor achieved but *lost*. Desire continually
collapses back into identification under the weight of the subject's
"disappointment," a disappointment prompted by the inadequacy
of the object to fill the measure of its desire. This fall appears to be
no different from the deflation any subject experiences when the
fantasized object of desire is finally encountered. Slavoj Zizek rightly
points out that the found object never coincides with the referent
of desire; when faced with the object of desire, the desiring subject
inevitably experiences a feeling of "this is not it."[26] What makes this
homosexual fall, this fall into homosexuality, more precipitous is the
fact that the subject's aspirations are more ambitious. This particular
subject has overstepped its bounds and desired too much. Those
who progress farthest in oedipalization apparently tumble hardest,
with enough momentum and force to reenter the preoedipal stage,
leaving desire, lack, and even injury behind. But what kind of fall,
in this pseudoscientific gravitational model, produces a homosexual
subject? "We do not . . . mean to maintain," Freud insists, "that every
girl who experiences a disappointment such as this of the longing for love that springs from the Oedipus attitude at puberty will
necessarily on that account *fall a victim to homosexuality*" (168;
emphasis added). Do some subjects carry within them a kind of
Icarus complex,[27] an inherent proclivity for falling? Or are certain
unpredictable Newtonian forces at work to pull any subject at any
moment back into the center of gravity Freud calls primary identification? If falling is the tropological model Freud selects to describe
homosexual identity formations, then what can be said exactly to
precipitate the fall?

Freud's excesses make their reentry at this point, for falling is
conceptualized as a response to a heavy burden: one falls under an
excessive weight, the weight of desire — a desire that can ultimately
function only in such a symbolics as synonymous with heterosexuality. For Freud, homosexual desire is oxymoronic; like women,
homosexuals (male and female) lack lack,[28] or lack a certain mature
relation to lack. By temporally positing homosexuality as antecedent
to the lack that inaugurates desire, Freud in effect drops the sexual-

ity out of homosexuality. It is not lack that defines a homo(sexual) subject but excess, the lack of lack: the surplus that precedes and delimits need, the unintelligible remainder that circumscribes the boundaries of the rational, the overness that must always come first to mark off the deviant from the normal. The excess associated with homosexuality, in Freud's inversive logic (his logic of inversion), holds the position of a "leftover" that comes "right before," with homosexuality assigned to the place of the firstness of any supplement.

In its popular incarnations, the surfeit that marks off homosexuality from its normative other, heterosexuality, is "gleaned" from the surface of the body: homosexuals are said to distinguish themselves by their extravagant dress, their exaggerated mannerisms, their hysterical intonations, their insatiable oral sex drives, and their absurd imitations of "feminine" and "masculine" behavior.[29] What we have in Freud's grammar of excess is a critical displacement of excess from the exterior to the interior; no longer a catalog of enculturating signs such as clothes, language, or style, excess shifts from surface index to subterranean force. Freud writes that his own patient betrayed none of the outward signs a Viennese medical profession expected to find in a homosexual woman, showing "no obvious deviation from the physical type, nor any menstrual disturbance" (154). It is true, Freud confesses, that the "beautiful and well-made girl" had her father's tall figure and sharp facial features, as well as his intellectual acuity, but "these distinctions are conventional rather than scientific," he concludes (154). Moreover, unlike her famous predecessor Dora, Freud's latest homosexual patient "had never been neurotic, and came to the analysis without even one hysterical symptom" (155). In every superficial respect, his new patient strikes Freud as completely unexceptional. Yet it is the very absence of conventional hysterical symptoms (coughing, aphasia, weeping, spasms, tics, etc.) or other external signs of neurosis that draws Freud ultimately to the conclusion that this woman's very normality is most irregular, her lack of "even one hysterical symptom" an indicator of the most abnormal or peculiar of states for a woman. This particular woman is excessively normal, her deviancy secured through an apparent psychological refusal of abnormality. Mimicry is transposed from the surface of the body to its psychical infrastructure as excess comes to designate something more than a style or a performance; excess for Freud marks a certain internal relation that defines the very structure of an emotional identification.

Mikkel Borch-Jacobsen, following Freud, explains the desire-identification dynamics this way: identification always *anticipates* desire; identification, rather than an object, "governs" (32), "orients" (34), "induces," and "predicts" desire (47). Identification, in effect, comes first, and the subject "dates" itself from this mimetic turn:

> Desire (the desiring subject) does not come first, to be *followed* by an identification that would allow the desire to be fulfilled. What comes first is a tendency toward identification, a primordial tendency which then gives rise to a desire; and this desire is, from the outset, a (mimetic, rivalrous) desire to oust the incommodious other from the place the pseudosubject already occupies in fantasy. . . . Identification brings the desiring subject into being, and not the other way around.[30]

This approach de-essentializes sexuality in a particularly useful way, for to show that desires are never originary is also to imply that there are no "natural" or "normal" libidinal impulses that may later get rerouted or "perverted" through an identification gone astray. However, what remains completely ungrounded in this explanation of desire and identification is the problematical notion of *identification* as a "primordial tendency." Freud leans heavily on a scientific model of entropy that posits the motor force of psychological change and sexual development as a drive toward sameness, a tendency toward mimesis: homophilic identification. While crucially naming the indispensability of homophilic identification to the production of sexual identity, Freud nonetheless sees mimeticism as a continual threat to the stability and the coherency of that identity. For Freud, I would suggest, the real danger posed by the desire/identification codependency is not the potential for an excess of desire to collapse back into an identification but the possibility for new forms of identification to generate ever-proliferating and socially unmanageable forms of desire.

"A Case of Homosexuality in a Woman" attributes the girl's sexual interest in young mothers to the eventual, perhaps even inevitable, collapse of her "strong desire to be a mother herself" (156), a change in object-choice brought about by the girl's oedipal disappointment at her failure to have her father's child — a failure made all the more visible by her own mother's midlife pregnancy. The first objects of the girl's sexual desire after the birth of her youngest brother, Freud tells us, are therefore "really mothers, women between thirty and thirty-five whom she had met with their children," and even though the girl eventually gives up actual motherhood as the "*sine qua non* in her love-object," analysis proves to Freud "beyond all shadow of doubt that the lady-love was a substitute for — her mother" (156).

While Freud directs his theoretical remarks, and the reader's attention, to the problem of an excess of desire reverting (back) into an identification, the example proffered by the details of the case history itself demonstrates exactly the opposite phenomenon: the possibility for an overly zealous identification ("the strong desire to be a mother") to give way to an equally powerful desire ("motherhood as a *sine qua non* in her love-object"). Apparently Freud's patient assumes her role too well, her excessive desire to be a mother the very trigger for her sudden desire to sleep with one. Yet the lurking danger posed by a too successful oedipalization signals exactly the paradox Freud refuses to see in his own reading, for to recognize this possibility would involve also, at the very least, entertaining the idea of heterosexuality as an inessential supplement and originary excess, or, in an even more radical (and, for Freud, untenable) formulation, allowing for the possibility that it is "absolute" or "exclusive" *hetero*sexuality that may be intolerable to the ego.[31] Moreover, Freud's tactical misreading of the actual workings of identification and desire in this particular case history permits him to deflect attention away from the enculturating and normative work of psychoanalysis: the attempt to effect "curative restorations" by carefully monitoring and limiting the range of a subject's identifications. The job of psychoanalysis, after all, is typically to reorient a culturally tabooed desire by first redirecting the identification that produced it — a task usually accomplished through the therapeutic use of transference.

Fallen Women

Freud's insistence upon the homosexual woman's "fall" into primary identification (preoedipal absorption with the mother) works effectively to exclude the woman who desires another woman from the very category of "sexuality," and it does so by insuring that any measure of sexual maturity will be designated as heterosexual object-choice "achieved" through the act of secondary identification (oedipal incorporation of a parental ideal). Freud sustains the notion of female homosexuality's presexual status by assuming, first, that same-sex desire is principally and finally an act of primary identification and, second, that primary identification is completely uninflected by the cultural markers associated with secondary identification. When the girl leaves the Oedipus complex, which marked her original entry into history and culture, and falls into the shadowy netherworld of primary identification, she drops out of sexual difference as well. But "primary" identification is itself a social process, already presupposing in the subject prior knowledge of the culturally weighted distinction between maternal and paternal roles, and assuming in advance at least an "intuition" of sexual difference.[32] Preoedipality is firmly entrenched in the social order and cannot be read as before, outside, or even after the Symbolic; the mother-daughter relation, no less than the father-daughter relation, is a Symbolic association completely inscribed in the field of representation, sociality, and culture. Freud explains his patient's homoerotic attachment to older women of child-bearing age as a rehearsal of the girl's early "mother-complex," a preoedipal, presexual state of nondifferentiation with the mother, while at the same time making this homosexual object-choice entirely dependent upon a (preceding) paternal identification. This contradictory insistence upon homosexuality's postoedipal return to a precultural fixation flatly contradicts the case history's repeated disclosures of the importance, in the formation of the girl's sexual identity, of specifically social ties between the girl, her family members, and the extrafamilial objects of her affections. Whom exactly the girl identifies *with* in her homosexual attachment to the lady is never entirely clear. While Freud ostensibly concludes that a masculine, paternal identification permits the girl's homosexual object-choice ("she changed into a man and took her mother in place of her father as the object of her love" [158]), his patient's suicidal plunge, which temporarily replaces the father's punitive anger with parental solicitude, suggests a feminine, maternal identification in which the girl continues to compete with her mother as rival for her father's love and attention (the mother "had herself suffered for some years from neurotic troubles and enjoyed a great deal of consideration from her husband" [149]). Equally indeterminate is the gendered identity of the love-object, insofar as the lady corresponds as much to the girl's masculine as to her feminine ideal: "[H]er lady's slender figure, severe beauty, and downright manner reminded her of the brother who was a little older than herself" (156).[33] With what in the other does the subject identify if not a particular familial or social ideal? Put slightly differently, what does the subject desire in the other if not a cultural reflection of what she herself aspires to be?

The scale of identification, in which the desiring subject rises and falls according to the strength of the pull and resistance of its elusive object, carries along with it a strong class connotation for Freud's patient. The girl, a member of the rising middle class, finds herself irresistibly attracted to "fallen women." Her current object of desire, a "demi-mondaine" (153) who has lost her reputation and fallen into "ignoble circumstances," inspires in the enamored young girl fantasies of chivalric rescue. The case history provides a strong suggestion that the "lady" is, in fact, a "lady-of-the-evening," a woman who maintains some semblance of her former class status by earning a living as a high-class prostitute: "[S]he lived simply by giving her bodily favours." But even before the girl's devotion to the lady, her "first passions had been for women who were not celebrated for specially strict propriety" (161). These early infatuations include "a film actress at a summer resort" (who first incites the ire of the girl's father [161]) and "a strict and unapproachable mistress" (who, Freud adds, is "obviously a substitute mother" [168]). For the girl, "bad reputation" in the love-object is "positively a 'necessary condition for love'" (161). All three of these mother-substitutes — the prostitute, the actress, and the teacher — occupy a class below the girl, but they also represent collectively a class of women who earn their living independently, outside of marriage and the heterosexual contract. Could it be that the force of the attraction exerted on the girl by these figures of desire is, in part, the lure of the economic independence and social mobility that they represent? The real provocation of the girl's impassioned devotion to these working ladies may issue not simply from the sex of her love-objects but from their "low" social standing as well. To a class-conscious Viennese society, the greatest threat posed by the girl's "homosexual enthusiasms" (168) is the ever-present possibility of what Freud diagnoses elsewhere as "the dangers of sexual relations with people of an inferior social class."[34]

This figuration of identification as a problem of height and scale, a matter of the ego's striving to reach up to an elevated object, further recalls the image of the young Freud reaching for the unattainable goods in his mother's cupboard. That one of Freud's earliest memories should summon up a fall during the preoedipal stage, a fall that inflicted a wound whose scar he bears with him into adulthood, may suggest Freud's unconscious fear that he has already been castrated and placed on a homosexual continuum along with the mother. Indeed, what Freud seems most anxious to disavow in his analysis of the young girl is his own identification with the feminine. Freud more or less admits directly to an identification with his patient's stern but loving father, "an earnest, worthy man, at bottom very tender-hearted" (149), and he seems convinced that his patient, as he tellingly puts it, "intended to deceive me just as she habitually deceived her father" (165). But this masculine identification masks a deeper, more disturbing feminine identification with the mother who "enjoyed her daughter's confidence concerning her passion" (149). The transferential role Freud frequently found himself playing in his therapeutic sessions was not exclusively nor even principally the familiar role of paternal prohibitor but more often the less comfortable role of maternal educator: substitute mother-figure imparting sexual knowledge to adolescent girls. In fact, as a male doctor speaking candidly on sexual subjects to girls in his professional care, regularly opening himself to charges of social impropriety and sexual prurience, Freud could not entirely escape (despite his best attempts to seek refuge behind the mantle of scientific knowledge) the "taint" of a feminine identification with the mother whose proper role is to educate her daughter on matters of sexual and social conduct. This is not the first time Freud has disavowed a strong feminine identification. In addition to Freud's much-discussed identification with Dora's hysteria, Jim Swan has uncovered Freud's unconscious identification with a pregnant woman in the dream of Irma's injection and an equally strong identification with his childhood nurse in the dream of "a little sheep's head." Freud himself was unable to make these connections, even though, as Swan points out, the idea of the therapist as a nurse to his patients is not in the least an uncommon theme in psychoanalytic literature.[35]

Fighting continually against the "low estimation" (149) in which psychoanalysis is held in Vienna, Freud perhaps more closely resembles the lady than any other stock figure in this extended family romance. Freud's own marginal social standing and his lifelong economic anxieties, in addition to his frank discussion of sexuality, all situate him structurally in the position of the lady, the fallen woman. But unlike the lady, Freud is unable to achieve any stature or prominence in his patient's eyes:

> Once when I expounded to her a specially important part of the theory, one touching her nearly, she replied in an inimitable tone, "How very interesting," as though she were a *grande dame* being taken over a museum and glancing through her lorgnon at objects to which she was completely indifferent. (163)

This overly clever comparison of his patient to a *grande dame* glancing through her lorgnon betrays Freud's sensitivity to the girl's cutting pretenses to class superiority. When, in a psychodrama like this one, the look carries such potent and castrating powers, not even Freud is immune to the discomfiture provoked by his patient's class condescension — an irritation that ultimately leads Freud to terminate the girl's treatment and to counsel his patient to see a woman doctor instead (164). "Retiring in favor of someone else" (159),[36] Freud beats a fast retreat, acting out the very rhetorical move that he identifies in this case history as one of the "causes" of homosexuality (159). Fixed by his patient's arrogant glance, much as the girl is herself arrested on the street by her father's disapproving look, Freud "falls" through his patient's fault. In a case history where reversible and elastic identifications keep the family neurosis in motion, Freud interestingly gets to play all the principal parts: father, mother, beloved, *and* girl.

Conclusion

The subject, governed by a drive to consume and to possess the object of its desire, must resist the call of primary identification (homophilia) if it is to succeed in its climb toward maturity, defined as object-relatedness (heterophilia). Primary identification — something of a redundancy in Freud — operates as the gravitational pull that perpetually threatens to capsize the subject under the excessive weight of its own regressive desires. In short, identification both precedes desire and strives to exceed it, propelled by its insatiable oral drive to swallow desire whole. In Freud's reading of identification and desire, homosexual desire is not even, properly speaking, desire. Rather homosexuality represents an instance of identification gone awry — identification in overdrive (or, one might say, oral drive). This overdrive is also implicitly a death drive: *cadere* (Latin for "to fall") etymologically conjures cadavers. For Freud every fall into homosexuality is *inherently suicidal* since the "retreat" from oedipality entails not only the loss of desire but the loss of a fundamental relation to the world into which desire permits entry — the world of sociality, sexuality, and subjectivity.

While desire is the province and the privilege of heterosexuals, homosexuals are portrayed as hysterical identifiers and expert mimics.[37] By strategically aligning "homo" with identification and "hetero" with desire, Freud, in spectacularly circular fashion, resubmits homosexuality to its own alleged entropic "tendencies," so that "homo" subsumes "sexuality" and identification incorporates desire. What Freud gives us in the end is a Newtonian explanation of sexual orientation in which falling bodies are homosexual bodies, weighted down by the heaviness of multiple identifications, and rising bodies are heterosexual bodies, buoyed up by the weightlessness of desires unmoored from their (lost) objects. This essay has attempted to demonstrate that such a mechanistic explanatory model is itself overburdened and constrained by the heaviness of its terms, terms that increasingly come to exceed the bounds and conditions of their founding logic. Precisely because desire and identification cannot be securely separated or easily prevented from turning back on one another, Freud's persistent attempt to read sexual orientation according to the laws of gravity and motion ultimately falls apart, splintering under the pressure of its own rhetorical weight.

NOTES

An early version of this essay was first presented at the Center for the Critical Analysis of Contemporary Culture at Rutgers University. I would like to thank all the participants of the 1990–91 seminar — in particular, Elin Diamond, Jay Geller, Marcia Ian, Cora Kaplan, David Toise, and Carolyn Williams — for their thoughtful and useful suggestions. Thanks also to Eric Santner for generously checking the German translations and to Eduardo Cadava, Walter Hughes, Geeta Patel, and Michael Warner, all of whom provided helpful commentary on the essay's final incarnation.

1. Sigmund Freud, "The Psychogenesis of a Case of Homosexuality in a Woman," in vol. 18 of *The Standard Edition,* trans. James Strachey (London: Hogarth Press, 1955), 145–72. The original text, "Über die Psychogenese eines Falles von weiblicher Homosexualität," can be found in vol. 12 of *Gesammelte Werke* (Frankfurt am Main: S. Fischer Verlag, 1968), 271–302.

2. The phrase is Jacques Lacan's, from Seminar I on *Freud's Papers on Technique, 1953–1954,* ed. Jacques-Alain Miller and trans. John Forrester (New York and London: W. W. Norton, 1988), 198. In its interest in the inverted, disorientating logic of the "pre" and the "post," this essay addresses, albeit from a different direction, many of the same theoretical problems discussed in Lee Edelman's analysis of the Wolf Man. In "Seeing Things: Representation, the Scene of Surveillance, and the Spectacle of Gay Male Sex" (in Diana Fuss, ed., *Inside/Out: Lesbian Theories, Gay Theories* [New York and London: Routledge, 1991]), Edelman returns to the question of "sexual suppositions" in the psychoanalytic constitution of male subjectivity, while my own reading of female homosexuality anticipates the problem of sexual *pre*suppositions. A comparative reading might also conclude that Edelman's (be)hindsight finds an epistemological counterpart in my own focus upon a circumscribed (be)foresight. While the cultural representations of lesbian sexuality as "foreplay" and gay male sexuality as "behindplay" (see Edelman, "Seeing Things," 104) may well overdetermine the staging of these particular theoretical "scenes," it strikes me that such investigations of the before and the behind (my own confrontation with the before postdating Edelman's entry into the behind) might more profitably be read back-to-back.

3. See Sigmund Freud, *Fragment of an Analysis of a Case of Hysteria* (1905), in vol. 7 of *The Standard Edition,* trans. James Strachey (London: Hogarth Press, 1953), 125–243.

4. Jacques Lacan, *"De la psychose paranoïaque dans ses rapports avec la personalité" suivi de "Premiers écrits sur la paranoïa"* (Paris: Editions du Seuil, 1975).

5. Julia Kristeva, *About Chinese Women,* trans. Anita Barrows (New York and London: Marion Boyars, 1977).

6. Catherine Clément, *The Lives and Legends of Jacques Lacan,* trans. Arthur Goldhammer (New York: Columbia University Press, 1983), 60.

7. Judith Butler's work is especially adept at relentlessly interrogating the specious logic of a before and an after, exposing how every before (what ostensibly comes first) is really an effect of the after (what it was thought to precede): for example, the preoedipal an effect of the oedipal, the prediscursive an effect of the discursive, the prejuridical an effect of the juridical, and so on. "Pre" formatives are read as "per" formatives in Butler's deconstruction of false foundationalisms. See *Gender Trouble: Feminism and the Subversion of Identity* (New York and London: Routledge, 1990).

8. I am grateful to Patricia Williams for her suggestion of this particular term and for her invitation to think more about the figure of inessentiality at the annual meeting of the American Association of Law Schools (January 1991); some of the following

remarks were formulated for that occasion on a panel devoted to the problem of "inessentially speaking."

9. Although unable to resist speculating on etiological foundations throughout his work on sexual inversion, Freud nonetheless seems peculiarly aware of the futility of doing so. He writes in the present case history: "So long as we trace the development from its final outcome backwards, the chain of events appears continuous, and we feel we have gained an insight which is completely satisfactory or even exhaustive. But if we proceed the reverse way, if we start from the premises inferred from the analysis and try to follow these up to the final result, then we no longer get the impression of an inevitable sequence of events which could not have been otherwise determined" (167).

10. "The Psychogenesis of a Case of Homosexuality in a Woman" may well be Freud's most overlooked case study; certainly compared to the volume of criticism generated by the Dora case history, the "Psychogenesis" paper has received surprisingly little attention. For some important exceptions to this critical silence, see Luce Irigaray, "Commodities among Themselves" in *This Sex Which Is Not One,* trans. Catherine Porter (Ithaca, N.Y.: Cornell University Press, 1985); Mandy Merck, "The Train of Thought in Freud's 'Case of Homosexuality in a Woman,' " *m/f* 11/12 (1986): 35–46; Judith A. Roof, "Freud Reads Lesbians: The Male Homosexual Imperative," *Arizona Quarterly* 46, no. 1 (spring 1990): 17–26; Diane Hamer, "Significant Others: Lesbians and Psychoanalytic Theory," *Feminist Review* 34 (spring 1990): 134–51; and Mary Jacobus, "Russian Tactics: Freud's 'Case of Homosexuality in a Woman,' " forthcoming.

11. Sigmund Freud, *Three Essays on the Theory of Sexuality,* vol. 7 of *The Standard Edition,* trans. James Strachey (London: Hogarth Press, 1953), 136–37.

12. Sigmund Freud, "Femininity," in *New Introductory Lectures on Psychoanalysis,* vol. 22 of *The Standard Edition* (London: Hogarth Press, 1964), 130.

13. Hélène Deutsch, "On Female Homosexuality," in Hendrik Ruitenbeek, ed., *Psychoanalysis and Female Sexuality* (New Haven: College and University Press, 1966), 125. Deutsch's essay was originally published in *The International Journal of Psychoanalysis* 14 (1933), the same year Freud's *New Introductory Lectures* appeared in print. See also Deutsch's *The Psychology of Women,* vol. 1 (New York: Bantam, 1973), 332–61. The Fenichel citation is taken from his work entitled *The Psychoanalytic Theory of Neurosis* (New York: W. W. Norton, 1945), 340.

14. For an interesting inversion of the regression/restoration binary, see John Fletcher's "Freud and His Uses: Psychoanalysis and Gay Theory," in Simon Shepherd and Mick Wallis, eds., *Coming On Strong: Gay Politics and Culture* (London: Unwin Hyman, 1989), 90–118. Fletcher sees lesbianism, and not its proposed psychoanalytic "cure," as the true restoration. To the degree that lesbianism *contests* castration, it can be read as "a restorative strategy which seeks to repair the losses, denigrations, thwartings that a patriarchal culture inflicts on the girl in her primary relation to the mother" (105).

15. Cathy Caruth, "The Claims of Reference," *The Yale Journal of Criticism* 4, no. 1 (1990): 194.

16. Sigmund Freud, *The Interpretation of Dreams,* vol. 5 of *The Standard Edition,* trans. James Strachey (London: Hogarth Press, 1953), 560. See also "Dreams and Telepathy," in vol. 18 of *The Standard Edition,* trans. James Strachey (London: Hogarth Press, 1955), 198.

17. Freud, "Dreams and Telepathy," 213.

18. Sigmund Freud, *The Psychopathology of Everyday Life*, vol. 6 of *The Standard Edition*, trans. James Strachey (London: Hogarth Press, 1960), 175.

19. I have discussed the implications of Freud's persistent attempts to dichotomize desire and identification in "Fashion and the Homospectatorial Look," *Critical Inquiry* 18 (summer 1992): 713–37. For a similar critique of Freud's insistence on the mutual exclusivity of subject and object, which focuses by contrast on Freud's theorization of *male* sexuality, see Michael Warner's "Homo-Narcissism; or, Heterosexuality," in Joseph A. Boone and Michael Cadden, eds., *Engendering Men: The Question of Male Feminist Criticism* (New York and London: Routledge, 1990), 190–206. Warner points out that the argument Freud offers to explain why a subject might choose one secondary identification over another is based entirely on recourse to the suspect notion of congenital predispositions: "[O]nly the child's 'sexual disposition' — i.e., its 'masculine' or 'feminine' bent — will determine the relative *weight* of these identification axes" (196; emphasis mine).

20. Sigmund Freud, *Group Psychology and the Analysis of the Ego*, vol. 18 of *The Standard Edition*, trans. James Strachey (London: Hogarth Press, 1955), 106.

21. See Philippe Lacoue-Labarthe, *Typography: Mimesis, Philosophy, Politics*, ed. Christopher Fynsk (Cambridge: Harvard University Press, 1989), 114. Lacoue-Labarthe is also one of the most astute readers of identification's inscription in the social field. His analysis of originary mimesis as imitation concludes with a challenge to those critics of psychoanalysis who seek to divest its key concepts of their critical politicality: "Why would the problem of identification not be, in general, the essential problem of the political?" (300).

22. Freud, *New Introductory Lectures*, 63.

23. Freud, *Group Psychology*, 107.

24. A simpler way to put this problem of desire slipping over and into identification is to say that it is possible to love someone so excessively and exclusively that one gradually becomes that person.

25. Kaja Silverman, "White Skin, Brown Masks: The Double Mimesis, or with Lawrence in Arabia," in *Differences: A Journal of Feminist Cultural Studies* 1, no. 3 (fall 1989): 25. Silverman helpfully suggests that we think of identification "not so much as the 'resolution' of desire as its perpetuation within another regime" (24).

26. Slavoj Zizek, *Looking Awry: An Introduction to Jacques Lacan through Popular Culture* (Cambridge: MIT Press, 1991), 92.

27. I am indebted to Alan Stoekl's identification of the Icarian complex, an "unconscious and pathological desire to fall," in the work of Georges Bataille. See Stoekl's introduction to Bataille's *Visions of Excess: Selected Writings, 1927–1939* (Minneapolis: University of Minnesota Press, 1985), xv.

28. Michèle Montreley, "Inquiry into Femininity," *m/f* 1 (1978): 83–102.

29. There can perhaps be no better, more playful, more mimetic response to such excessive parodies than more excess — a politics of mimesis. As recent work on camp, butch-femme, hermaphroditism, transvestism, and transsexualism has powerfully and performatively demonstrated, to be excessively excessive, to flaunt one's performance as performance, is to unmask all identity as drag. Central to each of these studies is Irigaray's slippery distinction between "masquerade" (the unconscious assumption of femininity) and "mimicry" (the deliberate and playful performance of femininity). The critical difference between masquerade and mimicry —

between the "straight" imitation of a role and a parodic hyperbolization of that role —
depends on the degree and readability of its excess. Mimicry works to undo masquerade by overdoing it, subverting the dominant system of sexual representation
by intentionally ironizing it. But without the telltale signs of excess, encoded in the
mimic's walk, speech, or dress, mimicry would be indistinguishable from masquerade, and the political utility of mimesis would be negligible. Excess, in other words,
is all that holds the two apart, for to fail in mimesis is usually to fail in being *excessive enough.* Currently, three of the most important works that attempt to theorize
the problematics of excess in the politics of mimesis are Carole-Anne Tyler's *Female Impersonators* (forthcoming); Marjorie Garber's *Vested Interests: Cross-Dressing
and Cultural Anxiety* (New York and London: Routledge, 1991); and Judith Butler's
Bodies That Matter (New York and London: Routledge, forthcoming).

30. Mikkel Borch-Jacobsen, *The Freudian Subject,* trans. Catherine Porter (Stanford, Calif.: Stanford University Press, 1988), 47.

31. Sandor Ferenczi's 1909 "More about Homosexuality" contains one of the
earliest suggestions in psychoanalysis that homosexuality may be the effect of an
"excessively powerful heterosexuality." See Ferenczi's *Final Contributions to the
Problems and Methods of Psychoanalysis,* ed. Michael Balint and trans. Eric Mos-
bacher (New York: Basic Books, 1955). Cited in Kenneth Lewes, *The Psychoanalytic
Theory of Male Homosexuality* (New York: New American Library, 1988), 146.

32. For an excellent discussion of the differences between primary and secondary
identification, see Mary Ann Doane's "Misrecognition and Identity" in Ron Burnett,
ed., *Explorations in Film Theory: Selected Essays from Ciné-Tracts* (Bloomington and
Indianapolis: Indiana University Press, 1991), 15–25. Regarding the problem of primary identification, Doane reasonably wonders: "Does it really define a moment
which is neuter, which pre-dates the establishment of sexual difference?" (21).

33. Lines like these, which suggest (on the part of the girl) a masculine object-
choice in addition to a masculine identification, lead Judith Roof to conclude that
Freud's theory of lesbianism amounts in the end to little more than a displaced
analysis of *male* homosexuality. See Roof's "Freud Reads Lesbians."

34. Freud, *Interpretation of Dreams,* 305. One of Freud's most interesting readings
of class conflict can be found in his analysis of a male patient's "sapphic dream"
where "above" and "below" refer not only to sexual parts but to social positions as
well. His patient's dream of laborious climbing reminds Freud of Alphonse Daudet's
Sappho, a book that Freud understands as a powerful "warning to young men not
to allow their affections to be seriously engaged by girls of humble origin and a
dubious past" (286).

35. Jim Swan, "*Mater* and Nannie: Freud's Two Mothers and the Discovery of the
Oedipus Complex," *American Imago* 31, no. 1 (spring 1974): 39. Swan hypothesizes,
reasonably enough, that Freud's resistance to acknowledging publicly his fear of a
feminine identification has everything to do with his anxieties over homosexuality
(27). Swan's essay remains one of the best and most suggestive readings of why
Freud waited until shortly after the death of his mother in 1930 to "discover" the
critical importance of preoedipality and the infant's primary erotic identification with
the mother.

36. Mandy Merck asks: "In insisting upon a woman analyst isn't Freud acting
precisely as he accuses his homosexual patient of doing?" ("Train of Thought," 44).
In "Russian Tactics," Mary Jacobus also provides a fascinating reading of Freud's

feminine identifications, arguing that "even more than the woman doctor in whose favour Freud 'retires,' the lady turns out to be a rival authority on lesbian and bisexual matters." Both Merck and Jacobus provide particularly useful accounts of the case history's opening rhetoric of courtly love and its closing allusion to surgical sex-change. I would like to thank Mary Jacobus for generously sharing with me her work in progress.

37. I am indebted to Marcia Ian for seeing the implications of my reading of Freud here better than I did.

How to Bring Your Kids Up Gay
Eve Kosofsky Sedgwick

In the summer of 1989, the United States Department of Health and Human Services released a study entitled *Report of the Secretary's Task Force on Youth Suicide*. Written in response to the apparently burgeoning epidemic of suicides and suicide attempts by children and adolescents in the United States, the 110–page report contained a section analyzing the situation of gay and lesbian youth. It concluded that because "gay youth face a hostile and condemning environment, verbal and physical abuse, and rejection and isolation from families and peers," young gays and lesbians are two to three times more likely than other young people to attempt and to commit suicide. The report recommends, modestly enough, an "end [to] discrimination against youths on the basis of such characteristics as . . . sexual orientation."

On October 13, 1989, Dr. Louis W. Sullivan, Secretary of the Department of Health and Human Services, repudiated this section of the report — impugning not its accuracy, but, it seems, its very existence. In a written statement Sullivan said, "[T]he views expressed in the paper entitled 'Gay Male and Lesbian Youth Suicide' do not in any way represent my personal beliefs or the policy of this Department. I am strongly committed to advancing traditional family values. . . . In my opinion, the views expressed in the paper run contrary to that aim."[1]

It's always open season on gay kids. What professor who cares for her students' survival and dignity can fail to be impressed and frightened by the unaccustomed, perhaps impossible responsibilities that devolve on faculty as a result of the homophobia uniformly enjoined on, for example, teachers in the primary and secondary levels of public school — who are subject to being fired, not only for being visibly gay, but, whatever their sexuality, for providing any intimation that homosexual desires, identities, cultures, adults, children, or adolescents have a right to expression or existence?

And where, in all this, is psychoanalysis? Where are the "helping professions"? In this discussion of institutions, I mean to ask not about Freud and the possibly spacious affordances of the mother-texts, but about psychoanalysis and psychiatry as they are functioning in the United States today.[2] I am especially interested in revisionist psychoanalysis, including ego-psychology, and in developments following on the American Psychiatric Association's much-publicized 1973 decision to drop the pathologizing diagnosis of homosexuality from its next Diagnostic and Statistical Manual (DSM-III). What is likely to be the fate of children brought under the influence of psychoanalysis and psychiatry today, post–DSM-III, on account of anxieties about their sexuality?

The monographic literature on the subject is, to begin with, as far as I can tell, exclusively about boys. A representative example of this revisionist, ego-based psychoanalytic theory would be Richard C. Friedman's *Male Homosexuality: A Contemporary Psychoanalytic Perspective,* published by Yale in 1988.[3] (A sort of companion-volume, though by a nonpsychoanalyst psychiatrist, is Richard Green's *The "Sissy Boy Syndrome" and the Development of Homosexuality* [1987], also from Yale.)[4] Friedman's book, which lavishly acknowledges his wife and children, is strongly marked by his sympathetic involvement with the 1973 depathologizing movement. It contains several visibly admiring histories of gay men, many of them encountered in nontherapeutic contexts. These include "Luke, a forty-five-year-old career army officer and a life-long exclusively homosexual man" (152); and Tim, who was "burly, strong, and could work side by side with anyone at the most strenuous jobs": "gregarious and likeable," "an excellent athlete," Tim was "captain of [his high-school] wrestling team and editor of the school newspaper" (206–7). Bob, another "well-integrated individual," "had regular sexual activity with a few different partners but never cruised or visited gay bars or baths. He did not belong to a gay organization. As an adult, Bob had had a stable, productive work history. He had loyal, caring, durable friendships with both men and women" (92–93). Friedman also, by way of comparison, gives an example of a *hetero*sexual man with what he considers a highly integrated personality, who happens to be a combat jet pilot: "Fit and trim, in his late twenties, he had the quietly commanding style of an effective decision maker" (86).[5]

Is a pattern emerging? Revisionist analysts seem prepared to like some gay men, but the healthy homosexual is (a) one who is already grown up and (b) acts masculine. In fact Friedman correlates, in so many words, adult gay male effeminacy with "global character pathology" and what he calls "the lower part of the psychostructural spectrum" (93). In the obligatory paragraphs of his book concerning "the question of when behavioral deviation from a defined norm should be considered psychopathology," Friedman makes explicit that while "clinical concepts are often somewhat imprecise and admittedly fail to do justice to the rich variability of human behavior," a certain baseline concept of pathology will be maintained in his study; and that baseline will be drawn in a very particular place. "The distinction between nonconformists and people with psychopathology is usually clear enough during childhood. Extremely and chronically effeminate boys, for example, should be understood as falling into the latter category" (32–33).

"For example," "extremely and chronically effeminate boys" — this is the abject that haunts revisionist psychoanalysis. The same DSM-III that, published in 1980, was the first that did not contain an entry for "homosexuality," was also the first that *did* contain a new diagnosis, numbered (for insurance purposes) 302.60: "Gender Identity Disorder of Childhood." Nominally gender-neutral, this diagnosis is actually highly differential between boys and girls: a girl gets this pathologizing label only in the rare case of asserting that she actually is anatomically male (e.g., "that she has, or will grow, a penis"); while a boy can be treated for Gender Identity Disorder of Childhood if he merely asserts "that it would be better not to have a penis" — *or*, alternatively, if he displays a "preoccupation with female stereotypical activities as manifested by a preference for either cross-dressing or simulating female attire, or by a compelling desire to participate in the games and pastimes of girls."[6] While the decision to remove "homosexuality" from DSM-III was highly polemicized and public, accomplished only under intense pressure from gay activists outside the profession, the addition to DSM-III of the "Gender Identity Disorder of Childhood" appears to have attracted no outside attention at all — nor even to have been perceived as part of the same conceptual shift.[7] Indeed, the gay movement has never been quick to attend to issues concerning effeminate boys. There is a discreditable reason for this in the marginal or stigmatized position to which even adult men who are effeminate have often been relegated in the movement.[8] A more understandable reason than effeminophobia, however, is the conceptual need of the gay movement to interrupt a long tradition of viewing gender and sexuality as continuous and collapsible categories — a tradition of assuming that anyone, male or female, who desires a man must by definition be feminine; and that anyone, male or female, who desires a woman must by the same token be masculine. That one woman, *as a woman,* might desire another; that one man, *as a man,* might desire another: the indispensable need to make these powerful, subversive assertions has seemed, perhaps, to require a relative deemphasis of the links between gay adults and gender-nonconforming children. To begin to theorize gender and sexuality as distinct though intimately entangled axes of analysis has been, indeed, a great advance of recent lesbian and gay thought.

There is a danger, however, that that advance may leave the effeminate boy once more in the position of the haunting abject — this time the haunting abject of gay thought itself. This is an especially horrifying thought if — as many studies launched from many different theoretical and political positions have suggested — for any given adult gay man, wherever he may be at present on a scale of self-perceived or socially ascribed masculinity (ranging from extremely masculine to extremely feminine), the likelihood is disproportionately high that he will have a childhood history of self-perceived effeminacy, femininity, or nonmasculinity.[9] In this case the eclipse of the effeminate boy from adult gay discourse would represent more than a damaging theoretical gap; it would represent a node of annihilating homophobic, gynephobic, and pedophobic hatred internalized and made central to gay-affirmative analysis. The effeminate boy would come to function as the open secret of many politicized adult gay men.

One of the most interesting aspects — and by interesting I mean cautionary — of the new psychoanalytic developments is that they are based on *precisely* the theoretical move of distinguishing gender from sexuality. This is how it happens that the *de*pathologization of an atypical sexual object-choice can be yoked to the *new* pathologization of an atypical gender identification. Integrating the gender-constructivist research of, for example, John Money and Robert Stoller, research that many have taken (though perhaps wrongly) as having potential for feminist uses, this work posits the very early consolidation of something called Core Gender Identity — one's basal sense of being male or female — as a separate stage prior to, even conceivably independent of, any crystallization of sexual fantasy or sexual object-choice. Gender Disorder of Childhood is seen as a pathology involving the Core Gender Identity (failure to develop a CGI consistent with one's biological sex); sexual object-choice, on the other hand, is unbundled from this Core Gender Identity through a reasonably space-making series of two-phase narrative moves. Under the pressure, ironically, of having to show how gay adults whom he considers well-integrated personalities do sometimes evolve from children seen as the very definition of psychopathology, Friedman unpacks several developmental steps that have often otherwise been seen as rigidly unitary.[10]

One serious problem with this way of distinguishing between gender and sexuality is that, while denaturalizing sexual object-choice, it radically *re*naturalizes gender. All ego-psychology is prone, in the first place, to structuring developmental narrative around a none-too-dialectical trope of progressive *consolidation* of self. To place a very early core-gender determinant (however little biologized it may be) at the very center of that process of consolidation seems to mean, essentially, that for a nontranssexual person with a penis, nothing can ever be assimilated to the self through this process of consolidation unless it can be assimilated *as masculinity*. For even the most feminine–self-identified boys, Friedman uses the phrases "sense of masculine self-regard" (245), "masculine competency" (20), and "self-evaluation as appropriately masculine" (244) as synonyms for any self-esteem and, ultimately, for any *self*. As he describes the interactive process that leads to any ego-consolidation in a boy:

> Boys measure themselves in relation to others whom they estimate to be similar. [For Friedman, this means only men and other boys.]

Similarity of self-assessment depends on consensual validation. The others must agree that the boy is and will remain similar to them. The boy must also view both groups of males (peers and older men) as appropriate for idealization. Not only must he be like them in some ways, he must want to be like them in others. They in turn must want him to be like them. Unconsciously, they must have the capacity to identify with him. This naturally occurring [!] fit between the male social world and the boy's inner object world is the juvenile phase-specific counterpoint to the preoedipal child's relationship with the mother. (237)

The reason effeminate boys turn out gay, according to this account, is that other men don't validate them as masculine. There is a persistent, wistful fantasy in this book: "One cannot help but wonder how these [prehomosexual boys] would have developed if the males they idealized had had a more flexible and abstract sense of masculine competency" (20). For Friedman, the increasing flexibility in what kinds of attributes or activities *can* be processed as masculine, with increasing maturity, seems fully to account for the fact that so many "gender-disturbed" (pathologically effeminate) little boys manage to grow up into "healthy" (masculine) men, albeit after the phase where their sexuality has differentiated as gay.

Or rather, it *almost* fully accounts for it. There is a residue of mystery, resurfacing at several points in the book, about why most gay men turn out so resilient — about how they even survive — given the profound initial deficit of "masculine self-regard" characteristic of many proto-gay childhoods, and the late and relatively superficial remediation of it that comes with increasing maturity. Given that "the virulence and chronicity of [social] stress [against it] puts homosexuality in a unique position in the human behavioral repertoire," how does one account for "the fact that severe, persistent morbidity does not occur more frequently" among gay adolescents (205)? Friedman essentially throws up his hands at these moments. "A number of possible explanations arise, but one seems particularly likely to me: namely, that homosexuality is associated with some psychological mechanism, not understood or even studied to date, that protects the individual from diverse psychiatric disorders" (236). It "might include mechanisms influencing ego resiliency, growth potential, and the capacity to form intimate relationships" (205). And "it is possible that, for reasons that have not yet been well described, [gender-disturbed boys'] mechanisms for coping with anguish and adversity are unusually effective" (201).

These are huge blank spaces to be left in what purports to be a developmental account of proto-gay children. But given that ego-syntonic consolidation for a boy can come only in the form of masculinity, given that masculinity can be conferred only by men (20), and given that femininity, in a person with a penis, can represent nothing but deficit and disorder, the one explanation that could *never* be broached is that these mysterious skills of survival, filiation, and resistance could derive from a secure identification with the resource-richness of a mother. Mothers, indeed, have nothing to contribute to this process of masculine validation, and women are reduced in the light of its urgency to a null set: any involvement in it by a woman is overinvolvement; any protectiveness is overprotectiveness; and, for instance, mothers "proud of their sons' nonviolent qualities" are manifesting unmistakable "family pathology" (193).

For both Friedman and Green, then, the first, imperative developmental task of a male child or his parents and caretakers is to get a properly male Core Gender Identity in place, as a basis for further and perhaps more flexible explorations of what it may be to *be* masculine — that is, for a male person, to be *human*. Friedman is rather equivocal about whether this masculine CGI necessarily entails any particular content, or whether it is an almost purely formal, preconditional differentiation that, once firmly in place, can cover an almost infinite range of behaviors and attitudes. He certainly does not see a necessary connection between masculinity and any scapegoating of male homosexuality; since ego-psychology treats the development of male heterosexuality as nonproblematical after adolescence, as not involving the suppression of any homosexual or bisexual possibility (263–67), and therefore as completely unimplicated with homosexual panic (178), it seems merely an unfortunate, perhaps rectifiable misunderstanding that for a proto-gay child to identify "masculinely" might involve his identification with his own erasure.

The renaturalization and enforcement of gender assignment are not the worst news about the new psychiatry of gay acceptance, however. The worst is that it not only fails to offer, but seems conceptually incapable of offering, even the slightest resistance to the wish endemic in the culture surrounding and supporting it: the wish that gay people *not exist.* There are many people in the worlds we inhabit, and these psychiatrists are unmistakably among them, who have a strong interest in the dignified treatment of any gay people who may happen already to exist. But the number of persons or institutions by whom the existence of gay people is treated as a precious desideratum, a needed condition of life, is small. The presiding asymmetry of value assignment between hetero and homo goes unchallenged everywhere: advice on how to help your kids turn out gay, not to mention your students, your parishioners, your therapy clients, or your military subordinates, is less ubiquitous than you might think. On the other hand, the scope of institutions whose programmatic undertaking is to prevent the development of gay people is unimaginably large. There is no major institutionalized discourse that offers a firm resistance to that undertaking: in the United States, at any rate, most sites of the state, the military, education, law, penal institutions, the church, medicine, and mass culture enforce it all but unquestioningly, and with little hesitation at even the recourse to invasive violence.

The books cited above, and the associated therapeutic strategies and institutions, are not about invasive violence. What they are about is a train of squalid lies. The overarching lie is that they are predicated on anything but the therapists' disavowed desire for a nongay outcome. Friedman, for instance, speculates wistfully that — with proper therapeutic intervention — the sexual orientation of one gay man whom he describes as quite healthy might conceivably (not have *been changed* but) "have shifted *on its own*" (Friedman's italics): a speculation, he artlessly remarks, "not value-laden with regard to sexual orientation" (212). Green's book, composed largely of interview transcripts, is a tissue of his lies to children about their parents' motives for bringing them in for therapy. (It was "not to prevent you from becoming homosexual," he tells one young man who had been subjected to behavior modification, "it was because you were unhappy" [318]; but later on the very same page, he unself-consciously confirms to his trusted reader that "parents of sons who entered therapy were ... worried that the cross-gender behavior portended problems with later sexuality.") He encourages predominantly gay young men to "reassure" their parents that they are "bisexual" ("Tell him just enough so he feels better" [207]), and to consider favorably the option of marrying and keeping their wives in the dark about their sexual activities (205). He lies to himself and to us in encouraging patients to lie to him. For instance, in a series of interviews with Kyle, the boy subjected to behavioral therapy, Green reports him as saying that he is unusually with- drawn — "I suppose I've been overly sensitive when guys look at me or something ever since I can remember, you know, after my mom told me why I have to go to UCLA because they were afraid I'd turn into a homosexual" (307); as saying that homosexuality "is pretty bad, and I don't think they should be around to influence children. . . . I don't think they should be hurt by society or any- thing like that — especially in New York. You have them who are into leather and stuff like that. I mean, I think that is really sick, and I think that maybe they should be put away" (307); as saying that he wants to commit violence on men who look at him (307); and as saying that if he had a child like himself, he "would take him where he would be helped" (317). The very image of serene self-acceptance?

Green's summary:

> Opponents of therapy have argued that intervention underscores the child's "deviance," renders him ashamed of who he is, and makes him suppress his "true self." Data on psychological tests do not support this contention; nor does the content of clinical interviews. The boys look back favorably on treatment. They would endorse such intervention if they were the father of a "feminine" boy. Their reason is to reduce childhood conflict and social stigma. Therapy with these boys appeared to accomplish this. (319)

Consistent with this, Green is obscenely eager to convince par- ents that their hatred and rage at their effeminate sons really is only a desire to protect them from peer-group cruelty — even when the parents name *their own* feelings as hatred and rage (391–92). Even when fully one-quarter of parents of gay sons are *so* interested in protecting them from social cruelty that, when the boys fail to change, their parents kick them out on the street, Green is withering about mothers who display any tolerance of their sons' cross-gender behavior (373–75). In fact, his bottom-line identifications as a clin- ician actually seem to lie with the enforcing peer group: he refers approvingly at one point to "therapy, be it formal (delivered by paid professionals) or informal (delivered by the peer group and the larger society via teasing and sex-role standards)" (388).

Referring blandly on one page to "psychological intervention directed at increasing [effeminate boys'] comfort with being male" (259), Friedman says much more candidly on the next page: "[T]he rights of parents to oversee the development of children is a long-established principle. Who is to dictate that parents may not try to raise their children in a manner that maximizes the possibility of a heterosexual outcome?" (260). Who indeed — if the members of this profession can't stop seeing the prevention of gay people as an ethical use of their skills?

Even outside of the mental health professions and within more authentically gay-affirmative discourses, the theoretical space for supporting gay development is, as I've pointed out in the introduction to *Epistemology of the Closet,* narrow. Constructivist arguments have tended to keep hands off the experience of gay and proto-gay kids. For gay and gay-loving people, even though the space of cultural malleability is the only conceivable theater for our effective politics, every step of this constructivist nature/culture argument holds danger: the danger of the difficulty of intervening in the seemingly natural trajectory from identifying a place of cultural malleability, to inventing an ethical or therapeutic mandate for cultural manipulation, to the overarching, hygienic Western fantasy of a world without any more homosexuals in it.

That's one set of dangers, and it is as against them, as I've argued, that essentialist and biologizing understandings of sexual identity accrue a certain gravity. Conceptualizing an unalterably *homosexual body* seems to offer resistance to the social-engineering momentum apparently built into every one of the human sciences of the West, and that resistance can reassure profoundly. At the same time, however, in the postmodern era it is becoming increasingly problematical to assume that grounding an identity in biology or "essential nature" is a stable way of insulating it from societal interference. If anything, the gestalt of assumptions that undergird nature/nurture debates may be in process of direct reversal. Increasingly it is the conjecture that a particular trait is genetically or biologically based, *not* that it is "only cultural," that seems to trigger an estrus of manipulative fantasy in the technological institutions of the culture. A relative depressiveness about the efficacy of social-engineering techniques, a high mania about biological control: the Cartesian bipolar psychosis that always underlay the nature/nurture debates has switched its polar assignments without surrendering a bit of its hold over the collective life. And in this unstable context, the dependence on a specified *homosexual body* to offer resistance to any gay-eradicating momentum is tremblingly vulnerable. AIDS, although it is used to proffer every single day to the news-consuming public the crystallized vision of a world after the homosexual, could never by itself bring about such a world. What whets these fantasies more dangerously, because more blandly, is the presentation, often in ostensibly or authentically gay-affirmative contexts, of biologically based "explanations" for deviant behavior that are absolutely invariably couched in terms of "excess," "deficiency," or "imbalance" — whether in the hormones, in the genetic material, or, as is currently fashionable, in the fetal endocrine environment. If I had ever, in any medium, seen any researcher or popularizer refer even once to any supposed gay-producing circumstance as the *proper* hormone balance, or the *conducive* endocrine environment, for gay generation, I would be less chilled by the breezes of all this technological confidence. As things are, a medicalized dream of the prevention of gay bodies seems to be the less visible, far more respectable underside of the AIDS-fueled public dream of their extirpation.

In this unstable balance of assumptions between nature and culture, at any rate, under the overarching, relatively unchallenged aegis of a culture's desire that gay people *not be,* there is no unthreatened, unthreatening theoretical home for a concept of gay and lesbian origins. What the books I have been discussing, and the institutions to which they are attached, demonstrate is that the wish for the dignified treatment of already gay people is necessarily destined to turn into either trivializing apologetics or, much worse, a silkily camouflaged complicity in oppression — in the absence of a strong, explicit, *erotically invested* affirmation of some people's felt desire or need that there be gay people in the immediate world.

NOTES

This essay was originally written for a panel on psychoanalysis and homosexuality at the Modern Language Association conference, December 1989. Several paragraphs of it are adapted from what became the introduction to my *Epistemology of the*

Closet (Berkeley and Los Angeles: University of California Press, 1990). Jack Cameron pointed me in the direction of these texts; Cindy Patton fortified my resistance to them; and Jonathan Goldberg helped me articulate the argument made here. The motivation for this essay, and some of its approaches, are immensely indebted to several other friends, as well — most particularly to conversations over a long period with Michael Moon.

1. This information comes from reports in the *New York Native,* 23 September 1989, 9–10; 13 November 1989, 14; 27 November 1989, 7.

2. A particularly illuminating overview of psychoanalytic approaches to male homosexuality is available in Kenneth Lewes, *The Psychoanalytic Theory of Male Homosexuality* (New York: Simon and Schuster, 1988; New York: Penguin/NAL/Meridian, 1989).

3. Richard C. Friedman, *Male Homosexuality: A Contemporary Psychoanalytic Perspective* (New Haven: Yale University Press, 1988).

4. Richard Green, *The "Sissy Boy Syndrome" and the Development of Homosexuality* (New Haven: Yale University Press, 1987).

5. It is worth noting that the gay men Friedman admires always have completely discretionary control over everyone else's knowledge of their sexuality; there is no sense that others may have their own intuitions that they are gay; no sense of physical effeminacy; no visible participation in gay (physical, cultural, sartorial) semiotics or community. For many contemporary gay people, such an existence would be impossible; for a great many, it would seem starvingly impoverished in terms of culture, community, and meaning.

6. American Psychiatric Association Staff, *Diagnostic and Statistical Manual of Mental Disorders,* 3d ed. (Washington, D.C.: American Psychiatric Association, 1980), 265–66.

7. The exception to this generalization is Lawrence Mass, whose *Dialogues of the Sexual Revolution,* vol. 1: *Homosexuality and Sexuality* (New York: Harrington Park Press, 1990) collects a decade's worth of interviews with psychiatrists and sex researchers, originally conducted for and published in the gay press. In these often illuminating interviews, a number of Mass's questions are asked under the premise that "American psychiatry is simply engaged in a long, subtle process of reconceptualizing homosexuality as a mental illness with another name — the 'gender identity disorder of childhood' " (214).

8. That relegation may be diminishing as, in many places, "queer" politics comes to overlap and/or compete with "gay" politics. Part of what I understand to be the exciting charge of the very word "queer" is that it embraces, instead of repudiating, what have for many of us been formative childhood experiences of difference and stigmatization.

9. For descriptions of this literature, see Friedman, *Male Homosexuality,* 33–48; and Green, *"Sissy Boy Syndrome,"* 370–90. The most credible of these studies from a gay-affirmative standpoint would be A. P. Bell, M. S. Weinberg, and S. K. Hammersmith, *Sexual Preference: Its Development in Men and Women* (Bloomington: Indiana University Press, 1981), which concludes: "Childhood Gender Nonconformity turned out to be more strongly connected to adult homosexuality than was any other variable in the study" (80).

10. Priding himself on his interdisciplinarity, moreover, Friedman is much taken

with recent neuroendocrinological work suggesting that prenatal stress on the mother may affect structuration of the fetal brain in such a way that hormonal cues to the child as late as adolescence may be processed differentially. His treatment of these data as data is neither very responsible (e.g., problematical results that point only to "hypothetical differences" in one chapter [p. 24] have been silently upgraded to positive "knowledge" two chapters later [p. 51]) nor very impartial (e.g., the conditions hypothesized as conducive to gay development are invariably referred to as *inadequate* androgenization [14], a *deficit* [15], etc.). But his infatuation with this model does have two useful effects. First, it seems to generate by direct analogy this further series of two-phase narratives about psychic development, narratives that discriminate between the circumstances under which a particular psychic structure is *organized* and those under which it is *activated,* that may turn out to enable some new sinuosities for other, more gay-embracing and pluralist projects of developmental narration. (This analogical process is made explicit on 241–45.) And, second, it goes a long way toward detotalizing, demystifying, and narrativizing in a recognizable way any reader's sense of the threat (the promise?) presented by a supposed neurobiological vision of the already gay male body.

The Construction of Heterosexuality
Janet E. Halley

The Supreme Court's 1986 decision in *Bowers v. Hardwick*[1] held that the due process clause does not protect what the Court was pleased to call "homosexual sodomy" from criminalization. Since then four circuit courts have held that the *Hardwick* case "forecloses [any] effort to gain suspect class status" under the equal protection clause for individuals deemed to be homosexuals.[2] These appeals panels, led by the D.C. Circuit in *Padula v. Webster,* have concluded that *Hardwick* foreclosed meaningful equality rights for "homosexuals" because the Supreme Court in that decision refused to invalidate "state laws that criminalize *the behavior that defines the class.*"[3]

As several commentators have observed, federal constitutional law provides some doctrinal grounds for insisting that a due process case is not binding precedent in the equal protection context.[4] But doctrinal arguments separating due process from equal protection analysis do not appear to be strong enough to overcome the apparently overwhelming commonsense appeal of the argument that, inasmuch as entry into the class can be made a felony, a fortiori it can become the basis for denial of federal employment, security clearances, subsidized housing, and so on. This definition is so culturally pervasive today that it appears with alarming frequency in other settings — it is pandemic among judicial, legislative, and executive decision makers, and can be detected outside specifically legal contexts as well.[5] This pervasiveness suggests that we are confronted here with a categorical practice that requires refutation in its own right.

Happily, the premise of *Padula* and the cases following it — that sodomy is the behavior that defines the class — can be challenged. Indeed, it seems to me to be a very timely moment to argue that equal protection theorizing should focus not, as it has until the last few years, on *categories,* but on *practices of categorization.* The searching examination of cultural identity formation that has been underway in feminist criticism, critical race theory, and queer critique in recent years should now be invoked in the development of legal strategy; and litigation should not be ignored as an important forum for the development and contestation of sexual-orientation identities. In the wake of *Hardwick* and *Padula,* the confluence of identity politics and legal practice is inevitable.

This essay is offered as a contribution, largely critical rather than constructive, to that argument. It explores, first, the proposition that legal definitions of the class of homosexuals persistently involve equally decisive, but far less visible, practices of constituting a class of heterosexuals. The two classifications are diacritical in the sense that they acquire definition and meaning in relation to one another: the fact that the more privileged class habitually hides its existence *as a class* doesn't mean that legal decision makers can afford to ignore it. Second, I propose that the difference *between* the categories homosexual and heterosexual is systematically related to differences *within* the category heterosexual. These differences aren't merely lexical, a matter of technical terminology and categorical structure; rather, they structure the social conditions in which the status "heterosexual" is given meaning and is attached to individual persons. Despite its representation as monolithic in its nonhomosexuality, heterosexuality as it operates in federal equal protection cases is a highly unstable, default characterization for people who have not marked themselves or been marked by others as homosexual. Finally, I contend that the threat of precipitous expulsion from the class of heterosexuals, and from all the material and discursive privileges enjoyed by members of that class, bribes class members into complicity with a pervasive representation of the class as coherent, stable, exclusively loyal to heterosexual eroticism, and pure of any sodomitical desires or conduct.

Part 1 of this article seeks to support these contentions by an internal critique of several important equal protection cases recently decided in federal court. Part 2 then turns to an alternative to the *Padula* definition, recently proposed by gay-rights litigators, in which intrinsic personhood (rather than sodomy) defines the class of homosexuals. I argue that this "personhood definition" includes within it so many key features of the *Padula* definition itself that I feel compelled to ask whether they're really different after all. Part 3 briefly sketches the theoretical constraints within which a less dangerous definitional strategy must be developed.

I

Three recent cases in which federal appellate courts have rejected equal protection challenges of gay men, lesbians, and bisexuals expose the dynamics at work when federal courts set out to generate a class of heterosexuals and to disguise its constitution.

Marjorie Rowland and the Town of Mad River

Marjorie Rowland was a closeted, nontenured guidance counselor at the public high school in Mad River — a town destined to live up to its name.[6] Her story starts with an episode in which she treated her own bisexuality as a secret about herself by disclosing it, carefully, to a single co-worker. This co-worker reported her disclosure to the school's principal. Some time later Rowland counseled the parent of a student confused about his or her sexual identity, advising the parent not to panic at this uncertainty. Fearful after this interview that her job might be threatened, Rowland confided the fact of the interview, and her bisexuality, to the school's vice-principal. Soon her sexual identity became a matter of public knowledge and the object of a local effort to get her fired. Throughout the growing turmoil, and with increasing publicity, Rowland continued to make confessions of her sexual identity. Finally she lost her job.

The majority opinion of the Sixth Circuit classified Rowland's first two disclosures as mere private utterances on matters of personal interest, and denied them the protection granted to public speech. It concluded: "[P]laintiff has attempted to make homosexual rights the issue in this case. However, her personal sexual orientation is not a matter of public concern."[7] The court designated Rowland as having a sexual orientation that is personal and intrinsic to herself, that emerges from her alone without the intervention of any public entity, and that exists without creating any implications for understanding the class of heterosexuals.

Justice Brennan, dissenting from the Supreme Court's denial of Rowland's petition for Supreme Court review, carefully delineated the false distinctions on which the Sixth Circuit's holding rested. First, he argued, no one can disclose personal homosexual or bisexual identity, even in the most secretive circumstances, without engaging in the current public debate over sexual orientation: "The fact of petitioner's bisexuality, *once spoken,* necessarily and ineluctably involved her in that debate."[8] And, second, that act of speech cannot then be distinguished from the sexual identity it reveals: "[P]etitioner's First Amendment and equal protection claims may be seen to converge, because it is *realistically impossible to separate her spoken statements from her status.*"[9]

To put it a bit differently, Marjorie Rowland's spoken statements *constituted* her status. Thus we vastly underestimate the complexity of the interaction between Rowland and the town of Mad River if we understand the town to have discovered a hidden *fact* — Rowland's bisexuality — and to have acted, wisely or foolishly, upon it. Both Rowland and the town of Mad River were engaged in a diacritical struggle — one in which the self-definition of both players was at stake. This should make visible what otherwise should remain hidden — Rowland's discursive exertions were made in interaction with a class of heterosexuals *also in the process of self-constitution.*

It is useful to remember here that student, whom I will arbitrarily denominate "he." At the time Rowland's narrative began, he was wavering anxiously at the threshold of sexuality, uncertain which little box — gay, straight, or bisexual — he would have to insert himself into. The underlying ambivalence of this student's erotic disposition may have survived the storm that swept Rowland from her job. But the storm will have accomplished its purpose if the student learns that, as long as he lives in Mad River, he should not disclose them to anyone again.

Mad River as a political entity emerges from the Rowland controversy *heterosexual.* And, assuming the student heeds his lesson in silence, the class of heterosexuals thus constituted will include him, despite his capacity for confusion about his sexual orientation. The resulting class of heterosexuals is a default class, home to those who have not fallen out of it. It openly expels but covertly incorporates the homosexual other, an undertaking that renders it profoundly heterogeneous, unstable, and provisional. It can maintain its current boundaries and even its apparent legitimacy only if the student and others like him remain silent. And until they speak, it owes its glory days as a coherent social category to its members' own *failure to acknowledge* its discursive constitution, the coercive dynamics of its incoherence.

James Miller and His Official Interpreters

If Marjorie Rowland and Mad River together indicate the way in which the incoherence of the heterosexual class operates as a bribe, the case of James Miller indicates how arbitrarily the threat underlying the bribe can be called in. Miller was a naval officer discharged under Navy regulations (since revised) that required that any person who had committed a homosexual act be separated from service as a homosexual. His equal protection challenge and that of two other naval officers also discharged under those regulations were consolidated in *Beller v. Middendorf*,[10] a Ninth Circuit case ultimately decided by then-Judge Anthony Kennedy. The court's analysis of plaintiff Miller's case displays an ugly tableau, with the "homosexual" reduced to the object of others' knowledge and as such to language so close to gibberish that it is worse than silence; and with the official knower founding the clarity of its discourse simply upon its power to enforce it.

Miller is represented in the published decision as profoundly equivocal on the subject of his sexual-orientation identity. He apparently confessed to committing homosexual acts while on leave in Taiwan and at some unspecified earlier time, yet he also "has at various times denied being homosexual and expressed regret or repugnance at his acts."[11] If we ask, on the basis of these facts, whether Miller was gay or straight, we miss the painful richness of his encounter with the Navy's gay-purgative policy and with the judicial decision makers to whom he appealed for protection. The importance of changing the question is suggested by the fact that it is impossible to understand Miller's statements as constituting an autobiography unproblematically descriptive of his identity before the discharge proceedings began or even during them. On one hand, we are not entitled to impute to Miller actual repugnance at homosexual activities (and thus a stable or reformed heterosexual identity) because his confession of this emotion might be cynically strategic. On the other hand, neither are we entitled to conclude that Miller's profession of repugnance was merely strategic and cynical: the scene is too redolent of the religious confessional, in which the penitent offers as a sincere self-articulation a form of self derived from the dominant discourse he confronts as his punisher.

Both sources of incoherence are attributable to the presence of a coercive inquisitor. This shadow figure is actually the crux of Miller's story — and can be revealed only if we shift our attention from the effort to assign a sexual-orientation identity to Miller, to the effort to describe the Navy's mode of "knowing" Miller as a homosexual and its assumption in doing so of a nonhomosexual positionality.

It is important to note the extent to which Miller's collapse as a self-identifying speaker simultaneously consolidates the authority, and the nonhomosexual identity, of his Naval interlocutors. If we assume that Miller has taken up a strategy of deception, we're entitled to conclude that Miller is insincere as to his sensation of remorse and his identification as heterosexual because of it; but we can't deduce from *that* what identity he would espouse absent material coercion. And even assuming sincerity, his declarations will bear only the most exiguous inferences because the Navy has imposed not only material but also definitional coercion — has conjoined its power to deprive Miller of a livelihood and an opportunity to serve with its power to limn the contours of the class of homosexuals. Indeed, if Miller has undertaken a sincere confession, he has legitimated the Navy in both its material and its discursive projects. Any actual contemporaneous heterosexuality Miller can attain depends not just on his self-description, but on the Navy's ultimate adjudication of his status as a class member — and Miller (if sincere) has agreed to that.

The contrast with Marjorie Rowland, although decidedly dysphoric, is instructive. While Rowland powerfully intervened in a public debate over homosexuality upon describing herself, in two ostensibly private conversations, as bisexual, Miller was drawn into that debate, and given a location in it, without consolidating the authority to describe himself. Instead, even as Miller claimed to expel himself from the class of homosexuals and to constitute himself as heterosexual, he was expelled from the class of heterosexuals and constituted as homosexual by an act of definitional power over which he had no control. That is, the disintegration of his authority to name himself indicates not merely Miller's unwillingness to be excluded from the Navy or his bafflement at the moralized binarism in which he was required to find a place; it also indicates that the class of heterosexuals gains at the moment of this exclusion what Miller has lost, the epistemological authority to know and to designate what (and who) a homosexual is.

The Ninth Circuit's decision is replete with signs that some of the naval and judicial decision makers involved in Miller's case were disconcerted by this exposure of the role sheer power played in their regime of knowing. Both the hearing board convened to consider Miller's discharge and the Senior Medical Officer who examined him balked at applying the Navy's strict act/status equation in his case. The board found that Miller had committed homosexual acts while in service, but recommended that he be retained. It is not clear from the published opinion whether this vote expressed a view that Miller was an erring heterosexual, a harmless homosexual, or a human being who could not be fit into rigid ideal categories.

The appellate opinion's summary of the Senior Medical Officer's evaluation suggests the more critical third alternative. According to Judge Kennedy's opinion, the medical expert found that Miller "did not *appear* to be *'a homosexual.'* "[12] Judge Kennedy's typography here recognizes the social artifice of the category "homosexual," a sign I was once willing to take as auspicious. But Judge Kennedy finally rendered these highly equivocal reports legally irrelevant, and stabilized the legal assignment of homosexual identity to plaintiff Miller, by interpreting the old Navy rules as creating absolutely no discretion in those charged with carrying them out.[13] In contrast to the cases of the other plaintiffs consolidated with Miller's, Kennedy concluded, "The case of Miller is closer but no less *clear*."[14]

"Clarity" here cannot emerge from any unequivocal evidence of Miller's sexual-orientation identity, for there is none. Instead it describes the epistemological confidence of the institutional decision maker in its definitional undertakings, while reducing the acute problematics of Miller's identity to silence. In the act of excluding James Miller, the heterosexual class denies its own definitional incoherence and constitutes itself as enjoying exclusive possession of the power to define heterosexual and homosexual classes, to know the truth about their inhabitants, to label indelibly, and to expel unilaterally.

Federal Judges and the Class of Sodomites

Judge Kennedy's "clarity" suggests that the definitional struggles that I've been describing in this essay engage not merely abstract cultural traditions of defining, and not only private citizens like Marjorie Rowland and James Miller, but actual federal judges. When federal judges undertake actual instantiations of the definitional categories homosexual and heterosexual, we might, then, think it fair to ask how the judge situates him- or herself, not only as knower but also as known.

The paradigmatic instances of such self-constitution appear, not surprisingly, in *Hardwick* and *Padula,* the cases that have given legal urgency to the definitional dynamics I'm trying to understand here. When the Supreme Court in *Hardwick* stamped a Constitutional imprimatur on laws criminalizing homosexual sodomy, and again when the D.C. Circuit in *Padula* reasoned that that crime defines the class of homosexuals, the deciding judges engaged in what Eve Kosofsky Sedgwick aptly described as the "speech act of a silence"[15] constituting their own exemption, as (putative) heterosexuals, from the punishment they deemed appropriate for homosexuals. What this act of silence occluded was the judges' own status as potential sodomites under relevant jurisdictions' statutory regimes.

Underpinning both cases is the Georgia statute up for review in *Hardwick.* That statute does not make any distinction between homosexual or heterosexual actors. Instead, it prohibits *anyone* from voluntarily engaging in "any sexual act involving the sex organs of one person and the mouth or anus of another."[16] Out of a challenge that the enforcement of this statute invaded the privacy rights Michael Hardwick enjoyed *as a person,* Justice White framed the matter in the following words: "[T]he issue presented is whether the Federal Constitution confers a fundamental right *upon homosexuals* to engage in sodomy."[17] Having posed the issue in that way, he held that Georgia's condemnation of "homosexual sodomy" validly expresses "majority sentiments about the morality of *homosexuality,*" indeed a "*presumed belief of a majority of the electorate in Georgia that homosexual sodomy is immoral and unacceptable.*"[18]

In these moves, Justice White's majority opinion generates a class of homosexuals *within,* even as it excludes that class *from,* an unmarked class of human persons all subject to the Georgia sodomy statute. Nothing covert in that: Justice White apparently felt no qualms about misreading the Georgia statute in the full light of day, for all to see. And yet the diacritical relation — the simultaneous generation of a class of heterosexuals — remains unacknowledged. Potentially felonious under the actual statute before the Court in *Hardwick,* the class of heterosexuals is allowed to drop silently out of the picture. Indeed, "dropping silently out of the picture" becomes a, perhaps *the,* salient characteristic of the class.

This silence is arresting as well in the *Padula* judges' refusal to grapple with the sodomy statute actually in force in the jurisdiction in which they sat when they made their ruling. For the *Padula* pronunciamento was uttered in Washington, D.C., where, as in Georgia, the law prohibits all sodomitical acts without regard to the gender of the actors.[19] If indeed felonious sodomy were the "behavior that defines the class" of homosexuals, then the class of homosexuals would potentially include every adult in the jurisdiction in which the judges sat. That is, if the decision were taken at its word, we would have to conclude that the judges themselves, no matter what their sexual orientation, are potential sodomites (and, to follow the logic to its end, actual homosexuals). But the decision requires us to correct its extravagant meaning: it is *homosexual* sodomy, not *felony* sodomy, that defines the class of homosexuals; that is, to make the decision make sense, we have to engage in an act of *assuming out of existence* the criminality of sodomitical acts involving persons of different genders.

This isn't just a blind spot: it is a gesture in the constitution of a class. And there is a bribe attached: the reward for joining in this misprision of the statute is that one can join the *Padula* judges in silently constituting the class of those who (mis)read themselves out of the target group of the vast majority of consensual sodomy prohibitions,[20] those who are exempt, those whose sexual conduct — even more, those whose sexual desires — are covered by a mantle of privacy and silence.

II

The definition of the class of homosexuals adopted by the D.C Circuit in *Padula v. Webster* might be called a "deviance definition" because it identifies the class by a transgressive sexual practice. It has not gone unopposed. A number of courts, dissenting judges, and academic commentators have resisted the argument that *Hardwick* controls in the equal protection context by adopting a very different definition of the homosexual class — what I call a "personhood definition," in which the class of homosexuals is defined by a form of personality shared by its members.

The good news is that this argument has formed the basis of a recent decision, *Jantz v. Muci,* in which Judge Kelly of the District of Kansas broke with *Padula* and held that discrimination based on sexual orientation warrants heightened scrutiny notwithstanding *Hardwick.*[21] The bad news is that the "personhood definition" underlying this decision does not actually take us very far from the definitional dynamics that can be detected in the acutely antigay decisions analyzed above. The personhood definition, like the deviance definition, presupposes that a class of homosexuals exists in nature, before the law. The apparent divergence of these two definitions sustains the illusion that the class of homosexuals is not continually being articulated through the processes — including the judicial processes — of definition. And once accepted, as we have seen, *that* illusion foments another: that the class of *heterosexuals* is stable, natural, and transparent. The convergence of these definitions should warn us that the focus of antihomophobic equal protection analysis should be not on the class of homosexuals but on the diacritics that produce it and its supposed "opposite."

So, how does the personhood definition work and how is it different from the deviance definition? The personhood definition as it is deployed in *Jantz v. Muci* and elsewhere attempts to make a dichotomy of homosexuals and heterosexuals on the basis of intrinsic personhood. It originates in a distinction between *sexual conduct* and *sexual orientation,*[22] so that the "class" of homosexuals, under this definition, is characterized not by a particular species of acts but by an "orientation" — and sexual orientation, the court found in *Jantz v. Muci,* is a "central and defining aspect of the personality

92   Janet E. Halley

of every individual."[23] Far from being defined by bodily acts, the "class of homosexuals" is defined by an intrinsic, even foundational fibre of personality.

Competing for legal recognition, then, are two conceptions of "the homosexual" that appear diametrically opposed — a definition that invokes a deviant act and a definition that invokes a conception of personhood. The differences in approach are easy to see. First, whereas the deviance definition invokes an objective act, the personhood definition dichotomizes subjectivities. Second, by referring only to an act, the deviance definition sets up a class of homosexuals without explicitly referring to or delineating a class of heterosexuals; the personhood definition, on the other hand, invokes a taxonomy of personalities — to borrow some language from *Jantz v. Muci*, "sexual orientation (whether homosexual or heterosexual)"[24] — that explicitly acknowledges an apparently complementary class of heterosexuals. And third, the deviance definition, with its clinical isolation of a particularized "behavior," apparently disengages the court itself from the ontological scene in which its class of homosexuals emerges (recall the posture of heterosexual immunity constructed in *Hardwick* and *Padula*), while the personhood definition implicates everyone — and that necessarily includes the person of the judge — in the totality it makes of its homo- and heterosexualities.

These two definitions thus apparently differ both in what they describe and in how they situate the authority making the description. And the personhood definition advanced in *Jantz v. Muci* appears to constitute a major improvement — not only in the holding it makes possible (the first favorable equal protection decision to issue from a federal court in years) but also in providing a culturally plausible way for judges and litigators steeped in the liberal tradition to articulate an antihomophobic discourse.

Ultimately, however, the personhood definition is not so terribly different from the deviance definition, in that each of them partakes of important ontological and epistemological characteristics that mark its apparent opposite. A kind of essentialism that covertly subtends the deviance definition, particularly as it has been applied in cases subsequent to *Padula*, rides on the surface of the personhood definition; and a kind of certainty and magisterial knowingness — in short, an objectivity — that quite patently marks

definitional stance reappears less frankly in the
's deployment of the personhood definition. For
therefore, the deviance and personhood defi-
features that should make us skeptical about

Tracing this correspondence between the deviance and personhood definitions requires an initial close reading of deviance-
definition cases, to specify the ways in which they locate "the
homosexual" as the essential object of heterosexual knowledge.
These essentialist entailments of the deviance definition emerge
clearly only in cases (unlike *Padula* itself)[25] involving a plaintiff
identified as gay or lesbian because of conduct *different from* the
acts that supposedly "define the class" of homosexuals. The Ninth
Circuit's decision in *High Tech Gays v. Defense Industry Security
Clearance Office* provides a striking example. Applicants for security clearances filed *High Tech Gays* as a class action, alleging that
the Department of Defense had violated their associational rights
and their right to equal protection by subjecting them to more rigorous approval procedures than those applied to other applicants,
all in an effort to screen out gay men and lesbians. In order to make
sense of the Ninth Circuit's decision in the appeal of Robert Weston, one of the named plaintiffs, we have to impute to the court an
essentialist understanding of the class of homosexuals.

The Ninth Circuit acknowledged that Weston was denied a security clearance "because his application revealed that he belonged
to a gay organization."[26] The Court of Appeals remanded with an
order commanding the district court to enter summary judgment
for the Department of Defense against all plaintiffs, *including Weston.* What that amounts to is a holding that, as a matter of law
and notwithstanding any particularized proof the plaintiffs might
be able to present at trial, they could not win and their complaint
had to be dismissed before trial. Because the court dismissed Weston's claims as well as those of the other named plaintiffs, the basis
for its holding applies even to him:

> [B]y [*sic*] the *Hardwick* majority holding that the Constitution confers
> no fundamental right upon homosexuals to engage in sodomy, and
> because homosexual conduct can thus be criminalized, homosexuals
> cannot constitute a suspect or quasi-suspect class entitled to greater
> than rational basis review for equal protection purposes.[27]

The ruling against Weston coheres only if the court has made a *legal conclusion* that Weston had committed criminalizable sodomy.[28] And the only basis on which such a conclusion could rest is Weston's willingness to be identified as a gay man. To reconstruct the court's apparent logic here: inasmuch as Weston was a gay man, he had, as a matter of law, committed sodomy. Sodomy, in the mind of the law, was essential to who Weston was.

In *benShalom v. Marsh* the Seventh Circuit had to perform a similarly essentialist move in its effort to bring plaintiff Miriam benShalom into a class of homosexuals defined by conduct. The court conceded that the Army had refused benShalom reenlistment not because of any homosexual acts but because she frankly identified herself as a lesbian.[29] The Seventh Circuit held that such admissions were "reliable evidence of a desire and propensity to engage in homosexual conduct."[30] Perhaps so. But there is more: illogically disregarding the possibility of exceptions, the court then proceeded to conclude that benShalom's profession of a lesbian identity was "*compelling* evidence that plaintiff has in the past and is likely to again engage in such conduct."[31] On that basis the court held that *Hardwick* required dismissal of benShalom's equal protection claims — that is, it held that there was *no way* benShalom could escape the imputation to her of criminal(izable) sodomy. Once again the deviance definition, apparently founded only on discrete acts of bodily conduct, insists that that conduct is an essential, foundational, and inescapable element of a gay plaintiff's character — of her personhood.

If sodomy is essential to homosexuality in cases relying on the deviance definition, homosexuality (and heterosexuality) are essential to personhood under the personhood definition. Indeed, what's so remarkable is the ease with which essentialist commitments can be discerned in expressions of the personhood definition. It's as though the judge writing the decision in *Jantz v. Muci* had the first chapter of Diana Fuss's book *Essentially Speaking* right at his side. As her first definition of essentialism, Fuss indicates that it is "a belief in true essence — that which is most irreducible, unchanging, and therefore constitutive of a given person or thing."[32] In *Jantz v. Muci,* the court determined that the sexual orientation "homosexuality" is not merely immutable, but moreover a "central, defining trait of personhood, which may be altered only at the expense of significant damage to the individual's sense of self."[33] Fuss goes on to describe the relationship between the social and the natural in an essentialist frame: "For the essentialist, the natural provides the raw material and determinative starting point for the practices and laws of the social."[34] And the *Jantz v. Muci* court goes on to conclude: "to discriminate against individuals who accept *their given sexual orientation* and refuse to alter that orientation to conform to *societal norms* does significant violence to *a central and defining character* of those individuals."[35]

I point out these correspondences with great pain and reluctance. Judge Kelly's decision in *Jantz v. Muci* is an amazing accomplishment, both for the plaintiff's attorneys and for Judge Kelly himself. In *so many ways* they got it right.[36] But the convergence of the two definitions on essentialism in this way suggests that the personhood definition was *already there* in the deviance definition. Although technically it offers a way of delinking *Hardwick* from the equal protection clause, the personhood definition exposes an unexpressed assumption of the deviance definition: that rigid, fixed sexual identities constitute the definitional essences of persons. The internal logic of the personhood definition would not be fundamentally offended if one proceeded to add to it the only additional requisite of the deviance definition: that the persons essentially committed to homosexual personhood are *thereby also* essentially committed to sodomitical action.

Not surprisingly, the convergence of the personhood and deviance definitions extends beyond the definitions they propose to their constructions of a stance from which to define. It was the argument of part 1, above, that a class of nonhomosexuals is diacritically constituted in practices of homosexual definition. To recapitulate, the deviance definition purports to found a class of homosexuals upon discrete bodily acts, without regard to the definition of any counterpart class. That counterpart class, purportedly having nothing to do with the foundation of a class of homosexuals and discernible only by rather ferocious tactics of unsympathetic reading, remains silent and invisible. Thus judges working with the deviance definition persistently fail to acknowledge the dichotomy they imply or their own agency and embeddedness within it. In the project of *Padula* "objectivity," however, a position from which the

class of homosexuals can be known is under construction even as
it is removed from view. This position is a class of *nonhomosexuals* who know what a homosexual is; who are at the same time
exempt from the definitional clarity to which homosexuals are subject; and who because of both of these features are exempt from the
discrimination to which "known homosexuals" are exposed. Both
their epistemological privilege and their exemptions are contingent,
however, on their continued silence about the heterogeneity and
fabricatedness of their class — on their acceptance of what I have
called the "bribe."

The covert assumption of deviance-definitional dynamics within
the personhood definition extends, I would argue, to the construction of the class of heterosexuals. Of course, at first glance they
seem to be different in this regard: the personhood formulation is
so much more frank than the deviance definition about the position
of privilege and authority from which the category of homosexuals
is discerned. At least those propounding the personhood definition
acknowledge that they are working within a homo/hetero-sexual
binarism, permit the inference that everyone has to deal with his
or her place in it, and thus implicitly place themselves in the same
world with the homosexual object of their knowledge. But under
the personhood definition these are natural categories, represented
to be already in place before the social activity of describing them
begins. Here again, then, we encounter a knower of the sexual
system who achieves a posture of objectivity, neutrality, and dis-
engagement. A deficit in this disengaged posture appears when, in
support of its conclusion that homosexual orientation is immutable,
the *Jantz v. Muci* court reasons as follows:

> Judge Norris [concurring in *Watkins v. United States Army*] has put
> the issue in terms the ordinary person (whether heterosexual or
> homosexual) can appreciate. If the government began to discriminate
> against heterosexuals, how many heterosexuals "would find it easy
> not only to abstain from heterosexual activity but also shift the object
> of their desires to persons of the same sex?"[37]

This passage is doing a lot of work. Ordinary people take two
shapes — and only two: heterosexual or homosexual. But the apparent symmetry of these two personal formations is belied by the
acute asymmetry imposed by the passage's rhetorical appeal. The

rhetorical question, though nominally addressed to every "ordinary person," actually asks: "*[H]ow many heterosexuals* 'would find it easy...?'" That is, the court's interlocutors are those who can register the horror a heterosexual would feel if invited or required to direct his or her sexual desire toward another person of the same sex — and that must be the class of heterosexuals. Not coincidentally, the class with the cognitive authority to give a rhetorically important answer to the question is also the class with the judicial and legislative authority to enforce its answer. Most decisively, this privileged class is represented to be entirely autonomous of its counterpart class of homosexuals, to be constituted by heterosexual desire that is not only *fixed* but *exclusive.*

Although the holding in *Jantz v. Muci* must gratify anyone seeking to fortify legal protections for gay men, lesbians, and bisexuals, this underlying act of definition should give us pause. For here the characteristics of *Padula* objectivity reemerge, altered in a key particular that reveals a new range for the exercise of homophobic power. Under both definitional regimes (nonhomo)(hetero)sexuals know what a homosexual is and are exempt from the discrimination to which homosexuals may be exposed. But unlike the class of "nonhomosexuals" implied in *Padula,* the class of "heterosexuals" delineated in *Jantz v. Muci* is subject to precisely the same degree of definitional clarity as that which specifies homosexuals. The personhood definition not only describes that class as a natural given; it also *specifies that membership in it requires exclusive and unchanging fidelity to heterosexual desire.* But insofar as this definition is a social representation emanating from a relatively empowered authority, we might more accurately say that it *exhorts* a class of heterosexuals *to represent itself* as united in exclusive and unchanging fidelity to heterosexual desire. Even as it sets in place a basis upon which to hold that discrimination against gay men, lesbians, and bisexuals will be subject to meaningful judicial scrutiny, the personhood definition reconfirms the bribe.

III

Hardwick and *Padula* are going to require gay-affirmative litigators to wrestle with identity politics. As Nan D. Hunter concludes in an essay soberly entitled "Life after *Hardwick*," the *Padula* decision and its progeny will require us to assure that essentialist claims about gay, lesbian, and bisexual identity no longer draw the limit of the constitutional protection we seek.[38] From this perspective, cultural criticism committed to the premise that cultural binarisms are pervasively textual should form an important theoretical resource for litigators, by providing insight into the ways in which gay, lesbian, and bisexual identities escape the *Padula* court's effort to consolidate them as sodomy. But the foregoing analysis also sounds a warning note, suggesting that such criticism cannot be the only theoretical resource for a post-*Hardwick* litigation strategy. Once we shift our attention from the dynamics that constitute the class of homosexuals to those that form and police the class of heterosexuals, a problem unanticipated in purely textualist critical theory emerges: the use of incoherent and multiple identities not to deconstruct a monolithic cultural binarism, but to enforce one.

In the legal practices that I have just described, definitional incoherence is the very mechanism of material dominance. When Rowland's student becomes heterosexual, and James Miller becomes homosexual, incoherence does not deconstruct but rather regulates a hetero/homo hierarchy. The bribe that diversifies the class of heterosexuals further draws our attention to the importance in definitional politics of material relations of power. The assumption that relations of dominance and subordination are purely discursive must give way to an analysis of the ways in which concrete exertions of power intervene to determine whether consolidations or dispersals of identity will, in a particular time and place, be liberating or oppressive.

To borrow Susan Bordo's formulation, "*both* 'naturalist' and 'textualizing' notions of the body are culturally situated" and "both are thus equally amenable to being historically utilized as coercive instruments of power."[39] And to borrow Eve Kosofsky Sedgwick's reflection on the limits of deconstruction per se:

> [A] deconstructive analysis of [the] definitional knots [exposed by
> the deconstruction of the binarism hetero/homosexuality], however
> necessary, [is not] at all sufficient to disable them. Quite the opposite:
> I would suggest that an understanding of their irresolvable instability
> has been continually available, and has continually lent discursive
> authority, to antigay as well as to gay cultural forces of this century.[40]

The next generation of constitutional arguments for gay, lesbian, and bisexual rights must accommodate the complexities suggested by these formulations. These arguments must be supple enough to explain why official imposition of fixed identities *and* the official administration of incoherent and labile ones undermine civic values; they must be capacious enough to claim constitutional protection not only for assertions of consolidated and even essentialist gay, lesbian, bisexual, and queer identities, but also for the choice to be queer.

At least two federal judges have indicated that life tenure does not strip the human mind of its capacity to conceive of alternatives to the *Padula* definition that do not depend on the personhood thesis.[41] The task now is to develop expressive, political, and civic models of sexual-orientation identity formation that will convince other judges.

NOTES

I want to thank Christine A. Littleton, Gerald Lopez, Nancy Sorkin Rabinowitz, Margaret Jane Radin, Deborah Rhode, and Carol Sanger for reading drafts of this essay, and audiences at Duke University in March 1992 and at the Critical Networks Conference in April 1992 for their helpful responses.

1. *Hardwick v. Bowers*, 478 U.S. 186, 106 S. Ct. 2841 (1986).

2. *Padula v. Webster*, 822 F.2d 97, 103 (D.C. Cir. 1987); *see also High Tech Gays v. Defense Indus. Security Clearance Office*, 895 F.2d 563, 571 (9th Cir. 1990); *benShalom v. Marsh*, 881 F.2d 454, 464–65 (7th Cir. 1989), *cert. denied*, 110 S. Ct. 1296 (1990); *Woodward v. United States*, 871 F.2d 1068, 1076 (Fed. Cir. 1989).

3. *Padula*, 822 F.2d at 103 (emphasis added).

4. Cass Sunstein, "Sexual Orientation and the Constitution: A Note on the Relationship between Due Process and Equal Protection," 55 *U. Chi. L. Rev.* 1161 (1989); Tracey Rich, "Sexual Orientation Discrimination in the Wake of *Bowers v. Hardwick*," 22 *Ga. L. Rev.* 773 (1988). But Rich provides no argument for disabling *Hardwick* in the equal protection context, and Sunstein's rationale is vulnerable to criticism. Sunstein distinguishes due process jurisprudence, which he approvingly characterizes as a cumulation of traditional legal values, from equal protection jurisprudence, which prohibits even time-honored forms of discrimination. It is the *Hardwick* Court itself, of course, that preeminently restricts due process rights to a recapitulation of past legal commitments. For a stern critique of that understanding of due process, see Frank Michelman, "Law's Republic," 97 *Yale L. J.* 1493 (1987).

5. For a catalog of examples, see my essay "*Bowers v. Hardwick* in the Renaissance," in Jonathan Goldberg, ed., *Queering the Renaissance* (Durham, N.C.: Duke University Press, 1993).

6. *Rowland v. Mad River Local School Dist.*, 730 F.2d 444 (6th Cir. 1984), *cert. denied,* 470 U.S. 1009 (1985).

7. *Rowland,* 730 F.2d at 451.

8. *Rowland,* 470 U.S. at 1012 (Brennan, J., dissenting) (emphasis added).

9. *Id.* at 1016 n. 11 (emphasis added).

10. *Beller v. Middendorf,* 632 F.2d 788 (9th Cir. 1980) (Anthony Kennedy, J.), *cert. denied sub nom. Beller v. Lehman,* 452 U.S. 905, *cert. denied,* 454 U.S. 855 (1981).

11. *Beller v. Middendorf,* 632 F.2d at 802 n.9.

12. *Id.* at 794 (emphasis added).

13. *Id.* at 801–5.

14. *Id.* at 802 n. 9.

15. Eve Kosofsky Sedgwick, *Epistemology of the Closet* (Berkeley: University of California Press, 1990), 3.

16. Ga. Code Ann. §16–6–2 (1984).

17. *Hardwick,* 106 S. Ct. at 2843 (emphasis added).

18. *Id.* at 2844, 2846 (emphasis added).

19. D.C. Code Ann. §22–3502 (1991). Residents of and travelers to the District of Columbia might wish to take note that the annotated code includes this general prohibition of fellatio, cunnilingus, and anal intercourse under the rubric "Sexual Psychopaths."

20. Facially neutral sodomy statutes are in force in nineteen jurisdictions; nine states target only homosexual sodomy for criminalization.

Jurisdictions with facially neutral statutes are: Alabama (Ala. Code §13A-6-60(2), 13A-6-65(a)(3) (1982)); Arizona (Ariz. Rev. Stat. Ann. §§13–1411, 13–1412 (1989)); District of Columbia (D.C. Code Ann. §22–3052 (1981)); Florida (Fla. Stat. Ann. §800.02 (West 1976)); Georgia (Ga. Code Ann. §16–6–2 (1984)); Idaho (Idaho Code §18–6605 (1987)); Louisiana (La. Rev. Stat. Ann. art. 27, §§553–54 (1987)); Maryland (Md. Code Ann. art. 27, §§553–54 (1987)); Massachusetts (Mass. Gen. L. Ann. ch. 35A, §§34–35 (1990)); Michigan (Mich. Comp. Laws Ann. §§750.158 (West 1991)); Minnesota (Minn. Stat. Ann. §609.293 (1987)); Mississippi (Miss. Code Ann. §97–29–59 (1972)); North Carolina (N.C. Gen. Stat. §14–177 (1990)); Pennsylvania (Pa. Stat. Ann. tit. 18, §3124 (Purdon 1983)); Rhode Island (R.I. Gen. Laws §11–10–1 (1981)); South Carolina (S.C. Code Ann. §16–15–20 (Law. Co-op. 1985)); South Dakota (S.D. Codified Laws §22–22–2 (1988)); Utah (Utah Code Ann. §76–5–403(1) (1990)); and Virginia (Va. Code §18.2–361 (1982)).

In addition to the facially neutral sodomy statutes just cited, Michigan has enacted three criminal statutes that distinguish between gay male, lesbian, and heterosexual encounters but that criminalize them in substantially identical terms. The statutes prohibit "gross indecency," a term that may include fellatio, and apply to acts between men, Mich. Comp. Laws Ann. §750.338 (West 1991); between women, Mich. Comp. Laws Ann. §750.338a (West 1991); and between a man and a woman, Mich. Comp. Laws Ann. §750.338b (West 1991). By their terms these statutes apply to private as well as public conduct.

The nine states that criminalize consensual, noncommercial sodomy only where the participants are of the same sex are: Arkansas (Ark. Stat. Ann. §5–41–1813 (1975)); Kansas (Kan. Stat. Ann. §21–3505 (1988)); Kentucky (Ky. Rev. Stat. §510.100 (1990)); Missouri (Mo. Rev. Stat. §566.090(1)(3) (West 1979)); Montana (Mont. Code Ann. §§45–2–101(20), 45–2–101(60), 45–2–101(61) (1989)); Nevada (Nev. Stat. §201.190 (1986));

Oklahoma (Okla. Stat. tit. 21, §886 (1983), a facially neutral statute that has been held to violate the state constitutional right to privacy when applied to heterosexual sodomy, *see Post v. State,* 715 P.2d 1105 (Ok. Crim. App.), *cert. denied,* 107 S. Ct. 290 (1986)); Tennessee (Tenn. Code Ann. §39–13–510 (Supp. 1990)); Texas (Tex. Penal Code Ann. §21.06 (1989)).

21. *Jantz v. Muci,* 759 F. Supp. 1543 (D. Kan. 1991); *see also, e.g., Watkins v. United States Army,* 875 F.2d 699, 726–26 (9th Cir. 1989) (en banc) (Norris, J., concurring). The academic authority most frequently cited in support of this definition is surely Lawrence H. Tribe, *American Constitutional Law* §16–33 at 1616 (1988); *see also* Note, The Constitutional Status of Sexual Orientation: Homosexuality as a Suspect Classification, 98 *Harv. L. Rev.* 1285, 1303 (1985).

22. *Jantz v. Muci,* 759 F. Supp. at 1458.

23. *Id.* at 1551.

24. *Id.* at 1457.

25. The D.C. Circuit deemed plaintiff Margaret Padula to be a "practicing homosexual," by which it apparently meant that she was a person to whom "homosexual status attaches" because she "engage[d] in homosexual conduct." *Padula,* 822 F.2d at 99, 102. The court further conflated "homosexual conduct" with the conduct that *Hardwick* held to be criminalizable. *Id.* at 103. Margaret Padula apparently did not dispute this logic. *Id.* It is probably necessary to remind ourselves that her designation as a sodomite is thus a legal fiction. But at least it is a designation with a discernible history. The cases examined in the text below provide no indication of why or how sodomitical acts were imputed to their lesbian and gay plaintiffs.

26. *High Tech Gays,* 668 F. Supp. 1361, 1366 (N.D. Cal. 1987).

27. *Hi Tech Gays,* 895 F.2d 563, 571 (9th Cir. 1990). For a vigorous dissent from denial of en banc review of this decision, and in particular of the ruling discussed above, *see High Tech Gays,* 909 F.2d at 379–80.

28. The court need not have made the prior assumption that, because Weston belonged to a gay organization, he could be nothing other than a gay man. Weston's identity as "gay" was already established when Weston and the other plaintiffs described themselves as gay in their complaint, 895 F.2d at 569, and when he became a representative under Rule 23 of a plaintiff class consisting only of "gay persons." *High Tech Gays v. Defense Indus. Sec. Clearance Office,* 909 F. Supp. 1361, 1366 (N.D. Cal. 1987), *rev'd in part, vac. in part and remanded,* 895 F.2d 563.

29. *benShalom v. Marsh,* 881 F.2d 454, 457 (7th Cir. 1989). This concession is based on findings made in benShalom's first lawsuit against the Army, filed in 1976. In that litigation, benShalom challenged her discharge by the Army, and ultimately won court-ordered reinstatement. When, thus reinstated, she sought to reenlist at the expiration of her original enlistment, the Army again sought to exclude her from service. She filed a second lawsuit challenging this second adverse decision. The regulatory posture of the reenlistment litigation is thus different from that of the discharge case, but the Army in both cases acted upon the same facts about benShalom's sexual-orientation identity. Those facts were found in the first litigation as follows: "petitioner had publicly acknowledged her homosexuality during conversations with fellow reservists, in an interview with a reporter for her division newspaper, and in class, while teaching drill sergeant candidates. There was no proof that she engaged in homosexual acts, or had done anything that could be interpreted as a homosexual

advance toward fellow reservists." *benShalom v. Secretary of the Army,* 489 F. Supp. 964, 969 (E.D. Wis. 1980).

30. *benShalom v. Marsh,* 881 F.2d 454, 464 (7th Cir. 1989).

31. *Id.,* 881 F.2d at 464.

32. Diana Fuss, *Essentially Speaking* (New York: Routledge, 1989), 2.

33. *Id.* at 1548. As Judge Kelly explicitly held in *Jantz v. Muci,* 759 F.2d at 1458 and 1458 n. 5, "immutability simply is not a prerequisite for suspect classification." For a discussion of the so-called immutability doctrine in equal protection law, and its application to cases involving discrimination on the basis of sexual-orientation identity, see Halley, "The Politics of the Closet," 36 *UCLA L. Rev.* at 915–932.

34. Fuss, *Essentially Speaking,* 3.

35. *Jantz v. Muci,* 759 F. Supp. at 1548 (emphasis added).

36. Judge Kelly held that immutability is not a prerequisite for heightened equal protection scrutiny; that antigay discrimination is invidious in the sense that it enforces counterfactual stereotypes of gay men and lesbians; that gay men and lesbians have borne a history of intense, pervasive, purposeful, and often violent discrimination; and that scattered legislative victories do not prove that gay men and lesbians can protect themselves in the political process without judicial intervention. *Jantz v. Muci,* 759 F. Supp. at 1548–50. He also held that the governmental defendant could not establish the rationality of its act of discrimination merely by asserting it. *Id.* at 1551–52. Anyone familiar with equal protection cases in this area will appreciate the rarity of these holdings.

37. *Jantz v. Muci,* 759 F Supp. at 1548 (*quoting Watkins v. United States Army,* 875 F.2d 699, 726 (9th Cir. 1989) (en banc) (Norris, J., concurring)).

38. Nan D. Hunter, "Life after *Hardwick,*" 27 *Harv. Civ. R. Civ. L. R. Rev.* 531 (1992).

39. Susan Bordo, "Postmodern Subjects, Postmodern Bodies," *Feminist Studies* 18 (1992): 159, 169.

40. Sedgwick, *Epistemology of the Closet,* 10.

41. See Judge Henderson's decision in *High Tech Gays v. Defense Indus. Security Clearance Office,* 668 F. Supp. 1361, 1368–72 (N.D. Cal. 1987) ("The Constitution protects an individual's right to express attraction, affection or love for another human being through sexual activity that does not constitute the specific acts that the Supreme Court in *Hardwick* held are not entitled to Constitutional protection"), *rev'd,* 895 F.2d 563 (9th Cir. 1990), *petition for reb'g en banc denied,* 909 F.2d 375 (9th Cir. 1990) (dissent of Judges Canby and Norris). And as Judge Canby observed in his dissent from denial of en banc review in *High Tech Gays,* "It is an error of massive proportions to define the entire class of homosexuals by sodomy." *Hi Tech Gays,* 909 F.2d at 380.

Part II

Get Used to It:
The New Queer Politics

Identity and Politics in a "Postmodern" Gay Culture: Some Historical and Conceptual Notes

Steven Seidman

Contemporary lesbian and gay male cultures evidence a heightened sensitivity to issues of difference and the social formation of desire, sexuality, and identity. As individuals we know what it means to be treated as different, to be rendered as a deviant other by folk and expert cultures, and to approach our bodies, desires, and identities with a deliberateness often lacking in mainstream straight society. Nevertheless, our existential awareness of the cultural politics of otherness has not necessarily been reflected in our dominant theories. For example, the new sociology and history of same-sex intimacies has been narrowly focused on the social origin and development of lesbian and gay male identities and communities among almost exclusively white, middle-class Europeans or Americans.

The theoretical and political limits of the post-Stonewall culture have become apparent. Social constructionist scholars seem to be rehearsing a monotone history of gay identity to a point of pointlessness. The arcane polemics between constructionists and essentialists has evolved into a sterile metaphysical debate devoid of moral and political import. Much of current lesbian and gay studies remains wedded to a standard Enlightenment scientistic self-understanding that, in my view, is inconsistent with its social constructionist premises. Gay identity politics moves back and forth between a narrow single-interest-group politic and a view of coalition politics as the sum of separate identity communities, each locked into its own sexual, gender, class, or racial politic.

I hold to the view that the currents of thought that now routinely

go under the rubric "postmodern" offer a cultural resource to imagine rethinking identity and politics. I approach postmodernism as
a broad cultural and intellectual standpoint that views science, and
all claims to knowledge, as moral and social forces and that is suspicious of systematizing, theory-building projects. Furthermore, in
place of the global, millennial politics of Marxism, radical feminism,
or gay liberationism, I view postmodernism as speaking of multiple,
local, intersecting struggles whose aim is less "the end of domination" or "human liberation" than the creation of social spaces that
encourage the proliferation of pleasures, desires, voices, interests,
modes of individuation and democratization.

I hesitate, however, to assume that postmodern thinking marks an
epochal shift to "postmodernity" or to a new sociohistorical era. I situate postmodern turns of social thought in relation to the evolution
of the left-wing of the new social movements. This is a claim I intend to initially press. Specifically, I make the case that postmodern
strains in gay thinking and politics have their immediate social origin in recent developments in the gay culture. In the reaction by
people of color, third–world-identified gays, poor and working class
gays, and sex rebels to the ethnic/essentialist model of identity and
community that achieved dominance in the lesbian and gay cultures
of the 1970s, I locate the social basis for a rethinking of identity and
politics.

Postmodernism and the New Social Movements

Postmodernism has come to signify, among other things, a phase of
historical development, a stage of late capitalism, a new aesthetic,
a sensibility, an epistemological break, the end of grand narratives,
and a new political juncture.[1] These disparate descriptions of the
postmodern reflect divergent social standpoints and agendas. Postmodernism is, to put it simply, a rhetorical figure whose meaning
is linked to the use to which it is put in a particular social context.

I approach postmodernism as a broad theoretical or intellectual
standpoint. I situate it in relation to the history of the new social
movements (NSM) in the 1970s and 1980s.[2] I argue that postmodern
cultural politics are promoted by the struggles between the NSM and
mainstream American society. Furthermore, the conflicts between

the NSM and the social mainstream are mirrored, in some important respects, within the NSM. It is this dual conflict that is pivotal to the formation of postmodern ways of thinking and politics.

The immediate context of the appearance of postmodernism in the United States is the break of the left from Marxism. I interpret postmodernism, at least one prominent current of it in the United States, as the standpoint of a post-Marxian left whose politics are tied to the NSM.

The shift in left politics in the 1970s and 1980s from the politics of class and labor to the post-Marxian social criticism of the NSM forms a pivotal social setting for the rise of a left postmodern social discourse. In the United States, the social base of Marxism has been significantly narrower than in Europe. Yet, Marxism was, for many postwar leftists, the dominant language of social criticism and political strategizing. Virtually all of the NSM, at least in their liberationist strains, initially (in the late 1960s and early 1970s) deployed Marxism as a model for a critical theory and politic. However, in each case, in the black, feminist, and gay liberationist movements, in the new-left and countercultural movements, conceptual and political strategies gravitated away from Marxism or abandoned it entirely. Marxism may have initially facilitated social criticism and political mobilization in the NSM, but its epistemic and political privileging of working-class politics rendered racial, gender, sexual, and other nonclass struggles secondary and marginal. In the end, these movements turned against Marxism to establish the legitimacy of their own sphere of struggle and their own social and discursive practices.

In the course of the 1970s the liberationist movements abandoned Marxism as both a model of social criticism and an organizing political strategy. Thus, while early radical feminists such as Millet and Firestone articulated their critique of sexism in the language of Marxism, their radical feminist heirs (e.g., Adrienne Rich, Andrea Dworkin, Mary Daly) elaborated a decidedly non-Marxian, cultural critique of sexism. By the mid-1970s, the left was socially, ideologically, and politically decentered. It was composed of a plurality of movements, each focused on its own particular project of building an autonomous community, evolving its own language of social analysis, and forging an oppositional politic.

The social fracturing of left politics was accompanied by a theoretical decentering. This entailed not only the narrowing of Marxism to a local sociopolitical and discursive project but a broader strategy of historicizing and politicizing all social discourse, including the disciplinary discourses of the human sciences.

To establish their own sociopolitical space the NSM had to contest Marxism's status as *the* science of society. Left critics challenged the Marxist claim to have revealed the essential social conflicts and laws of history. In particular, leftists criticized the Marxian notion that class struggle anchored in economic inequalities is the primary social division and site for political organizing. For example, feminists disputed the validity of applying a Marxian economic and class analysis to premodern kinship-based societies.[3] Indeed, many feminists contested the Marxian analysis of modern societies on the grounds that its organizing concept of production excluded sexual and household reproduction and failed to address the gendered texture of private and public life.[4] Marxism had the effect, moreover, of marginalizing gender struggles. Socialist-feminist efforts to graft a gender analysis onto Marxism have proved unsuccessful. In the course of the 1980s many feminists have repudiated Marxism; they have evolved their own critical discourse and politics that center on gender dynamics. The feminist critique had the effect of narrowing Marxism to a local conceptual and political project, one centered on labor and the dynamics of class.

These new oppositional movements have not been unified by any post-Marxian social theory. Totalizing efforts by neo-Marxists such as Althusser or Habermas have not proved compelling. Social criticism has splintered into a myriad of local discourses mirroring the social fracturing of the American left.

The relativizing of Marxism was part of a more general confrontation with the Enlightenment heritage. The NSM contested the claim of science to universal knowledge and its rationale that it promotes social progress through enlightenment. In fact, a central struggle of the NSM has been against science as a discourse that carries cultural and institutional authority. Unlike the oppression of labor, which is linked directly to political economic and class dynamics, cultural political struggles are pivotal to the NSM. The ways in which women, gays, lesbians, people of color, and the differently abled are oppressed are closely tied to stigmatizing public discourses and representations. These groups are, to be sure, oppressed by economic discrimination and social policy enforced by the state. However, whereas social oppression for blue-collar workers is rooted in economic and class arrangements, the oppression of the NSM is anchored in cultural representations. In particular, the human sciences — psychiatry, psychology, criminology, sociology — have played a key role in shaping the way Americans think about the body, self-identity, and social norms. The struggle over cultural production and representation has been central to the NSM. They have not only challenged particular constructions of identity that carry the authority of science but have contested the claim of science to epistemic authority. Thus, feminists have disputed scientific constructions of women as biologically destined to be wives and mothers; they have raised suspicions about representations that, under the sign of science, project women as emotional, nurturing, and other-directed — a characterization that warrants caretaking and servicing roles.[5] Similarly, lesbians and gay men have had to struggle against scientific-medical constructions of same-sex desire as symptomatic of an unnatural, abnormal, socially pathological human type — the homosexual.[6] At the heart of both the feminist and gay movements has been a politic that targets science and its institutional carriers — schools, hospitals, psychiatric institutions, prisons, scientific associations — as important creators of oppressive identity models and social norms.

As the NSM have contested the authority of science, we can observe postmodern strains in their discourses. The claim of science to value-neutrality and objectivity has been disputed; the privileging of science as a carrier of Truth has been challenged; Enlightenment legitimations that authorize science on the grounds of promoting social progress through eliminating error and ignorance have been questioned. In at least certain strains of NSM thinking, science has been reconceived as a culture-bound social practice that bears the mark of its sociohistorical embeddedness and the social interests of its producers. Viewed as a normative and social force, science has the effect of drawing moral boundaries, producing social hierarchies, and creating identities. Science is imagined as a discursive strategy implicated in heterogeneous power struggles.

The confrontation between the NSM and the social mainstream is only one social dynamic that has been productive of postmodern discursive strains. There are internal dynamics within these movements that reproduce this external struggle and that have been equally productive of a postmodern point of view — specifically, the struggles by individuals and groups who have been marginalized within these movements. They have contested the particular social interests that have achieved sociopolitical dominance in these movements and that project their own interests as universal. The clash between the periphery and center *within these movements* is a key source of postmodern thinking and politics.

In the remainder of this essay, I wish to at least partially redeem the claim linking the rise of postmodern social discourses to the internal dynamics of the NSM by focusing on the evolution of gay intellectual culture. My hope is that this approach might provide a useful standpoint from which to grasp the social and political significance of the rethinking of the politics of identity and difference that goes under the name of postmodernism or poststructuralism.

A brief resume of my argument. My starting point is gay liberation theory. I argue that liberation theory moved on a conceptual terrain decidedly different from its predecessor and successor. Liberation theory presupposed a notion of an innate polymorphous, androgynous human nature. Liberation politics aimed at freeing individuals from the constraints of a sex/gender system that locked them into mutually exclusive homo/hetero and feminine/masculine roles. Liberation theory and politics exhibit a kinship with what is now called postmodernism. Instead of evolving in this direction, however, liberationism gave way in the late 1970s to an ethnic/minority sociopolitical agenda. Although this model proved effective in socially mobilizing lesbians and gay men, its emphasis on a unitary identity and community marginalized individuals who deviated from its implicitly white, middle-class social norms. Moreover, its narrow single-interest-group politic proved ineffective in response to the conservative backlash in the late 1970s.

In the 1980s, there was a reaction to this ethnic/essentialist model by marginalized social interests (e.g., gay people of color and sex rebels), by activists wishing to renew a more radical gay politics, and by a new cadre of scholar-intellectuals trumpeting the politics of difference. While the ethnic/essentialist culture that grounded gay identity politics for two decades was under assault, a poststructuralist version of postmodern gay theory stepped forward as the true radical heir to a fading liberationist ideal. To the extent that

poststructuralism, like its political counterpart, Queer Natic
into a postidentity politic, its exquisite intellectual and polit̲̲̲ ̲̲̲
turing draws its power more from its critical force than any positive
program for change.

From the Politics of Liberationism to Ethnic Separatism

In the years preceding gay liberationism, mainstream homosexual
thought (represented in the publications of the Mattachine Society
and the Daughters of Bilitis) highlighted homosexuality as a condition of a segment of humanity.[7] Homosexuality was described as a
basic character trait. Indeed, many in the homophile movement, as
it was often called, believed that homosexuality was symptomatic
of a psychic abnormality. However, the underlying shared humanity of homosexuals and heterosexuals was thought to warrant the
elimination of discrimination.

Although many in the mainstream homophile movement described homosexuals as a minority, this difference was not celebrated. They did not promote the building of an autonomous
homosexual culture. Instead they interpreted the minority condition
of homosexuals as an unfortunate consequence of social discrimination. They sought to abolish the homosexual as a distinct social
identity. They intended social assimilation.

Gay liberation and the lesbian feminist movement challenged
mainstream homophile thinking. They contested the notion of
homosexuality as a condition of a segment of humanity; repudiated the idea of homosexuality as symptomatic of psychic or social
inferiority; and rejected a politics of assimilation.[8]

In the early years of gay liberation (1969–73), gay theory was not
unified. For the purpose of this essay, I distinguish gay liberation
and lesbian feminist theory. Gay liberation theory was not necessarily produced by and for men. Many lesbian-identified women
participated in its creation. In contrast, lesbian feminism was created by and for women. Lesbian feminism emerged, in part, as a
reaction against gay liberation, which was criticized as reflecting the
values and interests of men. It also developed in reaction to liberal
and radical feminist orthodoxy, whose priorities were said to be
those of heterosexual women.

Lesbian feminists repudiated the view of lesbianism as a type of sexual desire or orientation. They interpreted lesbianism as a personal, social, and political commitment to bond with women. A lesbian is, as the classic manifesto of lesbian feminism, "Woman-Identified Woman," declared, woman-identified.[9] The lesbian recognizes her unique kinship with female experiences and values. She makes a choice to center her life around women.

For lesbian feminists, lesbianism is not a condition or trait of some women; its not a sexual preference that marks women off from each other. Quite the contrary, lesbianism or being woman-identified is said to be a condition of all women. If some women fail to realize this, it is because in a male-dominated society they identify with male-imposed definitions that wed womanhood to heterosexual relations and roles.

Lesbianism is viewed as a political act. The decision to bond with women challenges male dominance that is said to be maintained through the institution of heterosexuality. To the extent that a woman's personal and social worth is defined by her relation to men (e.g., her role as wife and mother), she cedes control over her life to men. Lesbianism projects women as autonomous and equal to men. Lesbian feminism encourages women to become aware of their ties to other women; it intends to promote the growth of female values and modes of being by building an autonomous "womansculture."

In the early years of gay and women's liberation, lesbian feminism was pioneered by Sidney Abbott, Barbara Love, Rita Mae Brown, Ti-Grace Atkinson, Martha Shelley, and the women around the Radicalesbian and the Furies collectives. While lesbian feminism lost much of its organizational authority within the women's movement by the mid-1970s, it achieved an ideological prominence among feminists and lesbians as it was elaborated into what has come to be called cultural feminism. Many of the leading cultural feminists had their personal and ideological roots in lesbian feminism, for example, Adrienne Rich, Robin Morgan, Susan Griffin, Andrea Dworkin, Mary Daly, and Kathleen Barry.

Gay liberation theory materialized in the post-Stonewall period between roughly 1969 and 1973. Liberation theory appeared in newspapers such as *Come Out!, Rat,* and *Fag Rag.* There were few attempts to provide a totalizing historical theory from an affirmative gay standpoint.

Dennis Altman's *Homosexual Oppression and Liberation* is perhaps the only statement of liberation theory that compares to, say, Millet's *Sexual Politics* or Shulamith's *Dialectic of Sex*.[10] Although the author is Australian, he reports an extensive involvement in the American gay liberation movement. The book reflects, moreover, a decidedly American point of view, as it carries on a dialogue with the new left, American feminists, and gay writers.

Altman offers a grand narrative of the struggle of the homosexual subject for liberation against social oppression. Although he features the theme of homosexual oppression and the movement for liberation, the homosexual subject turns out to be a sociohistorical event. Humanity is not naturally divided into heterosexuals and homosexuals. The homosexual, as we know this figure in the postwar Western world, is not a universal human type but a historical product.

Although Altman rejects the essentialist premise of a transhistorical homosexual subject, he does not avoid an ontology of human sexuality. Drawing on the Freudo-Marxism of Marcuse's *Eros and Civilization,* he assumes "the essentially polymorphous and bisexual needs of the human being."[11] In this primeval condition, the self takes pleasure from all the parts of his/her body and from both genders. Altman maintains that societies impose upon humanity a repressive regime that channels our polymorphous eroticism into a narrow genital-centered, procreative-oriented heterosexual norm.

Gay liberation is a movement of human sexual liberation. It aims to institute a sexual regime in which sexuality is not defined by a mutually exclusive gender preference. A political strategy that centers on legitimating a homosexual identity perpetuates a divided sexual self and society. It does not contest a sexual regime that reduces eros as a genital-centered, penetrative sexual norm. Accordingly, sexual liberation should involve struggling against circumscribing eros to a romantic, marital, genital-and-penetrative sexual desire. Altman envisions a liberatory ideal that defends a diffuse body eroticism; the eroticization of everyday life; sexual exchanges that go beyond a romantic coupling; and approaching sex as a medium of procreation and love but also pleasure and play.

Gay liberation is more than a movement to liberate eros; it is a gender revolution. The struggle against the homo/hetero dichotomy is intertwined with the struggle against a sex-role system that views masculinity and femininity as mutually exclusive categories of gender identity. Altman views the binary sex and gender systems as mutually reinforcing. "There is a marked connection in our society between the repression of bisexuality [the creation of the homo/hetero roles] and the development of clearly demarcated sex roles."[12] The gender system is said to posit heterosexuality as a primary sign of gender normality. A true man loves women; a true woman loves men. "Sex roles are a first, and central, distinction made by society. Being male and female is, above all, defined in terms of the other: men learn that their masculinity depends on being able to make it with women, women that fulfillment can only be obtained through being bound to a man. In a society based on the assumption that heterosexuality represents all that is sexually normal, children are taught to view as natural and inevitable that they in turn will become 'mummies' and 'daddies.' "[13] To challenge the sex system and the tyranny of the homo/hetero classification system and to assert our innate bisexuality, challenges the bipolar gender system.

Although liberation theorists did not share all of Altman's ideas, there was a common core of liberation theory. For example, Allen Young's "Out of the Closet, into the Streets" described gay liberation "as a struggle against sexism."[14] Sexism means "a belief or practice that the sex or sexual orientation of human beings gives to some the right to certain privileges, powers, or roles, while denying to others their full potential. Within the context of our society, sexism is primarily manifested through male supremacy and heterosexual chauvinism."[15] In American society, sexism is responsible for the creation of a homosexual and heterosexual identity and a masculine and feminine identity that privilege heterosexual men.

Sexism denies the innate universality of homosexual and heterosexual, masculine and feminine desires and feelings. These roles — heterosexual and homosexual, man and woman — cut us off from parts of ourselves, set us against each other, and lead to the oppression of homosexuals by heterosexuals and women by men. Gay liberation is a struggle against heterosexism and sexism, as we would say today. Its aim is to liberate our homosexual and heterosexual, masculine and feminine desires in order to become whole.

Gay prefigures for Young a new human type — beyond narrow

roles and identities — where our inherent bisexual, androgynous nature is expressed in free, equal relationships and social bonds. "Gay is good for all of us. The artificial categories 'heterosexual' and 'homosexual' have been laid on us by a sexist society. Children are born sexual. To protect the power of straight men in a sexist society, homosexuality becomes prohibited behavior."[16] Young imagines lesbians and gay men as a vanguard pioneering sexual and human liberation. "Homosexuals committed to struggling against sexism have a better chance than straights of building relationships based on equality because there is less enforcement of roles. We have already broken with gender programming."[17]

Between 1969 and 1973 a new body of gay theory accompanied the rise of the gay liberation movement. It departed from previous homosexual theory that mirrored dominant medical-scientific ideas by conceiving of homosexuality as symptomatic of an abnormal psychic condition characteristic of a segment of humanity. It rejected the notion that liberation means the social assimilation of homosexuals. Instead, liberation theory posited humans as innately bisexual, polymorphous beings. Homosexuality and heterosexuality were not seen as mutually exclusive desires, psychic conditions, or human types; they were seen as universal aspects of humankind. Societies create regimes that make homo/hetero gender preference mutually exclusive master categories of sexual identity. Societies create a stigmatized, polluted homodesire; they create an oppressed homosexual minority. Moreover, this sexual regime is said to be implicated in a gender system that divides humans into masculine and feminine roles. The aim of gay liberation was to abolish a sex/gender system that privileges heterosexuality and men.

There are some key similarities between gay liberation theory and postmodern discourses. Liberation theorists view the validity of their own discourse as tied to their particular social-historical identity and interests. They do not write as universal intellectuals, to use Foucault's term for the standpoint of many modernist intellectuals.[18] The liberationist theorist Allen Young declares: "Because I am a white male homosexual, a New Yorker, a leftist, most of what I say is from that perspective. There are other homosexuals — Third World People, lesbians, transvestites — about whom I can say little. They speak for themselves."[19] Gay liberation theorists viewed themselves as local intellectuals, speaking to experiences of sexual and gender oppression that are mediated by conditions of class, race, nationality, and so on. Their own discourse is understood as moral and political. They intend to reconfigure the everyday language of sex and gender, to challenge conventional perspectives that maintain an oppressive sex/gender system, and to offer alternative visions of personal and social life. Although they retain a residue of essentialism in their notion of an original bisexual, polymorphous, and androgynous human nature, their accounts of sexual and gender dynamics are decidedly constructionist.

Their vision of liberation, moreover, parallels somewhat a postmodern concept that frames freedom as the proliferation of bodies, desires, pleasures, and forms of intimate life. However, liberationists retain a millennial notion of a liberated humanity free from constraining normative structures, a vision absent in most postmodern texts. Most postmodernists would not share, moreover, the strong vanguardism in these liberationist discourses. In a word, gay liberation theory may be described as a post-Marxian left discourse that leans in a postmodern direction yet retains much of the modernist legacy, in particular its millennialism and vanguardism.

Between the early 1970s and the mid-1980s, there transpired a shift in lesbian and gay male culture.[20] Gay men and lesbians went their separate ways. The tensions in the early gay liberation days evolved into a full-blown separatism, even though some lesbians still identified with an inclusive gay movement. A gay subculture was created largely by and for men. Moreover, many lesbians either identified with the women's movement or with the lesbian separatist project of forging a womansculture.

Interestingly, the developments in the lesbian and gay male subcultures of this time reveal important similarities. In particular, there was an emphasis on community building around the notion of a unitary lesbian and gay identity. Gay men created an institutionally complete subculture. Although the lesbian feminist subculture was less institutionally elaborated, its dense, informal, network-based character and its blending with feminist institutions gave to it a socially developed texture. Similarly, in both the gay male and lesbian subcultures, a focus on personal identity and lifestyle was central. In the gay male subculture, newspapers such as the *Advocate,* with its promotion of consumerism and expressive-hedonistic values, symbolized the personalistic emphasis of this community. Although the lesbian feminist culture was much more ideological, it too exhibited a preoccupation with lifestyle concerns, for example, female values and spirituality. Finally, in both the lesbian and gay male subcultures we can detect a movement away from a liberationist framework toward an ethnic/ethnic minority model, with an emphasis on cultural difference, community building, and identity-based interest-group politics.

From the Solidarity of Identity to the Politics of Difference

As a movement committed to liberating humanity from the mutually exclusive and limiting roles of the heterosexual/homosexual and the feminine/masculine, gay liberation came to an end by the mid-1970s. From a broadly conceived sexual and gender liberation movement, the dominant agenda of the male-dominated gay culture became community building and winning civil rights. The rise of an ethnic model of identity and politics in the gay male community found a parallel in the lesbian feminist culture, with its emphasis on unique female values and building a womansculture. However, whereas gay men represented themselves as an ethnic group oriented toward assimilation, lesbian feminists presented themselves as the vanguard of a gender-separatist politic.

As an ethnic identity model acquired cultural dominance in the lesbian feminist and gay male communities, previously muffled voices of dissent began to be heard in the cultural mainstream of these communities. Specifically, individuals whose experiences and interests were not represented in the dominant gay identity constructions criticized the ethnic model as exhibiting a white, middle-class bias. Simultaneously, the ethnic identity model was under attack by constructionist scholars who underscored the immense sociohistorical diversity of meanings and social arrangements of same-sex desire. Finally, the emerging prominence of poststructuralism provided a language to deconstruct the category of a gay subject and to articulate the dissenting voices in a postmodern direction.

The challenge to the dominance of an ethnic model, with its notion of a unitary gay identity and its emphasis on cultural difference, surfaced from individuals whose lives were not reflected in the dominant representations, social conventions, and political strategies. There transpired a revolt of the social periphery against the center, only this time the center was not mainstream America but a dominant gay culture. From minor skirmishes in the mid-to-late 1970s to major wars through the 1980s, the concept of a unitary lesbian or gay male subject was in dispute. Three major sites of struggle against the gay cultural center have been the battle over race, bisexuality, and nonconventional sexualities.

Conflicts around gender were divisive in the early years of the gay movement. The Gay Liberation Front, for example, was initially composed of both men and women. Yet conflicts between gay men and lesbians, heightened by the feminist critique of male domination, led some lesbians to withdraw from liberation organizations. Many of them, along with feminists who were disenchanted with liberal feminism, were central in pioneering radical feminism. Ultimately, the tensions between straight and gay radical feminists contributed to a separatist lesbian feminist movement. Gender conflicts have continued to be a divisive issue for the gay movement. In the 1970s and early 1980s, however, this tension was "resolved" by a split into two separate movements — one predominantly gay male and the other exclusively lesbian and heavily lesbian feminist.

Gender conflicts have not challenged the ethnic model since this tension was dealt with by constructing separate gay male and lesbian identities and communities. The race issue, however, has posed a major challenge to the construction of a gay subject and to the ethnic assimilationist and separatist tendencies of the gay male and lesbian feminist communities respectively.

Much of the discussion on race through the early 1980s was pioneered by women of color and had the women's movement as its primary reference. Yet, lesbian women of color played a pivotal role in this discussion and implicated the lesbian community in the race issue. For example, in an anthology by radical women of color, *This Bridge Called My Back,* the primary focus of its contributors is the racism of the women's movement. However, in a section entitled "Between the Lines: On Culture, Class, and Homophobia," the racism and classism of lesbian feminism are discussed.[21]

In a dialogue on lesbian separatism, Barbara Smith underscores the class- and race-based character of lesbian feminism: "Separatism seems like such a narrow kind of politics.... [It] seems to be only viably practiced by women who have certain kinds of privilege: white-skinned privilege, class privilege."[22] Smith goes on to say that many lesbian women of color will not find separatism a viable strategy not only for economic reasons but because of the racism of many lesbian feminists. Moreover, to the extent that lesbians of color must struggle simultaneously against the racism of white women, separatism impedes the building of alliances with men of color. Race is said to place lesbian women of color in a different relation to men than white lesbians. "You see white women with class privilege don't share oppression with white men. They're in a critical and antagonistic position whereas Black women and other women of color definitely share oppressed situations with men of their race."[23] Smith maintains that being an African-American lesbian is not a minor variation on an essentially common lesbian experience; it is not a matter of adding race to gender oppression. Rather, race alters the meaning and social standpoint of being a lesbian.

In the early 1980s, lesbians and gay men of color made the racism of the women's movement and their own ethnic communities the focus of their criticism. By the late 1980s, it was the gay culture that was subject to critical scrutiny. For example, in 1986, the first black gay male anthology, *In the Life,* appeared.[24] In his introduction, the late Joseph Beam protests the invisibility of the black gay male experience in gay culture:

> It is possible to read thoroughly two or three consecutive issues of the *Advocate* . . . and never encounter, in words or images, Black gay men. It is possible to peruse the pages of *212 Magazine's* special issue on Washington D.C. and see no Black faces. It is possible to leaf through any of the major gay men's porno magazines . . . and never lay eyes on a Black Adonis. Finally, it is certainly possible to read an entire year of *Christopher Street* and think that there are no Black gay writers worthy of the incestuous bed of New York gay literati. . . . We ain't family. Very clearly, gay male means: white, middle-class, youthful, Nautilized, and probably butch, there is no room for Black gay men within the confines of this gay pentagon.[25]

Beam identified a major problem, black invisibility in gay public life, and the reason, racism. Invisibility in gay life was mirrored in the African-American community. *In the Life* was intended to "end the silence that surrounded our lives."[26] By naming their experience, black gay men hoped to create a public presence, a community within the communities of gay and black.

The success of *In the Life* spawned a second black gay male anthology, *Brother to Brother.*[27] In his introduction, Essex Hemphill echoes Beam's view that the gay community reproduces the invisibility and devaluation of black gays in the African-American community and in mainstream America. "The post-Stonewall white gay community of the 1980s was not seriously concerned with the existence of black gay men except as sexual objects. . . . It has not fully dawned on white gay men that racist conditioning has rendered many of them no different from their heterosexual brothers in the eyes of black gays and lesbians."[28] Hemphill believes that the dominant gay male culture does not represent the experience of black men. "Gay" signifies the experience of a white, middle-class, urban culture organized around sex, consumerism, and civil rights.

Lesbian and gay men of color have contested the notion of a unitary gay subject and the idea that the meaning and experience of being gay are socially uniform. Indeed, they argue that a discourse that abstracts a notion of gay identity from considerations of race and class is oppressive because it invariably implies a white, middle-class standpoint. The Latino activist, Charles Fernandez, put it this way: "Reflected in the general public's image of the typical homosexual, in the lesbian and gay media's depiction of its target audience, in the movement's agenda and strategies, in the academy's methodology and theorizing, and in the lesbian and gay community's own self-understanding, is this movement's subject and protagonist: a white and middle-class person."[29] Moreover, many gay people of color contend that the remedy to the ethnocentric character of dominant — white and middle-class — gay constructions of identity, community, and politics involves more than acknowledging racial or class variations. Race is said to be as deeply embedded in the formation of a person's identity or as elementary in the shaping of social interest as sexuality.[30]

Gay people of color challenged the dominant gay identity discourse. This discourse assumes that individuals who share the same homosexual preference in a homophobic society share a common experience, outlook, and set of values and interests. Gay people of color objected: individuals do not have a core gay identity around which race or class add mere social nuance. Rather, individuals are simultaneously gay, male, African-American, Latino, or working-class, each identification being shaped and shaping the others.

The notion of a unitary gay identity has been fundamental to the evolving gay communities of the 1980s. Even more basic to the framing of gay life as an ethnic group has been the assumption that gender preference defines sexual orientation. The very possibility of framing homosexuality as a site of identity and ethnicity presupposes sexual object-choice as a master category of sexual and self-identity. Mainstream gay culture took over the privileging of a hetero/homo sexual-identity regime from mainstream America. Even lesbian feminists who redefined lesbianism as a personal, social, and political act of woman-identification did not contest the identification of sexual orientation with a hetero/homo gender preference. In discussions over bisexuality and nonconventional sexualities, the privileging of a hetero/homo sexual definition and the coding of sexuality by gender preference are questioned — a questioning that goes to the very heart of the ethnic model of being gay.

In their introduction to the anthology *Bi Any Other Name: Bisexual People Speak Out,* Loraine Hutchins and Lani Kaahumanu criticize the gay culture for perpetuating a sexual code that privileges sexual object-choice as definitive of sexual identity and that assumes identities neatly fold into a heterosexual or homosexual one.[31] This code erases or stigmatizes the experiences of those individuals for whom sexual orientation is not a mutually exclusive choice and for whom sexual object-choice does not adequately describe their sexual and intimate lives. "We're told that we can't exist, that we're really heterosexual or really gay, that nothing exists except these two extremes."[32]

Some individuals who identify as bisexual aim to legitimate this identity alongside a heterosexual or homosexual one. They do not contest the hegemony of a regime that deploys sexual object-choice as the master category of sexual identity. For others, however, bisexuality challenges the privileging of sexual object-choice. They aim to render gender preference as just one aspect of sexual orientation.

Gender is just not what I care about or even really notice in a sexual partner. This is not to say that I don't have categories of sexual attraction.... I have categories, but gender isn't one of them. I'm erotically attracted to intelligent people, to people with dark/colored skin and light eyes and hair, to people with a kind of sleazy, sexy come-on, to eccentrics. In some of those categories I am homo-erotic...; in others I am hetero-erotic.... To be perfectly frank, I can barely imagine what it's like to be a lesbian or a straight woman, to be attracted to women because they are female.... I feel like...I am color blind or tone deaf to a gender-erotic world.[33]

In "My Interesting Condition," Jan Clausen contests the privileg-ing of sexual object-choice as the basis of sexual identity.[34] She recounts the process of building an identity and a social life around same-sex desire. She underscores the virtues of a lesbian life — the dignity it confers, the friendships, the sense of purpose, the political empowerment. She describes her turmoil when, after having as-sumed a lesbian identity, she discovered a heterosexual passion.[35] From the vantage point of a lesbian culture that builds a socio-political identity on the grounds of an unequivocal same-sex desire, Clausen became "radically Other through the deceptively simple act of taking a male lover."[36] She refuses, however, to embrace a bisex-ual identity. In part, this reflects her general disenchantment with identity politics: "Throughout much of my adult life, the insights of identity politics have shaped my world view, informed my ac-tivism, my writing, and in many respects the conduct of my most intimate relationships.... On the other hand, I've often felt uneasy about the intensity of the lesbian feminist focus on identity. It some-times leads into an obsessive narrowing of perspective."[37] Clausen refuses to embrace a bisexual identity: "I have a second problem with 'identifying' as bisexual.... I do not know what 'bisexual' de-sire would be, since my desire is always for a specifically sexed and gendered individual. When I am with a woman, I love as a woman loves a woman, and when I am with a man, I love as a woman loves a man. So bisexuality is not a sexual identity at all, but a sort of anti-identity, a refusal...to be limited to one object of desire, one way of loving."[38] Clausen urges an anti-identity politics or a politics that resists identity on behalf of an affirmation of "being all the parts of who I am."[39]

Leaving aside, for the moment, the coherence of an anti-identity politic, Clausen gives expression to reservations many lesbian- and gay-identified individuals share about the ethnic framing of same-sex desire.[40] The ethnicization of gay desire has presupposed the privileging of gender preference to define sexual and social identity, which, in turn, has been the basis upon which a gay community and politics are forged. Although this ethnic model can claim some major social accomplishments, it reinforces broadly mainstream social norms that devalue desires, behaviors, and social bonds that involve attraction to both sexes. In challenging sexual object-choice as a master category of sexual and social identity, the bisexual critique suggests the possibility of legitimating desires other than gender preference as grounds for constructing alternative identities, communities, and politics. This brings us to the third site of debate: advocacy for nonconventional sexualities.

In the late 1970s and 1980s, the so-called sex debates served as a major locus for contesting the ethnic model. In these debates, the privileging of sexual object-choice for defining sexual identity and the notion of a unitary gay identity came under assault. The battles varied somewhat between the lesbian and gay male communities.[41]

In the lesbian context, protest was aimed at the ideological prominence of lesbian feminism and its cultural-feminist variant. Cultural feminists posited a unique and unitary female sexual nature (across the hetero/homo divide) as the ground of a sexual ethic. Sex was defined as an expression of intimacy, as a mode of sharing and showing love; sexual behavior should exhibit its essentially nurturing, tender, person-centered, and diffusely erotic nature. Legitimate sex should be embedded in long-term, intimate, committed relationships. Sex that is body-centered, motivated by carnal pleasure, casual, involved with role-playing, or promiscuous was defined as male-identified.

The cultural-feminist sexual ethic was viewed by many lesbians as narrowly reflecting the experience of a small segment of the lesbian community, namely some white, socially privileged, Eurocentric, mostly lesbian feminists. It was experienced as oppressive to lesbians whose sexual values differed. It rendered their desires, behaviors, and relationships marginal and deviant.

In the early 1980s, discontent with lesbian feminism and its cultural-feminist elaboration surfaced in a series of public skirmishes. The chief battle sites were around pornography and sadomasochism (S/M), but the central issue was the meaning of eros for women and for feminism. Cultural feminists seized the initiative.

Their antiporn anthology *Take Back the Night* alerted women to the dangers of eros — of a carnal, aggressive, male-identified desire.[42] Critics responded with *Women against Censorship* and the "Sex Issue" of *Heresies,* in which eros, as an aggressive, carnal, and lascivious desire, was owned as feminine and feminist.[43] In conferences, journals, magazines, newspapers, and novels, feminists and many lesbians owned desires that had been culturally claimed as masculine and, by lesbian feminists, as dehumanizing. A proliferation of dissenting sexualities found a voice, a feminine, indeed feminist, voice that shattered the notion of a unitary female sexual subject. For example, lesbians, who also spoke as feminists, stepped forward as advocates of S/M. How does lesbian identity politics accommodate women whose primary attraction is to women but whose chief sexual orientation is S/M and whose primary sexual alignments are with gay and straight men? Whereas S/M advocates, such as the San Francisco group Samois, defended discipline and bondage games for their erotic and spiritual qualities, voices surfaced that rationalized gender role-playing in the butch-femme mode as another, frequently misunderstood, erotic genre.[44] With publications such as *Pleasure and Danger, The Powers of Desire, Heresies, On Our Backs,* and in the writings of Pat Califia, Gayle Rubin, Dorothy Allison, Amber Hollibaugh, Susie Bright, and many others, the notion of a unitary female or lesbian sexual subject was replaced by a female and lesbian perspective that is prolific and heterogeneous in its sexual desires, behaviors, styles, and values.[45]

There was nothing comparable to the substantive ethics of lesbian feminism in the gay male subculture of the 1970s. Its sexual code leaned toward a strident libertarianism. There did materialize, though, a dominant intimate norm — couple-centered but nonmonogamous.[46] This sexual regime tolerated a great deal of diversity — for example, marriage-like arrangements but also casual sex, public sex, sex with multiple partners, sex between friends, and paid sex.

There were, however, limits to sexual choice, even if these were not as clearly spelled out as in lesbian feminism. By the early 1980s these limits were made clearer as marginalized sexualities began to speak the very language of identity and legitimacy that mainstream gay men voiced one decade prior. While a myriad of submerged sexual interests clamored for public recognition, affirmative identities and communities materialized around S/M and man/boy love, only to meet with a great deal of opposition.[47]

I will confine my remarks to S/M. By the early 1980s, there appeared gay male S/M bars, clubs, newsletters, magazines, and advocacy organizations.[48] They demanded that the dominant gay culture recognize their legitimacy, for example, by including them in public events and by accurate media representations. Whereas S/M advocates shared with the broader gay community a status as sexual minorities struggling for rights and legitimation, they were, in fact, a threat to the gay mainstream. S/M challenged the privileging of gender preference in defining sexual identity. Gay men who practice S/M may have exclusive sex with men, but they often define their sexual identity primarily in relation to their S/M practices. Although the gay male subculture may be more tolerant of S/M sex than the social mainstream, S/M practices have come under assault. Critics recycle arguments used against homosexuality to discredit S/M, for example, S/M as a sign of an unnatural, abnormal, immoral desire, or a symptom of social decline, cultural narcissism, or homophobia.[49]

As lesbians and gay men succeeded in building elaborated subcultures, as we have obtained a measure of public legitimacy, we have met with resistance not only from outside forces but from within. Perhaps our very success has allowed for the surfacing of internal discord. In any event, as a dominant sociocultural order materialized in the lesbian and gay male communities, individuals who felt excluded or marginalized formed their own subcultural identities, networks, and political agendas. They challenged a hegemonic culture. The dominant ethnic model of identity and community was accused of reflecting a narrow white, middle-class, Eurocentric experience. The very discourse of liberation, with its notion of a gay subject unified by common interests, was viewed as a disciplining social force oppressive to large segments of the community in whose name it spoke.

Paralleling the assertion of social difference by gays of color and sex rebels, a constructionist scholarship placed in doubt the rather commonplace assumption that "gay" connotes a unitary, transhistorical meaning. This scholarship aimed to relativize the concept of gay identity. In the late 1970s and early 1980s, writers such as Jonathan Katz, Jeffrey Weeks, Carroll Smith-Rosenberg,

John D'Emilio, and Lillian Faderman argued that the late twentieth-century Western experience of same-sex intimacies, and the terms used to describe it, are historically unique.[50] A central claim was that in the late nineteenth and early twentieth centuries, sex, including same-sex experience, became the basis of a sexual and social identity. The deployment of sex as a core identity facilitated the historically unique formation of a distinctively "gay" community and politics. Thus, modern terms such as "homosexual," "lesbian," and "gay male" presuppose a historically specific sexual and social system — one in which sexual object-choice is the basis of a core self-definition.

According to this new scholarship, the categories of homosexual, gay, and lesbian do not signify a common, universal experience. The gay subject invoked in subcultural discourses and representations is seen as a historical product. Thus, Carroll Smith-Rosenberg in her classic essay, "The Female World of Love and Ritual: Relations between Women in Nineteenth-Century America," maintained that there was no category of homosexuality in the nineteenth century and that sexual orientation at that time did not signal a sexual or social identity.[51] Moreover, she claimed that same-sex intimacies, including open, romantic involvements, were widely accepted, at least among middle-class women. It was not uncommon for intimate bonds between women to be maintained simultaneously with heterosexual marriage, without carrying any stigma or shame.[52] Similarly, in his impressive documentary histories and commentaries, Jonathan Katz insisted that same-sex experiences of intimacy in nineteenth-century America were not the same phenomena as what we mean by a homosexual or gay experience.[53] Katz documents the absence of a category of homosexuality — or heterosexuality — in American popular culture until the early twentieth century. A multiplicity of meanings were attached to same-sex desire, some signifying less a sexual than a gender phenomenon.[54] Although a great deal of debate has transpired around the precise dating of the origin of a homosexual identity, the general claim that the modern concept of the homosexual is implicated in a historically specific sociocultural configuration seems compelling.[55]

Social constructionism was proposed as a conceptual or epistemological strategy.[56] Nevertheless, it carried definite social and political resonances. It alerts us to the repressive consequences of imposing current Western perspectives on non-Western experiences. In an effort to advance contemporary intellectual and political agendas, many gay scholars generalized current Western categories. Constructionists criticize this strategy as ethnocentric, as having the consequence of erasing variant social and historical experiences.

Yet, social constructionism exhibits an ambivalent relation to the ethnic identity model. On the one hand, as we have seen, constructionism featured the social and historical formation of sexual meanings, and thereby challenged the supposed universality of current models of gay identity. On the other hand, constructionism reinforced the ethnic model by framing its project as investigating the historical rise and social formation of gay identity-based communities and politics. Indeed, social constructionism, at least the historical scholarship of the late 1970s through the 1980s, often served as a kind of celebration of the coming of age of a gay ethnic minority.

At the core of both the sociopolitical and scholarly assertion of difference is, at least implicitly, an assault upon a modernist culture — straight and gay — whose controlling logic of identity exhibits an intolerance toward particularity or difference. In its compulsion to classify, order, and generalize, to find grounds or foundations for its categories, forms of life, and conceptual strategies, gay culture — like the broader social mainstream — strains toward erasing difference, even as it prides itself on its celebration of the individual.[57] In its affirmation of the particular against the general, of difference against the power of identity, the social and intellectual developments I have identified exhibit a postmodern edge.

The Politics of Subverting Identity

Social constructionism recalls the standpoint of gay liberation. For example, by asserting the deeply social and historical character of sexuality, it encourages, at least implicitly, a culture of social activism. Sexual conventions can be changed through acts of social will. In addition, constructionism provides a language highlighting social differences that marginalized lesbians and gay men can appeal to in order to legitimate their demands for recognition.

Viewed from the standpoint of gay liberationism, however, social constructionism appears suspect. Unlike liberation theory that was closely aligned to the politics of the movement, constructionism is increasingly disconnected from the political impulses of the movement. Indeed, gay constructionism has been captured by primarily academic interests. The debate over constructionism has become a metaphysical one centered on unresolvable conflicts such as nature versus nurture or realism versus nominalism. Moreover, if the debates are not mired in a metaphysical quagmire, they are preoccupied with an equally sterile historical scholasticism that revolves around tracing the appearance of homosexual subcultures or dating the rise of a homosexual identity.

Furthermore, whereas liberation theory assumed an explicitly moral and political understanding of its own discourse, social constructionists are often wedded to scientistic presuppositions, claiming for their own approach an objectivity, value neutrality, and evidentiary-based truth. Indeed, many view a constructionist approach as superior precisely because it obtains true representations of reality in contrast to the ethnocentric distortions of essentialist conceptual strategies. While constructionists have uncovered ethnocentric bias in gay scholarship that universalizes present-centered, culture-bound perspectives, they have not applied the same suspicion to their own discourse. If categories of same-sex intimacies are marked by the sociocultural context of their origin, is not the same true of our categories of analysis? And, if representations are embedded in broad national environments, are they not likewise stamped by the more particular social traits of their producers, for example, their class, race, ethnicity, nationality, age, or gender? Gay social constructionists have been enthusiastic in taking over Foucault's historicism but decidedly less so when it comes to his understanding of human studies as a practical-moral social force.[58]

Many activists and intellectuals discontented with mainstream lesbian and gay male culture are looking back fondly to the agenda of gay liberation. Indeed, many who embrace the rhetoric of social constructionism do so, in part, because they see in it a warrant for radical social activism.

I share this discontent with mainstream lesbian and gay male cultural politics. I wish to recover the expansive social and political potential of liberation theory. Nevertheless, we need to be clear about its limitations. As I noted earlier, liberationists viewed their movement as one of sexual and gender liberation. Unfortunately, they understood emancipation as a release from homosexual/heterosexual and masculine/feminine roles. They challenged the dominant sexual/social regime by juxtaposing to it a polymorphous, androgynous ideal of a liberated — constraint-free — humanity. Wouldn't a liberated humanity, however, require stable identities, social roles, and normative constraints? Liberationists conflated the critique of rigid roles and identities with the critique of all identities and roles as signifying domination. In a word, liberationists projected a radically individualistic, utopian concept of emancipation. They lacked, moreover, a credible strategy to transform a stable, socially anchored gay/straight identity regime into a postidentity liberated order.

Liberationist theory emerged as a gay identity and community were coalescing. It assumed the social dominance of a system of mutually exclusive roles around sexual orientation and gender; it formed as an opposition movement to this regime but reinforced it by narrowing its agenda to abolishing this system.

Today lesbians and gay men find themselves in a very different situation. Our standpoint is that of an elaborated culture founded upon an affirmative identity. Many of us have built coherent and meaningful lives around this identity. Moreover, although we still encounter substantial opposition in the social mainstream, we have gained considerable social inclusion. The liberationist strategy of juxtaposing a postidentity model to current identities would seem to lack credibility today.

The present condition of communities organized around affirmative gay/lesbian identities yet exhibiting heightened conflicts around those very identities should be the starting point of contemporary gay theory and politics. Where gay liberation confronted a dialectic of identity and difference that revolved around straight/gay and man/woman polarities, currently these oppositions are multiplied a hundredfold as we introduce differences along the dimensions of race, ethnicity, gender, age, sexual act, class, lifestyle, and locale. Thus, the dominant liberationist opposition between gay/straight and gay/lesbian passes into divisions between, say, white/black gay, black/Latino gay, middle-class/working-class gay, or lesbian/lesbian S/M, and on and on. Contemporary gay culture is centered on social difference and the multiplication of identities.

A key issue we confront today is as follows: How can we theorize and organize politically our multiple differences in light of the suspicions surrounding the dominant mode of identity politics? One strategy has called for the abandonment or destabilization of identity as a ground of gay politics. In poststructuralist theorizing, we are urged to shift our focus from the politics of personal identity to the politics of signification, in particular, to the deconstruction of a hetero/homo code that structures the "social text" of daily life.[59]

Reflecting on the recent history of the exclusions and conflicts elicited around identity constructions, poststructuralists have abandoned efforts to defend or reconfigure identity politics by theorizing its multiple and interlocking character. Appealing to one's sexual, gender, or ethnic identity as the ground of community and politics is rejected because of its inherent instabilities and exclusions. Diana Fuss describes the Derridean understanding of identity as follows: "Deconstruction dislocates the understanding of identity as self-presence and offers, instead, a view of identity as difference. To the extent that identity always contains the specter of non-identity within it, the subject is always divided and identity is always purchased at the price of the exclusion of the Other, the repression or repudiation of non-identity."[60] In other words, repudiating views of identity as essence or its effect, poststructuralists propose that the identity of an object or person is always implicated in its opposite. "Heterosexuality" has meaning only in relation to "homosexuality"; the coherence of the former is built on the exclusion, repression, and repudiation of the latter. These two terms form an interdependent, hierarchical relation of signification. The logic of identity is a logic of boundary defining which necessarily produces a subordinated other. The social productivity of identity is purchased at the price of a logic of hierarchy, normalization, and exclusion.[61]

Furthermore, gay identity constructions reinforce the dominant hetero/homo sexual code with its heteronormativity. If homosexuality and heterosexuality are a coupling in which each presupposes the other, each being present in the invocation of the other, and in which this coupling assumes hierarchical forms, then the epistemic and political project of identifying a gay subject reinforces and reproduces this hierarchical figure. Poststructuralists recommend that this discursive figure become the focus of a "deconstructive" analysis in place of the construction of the gay subject.

In effect, poststructuralists urge an epistemic shift from the humanistic standpoint of the individual subject creating himself or herself to the standpoint of a "structural" order, in this case a signifying or cultural discursivity.

Some poststructuralists intend to move the analysis of homosexuality into the center of Western culture. Whereas identity political standpoints framed homosexuality as an issue of sexuality and minority politics, poststructuralists position hetero/homosexual symbolism at the very center of Western culture — as structuring the very core modes of thought and culture of Western societies. This is perhaps the chief contention of Eve Kosofsky Sedgwick, whose latest book begins with the declaration:

> *Epistemology of the Closet* proposes that many of the major nodes of thought and knowledge in twentieth-century Western culture as a whole are structured — indeed, fractured — by a chronic, now endemic crisis of homo/heterosexual definition. . . . The book will argue that an understanding of virtually any aspect of modern Western culture must be, not merely incomplete, but damaged in its central substance to the degree that it does not incorporate a critical analysis of modern homo/heterosexual definition.[62]

Sedgwick conjectures that the homo/heterosexual figure is the master cultural term marking not only sexual definitions but categorical pairings such as secrecy/disclosure, knowledge/ignorance, private/public, masculine/feminine, majority/minority, innocence/initiation, natural/artificial, same/different, health/illness, growth/decadence, urbane/provincial.[63] Poststructuralists urge an epistemic shift from the resisting gay subject to the analysis of the homo/hetero code and its pervasive structuring of modes of thought, knowledge, and culture whose themes are both sexual and nonsexual.

The surfacing of a poststructural standpoint is in response to the perceived impasse of current gay politics and theory. In particular, the movement of gay politics between radical separatism and assimilationism seems closely tied to its centering on identity. Poststructuralism aims to destabilize identity as a ground of politics and theory in order to open up alternative social and political possibilities; poststructuralists seem to be positioned as a sort of theoretical wing of Queer Nation, with its insistent opposition to normalizing, disciplining social forces; with its disruptive politics of subversion; and with its opposition to both the straight and gay mainstream.[64] Just as Queer Nation wishes to create a sort of unified block in opposition to global processes of domination and exclusion, poststructuralists, by repositioning homosexuality as a central social fact, intend to render their oppositional practices as broadly social and globally oppositional.

To what end is poststructural critique directed? If the premiere collection *Inside/Out* is exemplary of the poststructural turn, the chief domain of struggle is the multiple sites of cultural production, in particular, high-brow literary and popular culture.[65] The principal aim is to document the presence of the hetero/homo figure, to disclose its compelling discursive efficacy and culturally contagious character, and to deconstruct it by revealing the mutual dependency of the polar terms and the instability and susceptibility of the figure to be reversed and subverted. Underlying this politics of subversion is a vague notion that this will encourage new, affirmative forms of personal and social life, although poststructuralists are reluctant to name their social vision. The poststructural move seems troubling, moreover, to the extent that social practices are framed narrowly as discursive and signifying, and critical practice becomes deconstructive textual strategies. Insofar as poststructuralists narrow cultural codes into binary signifying figures, insofar as discursive practices are not institutionally situated, there is an edging toward textual idealism.

An additional doubt about the poststructural turn: Who is the agent or subject of the politics of subversion? The poststructuralist critique of the logic of identity ends in a refusal to name a subject. Indeed, I detect a disposition in the deconstruction of identity to slide into viewing identity itself as the fulcrum of domination and its subversion as the center of an anti-identity politic. For example, although Judith Butler often elaborates complex understandings of identity as both enabling and self-limiting, she, at times, conflates identity as a disciplining force with domination and a politics of subversion with a politics against identity. "If it is already true that 'lesbians' and 'gay men' have been traditionally designated as impossible identities, errors of classification, unnatural disasters within juridico-medical discourses, . . . then perhaps these sites of disruption, error, confusion, and trouble can be the very rallying points for a certain resistance to classification and to identity as such."[66] Butler's politics of subversion at times becomes little more than a kind of disruptive repetitive performance that works "sexuality *against* identity." But to what end?

The poststructural turn edges beyond an anti-identity politics to a politics against identity per se. Implicit in this subversion of identity is a celebration of liminality, of the spaces between or outside structure, a kind of anarchistic championing of "pure" freedom from all constraints and limits. A strong parallel with Queer Nation is, once again, apparent. Like the poststructural refusal of identity, under the undifferentiated sign of Queer are united all those heterogeneous desires and interests that are marginalized and excluded in the straight and gay mainstream. Queers are not united by any unitary identity but only by their opposition to disciplining, normalizing social forces. Queer Nation aims to be the voice of all the disempowered and to stand for the proliferation of social differences. In its resistance to social codes (sexual gender, race, class) that impose unitary identities, in rebelling against forces imposing a repressive coherence and order, Queer Nation affirms an abstract unity of differences without wishing to name and fix these. This positioning resembles the poststructural refusal to name the subject, as if any anchoring of the flux and abundant richness of experience marks the beginnings of conflict, domination, and hierarchy.

This very refusal to anchor experience in identifications ends up, ironically, denying differences by either submerging them in an undifferentiated oppositional mass or by blocking the development of individual and social differences through the disciplining compulsory imperative to remain undifferentiated. Poststructuralists, like Queer Nationals, hope to avoid the self-limiting, fracturing dynamics of identification by an insistent disruptive subversion of identity. Yet, their cultural positioning, indeed their subversive politics, presupposes these very identifications and social anchorings. Is it possible that underlying the refusal to name the subject (of knowledge and politics) is a utopian wish for a full, intact, organic experience of self and other?

I have noted a turn in poststructural gay theory beyond a critique of identity politics to a politics against identity. The latter seems driven by its centering on a politics of identity subversion and draws from both romantic and antinomian traditions for its cultural resonance. Its limit, if you will, is the continuing practical efficacy of the resisting gay subject. In other words, it fails to theoretically engage the practices of individuals organized around affirmative lesbian and gay identities. Although I am sure that poststructuralists would readily acknowledge that gay identities have developed in resistance to an administrative-juridico-medical institutional rendering of same-sex desires, acts, and social formations as a site of social oppression, their focus on subverting identity seems to abstract from this institutional struggle and the social origin and efficacy of identity politics.[67] Identity constructions are not disciplining and regulatory only in a self-limiting and oppressive way; they are also personally, socially, and politically enabling; it is this moment that is captured by identity political standpoints that seems lost in the poststructural critique.

If the issue is not identity versus nonidentity, if subjects and social formations cannot elude categories of identity, if, indeed, identity categories have enabling, self- and socially enriching qualities, then the issue is less their affirmation or subversion than analyzing the kinds of identities that are socially produced and their manifold social significance. In this regard, I would follow the poststructural move that recommends viewing identity as a site of ongoing social regulation and contestation rather than a quasi-natural substance or an accomplished social fact. Identities are never fixed or stable, not only because they elicit otherness but because they are occasions of continuing social struggle. Yet, I would not privilege, as many poststructuralists seem to, signifying practices and contestations but would connect these to institutional dynamics. I would, moreover, follow the poststructural turn in framing identities as social structuring forces or, to use Foucaultian terms, as disciplining forces whose consequences for the individual, social relations, and politics should be critically analyzed. However, to the extent that some poststructuralists reduce the regulating and disciplining force of identity constructions to modes of domination and hierarchy, I would object. This rendering edges toward a politics against identity, to a sort of negative dialectics. As disciplining forces, identities are not only self-limiting and productive of hierarchies but are enabling or productive of social collectivities, moral bonds, and political agency. Although the poststructural problematization of identity is a welcome critique of the essentialist celebration of a unitary subject and tribal politic, poststructuralism's own troubled relation to identity edges toward an empty politics of gesture or disruptive performance that forfeits an integrative, transformative politic.

The recent proliferation of critiques of identity politics, particularly under the guise of poststructuralism, gives expression to the sociopolitical assertion of difference that I sketched previously. In its critique of identity politics as normalizing and exclusionary, in its disruption of an illusory unity that masks difference and domination, in forcing us to view identities as political artifices, poststructuralism is valuable. To the extent, however, that poststructural critique edges toward an anti-identity or postidentity standpoint, to the extent that it folds into a politics of the disruptive gesture, it lacks coherence. At another level, insofar as poststructuralism encourages us to focus less on the formation of gay identities as grounds of an ethnic minority and urges us to analyze cultural codes, it pushes our inquiries beyond a sociology of a minority to a study of the structure and tensions of modern culture. Yet to the extent that poststructuralists reduce cultural codes to textual practice and to the extent that these practices are abstracted from institutional contexts, we come up against the limits of poststructuralism as social critique.

Foregrounding the Social: The Next Move?

The limits of identity politics revolve around its thinking of identity as a unitary phenomenon, whether its unity is produced by nature or society. Positing a gay identity, no matter how it strains to be inclusive of difference, produces exclusions, represses difference, and normalizes being gay. Identity politics strains, as well, toward a narrow, liberal, interest-group politic aimed at assimilationism or spawns its opposite, a troubling ethnic-nationalist separatism. Poststructuralism is a kind of reverse or, if you wish, deconstructive logic; it dissolves any notion of a substantial unity in identity constructions leaving only rhetorics of identities, performances, and the free play of difference and possibility. Whereas identity politics offers a strong politics on a weak, exclusionary basis, poststructuralism offers a thin politics as its problematizes the very notion of a collective in whose name a movement acts.

I sense the battle over identity politics beginning to grow tiresome, or perhaps it's my own weariness. The terms of the discussion are in need of a shift. In both defenders of identity politics and its poststructural critics there is a preoccupation with the self and the politics of representation. Institutional and historical analysis and an integrative political vision seem to have dropped out. Perhaps as the politics of backlash comes to an end, we can begin to entertain broader, more affirmative social and political visions. Central to a renewal of political vision will be thinking issues of self, subject, and identity as a social positioning, as marking a social juncture in the institutional, administrative, juridical organization of society, and as an axis of social stratification. As much as race, sexuality, gender, or class mark a site of self-definition and therefore implicate us in a politics of identity and representation, these categories serve as social and political markers. Sexual orientational status positions the self in the social periphery or the social center; it places the self in a determinate relation to institutional resources, social opportunities, legal protections, and social privileges; it places the self in a relation to a range of forms of social control, from violence to ridicule. Locating identity in a multidimensional social space features its macrosocial significance; we are compelled to relate the politics of representation to institutional dynamics.

In framing identity as a social positioning we need to avoid assuming that all individuals who share a social location by virtue of their gender or sexual orientation share a common or identical history or social experience. The notion that a hetero/homosexual social positioning creates two antithetical unitary collectivities, the former positioned as one of privilege while the latter is positioned as an oppressed and resisting subject, lacks coherence. While appealing to a collective interest is a condition of political mobilization, it is unnecessary and undesirable to invoke a substantialist understanding of group life.

A major shortcoming of sociological essentialism is that it assumes that each axis of social constitution — gender, sexual orientation, ethnicity, class — can be isolated. However, as many feminist and gay people of color have argued, these axes of social positioning cannot be isolated in terms of a set of common attributes and experiences since they are always intersecting and mutually inflecting. Individuals experience sexual orientation in a particular class-, race-, or gender-mediated way, and only so. While we may wish, from time to time, to differentiate these axes of social positioning and identification for specific intellectual and practical reasons, we must avoid reifying what are analytical and political moves.

Unfortunately, I can do no more at this point than offer these rather sketchy proposals. However, the general direction of my thinking should be clear. Let me give a quick forward-looking résumé.

I urge a shift away from the preoccupation with self and representations characteristic of identity politics and poststructuralism to an analysis that embeds the self in institutional and cultural practices. I favor a politics of resistance that is guided by a transformative and affirmative social vision. This suggests an oppositional politic that intends institutional and cultural change without, however, being wedded to millennial vision. In a postmodern culture, anticipation of the "end of domination" or self-realization pass into local struggles for participatory democracy, distributive social justice, lifestyle choice, or reconfiguring knowledges. I prefer a pragmatic approach to social criticism. Conceptual and political decision making would be debated in terms of concrete advantages and disadvantages; the values guiding such pragmatic calculus would receive their moral warrant from local traditions and social ideals, not foundational appeals. In a pragmatically driven human studies, I imagine critical analyses that address specific conflicts, aim to detail the logics of social power, and do not shy away from spelling out a vision of a better society in terms resonant to policy makers and activists. In this regard, I am less patient with generalizing, systematizing "theories" in the tradition of Marxism or radical feminism; such efforts promote social hierarchy and an exclusionary politics. I favor social sketches, framed in a more narrative rather than analytical mode, as responses to specific social developments and conflicts with specific purposes in mind. I think for example of the writings, mostly essays with a strong narrative cast, most moving back and forth between the personal and the institutional, of Cherrie Moraga, Minnie Pratt, Audre Lorde, Gloria Anzaldúa, and Barbara Smith, as exemplary. This, however, is a topic for another occasion.

NOTES

I wish to thank Linda Nicholson, Rosemary Hennessey, and Michael Warner for their helpful comments on earlier drafts of this essay.

A note on terminology: When the term "gay" is used without further qualification, I intend to refer to both men and women. Although I have followed current conventions in speaking of lesbians, gay men, women, African-Americans, and so on, I mean by this only individuals who identify as, say, men or lesbians. My preference would be to speak of individuals who are gay-identified or African-American-identified, so as to convey the sociopolitical meaning of such identity constructs.

1. Among the most influential statements of postmodernism as a sociocultural phenomenon are Jean Baudrillard, *For a Critique of the Political Economy of the Sign* (St. Louis: Telos Press, 1981); idem, *Simulations* (New York: Semiotext[e], 1984); idem, *In the Shadow of the Silent Majorities* (New York: Semiotext[e], 1983); Frederic Jameson, "Postmodernism, or the Cultural Logic of Late Capitalism," *New Left Review* 146 (1984); Andreas Huyssen, *After the Great Divide* (Bloomington: Indiana University Press, 1986); Jean-François Lyotard, *The Postmodern Condition* (Minneapolis: University of Minnesota Press, 1984); Richard Rorty, "Postmodern Bourgeois Liberalism" and "Cosmopolitanism without Emancipation: A Response to Jean-François Lyotard," in *Objectivity, Relativism, and Truth* (Cambridge: Cambridge University Press, 1991); Terry Eagleton, "Capitalism, Modernism, and Postmodernism," in *Against the Grain* (London: Verso, 1986); David Harvey, *The Condition of Postmodernity* (Oxford: Basil Blackwell, 1990); Donna Haraway, "A Manifesto for Cyborgs: Science, Technology, and Socialist Feminism in the 1980s," *Socialist Review* 15 (1985). A fine overview of postmodernism is provided by Steven Connor, *Postmodernist Culture* (Oxford: Basil Blackwell, 1989).

2. On the new social movements, see Manuell Castells, *The City and the Grassroots* (Berkeley: University of California Press, 1983); Jean Cohen, "Strategy or Identity: New Theoretical Paradigms and Contemporary Social Movements," *Social Research* 52 (1985); E. Crighton and D. S. Mason, "Solidarity and the Green: The Rise of New Social Movements in East and West Europe," in Louis Kreisberg, ed., *Research in Social Movements, Conflict and Change* (Greenwich, Conn.: JAI Press, 1986); Klaus Eder, "The New Social Movements: Moral Crusades, Political Pressure Groups or Social Movements?" *Social Research* 52 (1985); Jürgen Habermas, "New Social Movements," *Telos* 49 (1981); Alberto Melucci, "The New Social Movements," *Social Science Information* 19 (1980); Alain Touraine, *The Voice and the Eye* (London: Cambridge University Press, 1981). Regarding the tie between the new social movements and "postmodern" social thought, see my "Social Theory as Narrative with a Moral Intent: A Postmodern Intervention," in Steven Seidman and David Wagner, eds., *Postmodernism and Social Theory* (Oxford: Basil Blackwell, 1991), and my "Postmodern Anxiety: The Politics of Epistemology," *Sociological Theory* 9 (fall 1991); Michel Foucault, "Two Lectures," in *Power/Knowledge* (New York: Pantheon, 1980); Andreas Huyssen, "Mapping the Postmodern," in *After the Great Divide;* and Susan Bordo, "Feminism, Postmodernism, and Gender-Scepticism," in Linda Nicholson, ed., *Feminism/Postmodernism* (New York: Routledge, 1990).

3. See, for example, Gayle Rubin, "The Traffic in Women," in Rayna Reiter, ed., *Towards an Anthropology of Women* (New York: Monthly Review Press, 1975); Michelle Rosaldo and Louise Lamphere, eds., *Woman, Culture and Society* (Stanford, Calif.: Stanford University Press, 1974); Sherry Ortner and Harriet Whitehead, eds., *Sexual Meanings* (Cambridge: Cambridge University Press, 1981).

4. See, for example, Isaac Balbus, *Marxism and Domination* (Princeton, N.J.:

Princeton University Press, 1982); Jane Flax, "Do Feminists Need Marxism?" in The Quest Staff, eds., *Building Feminist Theory* (New York: Longman Quest Staff, 1981); Linda Nicholson, *Gender and History* (New York: Columbia University Press, 1986); Iris Young, "Beyond the Unhappy Marriage: A Critique of Dual Systems Theory," in Lydia Sargent, ed., *Women and Revolution* (Boston: South End Press, 1982).

5. See, for example, Barbara Ehrenreich and Deirdre English, *For Her Own Good* (New York: Doubleday, 1979); Kate Millet, *Sexual Politics* (New York: Ballantine, 1969); Naomi Weisstein, "Psychology Constructs the Female," in Anne Koedt et al., eds., *Radical Feminism* (New York: Quadrangle, 1973).

6. See, for example, Ronald Bayer, *Homosexuality and American Psychiatry* (New York: Basic Books, 1981); John D'Emilio, *Sexual Politics, Sexual Communities* (Chicago: University of Chicago Press, 1983); Jeffrey Weeks, *Sexuality and Its Discontents* (London: Routledge, 1985). The pivotal role that medical-scientific discourses continue to play in shaping same-sex desire is evidenced in the HIV/AIDS phenomenon. See Simon Watney, *Policing Desire* (Minneapolis: University of Minnesota Press, 1987); Cindy Patton, *Inventing AIDS* (New York: Routledge, 1990); and Douglas Crimp, ed., "AIDS: Cultural Analysis, Cultural Activism" *October* 43 (winter 1987).

7. My interpretation of the perspective of the Mattachine Society is based, in part, on my own reading of the *Mattachine Review.* I have also drawn from John D'Emilio, *Sexual Politics;* Toby Marotta, *The Politics of Homosexuality* (Boston: Houghton Mifflin, 1981); Del Martin and Phyllis Lyon, *Lesbian/Woman* (New York: Bantam, 1972).

8. On the gay liberation movement's challenge to the older homophile movement, see Barry Adam, *The Rise of a Gay and Lesbian Movement* (Boston: Twayne, 1987) and n. 7, above.

9. Radicalesbians, "The Woman-Identified Woman," in *Radical Feminism*. In addition to essays in the above anthology, see Nancy Myron and Charlotte Bunch, eds., *Lesbianism and the Women's Movement* (Baltimore: Diana Press, 1975); Ti-Grace Atkinson, *Amazon Odyssey* (New York: Links Books, 1974); Leslie Tanner, ed., *Voices from Women's Liberation* (New York: North American Library, 1971).

10. Dennis Altman, *Homosexual Oppression and Liberation* (New York: Avon, 1971).

11. Ibid., 74.

12. Ibid., 80.

13. Ibid., 81.

14. Allen Young, "Out of the Closets, into the Streets," in Karla Jay and Allen Young, eds., *Out of the Closets* (New York: A Douglas Book, 1972), 7.

15. Ibid.

16. Ibid., 29.

17. Ibid. Cf. Carl Wittman, "A Gay Manifesto," in *Out of the Closets.*

18. Foucault, "Truth and Power," in *Power/Knowledge.*

19. Young, "Out of the Closets," 7.

20. On the shift to a ethnic/separatist model, see Dennis Altman, *Coming Out in the Seventies* (Sydney: Wild and Woolley, 1979); idem, "The Gay Movement Ten Years Later," *The Nation,* Nov. 13, 1982; and idem, *The Homosexualization of America* (New York: St. Martin's Press, 1982); Michael Bronski, *Cultural Clash* (Boston: South End Press, 1984); Laud Humphrey, "Exodus and Identity: The Emerging Gay

Culture," in Martin Levine, ed., *Gay Men* (New York: Harper and Row, 1979); John Lee,"The Gay Connection," *Urban Issues* 8 (July 1979); Lillian Faderman, *Odd Girls and Twilight Lovers* (New York: Columbia University Press, 1991).

21. Cherrie Moraga and Gloria Anzaldúa, eds., *This Bridge Called My Back: Writings by Radical Women of Color* (Latham, N.Y.: Kitchen Table, 1984).

22. Barbara Smith and Beverly Smith, "Across the Kitchen Table: A Sister-to-Sister Dialogue," in *This Bridge Called My Back,* 121.

23. Ibid.

24. Joseph Beam, ed., *In the Life* (Boston: Alyson, 1986).

25. Joseph Beam, "Introduction: Leaving the Shadows Behind," in *In the Life,* 14.

26. Ibid., 17.

27. Essex Hemphill, ed., *Brother to Brother* (Boston: Alyson, 1991).

28. Essex Hemphill, "Introduction," in *Brother to Brother,* xviii.

29. Charles Fernandez, "Undocumented Aliens in the Queer Nation: Reflections on Race and Ethnicity in the Lesbian and Gay Movement," *Democratic Left* (May/June 1991): 9.

30. Efforts to conceptualize the intersection of race and sexuality are moving into the center of gay theorizing. See, for example, Cherrie Moraga, *Loving in the War Years* (Boston: South End Press, 1983); Beam, ed., *In the Life;* Hemphill, ed., *Brother to Brother;* Jewelle Gomez, "Imagine a Lesbian . . . a Black Lesbian," *Trivia* 12 (spring 1988); Jackie Goldsby, "What It Means to Be Colored Me," *Out/Look* 9 (summer 1990); Tomas Almaguer, "Chicano Men: A Cartography of Homosexual Identity and Behavior," *Differences* 3 (1991); Carla Trujillo, ed., *Chicana Lesbians* (Berkeley, Calif.: Third Woman Press, 1991).

31. Loraine Hutchins and Lani Kaahumanu, "Bicoastal Introduction," in Hutchins and Kaahumanu, eds., *Bi Any Other Name* (Boston: Alyson, 1991).

32. Ibid., xx.

33. Jane Litwoman, "Some Thoughts on Bisexuality"; cited in *Bi Any Other Name,* 5.

34. Jan Clausen, "My Interesting Condition," *Out/Look* 7 (winter 1990).

35. Ibid., 13.

36. Ibid.

37. Ibid., 17.

38. Ibid., 18–19.

39. Ibid., 21.

40. For a different perspective on ethnicity and gay identity, see Steven Epstein, "Gay Politics, Ethnic Identity: The Limits of Social Constructionism," *Socialist Review* 17 (May-August 1987).

41. For overviews of the sex debates, see Steven Seidman, *Embattled Eros* (New York: Routledge, 1992); Ann Ferguson, *Blood at the Root* (London: Pandora Press, 1989); Shane Phelan, *Identity Politics* (Philadelphia: Temple University Press, 1989).

42. Laura Lederer, ed., *Take Back the Night* (New York: William Morrow, 1980).

43. Varda Burstyn, ed., *Women against Censorship* (Toronto: Douglas and McIntyre, 1985); "Sex Issue," *Heresies* 12 (1981); see also Feminist Anti-Censorship Task Force, eds., *Caught Looking* (Seattle: Real Comet Press, 1986).

44. Samois, *Coming to Power* (Boston: Alyson, 1982); Joan Nestle, "Butch-Fem Relationships," *Heresies;* idem, "The Fem Question," in Carole S. Vance, ed., *Pleasure and Danger: Exploring Female Sexuality* (Boston: Routledge and Kegan Paul, 1984);

Wendy Clark, "The Dyke, the Feminist, and the Devil," *Feminist Review* 11 (summer 1982).

45. See, for example, Dorothy Allison, "Lesbian Politics in the '80s," *New York Native,* December 7–20, 1981; idem, "Sex Talk," *New York Native,* July 29–August 11, 1985; idem, "Sexual Babel," *New York Native,* April 11–24, 1983; Susie Bright, "Year of the Lustful Lesbian," *New York Native,* July 30–August 12, 1984; Pat Califia, "What Is Gay Liberation?" *The Advocate,* June 25, 1981; idem, "A Secret Side of Lesbian Sexuality," *The Advocate,* December 27, 1979; idem, *Sapphistry: The Book of Lesbian Sexuality* (Tallahassee: Naiad Press, 1980); Amber Hollibaugh, "The Erotophobic Voice of Women," *New York Native,* September 26–October 9, 1983; idem, "Desire for the Future: Radical Hope in Passion and Pleasure," in *Pleasure and Danger;* Gayle Rubin, "Thinking Sex: Notes for a Radical Theory of the Politics of Sexuality," in Vance, ed., *Pleasure and Danger,* 267–319; Deirdre English, Amber Hollibaugh and Gayle Rubin, "Talking Sex: A Conversation on Sexuality and Feminism," *Socialist Review* 11 (July–August 1981).

46. See Steven Seidman, *Romantic Longings* (New York: Routledge, 1991), chap. 6.

47. See Weeks, *Sexuality and Its Discontents.*

48. On the rise of a lesbian and gay S/M subculture, see Pat Califia, "A Personal View of the History of the Lesbian S/M Community and Movement in San Francisco," in Samois, *Coming to Power;* Geoffrey Mains, *Urban Aboriginals* (San Francisco: Gay Sunshine Press, 1984); Arnie Kantrowitz, "From the Shadows: Gay Male S/M Activists," *The Advocate,* May 29, 1984.

49. See, for example, Craig Johnson, "S/M and the Myth of Mutual Consent," *New York Native,* May 29–June 11, 1985; Seymour Kleinberg, *Alienated Affections* (New York: St. Martin's Press, 1982).

50. Social constructionism has been pioneered by Michel Foucault, *The History of Sexuality,* vol. 1, *An Introduction* (New York: Pantheon, 1978); Jonathan Katz, *Gay/Lesbian Almanac* (New York: Harper and Row, 1983); Carroll Smith-Rosenberg, "The Female World of Love and Ritual," in *Disorderly Conduct* (New York: Oxford University Press, 1985); Jeffrey Weeks, *Coming Out* (London: Quartet, 1977).

51. Smith-Rosenberg, "Female World."

52. Ibid. Cf. Lillian Faderman, *Surpassing the Love of Men* (New York: Morrow, 1981).

53. Jonathan Katz, *Gay/Lesbian Almanac.*

54. Jonathan Katz, "The Invention of the Homosexual, 1880–1950," in *Gay/Lesbian Almanac.* Cf. George Chauncey, Jr., "Christian Brotherhood or Sexual Perversion? Homosexual Identities and the Construction of Sexual Boundaries in the World War One Era," *Journal of Social History* 9 (1985).

55. David Halperin has pressed constructionism in perhaps the most consistently historicist direction. He argues that there is a radical discontinuity with regard to the presuppositions about sexuality between the Greeks and the moderns. He proposes that modern Western sexual codes are underpinned by the assumption of a core sexual self revealed by sexual object-choice. Sexuality is viewed as a site where the truth of the self is revealed; sex is framed as a mode of social bonding. In ancient Greece, there was no such notion of a distinctively sexual nature to humanity. Sexuality was thought of less as a self-defining expression than as an act of reception and penetration. Sex was less a mutual social bond than a polarizing experience,

142   Steven Seidman

dramatizing social hierarchy. The master categories of sexual experience did not center on gender preference but revolved around active and passive roles. Sexual experience reenacted a public hierarchical social order. See David Halperin, *One Hundred Years of Homosexuality* (New York: Routledge, 1990), 30–31.

56. Many of the major statements of social constructionism have been collected in Edward Stein, ed., *Forms of Desire* (New York: Garland, 1990). Also, see *Homosexuality, Which Homosexuality?* International Conference on Gay and Lesbian Studies (London: CMP, 1989); and Lawrence Mass, ed., *Homosexuality as Behavior and Identity*, vol. 2: *Dialogues of the Sexual Revolution* (New York: Harrington Park Press, 1990).

57. Cf. Zygmunt Bauman, *Modernity and Ambivalence* (Ithaca, N.Y.: Cornell University Press, 1991).

58. I urge that gay theory substitute postmodern for modernist premises. Standard modernist science justifies itself by its claims to objectivity and truth, the growth of knowledge, and its role as an agent of enlightenment. A postmodern perspective will describe modernist social science as itself a major force in the production of bodies, sexualities, institutional orders, and social hierarchies. It interprets the modernist language of truth, objectivity, value neutrality, and scientific and social progress as a symbolic, rhetorical code that conceals a will to power. All discourse is viewed as embedded in a specific social configuration and exhibiting a partial, value-laden, interested standpoint. The kind of postmodern approach I am recommending favors pragmatic, justificatory strategies that underscore the practical and rhetorical character of social discourse. Similarly, I urge abandoning grand theories and metanarratives in favor of genealogies, historical deconstructionist analyses, and local social narratives. On postmodern criticisms of conventional social science and the development of a distinctive postmodern social studies, see Linda Nicholson, ed., *Feminism/Postmodernism* (New York: Routledge, 1990); and Steven Seidman and David Wagner, *Postmodernism and Social Theory* (Oxford: Basil Blackwell, 1992).

59. On poststructural gay theory, see Diana Fuss, ed., *Inside/Out: Lesbian Theories, Gay Theories* (New York: Routledge, 1991); Ronald Butters et al., eds., *Displacing Homophobia* (Durham, N.C.: Duke University Press, 1989); Joseph Boone and Michael Cadden, eds., *Engendering Men* (New York: Routledge, 1990).

60. Diana Fuss, *Essentially Speaking* (New York: Routledge, 1989), 102–3.

61. See Fuss, "Introduction," *Inside/Out*, 1.

62. Eve Kosofsky Sedgwick, *Epistemology of the Closet* (Berkeley: University of California Press, 1990), 1.

63. Ibid., 11, 71–72.

64. See the symposium "Queer/Nation," *Out/Look* 11 (winter 1991).

65. See Fuss, ed., *Inside/Out*.

66. Judith Butler, "Imitation and Gender Insubordination," in *Inside/Out*, 16.

67. See the relevant comments by Michael Warner in his introduction to the present volume.

Tremble, Hetero Swine!

Cindy Patton

This essay is *outré,* madness, a tragic, cruel fantasy, an eruption of inner rage, on how the oppressed desperately dream of being the oppressor. We shall sodomize your sons, emblems of your feeble masculinity, of your shallow dreams and vulgar lies.... All laws banning homosexual activity shall be revoked. Instead, legislation shall be passed which engenders love between men.... We will raise vast, private armies, as Mishima did, to defeat you.... The family unit... will be destroyed.... Perfect boys will be conceived and grown in the genetic laboratory....

Tremble, hetero swine, when we appear before you without our masks.[1]

For many readers, the above will be evident as a gay revenge fantasy. Because the author constructs his parodic identity through a campy desire to reverse the roles of oppressor and oppressed rather than arguing for the ordinariness of homosexuality, we might surmise that the author is a gay liberationist or Queer Nationalist. The arch style works because we also recognize the essay's foil: paranoid new-right conspiracy theories.

But this hermeneutic of queer identification is only part of the story. I cite the above essay as I encountered it in a 1989 issue of the right-wing periodical *New Dimensions,* a special issue devoted to "the truth" about AIDS. Apparently irony-proof, *New Dimensions's* editor interprets the essay as a statement of the gay movement's political plan. Accompanied by a sidebar detailing the "legislative goals of the homosexual movement," the article (which appeared in *Gay*

Community News as "The Homoerotic Order") is reprinted under the title "The Homosexual Mentality" with the following warning:

> Homosexual relations are indisputably the major cause of the AIDS epidemic in the Western world. But what is the mentality and the political agenda of homosexuals? WARNING: The material on this page, written by homosexual political activists, may be offensive to some people.[2]

Apparently, hetero swine do *not* tremble. Instead, they arm themselves with their own sense of a new-right identity, formed in opposition to what they understand to be a dominant culture in the grip of homosexual activists.

Boston's *Gay Community News,* along with California's *The Advocate,* is the new right's major source of information about gay politics and attitudes. But *New Dimensions* reproduces this article indirectly, using a complex set of citations to avoid reading the piece as a satire of the right's own beliefs. The editor reprints the article in full, acknowledging that it once ran in the *Gay Community News,* but citing its source as the *Congressional Record,* where presumably it had been submitted by a right-wing congressman as part of the Helms Amendment debates, about six months after the piece originally appeared. In addition to avoiding questions about how *New Dimensions*'s editor came to be reading a gay newspaper, citing the *Congressional Record* serves to establish the article's place in public discourse. The new right frequently employs this show-and-tell strategy, complete with disclaimers stating that the collector's reluctance to bring such "filth" out of the shadows was offset by the need to show the opposition for what it (allegedly) is. The double citation and freestanding full reproduction of the article legitimate the sentiment and style of the article as *the* identity against which new-right resistance must operate. By citing the *Congressional Record,* the editor of *New Dimensions* erases the parodic nature of the original article; by acknowledging that it originally ran in *Gay Community News,* he gives it the force of a serious statement by the "homosexual movement" as a whole. The sidebar chronology of the new right's version of the gay movement's ascendancy further distances the piece from parody and places it instead in the realm of political history.

Both gay and new-right identity operate by invoking parodies of the other; but gay identity frequently also uses the narrative device of "coming out" stories as instructive parables. The new right must cope with these claims to empirical self-understanding; homosexual self-knowledge is reconstructed as a kind of delusion that, in "coming out" and committing itself to the public state, forms positive evidence of perversion for the nonhomosexual, who, as part of his/her reciprocal identity, is capable of "seeing through" the cultural denial of the danger of always present but unacknowledged homosexuality. This maneuver is epistemologically central to the new right's identity claim and situates the new right as able and required to reinstruct a morally lobotomized society that has forgotten the danger of the homosexual.

It is ironic that the new right seems to have gained power in part in response to the moderate gains of the gay civil rights movement and the increased visibility it has afforded many lesbians and gay men. But similarly, the gay movement capitalized on the bold and vicious opposition to it that was generated by a general societal homophobia, even if this strategy and the movement's rhetoric could not erase the reality that violence was exacted on gay people by homophobes, but not the reverse. Using texts from the new right, I will argue in a moment that the mutual focus on the new-right/gay-movement oppositional dyad not only helped consolidate the internal identities of each groups, but was also used by each to promote general societal *dis*identification with the other: if neither group could reasonably hope to recruit many outsiders to its identity, promoting disidentification produced at least temporary allies.

The form of this deadly dance suggests that what is at stake is not the content of identities but the modes for staging politics through identity. The identity claimed in post–World War II discourses of civil rights is performative, less a discovery of self by people who were once shackled by a false consciousness than an effect of a rhetoric designed to reshape the ways in which political subjects are formed. Instead of understanding identity in an ego-psychological or developmental framework, I will argue that identity discourse is a strategy in a field of power in which the so-called identity movements[3] attempt to alter the conditions for constituting the political subject.

As the recitation of the *Gay Community News* article in *New Di-*

mensions suggests, gay and new-right identities define each other relationally, by a rhetorical reversal and counterreversal. Rhetorical reversal is one of the fundamental principles of the identity discourses of the post–World War II movements. Black, women's, and gay liberation typically "reclaimed" derogatory terms that were considered part of the hegemonic vocabulary and symptomatic of pervasive, stereotypical, negative societal attitudes. For example, the slogans "black is beautiful" and "gay is good" were designed to reverse the perception that African Americans could not conform to (white) standards of beauty and that homosexuals were bad citizens. Sometimes the appropriations take the form of recontextualizing terms — nigger, queer, girls, bitches — when used inside the group to which these terms once signified submission.

The new right performs a second reversal that is more than merely restating the position of the hegemony against which the progressive minorities stage their identities. Although using the hegemonic significations — "white, heterosexual, family-oriented" — the new right takes up its position as another minority, but one constituted in relation to the homophile and feminist Rainbow Coalition of minorities now read by the new right as the dominant society. The new right must perpetually reestablish the dominance of this implausible aggregation of special-interest groups; through citational practices similar to that discussed above, the new right incites homosexual speech in order to create a simulacrum homosexual movement whose epistemological structure is the speaking out of its inner (if perverse) certainty about its homosexual nature. The evidence (speeches, chronologies) of this phantom movement is then reversed to constitute the new right's objectivating knowledge structure — the new right images the public declarations of gay coming out as purloined information consolidated and managed through conspiracy theories. Thus, gay and new-right identities are lopsided counterparts. Gay identity comes from spilling the beans, from coming out of the closet to claim the other's derogatory speech as one's inverted reality. New-right identity cloisters self-revelation, reinterprets proud gay speech as confessions to the distinctive perversion that gay liberation's reversal sought to expose as fraud. If coming out says, "We're queer, we're here, get used to it," new-right identity appropriates this to say, "We knew it," and to society, "We told you so." What operates as a performative act of identity assertion for "queers" is read by the new right as *descriptive,* as not performative at all.

A second fundamental principle of identity discourse seems to have been lost from view in the debate about postmodernism and postidentity politics. Implicit in the differing modes of identity construction are claims about political formation, about forms of governmentality, about the difference between modernity and postmodernity. To the extent that groups like ACT UP or Queer Nation have, largely due to their sophisticated use of cynical media practices, been associated with postmodernism,[4] other forms of gay political labor have been implicitly identified as "bad old modernist." But more than standing for the discovery of a self, identities suture those who take them up to specific moral duties. Identities carry with them a requirement to act, which is felt as "what a person like me does." There is a pragmatic, temporal aspect to identities, whether we believe in them or not: the requirement to *act* implicit in even transient identities means that those who inhabit them feel they must do something and do it now. This produces a kind of closure, but that does not mean that identities are or become effectively essential: the stabilization of identities appears to be ineluctably essentialist only when we treat them in the realm of the imaginary, with its apparent promise of infinite possibilities for performance and reperformance. Instead, I propose here that we treat identities as a series of rhetorical closures linked with practical strategies, implicit or consciously defined, alliances and realliances that in turn affect the whole systems for staging political claims. As I will show, it is most importantly in the play of shifting pragmatics of alliance formation (what I will call deontic closures in order to indicate the performative and pragmatic dimensions, rather than imaginary dimensions) that identity rhetorics perform their work.

There are at least two forms of group identity, affiliative and exclusionary. The first is characterized by strategies of identification while the second is characterized by strategies of disidentification. Particular social identities (African-American, gay) will combine affiliative and exclusive identities — a person can inhabit either, or a mix of identifications and disidentifications — and it is from the relations of these identity procedures and the closures they produce that political subject formation occurs in postmodernity.

When I suggest that identities operate deontologically in a field of power, I mean field in Bourdieu's sense of a domain in which there are shifting, ongoing, and appropriative constructions of difference, in this case, differences of moral duty signified by proposing attributes as proper to contended identities. If it has seemed impossible to arbitrate between accomplished identities, this is because identities refer to each other to create distinctions of moral duty. This is why gay liberation and new-right rhetorics haunt each other, perpetually shifting their identificatory alliances. It is crucial to recognize these reorganizations, and in a moment I will detail a shift in new-right identity that simultaneously opposes homosexuality and embraces black conservatism. In this redistribution of moral duty the new right reconstructs its identity to oppose both white supremacist identity and black racial identity, to which gay liberation identity is likened.

"Resistance" in the context of these problematics of the subject might best be understood as a battle over the grammar of identity construction rather than a process of stabilizing the production of particular, individually appropriable identities. While resistance may occur through arch rearrangements of established identities, identity must be understood as performatively linking signifiers of social identity with duties to act: identity operates performatively in a practical and temporary space, a situation, if you will. Thus, identity constitution is less an achievement than an effect and is symptomatic of the shifts occurring in postmodern governmentality. A "real" state no longer simply institutes categories for political engagement; instead, competing rhetorics of identity interpellate individuals to moral positions that carry with them requirements for action. Identity is an issue of deontology, not ontology; it is a matter of duties and ethics, not of being.

New-Right Knowledge and Civil Rights Discourse

Homosexuals, according to the new right, have ascended to power largely because they can recognize each other when ordinary citizens (and especially the homosexuals' own wives) cannot. Gay people's "intraspecies radar" is deployed to make claims to minority status that Patrick Buchanan argues rest on inaccurate numerical claims originating in the "great hoax of Dr. Kinsey."[5] Despite the attempt to trump gay claims to civil rights by deploying epidemiologic data that confuse identity and acts that facilitate the transmission of HIV, Buchanan's now much-cited article makes a crucial capitulation to civil rights discourse. Buchanan doesn't question the validity of minority claims to civil rights in general; he just argues that homosexuals have duped Americans into accepting us based on an inflation of numbers. Adding credibility to his argument by citing New York Public Health Commissioner Stephen C. Joseph's controversial 1988 decision to lower projections for the number of AIDS cases in the city, Buchanan recommends that other public health officials "blow the sewer cap off Kinsey's monumental reputation, re-establish homosexuality as the 1-in-50 aberration, [and] expose the Gay Rights movement as a paper tiger."[6] Buchanan's progression of citations produces a deontic closure for new-right sympathizers that demands a course of activism in relation to the public health system, pitting (David) Joseph against (Goliath) Kinsey to produce a "fact" that will deflate (detumesce?) the gay movement.

This highlights the crucial difference between the new-right/ neo-conservative approach and the more overtly genocidal approach of the far right. The new right is operating within the domains of identity construction and is attempting to alter the power relation between identity and postmodern administrative apparatus like civil rights by defining what critical mass is required to establish the status of minority. Far from constituting an antiquated political impulse that seems still marginal at the voting booth, the new right engages in the battle to constitute the rules of identity formation that I am arguing constitute postmodern governmentality. Crucial to this battle is the constitution of a new-right identity that links an epistemological superiority to a moral duty. New-right identity is constructed through an asymmetry of knowledge and self-knowledge: occupying the hazardous space of being able to "know it when you see it" while evading the charge that it "takes one to know one."[7]

The new right's system of knowing contains a fragile logic, as is evident in the legal defense offered (and usually accepted) when queer-bashers argue that they acted because the person they beat up was making sexual overtures to them. There is a suggestion that the extreme of violence might have been due to an unconscious apprehension of the defendant's latent homosexuality. But queer-bashing cases are not really about whether the violence was committed or justified. Clearing the queer-basher of charges (the usual outcome until a few recent decisions) also clears him of the taint of latent homosexuality; the queer-basher's (and queer-hunter's) ability to "know" who is gay (here, by "knowing" he was coming on) is established as epistemologically superior to the victim's ability to deploy his intraspecies radar (even though this was not offered as part of the prosecution). The new right trades on this cultural commonplace by asserting that the identity that homosexuals claim as a form of self-knowledge is actually a delusion. This is most evident in the new-right strategy in which the speech of the supposedly covert conspiracy of homosexuals is wholly appropriated and read back as positive evidence, as in the exchange between *New Dimensions* and *Gay Community News* cited above.

New-right identity requires the perpetual if shifting assertion that it knows the truth about the "other," a truth it seeks to establish by enlisting any and all institutional and noninstitutional forms of knowledge construction. The far right continues its traditional concern with racial purity; here, issues of knowledge and self-knowledge circulate around the fear that a white person's history could contain an African. The new right's perpetual evacuation of its "other" — homosexuality — cannot be solved through establishing individual genealogies; the possibility of turning into a queer (or turning out to be queer) is a perpetual present. Fear of miscegenation and fear of latent homosexuality both serve as visceral but fragile tropes of self-knowledge and self-delusion, although as we saw in the Thomas-Hill controversy (with Thomas's "white wife" and the tabloids' suggestion that Hill might be a lesbian), the latter seems to be ascendant in the new right's pantheon of terrors.

Precisely because the logics of the far and new rights can still operate in tandem in relation to policing sexuality (rather than race) the efforts of the Rainbow Coalition to forestall internal competition on the grounds of civil rights prove inadequate; the battle over identity constitution in which queers and the new right are overtly engaged invokes and reconstructs resistance to racism. The political issue is not just building the largest coalition, but in how we constitute our memory of resistance, and consequently, on whose behalf we feel obliged to act. I want to show how the new right recasts racial identity and mates Western and black civil rights histories to exclude feminist and gay claims to civil rights.

The New Right: Refiguring Identity

Howard Winant[8] has noted that the right has a range of politics in regard to race, and this is true of rightist positions in relation to homosexuality, as I have argued elsewhere.[9] What is crucial for our purposes here is to note that the far right, with its militarist associations like the Klan and neo-Nazi groups, is centrally organized around an oppositional identity that from the Reconstruction through the New Deal has been articulated in terms of racial purity.[10] In the post–World War II era, this began to be articulated directly as a "white" identity. While it may seem paradoxical to mark the unmarked category in this way, it is crucial for neo-fascist racist discourse to produce as a rhetorical effect a white identity that sees itself as distinct from the unmarked nonidentity of the (white) hegemonic middle class. This racist white identity operates as importantly against the nonvigilant "race-mixing" white as it does against the "nonwhite."

The new-right and neo-conservative movements have a rather different view of race. The new right and neo-conservatives have courted conservative African Americans and "Hispanics" since the 1970s: Justice Clarence Thomas is only one of the recruits. Thomas had been writing for new-right and neo-conservative periodicals for over a decade, and is listed as an important black leader in Richard Viguerie's 1981 new-right manifesto, which has a "coming out" feel in listing the names and "rightist" credentials of dozens of people he considers the current and rising leaders of a new movement to reclaim the social space of America. The free-market ethos of the new right and neo-conservatives permits the assimilation of people of color if race is erased as an issue. The civil rights movement is gingerly embraced through a kind of octoroon approach to history in which a partial racial heritage can be "made white" through persistent re-breeding/reading. The role of the far right in sustaining racial hatred is suppressed in favor of constructing the liberals and their welfare state as the cause of black underdevelopment.

This rhetorical co-optation of the black civil rights movement is crucial in holding the line against *gay* claims to civil rights. In the following passage, David Pence invokes a popular memory of black resistance, then deploys it as a trope in transhistorically linked biblical and contemporary holocausts, both neatly "explained" by the attempt of homosexuals to attain civil status:

> Most individuals who were not involved in the civil rights movement against racism tend to lump the traditional civil rights movement with the later feminist and gay liberation campaigns. This hijacking of the freedom train by middle class careerists and sexual adolescents has virtually destroyed the real civil rights movement.... The early civil rights movement did not try to build identity on skin color but affirmed the common humanity, the common Creator and the common citizenship of each of us.... [T]he gay lobby [is] a middle class special interest group which has squandered the moral authority of the old civil rights movement and captured many of the government jobs in human rights agencies formerly held by racial minorities.... The road to Selma did not lead to the right to sodomy.[11]

Notice the reconstruction of black identity as a *non*racial identity constituted through "common humanity" rather than "skin color." Pence clearly sees gay liberation as based in a "trait" like skin color; the assertion of trait-loyalty is *opposed* to common citizenship. To make matters worse, queers are supposed to have taken minority jobs.

The invocation of Selma is crucial: the new right and neo-conservatives generally promote a long view of Western tradition. In *Cultural Conservatism: Toward a New National Agenda,* the popular manifesto of what has evolved into the political correctness debates, William Lind and William Marshner argue that

> cultural conservatism is the belief that there is a necessary, unbreakable, and causal relationship between traditional Western Judeo-Christian values, definitions of right and wrong, ways of thinking and ways of living — the parameters of Western culture — and the secular success of Western societies: their prosperity, their liberties, and the opportunities they offer their citizens to lead fulfilling, rewarding lives.... [T]raditional values and virtues are required not only to create a society that is free and prosperous, but also for individual fulfillment.[12]

In the context of this now well-articulated notion of survived forms of morality (the "Western" or "Judeo-Christian tradition"), the invocation of Selma (oddly enough, site of civil rights accomplished) serves to reconstruct a powerful popular memory of resistance. This incorporates African Americans into the traditional values, if they choose to join, but refuses a place for feminists and gays. The triple historical citation in Pence — Western civilization generally, black civil rights, the biblical destruction of Sodom — is collapsed into the linear figure of a road: the crumbled metanarrative of Western progress appears humbly here as common humanity in a common creator, which should embody the "true" rights achieved in a reorganized memory of the black civil rights movement. And the sibilant, stunning double metonymy, Selma/Sodom, is metaphorized as opposite ends of a road: if the destruction of Sodom somehow marked the beginning of true (black) civil rights, then to situate Sodom and Selma in the same place reverses (in fact, implodes) the progress of black civil rights. This rendering of the imputed map of a moral terrain in which Sodom and Selma marked opposite places asks the reader to bend the map, to entertain moving Sodom(y) to Selma.

Queer Coming and Going

AIDS has provided a sophisticated screen for constituting and reconstituting identities, and a deadly opportunity to link specific institutional practices with both gay assertions of self-knowledge and new-right assertions that homosexuality is an object of scientific knowledge. Importantly, if race had once served as a quasi-genetic metaphor for visualizing and policing difference, HIV, as a form of genetic interference, now provides the vessel for essentializing differences. In an interview with the editor of the rightish periodical *New Dimensions,* right-wing AIDS expert Gene Antonio explains why HIV antibodies don't stop the virus. The interviewer is confused and believes that people who get HIV are, due to drug use or homosexual practices, intrinsically weak. Antonio explains that "even if you had a healthy immune system and you got a transfusion of AIDS-infected blood, you're dead." They continue:

Antonio: . . . Once you're infected with the virus, you are always infected. The virus incorporates itself into the very genetic material of cells, so that all subsequent progeny cells are going to be infected.

ND: It's actually altering your genetic identity.

Antonio: Exactly. That's a very good way of putting it. You are now a permanent, genetically stamped AIDS-carrier.[13]

What's crucial here is the reversal of identity construction — AIDS discourse has a curious retrograde motion that I have called "the queer paradigm":[14] you can begin as a queer, and therefore as uniquely susceptible to AIDS, but whatever your cultural status, once you test positive for the HIV antibody, regardless of how you contracted the virus, you become nominally queer. The above exchange operates on the same logic, adding a genetic (i.e., indisputably biomedical) basis. Queerness may be genetically determined, as in the much-hyped recent twin and hypothalamus studies, but if you weren't queer before, HIV will "alter your genetic identity," make you a "permanent, genetically stamped AIDS-carrier."

The virus operates as a mobile metaphor in AIDS discourse generally. The virus and pseudoscientific concepts connected with it work overtime to prove the unique susceptibility of homosexuals to viral infection. In "The Spiritual Significance of Viral Infection," *New Dimensions* contributors Paul Bahder and Teresa Bahder explain that the virus

> is not a living thing and it has no will, no locomotion, no power of its own.
>   The mere presence of a virus does not necessitate infection because no virus can force itself onto a totally healthy cell. Some kind of receptivity on the part of the human cell is required to accept this kind of delivery.... It is an active process on the part of the recipient that is required before an infection can take place. It is not that we are innocent victims of a virus, but that we actively participate in acquiring a virus. It takes work and effort on the part of a living cell to absorb the inert, lifeless substance from within the wrappings of the virus.[15]

This veiled allusion to homosexuality in general, especially a *chosen* homosexuality, where even the "passive partner" is doing "work," sounds very much like Antonio's description of homosexual sex generally. The visceral, corporeal rhetoric about homosexuality serves to constitute its other (new-right identity) as endowed with a "natural" and "gentle" sexuality:

Activities involving severe bodily abuse and personal degradation
are an integral part of the repertoire of homosexual behavior.
The damaging practice of sodomy by itself can be classified as a
sadomasochistic act.[16]

An anatomical explanation is offered to separate the homosexual
from the heterosexual, implicitly retaking the once unmarked category of "heterosexual," marked "straight" within gay liberation
discourse, as the natural category:

Among male homosexuals, sodomy or anal intercourse is the act
substituted for heterosexual penile-vaginal coitus.
Physiologically, the rectum is designed for the expulsion of feces.
When sodomy is performed, the peculiar forced inward expansion
of the anal canal results in a tearing of the lining as well as bleeding
anal fissures.[17]

Antonio's "trauma of sodomy"[18] is combined with the fear of the
gay conspiracy's intention to recruit in (no doubt Mr. and Mrs.)
Bahder and Bahder's[19] explanation of how viruses work. Again, we
see the double reversal through which the new right reoccupies
the unmarked "dominant" category with an identity. A complete
psychology is offered to explain the moral difference between the
homosexual (and also the "cancer-prone" lifestyle, which is linked
to feminist critiques of gender roles) and "normal" lifestyle, complete with a concept of the "will" to recruit and the will to resist. In
this viral allegory, a new-right identity forces its deontic closure to
demand an alliance with an unstated set of traditional values:

A virus possesses the information on how to replicate in its own
image, but it has no means of doing it since it has no life. The
misinformation that is extracted from inside of a virus is used by a
living cell to produce more viruses instead of the molecules that are
necessary for its own healthy functioning. . . . No longer following its
own "understanding," the living cell now does something unthinkable,
something unreasonable. It departs from what it knew and it follows
what it has been told. . . .
   The "trauma" of viral infection can be understood by comparing it
with the psychological traumas that alter people's very identities. . . . [A]
virus "makes" a cell suspend its own healthy activity in favor of
replicating more viruses and in the end damaging itself. . . .

The suppression of a healthy and balanced functioning in the community of cells eventually leads to a rebellion.... [T]he body's immune system fails to discern that the rebellion will eventually destroy the whole system and consequently it "closes its eyes" on the disorder, because the external pressure is overwhelming and a revolution seems justified....

The AIDS virus is different from others in that it doesn't just destroy body cells. It kills...the very cells that are supposed to alert the body of a foreign intrusion. It destroys the body's ability to recognize what is wrong and thus enters the system camouflaged, unseen....

Total confusion of identities, accepting a new set of loyalties to the virus and abandoning one's true roots, that is really what AIDS is all about.[20]

The pathologizing and visceral representation of sodomy operates in tandem with the insistent copula of sodomy and gay identity to produce the stable "confusion" of identity that new-right identity may oppose. The closure of new-right identity is precisely its calm, clear ability to steer an unbalanced America back to the tried and true path of proper childbearing (to gain a proper "understanding"), drawing the line against "misinformed" claims to civil rights by those who "have no life [i.e., procreative power] of their own," and restore the capacity to recognize "foreign intrusion" (sodomitical penetration? Russian infiltration?). In short, to open and focus America's bleary eyes to disorder.

Geopolitically Queer

The paranoia about homosexuality's global dangers also lies in its capacity to demodernize and decivilize its practitioner. Sodomy is not only the "act" in which HIV may enter a body, but also the source of casual transmission, as Antonio argues in his widely distributed *The AIDS Cover-Up? The Real and Alarming Facts about AIDS:*

During sodomy, the biological design of the rectum combined with the aggressive properties of sperm expedite their substantial entrance into the bloodstream....

The weakening of the sphincter through repeated sodomy results in fecal incontinence and the dribbling of blood-stained contaminated stool. The involuntary depositing of the AIDS virus infected fecal secretions on the benches in locker rooms, toilet seats and elsewhere also creates a potential for spread by this route.[21]

As I have argued elsewhere,[22] this linkage of sodomy and AIDS, which is then metonymically projected to link the incontinent homosexual with the continent (body) of Africa, serves not only as a trope for consolidating new-right identity as (white) Western and heterosexual, but also, through its more scientific representations, serves as the basis for conducting suspect medical research in "Africa." *New Dimensions* editor and principal author, David Masters, in a sidebar to an article by Dr. John Seale, the right-wing British venereologist who prepared the National Front's secret AIDS-containment plan, proposed to but rejected by the House of Commons,[23] makes this fantasmatic but scientized connection between Africa and the "homosexual":

> Medical experts explain that the "biological environment" of major parts of Africa is very similar to that of the practicing homosexual. That is, because of the extreme poverty and ignorance in that part of the world, basic sanitation is not observed; food and water are often contaminated with sewage.... In other words, researchers contend that both groups, homosexuals as well as a large proportion of the population of parts of Africa, engage in practices which grossly violate the laws of natural protection against disease.[24]

While "practicing homosexuals" or "gays" are projected as categories of subject, the new right also attempts to strip "sodomy" and "homosexuality" of their attachment to persons who could, for example, stake claims for civil status and rights. Masters introduces the special issue on AIDS in an editorial entitled "War of the Worlds":

> In recent years the dangers of toxic waste, noise, and water pollution, and radon gas, to name a few, have become major topics of great societal concern. Numerous laws regarding the proper handling and disposal of wastes and environmental endangerment have been established to arrest the harmful effects of such problems. Yet, an insidious social disease known as AIDS is sweeping over our country and the world, politically protected by many of the same lawmakers and trusted icons of society who purport to save us from environmental danger.[25]

Here, the careful geopolitical syllogism that connects the Western homosexual and the African is despatialized. The "social disease known as AIDS" is actually homosexuality. "Political protection" encompasses the argument that Sodom(y) is not Selma (the legitimate claim to civil rights); if civil status is not properly a right, it can only be conveyed as a protection, and here by "icons of society" who protect us from the natural environment, but not from the unnatural "environmental danger" of homosexuality.

Conspiracy

If the eugenic urge in the new right's environmental and spatial metaphors is not fully evident, it becomes clearer in reverse as genocidal paranoia under the guise of public health recommendations:

> *Antonio:* All of these bath houses should be closed. They are the teeming, breeding grounds of AIDS infection, and they're wide open. In fact, they're opening new ones.
>   The way they look at it, "I've got it, so I may as well go for the gusto and sodomize myself and others into oblivion. And women too." There has been a call in some homosexual publications to go and have sex with as many women as possible so that they can inject it into the general population.[26]

Paranoia about homosexuals who would go so far as to engage in that reviled and disgusting act of heterosexual intercourse is not Antonio's only fear. The assertion of gay identity as the fulcrum for civil rights and social tolerance forced the new right to modify older rightist conspiracy theories, transforming the conspiracy hunter's task from unmasking a plot among secret perverts to deconstructing publicly claimed identities as rhetorical perversions of the very language of political discourse. In pre–gay liberation homosexual witch-hunts, homosexuals were presumed to be attempting to hide, perhaps even from themselves: the notion of latency resided entirely on the side of homosexuality, instead of sliding uncomfortably into a potential element of polymorphous heterosexuality. A well-trained observer could pick out the ineluctable clues — a limp wrist, preference for certain kinds of luggage, ways of moving and speaking.[27] Although homosexuals suffered as much as Communists from the witch-hunts of the House Committee on Un-American Activities,[28] the committee's imputed rationale for homosexuals' alleged "un-American" activity was unclear: while homosexuals operated in a conspiratorial manner, their main objective was to avoid detection and increase the reach of their perversion. The far right played an important role in the production of the combined Communist/homosexual conspiracy: numerous people created and distributed lists of people with alleged Communist or homosexual connections.[29] This process of list-management exposed those listed by condensing a variety of long-standing figures of otherness (homosexuals, Jews, immigrants, those in the business of producing mediated images) into a single category of "un-American," with its connotations of conspiracy, infiltration, penetration. Few of the "conspirators" invented by the right-wing list-makers made any secret of their involvement in political activities. The Communist party was not illegal, and attending public meetings was certainly protected under the First Amendment. Indeed, the process of blacklisting created the need to maintain some secrecy about such benign activities. Homosexuality was more clearly the subject of secrecy even when it was conditionally permissible, ironically, for example, in HUAC hatchet man Roy Cohn's case. Part of the power of the HUAC assault may have come from combining the ever-present secret of homosexuality with the retrospective secret of Communist sympathizing, fusing the most plausible figure of passive hiding (the homosexual closet) with the most terrifying figure of military defeat (communism).

This ideological construction of homosexuals as penetrators is the midpoint in a shift from the early twentieth-century[30] construction of the homosexual as a doubly deviant (in object and aim) mutual masturbator or effeminate cocksucker to the sinister wielder of a dangerous phallus in AIDS discourse.[31] As we will see in a moment, the discourse on HIV transmission within the "gay community" — in both mass media and new-right discourse — emphasizes reception, while the possibility of crossing-over into the "heterosexual community," via bisexual men, emphasizes penetration (of unsuspecting women). In fact, the proposition of the concept of community by gay people created the conditions for the refiguring of the fluid mainstream into the bounded "heterosexual community" and permitted a shift in metaphor from the subculture envaginated in the body of dominant culture to two cordoned entities requiring a passage or penetration. That the bisexual men who form the HIV "bridge" must also have been penetrated in order to have become infected is elided, or, rather, repressed, in order to recuperate the bisexual male as mainly heterosexual, at least insofar as his identity is still contingent upon being the inserting partner in the crucial, identity-bestowing act of intercourse.

Only a decade after HUAC, when homosexuals "came out" in apparently large numbers, this kind of conspiracy-unmasking tactic lost its bite. Now, instead of exposing individual members of a general conspiracy, the new right treats homosexuals as a "lobby" of open manipulators of institutions, especially the mass media where they promote "positive" image disinformation about themselves. New-right conspiracy smashing takes the form of exposing the ugly "truth" of a "perversion" the American public has been lulled into accepting as a "right." In the direct-mail empire conceived and once controlled by the now financially ruined Richard Viguerie, list-management reverses its epistemological grip: direct mail becomes a political weapon capable of operating outside the mainstream media that the new right views as in the clutches of the homosexual lobby. The metaphoric relation between the body politic and its rebellious parts is reversed: instead of operating from the body as a kind of radiation therapy directed at lumps of Communist or homosexual incursion, the new right exists within an incontinent homophilic (and feminist) body as a kind of vaccine. Where anti-Communist lists identified the true identity of a minority for the majority, new-right direct-mail pleas reinterpret mainstream culture as perverse for those listed.[32]

In the insistent linking of AIDS and homosexuality, right-wing conspiracy logic has extended the range of homosexual infiltration. Where homosexuals under the HUAC assault had no clear agenda, the gay liberation movement is seen to have a clear and active political agenda underneath what the new right interprets as the gay claims to be left alone (i.e., to be protected from discrimination). For convoluted reasons (they can't face the moral weight of what tolerance of homosexuals has wrought;[33] they are "morally lobotomized"),[34] doctors and public health officials are said to have been taken over by and to have helped homosexuals systematically misinform each other about various aspects of the epidemic. In an outrageous displacement of responsibility for the genocide of HIV disinformation, Seale connects the terror that hidden codes could establish one's "genetically stamped" identity with the fear that, at least to the heterosexual other, homosexual significations are impenetrable:

> Most [homosexuals] in the professions are only identifiable as homosexuals to other men with similar tastes — few have "come out" and even the wives of those who are married are usually unaware of their habits. Hence they automatically form a type of secret society without even trying, with wide ramifications across professional, institutional, and national boundaries.[35]

Identity and Postmodern Governmentality

These readings of new-right material suggest not only that the new right is strategically intertwined with the liberationist, identity-based movements, but also that a new form of governmentality, concerned with the rules by which groups may claim subject status, is emerging. The identitarian politics now stressed by the apprehension of multiple and conflicting identities within movement members as well as by the claims of once mainstream persons (white, middle-class, heterosexual men) to be a "minority" were born in a modernist and essentializing impulse. Identity served as a useful strategy for extending representation, both expanding the content of what might count as a subject and increasing channels of access to an already constituted polis and quickly became the principal means of staging political claims. However, with the emergence of group identities that make no reference to a transcendent essence (as in both Queer Nation and the new right) the political presence no longer requires the pretense of representing some prediscursive constituency. Identity now functions not so much to retain a representational space or define a trajectory toward cultural autonomy as it operates as a holograph of what the appropriate subject of a new form of governance might look like. The referents of identities are now less important than the capacity to look like an identity at all.

The battle over identity has been misunderstood by critics and practitioners alike. When identity-based politics are understood as related to modernist political formations, they do seem to employ an essentialist understanding of the identity as a psychological and communal accomplishment. However, a slight change of angle to explore the interrelation between claims to identity constitution suggests that identity politics is coextensive with (perhaps both constitutive of and constituted by) a shift from the modernist state to a postmodern condition of governmentality.

Current theory and, as I will argue in a moment, especially queer theory have become confused about the issue of identity because there are a range of competing populist and academic concepts of identity, as well as important differences between European and U.S. political experiences of calls to identity. I want to propose a more specific understanding of identity in the U.S. context, which is linked with larger issues of governmentality and social theory. As I suggested in my discussion of new-right identity, identity is a rhetorical effect that (1) elides its construction, (2) implies or re-narrates a history, (3) produces a deontic closure, and (4) operates performatively within a field of power in which citational chains link symbols and political subject position.

Metasocial Claims

There are multiple forms of identity, some linked with radically liberationist efforts, and some linked with radically fascist, genocidal efforts. European theorists, I think, are more conscious of the ambivalence of the idea of identity, not least because identity there is more recently, and currently, associated with both Nazism and "progressive" neo-nationalisms linked to territorial claims. Alain Touraine describes "two faces of identity" that appear to emerge in postindustrial society, both of which oppose the existing social roles, but one form of which is popular and one of which originates in the state:

> In the case of most societies, the appeal to identity relies upon a metasocial guarantor of social order, such as the essence of humanity or, more simply, one's belonging to a community defined by certain values or by a natural or historical attribute. But in our society the appeal to identity seems more often to refer not to a metasocial guarantor but to an infrasocial and natural force. The appeal to identity becomes an appeal, against social rules, to life, freedom, and creativity. Finally, the State itself appeals to identity against social roles, and attempts to impose the idea of a unity above all forms of particular belongings. A national State, for example,

appeals to citizenship, and, through it, to patriotism against all social, professional, and geographical differences. The individual or collective appeal to identity is thus the obverse of social life. Whereas the latter is a network of relations, the locus of identity is all at once that of individuals, communities, and States.[36]

Touraine's argument that both state and local identities are antisocial undercuts social constructionist sociology, which focuses on identities in relation to social roles constituted *against* nature or the state. In Touraine's view, there are both essentialist and antiessentialist concepts of identity. In general, suggests Touraine, "infrasocial" principles (including nature) are the court of appeals for identity claims that appear to be "essential"; however, it is important to distinguish between claims to transcendent, foundational categories and claims *against* social roles. The idea of social roles seems to arise within late modernity and in part to facilitate reintegration into the social whole of fracturing identities (especially geopolitical and national) through naturalizing things like race and gender. This naturalization of modernity's social roles seems to have promoted an identity strategy (still existing in pluralist liberal and left discourse) that copes with the proliferation of subject-linked differences through a teleological narrative that can collapse everyone into a transcendental subject. The "metasocial guarantor" here is the metanarrative of modernity itself. To stage claims to identity, however ineluctably sutured to the claimants' personal sense of psychic integrity, is to stage a claim *against* the self-naturalizing *social* roles that social constructionists have so eloquently described. That is, as long as identity is deconstructed within the framework of modernity, identities will appear to be claims to a natural self underneath the tyranny of modernity's own social roles. But this is to take the "native story" of identity claimants too seriously; it is to accept the story identities must tell in order to stand up within the modernist metanarrative as the only story they have to tell. If identities, however crude the translation, are allowed to speak not against the social roles within the modernity that birthed them, but against social integration as a whole, it begins to appear that identities are claims against the modern governmentality altogether. As content-empty spaces of signification designed strategically to link through rhetorics of moral duty, identities oppose rather than operate through ontological claims. The fact that the identity rhetorics associated with civil rights movements emphasize "being who we are" is a matter of strategic gloss. Queer Nationalists, the new right, and the homeys of East Los Angeles don't "be" — they "do" what they have to and by any means necessary (echoing Malcolm X).

The state forms of identity, while similar to older integrative appeals to the nation, are also importantly different and postmodern. As Touraine notes, patriotism (conserving an already existent national) and neo-nationalism (claims to a new national) are appeals against the integrative social order.[37] Severed from their earlier role of defining the relation between local and national interests and between the interests of competing collectivities defined as nations, nationalist rhetorics can now float free from the geopolitical boundaries they once referenced. Touraine's discussion goes some distance in explaining why, for example, Queer Nation read as a kind of nationalist identity causes concern for other gay activists who are still haunted by the deployment of national identity in Nazism, or, for that matter, in the United States's own Aryan Nation. We may be able to sort out some of these political differences and develop a postidentitarian political strategy if we understand how the state has begun to shift under the pressure of both the claims to and deconstructions of identity in the post–World War II era. I want to approach this larger problem of identity through the complaint that recent queer theory has been better at pointing out the essentialist moments and problems of identity than it has been in suggesting a postidentitarian politics.

Queer Theory: Reading on the Literary Side

The near hegemony in gay studies of deconstructive and psycho-analytic techniques, at least as evidenced in the selection and reception of papers at a recent conference at Rutgers, has upset both newer activists who want ways of thinking about what to do *now* and more tenured scholar-activists whose work outside the (in reality quite narrow) arena of literary criticism seems to have been forgotten.[38] While much interesting work continues to interrogate how modes of identity construction and/or ontological claims to being-types themselves construct the field of power, the social-construction/essentialism debate seems to have degenerated into attempts to decide which claim about the project of subjectivity is best.[39] This judgment is based either on some notion of political effectiveness, which elides the modes through which claims to identity themselves reconstitute the political space that identity stabilizers are attempting to engage, or on how nearly performed identities evade hypostatization.

Eve Kosofsky Sedgwick's *Epistemology of the Closet* is an elegant and compelling assault on the attempt to adjudicate between these two positions.[40] Instead, she urges us to understand how both kinds of claims enact different but mutually inscribed systems of knowability, which operate simultaneously among queers and in the form of assaults from the larger culture. She argues forcefully that essentialist and constructionist impulses are asymmetric, and this in part accounts for their resistance to adjudication or dialectical resolution. I have followed her opening here to suggest that the two contending "gay" epistemological structures operate within a field of power in which modes of knowledge of the subject constitute capital. Both are also enmeshed with the new right, another identity movement that is equally confused about how it can know who it is.

Moving from the foregrounding and deconstruction of epistemological structures to my analysis of such epistemological claims as but one *means* of gaining power through rhetorics of identity has forced me into the "social," a domain abandoned by recent gay theorizing. I hope I have convincingly shown that social theory, too, can escape the accusation of essentialism. Postmodern social theory appears as a relatively new move within queer theory, but only because the preconditions for gay studies have begun to slip from view. In fact, my theorizing is the grandchild (gay intellectual generations seem to be about five years) of social constructionist work conducted at the margins of traditional social sciences by people like Esther Newton, Gayle Rubin, Carole Vance, Gilbert Herdt, Jeffrey Weeks, and Dennis Altman, people who were obligatory citations for gay theorists only a few years ago before more textually based forms of queer theory achieved dominance at conferences and in gay studies collections. Thus, I want to draw attention to an implicit problem in the social-construction/essentialism debates as understood by textual critics (but not social theorists), which Sedgwick's new work partially attacks and partially reconstitutes, and which, equally, is responsible for the tendency in Judith Butler's *Gender Trouble* to provide complex accounts for how certain notions of identity elide their own construction, and yet, in the end, to be incapable of saying much useful about how to proceed given that gay liberation, just to take one example, is substantially indebted to precisely this hat trick.[41]

By implicitly referring to a modernity that, logically, their interventions should be therapeutically "forgetting," literary deconstruction and psychoanalytically oriented critique either stand as archeologies of a past knowledge/power system or obfuscate the political effects of current formations by speaking of "the social" in modernist terms. When deconstructionist critical techniques are innocent of the parallel debates among postmodern "social" theorists, there is a palpable gap between the "bad things" that happen in the "real world" and the logics of homosexual construction/disappearance uncovered as formal operations of literary (or popular) texts. For all their compelling brilliance, their deep affinity for the local and civil plight of queers, deconstructive and psychoanalytic approaches seem unsuccessful at connecting their crucial "reading" technique with the modes of constitution of, especially, civil–rights–linked identity.

It's not that we don't all resonate with the problematics evoked in the complex and detailed deconstructions, but the specificity needed for understanding the *constitution* of identities in the civil sphere now lags behind the techniques for deconstructing them. In fact, we may be deconstructing straw versions of the complex minority identities. Like Michel de Certeau's description of opinion formation that operates through citing hegemonic beliefs one is "above" holding,[42] deconstructionists may believe in the imputed essentialist identities much more than those in the political sphere who are purported to have them. There is little question that a major part of post-Stonewall gay politics has involved staking claims parallel to those of the more successful black civil rights movement and that the *logic* of such claims is ambivalently essentialist. However, this is to confuse the efforts of those inhabiting "oppositional" identities, often at substantial cost, for the *rules of the game* of identity, as ongoingly constituted in a field of power in which a modicum of safety is won. Despite excellent accounts of differences within "gay identity,"[43] until we stop insisting that identity per se is essentialist, the uses "ordinary gay people" make of these (and other — white, female, Southern) identities will remain untheorized, unknown, unavailable to thoughtful strategies of intervention. Pierre Bourdieu[44] cautions against assuming that those who are "best" at a game are most able to describe its rules; the ardently expressed attachments to gay identity among movement leaders are probably the least secure accounts of how identities can convey political capital for those who claim to be gay. Quotidian uses of identities must be understood in the context of a struggle to control the general rules of identity construction. The plainly essentializing logics within this field must be viewed as options deployed in a deadly game of queer survival, not as "foundations" for "identity."

At present, neo-Marxist cultural studies and poststructuralist social-construction theory are somewhat out of step concerning what was once called mass culture. This has produced an incoherent set of critical practices in which the "social" is deconstructed and evacuated, but a "cultural" (albeit more fun to study) is reinserted in the same place. Put another way, postmodern rhetorical theories are used to critique the modern social formation, but then a (modernist) hermeneutic of suspicion is deployed to "read" resistance within postmodern culture. Although ground-breaking in many respects, the early Birmingham School work on subcultures fell into precisely this conundrum: it in effect substituted a worn-out social with a polished-up cultural when it tried to explain mass culture as a principal site of identity construction. This approach assumes that mass culture is uniformly interpreted and serves as the principal paradigm for identity construction for individuals or microgroups. This crypto-psychology views the social as a series of functional roles and assumes a "political" cleaved off from prediscursive subjectivities and mediated through a "culture": a political-economic base instantiates social identity through "culture." This cultural Marxist approach assumes that the process of group identification that produces images and products prevents action within a separate sphere in which the real or unpleasant (depending on your relation to it) business of political power operates.

In neo-Marxist cultural studies, "cultural activism" (say, rap music or Queer Nation shopping trips) is of course important, but precisely how it gets its grip on the supposed "real" conditions of, say, street-gang violence or queer-bashing, is unclear. Glorifying cultural activism relies on — even while disguising its roots in — a base–superstructure metaphor in which the distinction between production and consumption embedded in Marxian notions of the alienation of labor is used to explain that the "work" of operating within and alongside images and artifacts is a *cultural* resistance to the other, passive, absorptive *social* relation of consumption.

These valorized antihegemonic interpretations assume that resistant masses are doing "something else" when they consume popular culture; the critic must attribute (or ethnographically "discovers") a hegemonic interpretation that resistant consumer practices are supposed to thwart. These claims make strategists of the consumer and the critic and assume a transcendent, intersubjective experience of oppression as the source of their mutual chafing against the banality of mass culture. But we have no reason to believe that this hegemonic interpretation is more than an attributed one, fabricated by the vast majority who disdain it in order to feel resistant to it. If the supposed hegemonic interpretation is something the various consumers and critics invent as a focus for an identificatory disdain, as de Certeau suggests, then the self-styled resistant vanguard is, numerically, the complicit majority.[45] The taking up, by a numerical minority of hyper-conservatives, of a "dominant" identification produced through a shared disdain for the views of the numerically superior (if fragmented) minorities is the more bizarre postmodern phenomenon: this is the political significance of the double reversal that I have described as constitutive of new-right identity. As I showed earlier, the new right reoccupied the ideology identified as mainstream by various minorities engaged in discourse reversals, only as a minority identity, not as the nonidentity of the majority. The new right took up an existing political position and claimed it as identity after the fact.

While it is possible to change the conceptual hierarchy among social, political, and cultural arenas, having once separated them it is not so easy to get rid of them since administrative technologies have grown up around both liberal modes of integrative management and Marxist strategies of organizing resistance. The identity-based movements' claim that the personal is political shows an impulse to dedifferentiate at least the public/domestic split. However, the tendency to valorize the subversive efficacy of cultural workers continues to separate the cultural and the public, reinscribing the cultural as private (as a feminized political?), without showing the conceptual dependence of notions of subversion on the concept of "public." It seems to me that an important part of the radical postmodern project is deconstructing not only binary metaphors but also the means by which the production of the political, social, and cultural are achieved, and to what effect.

The problem of denaturalizing the split between the social, cultural, and political and at the same time respecting the achievements of movements that have operated within those arenas has resulted in poststructuralist and especially postmodernist social theory being misunderstood as promoting a kind of apolitical pluralism. Those who adopt a detotalizing posture (i.e., in disavowing structuralism and foundational theories) are accused of promoting an astructuralism of the local that has other, necessarily totalizing, effects. To some extent, at least within U.S. academic practice, pluralizing *methods* — without more rigorously theorizing how, or in service of *what,* different readings might exist — suggests that, in principle, everything is placeable, explicable.

At least in the neo-pragmatism most publicly exemplified by Richard Rorty, there is avoidance of the fact that readings conflict in ways that have profound implications for how people are allowed to live. As Jean-François Lyotard suggests,[46] alternate readings (or redescriptions in Rorty's[47] terms) are at some point no longer merely rhetorical: they force closures, define the rules of debate, and exact an admission price from those entering the polis. Rorty tries to avoid this unpleasantness when he raises to a moral principle what is already the common practice in the postwar United States: we live and let live in private, in the expanding "social," and only fight about things that are in the public, the political. But social spaces are both preemptive and expandable: our current belief in an infinitely expandable social is a rhetorical effect of the proliferating identity movements of the 1960s and 1970s. This resulted from the invention of the concept of civil rights and its extension "privacy"; and at the same time this created the space for the new right to emerge by asserting the *preemptive* nature of social spaces, a position that appears fascist in the context of pluralism since in taking their space, the new right knocks others out of the game.

Pluralism tries to get us out of such conflicts by inventing "culture" as something groups possess independently of the ability to stake a claim in the social space and without needing to make their sociality evident as political claims. Indeed, while minoritizing politics have protected the cultural as private, they have worked to make the social public, *political* — a kind of legal and moral nationalization of "property" (voteless blacks, women, youth) that was once held privately by the dominant, white, male, upper/middle class. Homosexuals' attempts to gain protection to practice sex as private has produced a legal paradox: to insert privacy into the already accepted package of civil rights (to political participation, equal access, protection from discrimination) requires establishing lesbians and gay men as a publicly inscribed class. In the most immediate sense, a gay person must "come out" in order to get the right to privacy.

Rorty recognizes that the recent strategy of politicizing the social becomes unadministrable under current legal practices (if only, for example, because some heterosexual white males now want to claim themselves as a "minority"). His solution is to reverse the expansion of the social into the political by limiting the stakes (and size) of the public: he uses "pain" as the criterion for overriding the standoff of pluralist doubt in favor of intervention:

> The self-doubt [about our own sensitivity to the pain and humiliation of others] seems to me the characteristic mark of the first epoch in human history in which large numbers of people have become able to separate the question "Do you believe and desire what we believe and desire?" from the question "Are you suffering?" In my jargon, this is the ability to distinguish the question of whether you and I share the same final vocabulary from the question of whether you are in pain. Distinguishing these questions makes it possible to distinguish public from private questions, questions about pain from questions about the point of human life.[48]

Although this earnest plea seems reasonable, the ways an issue or event might pass from the private into the public are unclear. Between the private and unadjudicable and the agon of the public is the space of redescription, where people attempt to persuade others to their "final vocabulary" (something like Wittgenstein's concept of language game).[49] While Rorty acknowledges that power and redescription are linked, his attempt to reduce the question of doing the right thing to being able to recognize when we might humiliate or inflict pain fails to recognize the importance of re-description in defining what will register as pain, the possibility that redescription itself may be a form of humiliation.[50] While Rorty proposes an interesting distinction between the public and pri-vate that goes some distance in providing a basis for judgment that is imbedded in institutions rather than metasocial claims, he has gone very little distance from the sophistic ideal of a polis in which good men speak well: unless we permit him a predis-cursive "pain" that can somehow be communicated, if only we learn to listen, then Rorty cannot escape the possibility that re-descriptions will be in fact *about* making claims to pain. Rorty has taken a long trip to realize what the social movements al-ready knew: to participate in even a limited public, an interlocutor must establish personhood (the ability to have one's experience of pain counted). But instead of figuring out a way to promote pain speech, Rorty has taken up this claim from the side of the reluctant subject who discovers he has been hurting people and now wants to construct a discourse that will stop him before he kills again. I dwell on Rorty because his notion of redescription, developed from literary reading techniques and in the wake of postorientalist anthropology, is exemplary of a kind of abject Amer-ican neo-imperialism that — precisely through its evocation of its own self-consciousness of its uncomfortable place of global, local, and representational domination — shows what can happen when European poststructuralism is "redescribed" through the century-old liberal pragmatism that has both aided and infantilized identity politics.

A better reading of poststructural social theory that evades the avuncular tyranny of liberal pluralism would view notions of the social, political, and cultural as descriptions of relations of gov-ernmentality, forms of constituting or evading subject positions in relation to the apparatus of the modern state. Produced *through* the discourses of liberal pluralism, Marxism, and the identity move-ments, these subject positions are now differentially sustained by institutional practices. The task of the critic and activist would be to unravel the historic and conditional relations of forms of claims-making and look for ways to stage claims that better meet the desires of, say, gay liberation, feminism, or a Rainbow Coalition.

Governmentality and Gay Identity:
The Space of Queerness

The modern liberal state has an overt concern with coordinating and integrating different claims on resources and power. In this organic notion of governmentality, it makes sense to differentiate interests in order to place them under different forms of control that can be generally subsumed under a governing body whose legitimacy is staged through the appearance of consent in democratic representation. Here, "politics" is equated with state management and the direct process of achieving representation (elections, certainly, but also the hiring power — "affirmative action" — through which elective positions assert power under the illusion of representativeness). The "social" means issues affecting daily life, extrarepresentational issues like equitable distribution of resources ("poverty"), the environment, and "lifestyle."

If the modern state's business was to legitimate its existence in the absence of theological justification, to produce itself as a visible, secular, central organizational force Foucault describes so well, then the postmodern state seems concerned to recede from visibility, to operate blindly as a purely administrative apparatus to an apparent market democracy. If the modern state had to describe its existence in terms of reason, suggesting in one way or another that it was an outcome of the social contract, capable of organizing consent and policing deviation, the postmodern state has to pose itself as capable of administering an incoherent, incommensurable plurality of interests. The modern state integrates social factions to resolve conflict; the postmodern state holds pluralities apart. Instead of invoking an organicist logic that links the nation to the individual through increasingly smaller collectivities like the province, the township, and the family, the postmodern state proposes lateral linkages, communities or consumption units held in relation to one another and operating through the commercial logic of a free market that circulates rather than negotiates freedoms.

If modernity conceived power in blocks that operate entropically, postmodern power circulates, disperses, intensifies. The fields of power operative in postmodernity may be more importantly about the constitution of governable subjectivities than they are about the constitution of a governing state. Certainly, the two are connected, ideologically and practically. However, the crucial difference lies in the constitution of identities: it may be that essentialist and social constructionist claims are unadjudicable because accession to power — the constitution of governmentality — is now accomplished through, rather than a precondition of, making good on claims to identity.

The crucial battle now for "minorities" and resistant subalterns is not achieving democratic representation but wresting control over the discourses concerning identity construction. The opponent is not the state as much as it is the other collectivities attempting to set the rules for identity constitution in something like a "civil society." The problem is not one of cognitive or psychic dissonance — that is, that the right, for example, will not allow us to feel or be who we want to be, but that the terms for asserting identity *are* the categories of political engagement. The discursive practices of identity and the actors who activate them produce the categories of governmentality that engender the administrative state apparatus, not vice versa. It is as important to look at the battles taking place within the field of power in which accomplishment of "identities" operates as political capital — say, between the right and gays — as it is to see how their variously constituted identities interact with the administrative units.

Thus, identity as an effect comes into play at the threshold of what de Certeau,[51] following Derrida,[52] calls "the proper," at the threshold of engagement with constituted social and political institutions. As I have tried to show, this narrower sense of identity involves performativity, the ability to operate through citation within a field of power in which oppositional pairs are discernible against a backdrop of institutions and spaces. Institutions could be history or the courts, and spaces could be the social, gender, the nation. This is the place in which the new right invokes homophobia but a homophobia contingent on the continued construction of isolatable "gay identities."

If agents in possession of gay identities make demands for minority status within the political sphere, this is not because acquisition of gay identity strips away ideology and allows a homosexual body to realize its desire for civil rights that are simply waiting around for the asking. Rather, the demand for civil rights is an intrinsic effect of coming-out rhetoric, altering both the meaning of civil rights and the meaning of homoerotic practices. Coming-out rhetoric, in effect, articulates gay identity to civil rights practices, articulates homo-erotic practices to the political concept of minority. The person who takes up a post-Stonewall gay identity feels compelled to act in a way that will constitute her or himself as a subject appropriate to civil rights discourse, and thus, deserving of the status accruing to successful claims to minority status. In the process of queer enunci-ation, the meaning of civil rights, indeed, the capacity to hold apart the political and social, the public and private, have been radically altered.

The innovation of gay identity was not so much in making homo-sexuality seem acceptable to the homosexual, but in creating a crisis of duty in gays who could "come out" (in some sense, leave the private/social). In linking the demand for acceptance by society with the instantiation of identity in oneself, gay liberationists want society to take a stand for or against specific or specifiably "gay" per-sons. All identities effect these deontic closures: in fact, as I have argued above, the achievement of identities is precisely the staking out of duties and alliances in a field of power. Postmodern mini-narratives of individual and collective moral legitimacy are replacing the rational metanarratives — like the social contract, pluralism, and democracy — that characterized state legitimation in modernity.

Reading Queer, Living Here

Queer theory has developed detailed and productive ways of read-ing: queers are nothing if not good readers. In this sense, we are the paradigmatic case of the postmodern subject, constructed both through reading and as a rhetorical effect of reading. But having opted for the deconstructive reading heavily influenced by recent orthogonal criticisms of canonical literature over much of post-structuralist social theory, we've done less well at situating our reading and our *being read off* in larger fields of power. We may have committed both of Bourdieu's crimes: as critics, we may have misrecognized our own method of inquiry as coextensive with the objects' *modus operandi,* but also, since we have deployed our secret "queer knowledges," in essence, have been the archaeolo-gists (and architects) of our own marked desires, we have believed our native stories. I have tried here to revisit social theory from the place of queer readings, suggesting an alternate way of understanding identity with the hope of enabling more articulate strategies of "resistance" in the postmodernity that seems to have made it problematic to posit ourselves as subjects.

I have continued to hammer away at the notion of identity because, whether we like it or not, the crucial if now somewhat contradictory battles for civil rights and for destabilizing the homosexual signification that becomes fuel for medical, social, and "private" policing still depend on theorized and deployed notions of identity. We once embraced the notion of inherent identities because it was strategically useful: we should question identity now not for formal reasons (Is it essentialist?) but because one form of identity rhetoric may fold us back into the same structures of "oppression," for lack of a better term. Indeed, the highly circumscribed visibility that identity and its public representation afford seem to spawn sublime new oppressions — stereotyping of the severe dyke (arguing for abortion rights) and clean-cut (no doubt HIV-positive) fag lawyer, invisibility of most other forms of homosexual performance, hate crimes and their accounting. This it not just a problem of messy analytic categories: we live the political reality of our identity effects. If deconstructive readings of identities have produced anxiety for those who need them in order to make practical political claims, then reinterpreting identities as strategic systems with pragmatic purposes and unintended effects may make it easier to forge new strategies (with or without "identities"), and certainly make easier alliances between styles of queer practice.

NOTES

1. "The Homoerotic Order," *Gay Community News;* cited in "The Homosexual Mentality," *New Dimensions,* 1989, 28–29.

2. "Homosexual Mentality," 28.

3. There are various terms in current use to describe the movements that have occurred since World War II, that is, in what many would call late capitalism, postindustrial society, or postmodernity. I prefer the term "identity movements" for those groups who claim a personal identity that is linked to a "natural" ethnic, racial, or social/psychological trait that members of the group are supposed to have. Other social movements — often lumped together under the general term "new social movements" — may make identity claims, but these refer to the group itself, without making the claim that something like a preconsciousness of an intrinsic condition existed prior to the group. Thus, peace, green, and alternative lifestyle movements differ from the black, gay, or women's movements in that they are not claiming the

existence of a class consciousness. I will briefly discuss the problems in conceiving the "social" in which these movements are thought to exist, a topic I take up in greater detail elsewhere.

4. Douglas Crimp and Adam Rolston, *AIDS Demo Graphics* (Seattle: Bay Press, 1990); Cindy Patton, *Inventing AIDS* (New York: Routledge, 1990).

5. Patrick Buchanan, "The Great Hoax of Dr. Kinsey," *New Dimensions,* 1989, 50.

6. Ibid.

7. Eve Kosofsky Sedgwick, *Epistemology of the Closet* (Berkeley: University of California Press, 1990).

8. Howard Winant, "Postmodern Racial Politics: Difference and Inequality," *Social Review* 20, no. 1 (1990).

9. Cindy Patton, *Sex and Germs: The Politics of AIDS* (Boston: South End Press, 1985).

10. Michael Omi and Howard Winant, *Racial Formation in the United States from the 1960s to the 1980s* (New York: Routledge and Kegan Paul, 1986).

11. David Pence, "Address to Physicians, Grand Rapids, Michigan, November 4, 1987," in *Vital Speeches,* December, 1987.

12. William Lind and William Marshner, *Cultural Conservatism: Toward a New National Agenda,* Free Congress Research and Educational Foundation (Lanham, Md.: UPA Inc., 1987), 8.

13. Gene Antonio, "AIDS: The Real Dangers of Casual Transmission" (interview with David Kupelian), *New Dimensions,* 1989.

14. Patton, *Sex and Germs;* idem, *Inventing AIDS.*

15. Paul Bahder and Teresa Bahder, "The Spiritual Significance of Viral Infection," *New Dimensions,* 1989.

16. Gene Antonio, *The AIDS Cover-Up? The Real and Alarming Facts about AIDS* (San Francisco: Ignatius Press, 1986), 40.

17. Ibid., 34.

18. Ibid.

19. Bahder and Bahder, "Spiritual Significance."

20. Ibid., 51–52.

21. Antonio, *AIDS Cover-Up,* 38, 36.

22. Patton, *Inventing AIDS;* idem, "Containing 'African AIDS': The Bourgeois Family as Safe Sex," in Andrew Parker et al., eds., *Nationalisms and Sexualities* (New York: Routledge, 1992), 265–84.

23. Although they are connected by funding, agendas, and cross-citation, there are important differences in the American and British new rights. The American new right, as I am establishing here, operates solidly within the civil rights/identitarian rhetoric characteristic of post–World War II, U.S. political discourse. In the wake of Thatcherite privatization and home-rule doctrines, which specifically prohibited local use of government monies on projects that "promoted homosexuality and pretended families," an important segment of the nonsectarian British left began efforts to pass a bill of rights on the U.S. model, which would reimagine citizenship along the lines of civil rights rather than national membership. The British new right has responded to this attempt to "Americanize" the concept of British citizenship by combining notions of civil identities with more traditionally European notions of national identity.

24. David Masters, in John Seale, *New Dimensions,* 1989.

25. David Masters, "War of the Worlds," *New Dimensions,* 1989, 5.

26. Antonio, "AIDS: The Real Dangers," 16.

27. Toby Marotta, *The Politics of Homosexuality* (Boston: Houghton Mifflin, 1981); John D'Emilio, *Sexual Politics, Sexual Communities* (Chicago: University of Chicago Press, 1983); Lee Edelman, "Seeing Things: Representation, the Scene of Surveillance, and the Spectacle of Gay Male Sex," in Diana Fuss, ed., *Inside/Out: Lesbian Theories, Gay Theories* (New York and London: Routledge, 1991); and Lee Edelman, "Tearooms and Sympathy, or, the Epistemology of the Water Closet," in Parker et al., eds., *Nationalisms and Sexualities,* 265–84.

28. Joan Nestle, *A Restricted Country* (Ithaca, N.Y.: Firebrand Books, 1987).

29. Alan Crawford, *Thunder on the Right: The "New Right" and the Politics of Resentment* (New York: Pantheon, 1980).

30. Sigmund Freud, "The Sexual Aberrations," in *Three Essays on the Theory of Sexuality* (New York: Basic Books, 1963).

31. Cindy Patton, "Fear of AIDS: The Erotics of Innocence and Ingenuity," *Imago,* forthcoming.

32. Patton, *Sex and Germs.*

33. Seale, *New Dimensions,* 1989, 24.

34. Antonio, "AIDS: The Real Dangers," 16.

35. Seale, *New Dimensions,* 1989, 24.

36. Alain Touraine, *The Return of the Actor* (Minneapolis: University of Minnesota Press, 1988), 75–76.

37. Ibid.

38. Lisa Duggan, "Theory and Practice," *Village Voice Literary Supplement,* June 1992.

39. Lisa Duggan, "Making It Perfectly Queer," *Socialist Review,* spring 1992.

40. Sedgwick, *Epistemology.*

41. Judith Butler, *Gender Trouble: Feminism and the Subversion of Identity* (New York: Routledge, 1990).

42. Michel de Certeau, *The Practice of Everyday Life* (Berkeley: University of California Press, 1988).

43. D'Emilio, *Sexual Politics;* Marotta, *Politics;* Dennis Altman, *The Homosexualization of America* (Boston: Beacon Press, 1982).

44. Pierre Bourdieu, *Outline for a Theory of Practice* (Cambridge: Cambridge University Press, 1972).

45. De Certeau, *Practice,* 1988.

46. Jean-François Lyotard, *The Postmodern Condition: A Report on Knowledge* (Minneapolis: University of Minnesota Press, 1979).

47. Richard Rorty, *Contingency, Irony, and Solidarity* (Cambridge: Cambridge University Press, 1989).

48. Ibid., 189.

49. Ibid., 89–90.

50. Ibid., 88.

51. De Certeau, *Practice,* 1988.

52. Jacques Derrida, *Positions* (Chicago: University of Chicago Press, 1981).

Lesbian Bodies in the Age of (Post)mechanical Reproduction
Cathy Griggers

What signs mark the presence of a lesbian body?

Writing the lesbian body has become more common of late, making reading it all the more difficult. Less hidden, and so more cryptic than ever, the lesbian body increasingly appears as an actual variability set within the decors of everyday discourses. Signs of her presence appear on the cover of *ELLE,* for example, or in popular film and paperback detective mysteries as both the sleuth *and* femme fatale, in texts that range from Mary Wing's overt lesbian thriller *She Came Too Late* (1987) to the conflicted, symptomatic lesbian subplot in Bob Rafelson's *Black Widow* (1986). She appears disguised as a vampire in Tony Scott's *The Hunger* (1983), and masquerading as the latest American outlaw hero in *Thelma and Louise* (1991). On television, she's making her appearance on the evening soap *L.A. Law,* and she virtually made MTV via Madonna's *Justify Your Love* music video (1990). When MTV censored the video, she appeared on ABC's *Nightline* instead, under the guise of "news." Elsewhere, in the latest lesbian mail-order video from Femme Fatale — a discursive site where the lesbian imaginary meets the sex industry — you can find her on all fours and dressed in leather or feathers, or leather *and* feathers, typically wearing a phallic silicone simulacrum. Amidst controversy, she appeared in the trappings of San Francisco's and London's lesbian bar culture passing as a collection of art photographs in Della Grace's *Love Bites* (1991).[1] In the summer of 1992, PBS broadcast a BBC production depicting the torrid affair between Violet Treyfusis and Vita Sackville-West into the living rooms of millions of devoted Public Broadcasting viewers as part of Masterpiece Theatre, with an introduction by Alistair Cook. Meanwhile, Susie Bright made more lesbian sexual reality in 1992 with her new *Susie Bright's Sexual Reality: A Virtual Sex World Reader,* published by Cleis Press and quickly selling out of its first printing. Lesbian computer nerds quietly wait for Bright to assist in the world's first virtual sex program designed by a lesbian. Same-sex sex between women is already a menu option on the popular on-line *Virtual Valerie,* along with a menu for a variety of sex-toy applications. Let's face it: lesbian bodies in postmodernity are going broadcast; they're going technoculture; and they're going mainstream.[2]

In the process of mainstreaming, in which minoritarian and majority significations intermingle, the lesbian body of signs is exposed as an essentially dis-organ-ized body.[3] *The* lesbian is as fantasmatic a construct as *the* woman. There are women, and there are lesbian bodies — each body crossed by multiplicitous signifying regimes and by different histories, different technologies of representation and reproduction, and different social experiences of being lesbian determined by ethnicity, class, gender identity, and sexual practices. In other words, as lesbian bodies become more visible in mainstream culture, the differences among these bodies also become more apparent. There is a freedom and a loss inscribed in this current cultural state of being lesbian. On the one hand, lesbians are given greater exemption from a categorical call that delimits them from the cultural spaces of the *anytime, anywhere.* On the other hand, the call of identity politics becomes increasingly problematic.

The problem of identity is always a problem of signification in regard to historically specific social relations. Various attempts have been made to locate a lesbian identity, most inculcated in the grand nominalizing imperative bequeathed us by the Victorian taxonomies of "sexual" science. Should we define the lesbian by a specific sexual practice, or by the lack thereof? By a history of actual, or virtual, relations? Can she be identified once and for all by the presence of a public, broadcast kiss, by an act of self-proclamation, or by an act of community outing? Should we know her by the absence of the penis, or by the presence of a silicone simulacrum? Surely this material delimitation may go too far: For shouldn't we wonder whether or not a lesbian text, for all that, can be written across the body of a "man"? I can point to the case of male-to-female transsexuals who cathect toward women, but why should we limit the problematic to its most obvious, symptomatic manifestation?[4]

The question of a lesbian body of signs always takes us back to the notion of identity in the body, of body as identity, a notion complicated in postmodernity by alterations in technologies of reproduction. Walter Benjamin observed in "The Work of Art in the Age of Mechanical Reproduction" that mechanical reproduction destroyed the aura of the original work of art and, more importantly, provided a circuit for mass mentalities and thus an access code for fascism in the twentieth century.[5] We might recall in regard to this observation Hitler's admission that without the electronic reproduction of his voice over the radio, he could never have conquered Germany. For the sake of thinking the future of lesbian bodies in postmodernity, I want to recall Benjamin's critique of the state's techno-fetishization of technologies of reproduction in the context of contemporary lesbian bodies — bodies working under a signifying regime of simulation and within an economy of repetition. Jean Baudrillard[6] has defined postmechanical reproduction as the precession of simulacra, the accession of post–World War II, postindustrial culture to a state of hyper-reality. This state is reached when cultural reproduction begins to refer first and foremost to the fact that there is no original. For Jacques Attali,[7] postmechanical reproduction marks the difference between an economy of representation, in which representative power is used to maintain belief in the harmony of the *socius,* and an economy of repetition, characterized by the repetitive mass production of all social relations and the silencing of disorder by a bureaucratic power that operates in the ambiance of a deafening syncretic flow of mass productions. The cultural reproduction of lesbian bodies in the age of (post)mechanical reproduction, that is, in an economy of simulacral repetition, has more than ever destroyed any aura of an "original" lesbian identity, while exposing the cultural sites through which lesbianism is appropriated by the political economy of postmodernity.

Benjamin noted that the aesthetic debates over the status of photography as "art" obscured the more crucial question of whether the invention of photography hadn't transformed the very nature of art. Similarly, the appearance of the public lesbian, particularly after World War II liberated her from a depression economics, raises the question of whether the "nature" of the feminine hasn't substantively changed in postmodern culture. The point is that the political economy of (post)mechanical reproduction is altering traditional values and expressions of gendered social identities as subjects of history. The subjective transformation that Benjamin was on the verge of articulating in the years approaching World War II involved the relation of technologies of representation to the human body in regard to identification. In Benjamin's reading of the broader effects of photography and film, the audience's identification had shifted from the actor (Hitler) to the camera (technology). Technical reproduction not only changes the reaction of the masses to art, it calls the masses into being in their late modern and postmodern forms as subjects, not of nature, but of technology.[8]

We are at a moment of culture, for example, when phallic body prostheses are being mass-produced in the merger of the sex industry with plastics technologies. *On Our Backs* is not the only photojournal to market artificial penises. Even *Playgirl,* marketed primarily to straight women, carries pages of advertisements for a huge assortment of phallic simulacra. We're left to wonder what these women might eventually think to do with a double-ended dildo. But there's no mistaking that the lesbian assimilation of the sex-toy industry is reterritorializing the culturally constructed aura of the phallic signifier. By appropriating the phallus/penis for themselves, lesbians have turned technoculture's semiotic regime of simulation and the political economy of consumer culture back against the naturalization of masculinist hegemony. Once the penis is mass-reproduced, any illusion of a natural link between the cultural power organized under the sign of the phallus and the penis as biological organ is exposed as artificial. The reproduction of the penis as dildo exposes the male organ as signifier of the phallus, and not vice versa — that is, the dildo exposes the cultural organ of the phallus as a simulacrum. The dildo is an artificial penis, an appropriated phallus, and a material signifier of the imaginary ground for a historically manifest phallic regime of power.

The effect on lesbian identities of this merger between the sex industry and plastics technologies is typical of the double-binds characteristic of lesbianism in postmodernity. Ironically, the validity of grounding phallic power and gendered identity in the biological sign of difference in the male body is set up for cultural reinvestigation and reinvestment once the penis itself is reproduced as signifier, that is, in the very process of mass-producing artificial penises as a marketable sign for the consumption of desiring subjects, including subjects desiring counterhegemonic identities. At the same time, the commodification of the signifier — in this case the penis as signifier of the phallus — obscures the politico-economic reproduction of straight-class relations by channeling lesbian signification from the unstable and uncertain register of the *Real* to the overly stable, imaginary register of desire of the fetish-sign (i.e., the repetitive channeling of desire into the fixed circuit that runs from the penis as phallus to the phallus as penis in an endless loop). In other words, if working-class and middle-class urban lesbians and suburban dykes can't afford health care and don't yet have real national political representation, they can nonetheless buy a ten-inch "dinger" and a matching leather harness, and they can, with no guarantees, busy themselves at the task of appropriating for lesbian identities the signs of masculine power. This situation provides *both* a possibility for self-reinvention and self-empowerment *and* an appropriation of lesbian identities — and their labor, their leisure, and their purchasing power — into the commodity logic of technoculture.

At the same time, new reproductive technologies, including artificial insemination by donor (AID), in vitro fertilization (IVF), surrogate motherhood, Lavage embryo transfer, and tissue farming as in cross-uterine egg transplants, are both reterritorializing and reifying biological relations to gendered social roles.[9] The "body" is breaking up. I'm not talking just about the working body, the confessing body, the sexual body. These are old tropes, as Foucault showed us. In postmodernity, even the organs are separating from the body. That these organs are literal makes them no less organs of power. The womb is disjunct from the breast, for example, the vagina from the mouth that speaks, the ovaries and their production from the womb, and so on, and so on. The lesbian body's relation to these reified technologies is entirely representative of the contradictions of lesbian subject positions in postmodernity. While new reproductive technologies generally reinforce a repressive straight economy of maternal production, body management, and class-privileged division of labor, the technology of cross-uterine egg transplants, although highly regulated economically, finally allows a lesbian to give birth to another lesbian's child, a fact that to date has gone entirely unmentioned by either the medical community or the media.[10]

The point is that the bodies that are the supposed ground of identity in essentialist arguments — arguments that assert we are who we are because of our bodies — are both internally fragmented in response to the intrusions of biotechnologies and advanced surgical techniques, including transsexual procedures, and externally plied by a variety of technologically determined semiotic registers ranging from the sex-toy industry to broadcast representation. As a result, lesbian identities are generating a familiar unfamiliarity of terms that San Francisco's lesbian sexpert, Susie Bright, has been busily mainstreaming on the "Phil Donahue Show" — terms as provocative as female penetration, female masculinity, S/M lipstick dykes, and lesbian phallic mothers.

While all social bodies are plied by multiple regimes of signs, as Deleuze and Guattari as well as Foucault have repeatedly shown, lesbian bodies in the age of (post)mechanical reproduction are particularly paradigmatic of a radical semiotic multiplicity. This situation is hardly surprising. That lesbians are *not* women because women are a class defined by their relation to men — a statement Monique Wittig[11] has popularized — doesn't mean we know exactly what a lesbian is. The "lesbian," especially the lesbian who resists or slips the always potential sedimentarity in that term, marks a default of identity both twice-removed and exponentially factored. Lesbians in the public culture of postmodernity are subjects-in-the-making whose body of signs and bodies as sign are up for reappropriation and revision, answering as they do the party line of technology and identity.

This double call of technology and identity complicates our understanding of lesbian bodies as minority bodies — a definition that locates lesbians within the discourse of identity by their differences from the majority bodies of the hetero woman and man. If Wittig wants to envision lesbians as "runaway slaves with no other side of the Mississippi in sight,"[12] perpetual and permanent fugitives, it's also undeniable that lesbians are at the same time, and often in the same bodies, lesbians bearing arms, lesbians bearing children, lesbians becoming fashion, becoming commodity subjects, becoming Hollywood, becoming the sex industry, or becoming cyborg human-machinic assemblages. And from the alternative point of view, we are also bearing witness to the military becoming lesbian, the mother becoming lesbian, straight women becoming lesbian, fashion and Hollywood and the sex industry becoming lesbian, middle-class women, corporate America, and technoculture becoming lesbian, and so on. That is, the lesbian body of signs, like all minority bodies, is always becoming majority, in a multiplicity of ways. But at the same time, in a multitude of domains across the general cultural field, majority bodies are busy *becoming lesbian*.[13] This notion of the transsemiotics of identities follows from Deleuze/Guattari's schizoanalysis of the postulates of linguistics, in which the linguistic notion of minority language produces its meaningful variance from a rhizomatic, not oppositional, relation to its majority others.

In the lesbian cultural landscape of postmodernity, essentialist arguments about feminine identity are more defunct than ever, while Wittig's lesbian materialist analysis of straight culture is more urgent than ever and more problematic. Even if the first social contract underpinning dominant class relations in later industrial capitalism is still the heterosexual contract, as Wittig premises in *The Straight Mind,* the cultural variables for negotiating the space of that social contract are undergoing reconfiguration in postmodernity in ways that Wittig overlooks. This is why it's crucial to think the question of contemporary lesbian bodies in the specific context of the breakdown of ontological discourses in the shift from modernity to postmodernity, because in that shift the Cartesian, total subject that Wittig wants to claim as a right and as the political goal of lesbian identity politics is more and more manifestly undergoing splittings and fragmentations.[14] The decentralization of the post-Cartesian subject of postmodern culture is not antithetical to the dis-organ-ized political economy of postindustrial society, as Deleuze and Guattari have argued in the two volumes of *Capitalism and Schizophrenia*.[15] Indeed, capitalism itself produces schizoid subjectivity as a cultural state of being. For example, the notion of self in consumer discourse as a state that can be perpetually reconstructed according to one's desire and the reification of that desire into the reproduction of class relations have, in the case of lesbians, set a political economy of signs based on the commodification of selves in contention with compulsory heterosexuality and the cultural function it and the nuclear family serve in reproducing the labor force.

Setting lesbian identities first within the context of postmodern culture suggests two further clarifications to Wittig. First, any materialist analysis of a lesbian revolutionary position in relation to straight women as a class has to begin with one irreducible conundrum of postmodernity in regard to lesbian identities. The cultural space for contemporary lesbian identities to exist — economic freedom from dependence on a man — is a historical outcome of late-industrial capitalism's commodity logic in its total war phase in the first half of the twentieth century.[16] Lillian Faderman has thoroughly documented, in *Odd Girls and Twilight Lovers,* this historical occurrence and its outcomes for urban lesbian identities, particularly during World War II recruitment and during the military purges of homosexuals in the decade following the war that sent large numbers of lesbians to urban port cities.[17] Women, particularly single women, comprised a large proportion of the substitute bodies required by the state to maintain performativity criteria established before each world war or to meet the accelerated industrial needs of total war and reconstruction. This is one of the undeniable conditions of women's entry into the work force and the professions in the United States, including the academy, and of their assimilation into the commodity marketplace beyond the domestic sphere that, along with the 1960s civil rights movement, helped to set up the possibility of the 1970s women's movement.[18] This is also part of the history of the cultural production of lesbian bodies as we know them today.

In other words, and this is my final clarification to Wittig's reading of lesbian positionality, lesbians are becoming nomad runaways *and* becoming state *at the same time.* And it's at the various sites where these interminglings of bodies take place that the cultural contradictions will be most apparent and therefore the political stakes greatest. These sites include any becoming majoritarian of the minoritarian as well as the becoming minor of majority regimes of signs, and in each of these sites the political stakes may not be equivalent. This political complication results from the theoretical challenge to materialist social analysis presented by the failure of poststructural linguistics adequately to map cultural dialects *except* as unstable and constant sites of transformation. These kinds of subcultural variance and continuous historical transformation have to be factored in any lesbian materialist modeling system if we are to continue the work Wittig has launched not only toward a lesbian materialist critique of straight-class relations, but toward a materialist critique of lesbianism itself.

A discursive multiplicity of differences has to be seen as *both* a pragmatics of appropriation by straight culture *and* as signs of actual historical and material differences within subcultural groups. It's not enough to say that our discursive differences obfuscate the material reproduction of our class relations. Yet the material manifestations of the discourse of technology have made the lines between discourse, culture, and actual social bodies increasingly difficult to distinguish. If Wittig would identify lesbians by their refusal to take on the identity of the class that provides the labor and bodies for reproducing the labor force, for example, that distinction can no longer be so easily made. Reproductive technologies and economic independence have made it even more common for lesbian bodies to be maternal bodies, if not maternal bodies bearing the phallus. The materialist mapping of lesbian identities in postmodernity will therefore have to calculate relations among commodity logic, racially segmented and gendered classes, technologies of reproduction and simulation, and a war-machine partially exterior to the state in spite of its historical appropriation under the regime of global security and within the military-industrial-labor-foreign-aid complex. Consider, for example, the yet hypothetical but virtually real instance of the feminine cyborg assemblage made manifest in a female F-16 pilot executing desert bombing raids. When this virtual state of events becomes actual, my first question will be, Is she a lesbian body?

Cultural mappings of lesbian bodies will also have to include interminglings among "minorities." These specific sites of mixing and transformation will shape the political stakes and the political strategies for a lesbian feminist/Queer Nation alliance, and any possible alliance between that configuration and ethnic minorities. Take the case, from the 1950s to the present, of lesbians becoming only with much difficulty lesbian feminists, and then becoming after even more struggle lesbian feminists of color (these hybridities were always present, of course, but for years remained invisible within the "minority" social bodies of feminism or African Americanism or Hispanic Americanism). The history of this particular struggle over

the interminglings of minoritarian social bodies is entirely representative of the dilemmas facing the traditional political notion of
identity politics grounded in a totalized, stable, and fixed subject.
In a parallel although disjunct cultural scene, there is the instance
of lesbians assimilating gay male sexual practices and the identities they mobilize — which San Francisco knows better than any
other U.S. city. Such states of hybridity are made visible respectively by Audre Lorde's biomythography as a black lesbian feminist
in *Zami*[19] and Della Grace's photographs for a leather-lesbian identity politics in *Love Bites* (1991). In Grace's portrait of "Jane, Jane,
Queen of Pain" we see a lesbian body appropriating the codes of
straight porn while assimilating S/M sexual practices arising specifically out of the situationality of gay male bar culture. Grace's images
and Lorde's candid self-portrayal, along with all the other mass-
produced representations of lesbian bodies currently circulating in
popular culture, remind us of the ways in which lesbian bodies are
crossed by multiplicitous regimes of signs.

Indeed, the potential power of lesbian identity politics in the current historical moment comes from its situatedness and alliances
among feminist, gay male, and civil rights activisms. Some lesbian
bodies are a current site of contention in the women's movement,
particularly over the issue of S/M practices and porn, because of
their greater affinities with gay males than with straight women.
Furthermore, the activist politics of ACT UP in the face of the
ideological epidemic of significations surrounding AIDS represent
for many lesbians a better strategy of cultural politics than the
consciousness-raising discourses traditionally authorized by NOW.
But in the face of direct losses on the ground gained in the 1960s,
1970s, and 1980s on women's issues — right to abortions and birth-
control information, right to protection from sexual harassment in
the workplace, right to have recourse to a just law in the case of
rape — the Queer Nation/straight-feminism alliance will be crucial
to the future of lesbian cultural politics.

This state of being lesbian in the age of postmechanical reproduction does not eradicate radical politics, but asks that we refigure
our understanding of identity politics as a politics of transformation and hybridity as well as resistance, indeed a politics working
from both inside and outside straight technoculture and the race
and class structures that it reproduces. Haraway's "A Cyborg Mani-

festo"[20] theorizes one direction that lesbians can mobilize for further developing alliance-based, unintegrated networks of power in the cultural game of identity politics. The strategy of making cyborg assemblages of bodies and technologies proposed by Haraway should have a special valence for lesbians, who as a group have a history of playing with body assemblages against which straight women's masqueradings pale by comparison.

If feminisms and Marxisms have run amuck on Continental theoretical imperatives to construct a revolutionary subject that premises metaphysical identity closure, as Haraway argues, cyborg bodies, "stripped of identity," are free to rewrite the texts of their bodies and societies without the limit-texts of god/man, self/other, culture/nature, male/female.[21] Bearing the banner of subjects-as-etching-machines, cyborg politics would be the politics of multiplicitous coding practices and noise in a system of perfect communication, a politics of many in the place of one, of hybrids in the place of boundaries. For those who have experienced the dominations of the "autonomous" self, to etch the microsurfaces of the encoding social body as something less and more than a "one" may be an empowering reconceptualization of the "family of man."

Take camp struggles over straight semiosis, for example, which gay and lesbian subcultures have always understood as a style of everyday cultural politics and survival and not as prepolitical (a reading commonly produced by straight "politicized" subjects). If we premise that the body is not outside textuality, that the body is itself a field of signification, a site for the production of cultural meanings and ideological reifications, then we have to admit that you play the game this way or that, you choose to pass or not within this scene and the next, but you can't choose to stop playing with signs, with your own *material* production as a cultural (i.e., visibly signifying) body.

If we admit that social bodies only exist in a process of constant historical transformation, then there are only hybrid bodies, moving bodies, migrant bodies, becoming bodies, machinic-assemblage bodies. And in relation to bodies of signs in postindustrial capitalism, even in the case of the most organ-ized signifying regimes, Deleuze and Guattari insist there are only *trans*semiotics.[22] It's futile then to ask what subjectivities *essentially* exist inside and alongside the transversed social bodies of postmodernity. Too many challenges facing lesbian cultural politics are rendered invisible by a discourse of essentialism. It is in this regard that Haraway's vision of unnatural, hyper-constructed social bodies in their potential, if blasphemous, positivity provides an empowering alternative strategy for thinking lesbian bodies and organ-izing lesbian cultural politics into a material (if monstrous) body of power. But thinking this circuited body that might order lesbian organs of power with and within other assemblages of identity and being will require not only Benjamin's critique of the state's techno-fetishization of technologies of reproduction, but Wittig's lesbian materialism, as well as Deleuze and Guattari's schizoanalysis of being in capitalism.

When we take up Haraway's cyborg project *for* lesbianism, for example, Wittig's essays on the political economy of lesbianism should remind us that the sites of political struggle over lesbian cyborg affinities will solidify around the historically and materially determined pragmatics of *who* gets to produce cyborg bodies, who has access, who provides the laboring and component bodies, and who becomes and who buys the commodities re-produced. If we accept that the body exists in an assemblage with technology, the "human" body itself may well appear subordinate to the cyborg body of which it is a part. Thus cultural politics not only comes in conflict with the ideal of the totalized bourgeois subject, but comes into being encrypted in and by dominant signifying regimes of the state (such as media politics, the commodification of desires, new reproductive technologies, Star Wars, techno-progress, C_3I, and globalization). The problem of organ-ized agency will take on a dimensionality involving spatial and temporal coordinates of multiplicitous, rhizomatic collective social "identities." In each case, we'd have to reconsider where a cyborg body begins and ends (the limits of the text), for example, or when an exteriority is also an interiority. And who will have ownership of the means of cyborg production and reproduction?

Lesbian bodies are not essentially counterhegemonic sites of culture, as Wittig might like to theorize. The lesbian may not be a woman, as she argues in "One Is Not Born a Woman," yet she is not entirely exterior to straight culture.[23] Each lesbian has a faciality touching on some aspect of a majority signifying regime of postmodernity, whether that be masculinity/femininity, motherhood, race or the nation-state, the sex industry, technologies of simulation, surgical techno-plasties, the commodification of selves and knowledges, reproductive technologies, or the military under global capitalism. Lesbians are inside and outside, minority and majority, *at the same time*.

Lesbian bodies have always presented a challenge to essentialist notions of feminine identity, and never more so than when lesbians are set in the historical context of postmodernity. The cultural period in late-industrial and postindustrial society during World War II and in the fifty years since is their historical heyday. Lesbian bodies came of age under the specter of a holocaust that could reach finality only by the injection into the global symbolic of a nuclear sublime so horrific as to arrest all prior signification. Their agencies must be agencies that work with the reduced political rights of a worldwide civilian population under the new military regime of global security (Virilio). They are proffered a variety of prostheses and self-imaging technologies, in fact, a variety of bodies, as long as they meet the performativity criterion of commodity logic. And if they are runaways, they're running from the very political economy that produced their possibility. This is their double bind. For all these reasons, the immediate challenge facing lesbian bodies in postmodernity is how to make a dis-organ-ized body of signs and identities work for a progressive, or even a radical, politics.

NOTES

1. Della Grace, *Love Bites* (London: GMP, 1991).

2. Photographic and electronic imaging media — including photo-journals, popular film, broadcast and cable TV, home-video, and on-line transmissions — have mainstreamed lesbian images by disseminating them to broadcast audiences. The popular controversy over Madonna's *Justify Your Love* music video, which appeared late in 1990, exemplifies the continual process of semiotic assimilation. In this postmodern conundrum, Madonna not only *becomes lesbian* for a portion of the tape, but the lesbian subtext becomes, if not MTV, then broadcast news — specifically ABC's *Nightline*, which aired the video in its entirety to millions of late-night television viewers. *ELLE*'s butch-femme aesthetic — which has managed not to "go too far," as Madonna's video did — is successfully becoming majority fashion-feminine for a growing segment of the middle-class and upper-middle-class women's market. *L.A. Law* in the meanwhile is mainstreaming for prime-time soap audiences the everyday aporias of how to comport oneself with, as, and for a lesbian. *Thelma and Louise,* making the cover of *Time* the summer of its release with a photograph of Sarandon and Geena Davis looking both butch *and* exactly like each other under the heading "Why *Thelma and Louise* Strikes a Nerve" (June 24, 1991), is just another event in a long series of discursive assimilations that are producing the popular cultural

generation of the new butch-femme. Lesbians are both out and they are "passing" as versions of normative femininity.

3. The dis-organ-ized body, in Deleuze and Guattari's (1987) micromental study of capitalism and schizophrenia, is the Body without Organs (BwO) (Gilles Deleuze and Félix Guattari, *Capitalism and Schizophrenia* [Minneapolis: University of Minnesota Press, 1983, 1987]).

4. See Sandy Stone's account of and critique of the "gender dysphoria syndrome" in "The Empire Strikes Back: A Posttranssexual Manifesto," in *Body Guards*.

5. According to Walter Ong, mechanical production began with the reification of the oral world/word into print. Typography "literally" made the word into a commodity (*Orality and Literacy* [New York: Routledge, 1985], 119, 131).

6. Jean Baudrillard, *In the Shadow of the Silent Majorities* (New York: Semiotext[e], 1983).

7. Jacques Attali, *Noise* (Minneapolis: University of Minnesota Press, 1985).

8. Benjamin's discourse comes close to a discourse of degenerescence and decadence anchored in a notion of the natural when he reads mechanical reproduction as a process of cultural "liquidation," and when he approaches the historical object as if it were analogous to the aura of the "natural" object. He's reluctant to let go of the modern notion of history as comprised of objects bearing the same permanence and value as nature, and for good reason — fascism was obviously in its pragmatics a project of rewriting history. This is the contradiction of any nationalist totalitarian regime of signs: its fetishization of technologies at the very same time that it mobilizes remnant traces of a romantic notion of the "natural" *socius*. Perhaps Benjamin couldn't bring himself to say in public that the "authority" of the traditional cultural heritage that he appeals to in the face of fascism is itself purely constructed — depending on its own class structures and techniques of representation for reproduction and enforcement. The (constructed) authority of this "original" heritage in the minds of the masses would be appropriated more easily than anyone could have imagined by fascist dream machines using the new technologies of mass reproduction, epitomized in the Nazi's use of broadcast radio and the newsreel — media that Benjamin correctly recognized as new forms of armaments ("Work of Art," 213). The Nazi's genocidal program would demonstrate that history *could* be rewritten, in a matter of a few years, and that the "real" history that should have saved the world from the kind of contorted fantasy of national history and identity that was cathected onto Hitler had no *essential* authority whatsoever. Fascism, in fact, proceeds as a possibility from the very moment that the masses come to perceive themselves as the technologized subject of nature, and no longer as object of nature.

9. Gena Corea, *The Mother Machine: Reproductive Technology from Artificial Insemination to Artificial Wombs* (New York: Harper and Row, 1986); Christine Overall, *The Future of Human Reproduction* (Ontario: Women's Press, 1989).

10. The legal implications of this scenario await testing in regard to the law recognizing both the biological mother and birth mother as legal parents bearing full rights. I'm assuming in the scenario an artificial insemination by anonymous donor (AID).

11. Monique Wittig, *The Straight Mind* (Boston: Beacon Press, 1992).

12. Ibid.

13. The more this process of becoming minority occurs, however (and, of course, it's always occurring), the more difficult it becomes for the majority body to "resist

infiltration," and the more necessary it becomes for dominant straight culture ("traditional values coalitions," etc.) to protect all borders fronting on otherness. "Resisting infiltration" suggests a paranoid posture — one that denies the constant process of psychic auto-organization and reorganization, a process made visible particularly by subcultural collective identities organized around the erotic cultivation of the intersubjective transactions and psychic instabilities common to amatory relations. For this reason, Julia Kristeva describes amorous relations as the *vertigo of identity* (*Tales of Love* [New York: Columbia University Press, 1987]). Rather than return the gaze of a body functioning manifestly as a collapsed inside/outside system in interaction with a multidimensional and fluid (i.e., excessive, unnatural, monstrous) psychic system, the paranoid will take flight to a prolapsed symbolic, thereby stabilizing the illusion that identity is a stable relation to a fixed sign formation (i.e., a natural signatory relation of self to others).

14. See Wittig's argument for a lesbian total subject in "The Mark of Gender," in *Straight Minds.*

15. Deleuze and Guattari, *Capitalism and Schizophrenia.*

16. See Rudy Willis, *Total War and Twentieth-Century Higher Learning: Universities of the Western World in the First and Second World Wars* (Cranberry, N.J.: Farleigh-Dickinson University Press, 1991), particularly the chapter "Substitute Bodies."

17. Lillian Faderman, *Odd Girls and Twilight Lovers: A History of Lesbian Lives in America* (New York: Columbia University Press, 1991).

18. The 1970s women's movement and the 1960s African-American civil rights movement shared some of the same problematic ties to the war machine, through the substitute bodies recruitment policy in U.S. universities during World War II and through the G.I. Bill.

19. Audre Lorde, *Zami* (Freedom, Calif.: Crossing Press, 1983).

20. Donna Haraway, "A Cyborg Manifesto," in *Simians, Cyborgs, and Women: The Reinvention of Nature* (New York: Routledge, 1991).

21. Ibid., 176.

22. Deleuze and Guattari, *Capitalism and Schizophrenia.*

23. Wittig, *Straight Mind.*

Queer Nationality

Lauren Berlant and Elizabeth Freeman

> *Now the skins felt powerful and human. They became lords of sounds and lesser things. They passed nations through their mouths. They sat in judgment.*
>
> Zora Neale Hurston,
Their Eyes Were Watching God

> *We Are Everywhere. We Want Everything.*
>
> Queer Nation, Gay Pride Parade,
New York 1991

I Pledge Allegiance to the F(l)ag

At the end of Sandra Bernhard's *Without You I'm Nothing,* the diva wraps herself in an American flag. This act, which emblazons her interpretation of Prince's "Little Red Corvette," culminates her performance of feminine drag, feminist camp. Staging not a cross-dressing that binarizes sex but a masquerade that smudges the clarity of gender, Bernhard frames "woman" within a constellation of sexual practices whose forms of publicity change by the decade, by subcultural origin, by genres of pleasure (music, fashion, political theater), and by conventions of collective erotic fantasy. But having sexually overdressed for the bulk of the film, Bernhard strips down to a flag and a sequined red, white, and blue G-string and pasties, and thus: exposes a national body, her body. This national body does not address a mass or abstract audience of generic Americans;

nor does it campily evoke a "typical" American citizen's nostalgia for collective memory, ritual, and affect. Bernhard flags her body to mark a fantasy of erotic identification with someone present, in the intimate room: it is a national fantasy, displayed as a spectacle of desire, and a fantasy, apparently external to the official national frame, of communion with a black woman whose appearance personifies "authenticity."

At the same time, also in 1990, Madonna responded to a civic crisis marked by voter apathy among youth by performing in a pro-voting commercial stripped down to a bikini and wrapped alluringly in an American flag. In this commercial the blond bombshell is flanked by a black and a white man dressed in the clone semiotic that flags a certain East Coast urban gay community style. These men sing "Get Out and Vote" in discordant comic harmony with Madonna, while they wave little flags and she flashes her body by undulating a big one.

On March 24, 1991, the *Chicago Tribune Magazine* featured the Gulf War as a fashion event. Adding to the already widely publicized rush by citizens to own their very own gas masks and military fatigues, supplementing the fad for patriotic T- and sweatshirts bearing American flags and mottoes like "These colors won't run," this style section, titled "Red, White, and You," featured the new rage in feminine fashion: red, white, and blue. Mobilized by the patriotic furor generated by the war, women en masse were signifying through the color combination and not the icon, capitalizing on the capacity of the flag's traces to communicate personal politics without explicit polemic. The dissolution of the flag into flagness also protected the consumer from being charged with desecrating the flag, should it become stained with food or sweat, or singed with the dropped ashes of a cigarette.

In 1991, *RFD*, a magazine for rural gays with connections to the Radical Faeries, featured the image of a naked young white man with an erection on a pedestal, set against the background of an American flag. Two captions graced this portrait: "Bring our boys home and whole this solstice peace now!" and "What could be more American than young, hard man/boy flesh?"

A rhetorical question? Having witnessed this rush to consume the flag, to fuse it with the flesh, we conclude that at present the nation suffers from *Americana nervosa,* a compulsive self-gorging on ritual images. This grotesque fantasy structure was paraded in the 1988 presidential election by the Republican flap over whether citizens should be legally obliged to say the Pledge of Allegiance. It was further extended from mass public struggle into the Supreme Court by constitutional battles over whether the flag should be exposed to mortality's contagion in the form of its own ashes or dirt, and has recast national patriotism as a question not of political identity, but of proper public expression, loyal self-censorship, and personal discipline. No longer is the struggle to secure national discursive propriety located mainly on the general terrain of "freedom of speech," state policies against certain sexual practices, and the regulation of privately consumed sexual images within the U.S. mail: the struggle is now also over proper public submission to national iconicity, and over the nation's relation to gender, to sexuality, and to death.

If, in the wake of the election and the remilitarization of America, official patriotic discourse casts the American flag in an epidemic crisis, and struggles to manage its public meaning through a sublime collectively manufactured consent, the consumption of nationality in the 1990s appears motivated not by a satisfaction that already exists but by a collective desire to reclaim the nation for pleasure, and specifically the pleasure of spectacular public self-entitlement. Queer Nation has taken up the project of coordinating a new nationality. Its relation to nationhood is multiple and ambiguous, however, taking as much from the insurgent nationalisms of oppressed peoples as from the revolutionary idealism of the United States. Since its inception in 1990 it has invented collective local rituals of resistance, mass cultural spectacles, an organization, and even a lexicon to achieve these ends. It aims to capitalize on the difficulty of locating the national "public" whose consent to self-expression founds modern national identity.[1]

Queer Nation's outspoken promotion of a national sexuality not only discloses that mainstream national identity touts a subliminal sexuality more official than a state flower or national bird, but also makes explicit how thoroughly the local experience of the body is framed by laws, policies, and social customs regulating sexuality. Queer Nation's tactics of invention appropriate for gay politics both grass-roots and mass-mediated forms of countercultural resistance from left, feminist, and civil rights movements of the "sixties" —

the ones that insisted that the personal is political, engaging the complex relation between local and national practices. Also, in the retro-nostalgia impulse of postmodernism, Queer Nation redeploys these tactics in a kind of guerrilla warfare that names all concrete and abstract spaces of social communication as places where "the people" live, and thus as "national" sites ripe both for transgression and legitimate visibility.[2] Its tactics are to cross borders, to occupy spaces, and to mime the privileges of normality — in short, to simulate "the national" with a camp inflection. This model of political identity imitates not so much the "one man one vote" caucus polemic mentality of mainstream politics, but rather the individual and mass identities of consumers: Queer Nation, itself a collection of local affinity groups, has produced images, occupied public spaces of consumption like bars and malls, and refunctioned the culture of the trademark.[3] Exploiting the structures of identification and the embodied and disembodied scenes of erotic contact, substitution, publicity, and exchange so central to the allure of nationalism and capitalism, Queer Nation operates precisely in the American mode.[4]

In this essay we seek to understand the political logic of Queer Nationality and to trace the movement's spectacular intentions and effects. We will, in the next three sections, describe Queer Nation in its strongest tactical moments, as when it exploits the symbolic designs of mass and national culture in order to dismantle the standardizing apparatus that organizes all manner of sexual practice into "facts" of sexual *identity*,[5] as when it mobilizes a radically wide range of knowledge — modes of understanding from science to gossip — to reconstitute "information" about queerness, thus transforming the range of reference "queer" has by multiplying its specifications.[6] Whether or not Queer Nation survives as an organization past the present tense of our writing,[7] the movement provides us with these discursive political tactics not simply as fodder for history but also as a kind of incitement to reformulate the conditions under which further interventions into the juridical, policy, and popular practices of contemporary America must be thought and made.[8]

This demands an expanded politics of description. We might say, "an expended politics of *erotic* description," but crucial to a sexually radical movement for social change is the transgression of categorical distinctions between sexuality and politics, with their typically embedded divisions between public, private, and personal concerns. The multiplicity of social spaces, places where power and desire are enacted and transferred, needs to be disaggregated, specified: the abstract, disembodied networks of electronic visual, aural, and textual communication; the nationalized systems of juridical activity and official public commentary; the state and local political realms that are not at all simply microcosmic of the national; the manifestly pleasuring or money-making embodiments of local, national, and global capitalism; the random or customary interactions of social life — this sentence could, and must, go on interminably. These spaces are hard to describe because they are all unbounded, dialectically imagined, sometimes powerful, sometimes irrelevant to the theory, practice, and transformation of sexual hegemony. Whatever they are, at the moment they are resolutely national. Queer Nation's nationalist-style camp counterpolitics incorporates this discursive and territorial problem, shifting between a utopian politics of identity, difference, dispersion, and specificity and a pluralist agenda in the liberal sense that imagines a "gorgeous mosaic" of difference without a model of conflict. Our final section, "With *You* Out We're Nothing, and Beyond," supports and extends Queer Nation's contestation of existing cultural spaces, but seeks to reopen the question of nationalism's value as an infidel model of transgression and resistance: for the very naturalizing stereotypes of official nationality can inflect even the most radical insurgent forms. In other words, this is an antiassimilationist narrative about an antiassimilationist movement. However, it must be emphasized that disidentification with U.S. nationality is not, at this moment, even a theoretical option for Queer citizens: as long as PWAs (Persons with AIDS) require state support, as long as the official nation invests its identity in the pseudoright to police nonnormative sexual representations and sexual practices, the lesbian, gay, feminist, and queer communities in the United States do not have the privilege to disregard national identity. We are compelled, then, to read America's lips. What can we do to force the officially constituted nation to speak a new political tongue?

Recently, official America has sought to manage an explicit relation between national power and the vulnerable body by advertising an unironic consecration of masculine military images and surgical incisions into the borders of other sovereign nations; Queer Nation, in dramatic contrast, produces images in response to the massive violence against racial, sexual, gendered, and impoverished populations within the U.S. borders, a violence emblematized by but in no way limited to the federal response to AIDS. A brief history of the movement will help to explain the genesis of its polymorphous impulses. Founded at an ACT UP New York meeting in April 1990, Queer Nation aimed to extend the kinds of democratic counterpolitics deployed on behalf of AIDS activism for the transformation of public sexual discourse in general. Douglas Crimp and Adam Rolston's *AIDS Demo Graphics* is to date the fullest and most graphic record of ACT UP's intervention into local, state, and national systems of power and publicity.[9] This specification of mainstream sites of power was made necessary by federal stonewalling on the subject of AIDS treatment, support, and education among institutions in the political public sphere, where the bureaucratic norm is to disavow accountability to vulnerable populations. ACT UP recognizes the necessity to master the specific functions of political bureaucracies and to generate loud demands that these live up to their promise to all of "the people." Among other strategies, it exploits the coincidence between national and commercial spectacle by pirating advertising techniques: an alliance with the political artists called Gran Fury has produced a sophisticated poster campaign to transform the passive public space of New York into a zone of political pedagogy. Queer Nation takes from ACT UP this complex understanding of political space as fundamental to its insistence on making all public spheres truly safe for all of the persons who occupy them, not just in psychic loyalty but in everyday and embodied experience. To be safe in the national sense means not just safe from bashing, not just safe from discrimination, but safe *for* demonstration, in the mode of patriotic ritual, which always involves a deployment of affect, knowledge, spectacle, and, crucially, a kind of banality, ordinariness, popularity.

Through its activism Queer Nation seeks to redefine the community — its rights, its visibility — and take it into what's been claimed as straight political and social space. "QUEERS READ THIS" asks to be read as the accompanying declaration of nationalism. It says: In this culture, being queer means you've been condemned to death; appreciate our power and our bond; realize that whenever one of us is hurt we all suffer; know that we have to fight for ourselves because no one else will. It says, this is why we are a *nation* of queers, and why you must feel yourself a part. Its language seems to borrow from other, equally "threatening" power movements — black nationalist, feminist separatist.[10]

The key to the paradoxes of Queer Nation is the way it *exploits* internal difference. That is, Queer Nation understands the propriety of queerness to be a function of the diverse spaces in which it aims to become explicit. It names multiple local and national publics; it does not look for a theoretical coherence to regulate in advance all of its tactics: all politics in the Queer Nation are imagined on the *street*. Finally, it always refuses closeting strategies of assimilation and goes for the broadest and most explicit assertion of presence. This loudness involves two main kinds of public address: internal, for the production of safe collective queer spaces, and external, in a cultural pedagogy emblematized by the post–Black Power slogan, "We're here. We're queer. Get used to it." If "I'm black and I'm proud" sutures the first-person performative to racial visibility, transforming the speaker from racial object to ascendant subject, Queer Nation's slogan stages the shift from silent absence into present speech, from nothingness to collectivity, from a politics of embodiment to one of space, whose power erupts from the ambiguity of "here." Where?

Inside: I Hate Straights, and Other "Queeritual" Prayers

Nancy Fraser's recent essay on postmodernity and identity politics argues that countercultural groups engage in a dialectic with mainstream public culture, shifting between internal self-consolidation and reinvestment of the relatively essentialist "internal" identity into the normalizing discussions of the mass public sphere.[11] In this dialectic, the subaltern indeed becomes a speaking player in her own public identity, for the public is an intelligibly "dominant" space characterized by collective norms. Fraser's model does not work for Queer Nation, which neither recognizes a single internal or privatized interest nor certifies one "mainstream" whose disposition constitutes the terrain for counterpolitics. This distinguishing mark of Queer Nation — its capacity to include cultural resistance, opposition, and subcultural consolidation in a mix of tactics from identity politics and postmodern metropolitan information flows —

will thus govern our "inside" narrative. We will shuttle between a dispersed variety of Queer National events, falsely bringing into narrative logic and collective intentionality what has been a deliberately unsystematized politics.

If there is one manifesto of this polyvocal movement, defining the lamination of a gay liberation politics and new gay power tactics, it is, famously, the "I Hate Straights" polemic distributed as a broadside at the gay pride parades in New York and Chicago in the summer of 1990. "I Hate Straights," printed (at least in Chicago) over the image of a raised clenched masculine fist, is a monologue, a slave narrative without decorum, a manifesto of rage and its politics. Gone, the assimilationist patience of some gay liberation identity politics; gone, the assertive rationality of the "homosexual" subject who seeks legitimacy by signifying, through "straight" protocols, that "civilization" has been sighted on the cultural margin.[12]

"I Hate Straights," instead, "proceeds in terms of the unavoidable usefulness of something that is very dangerous."[13] What is dangerous is rage, and the way it is deployed both to an "internal" audience of gay subjects and an "external" straight world. The broadside begins with personal statements: "I have friends. Some of them are straight. Year after year, I see my straight friends. I want to see them, to see how they are doing, . . . [and] [y]ear after year I continue to realize that the facts of my life are irrelevant to them and that I am only half listened to." The speaker remains unheard because straights refuse to believe that gay subjects are in exile from privilege, from ownership of a point of view that American social institutions and popular cultural practices secure: "[I]nsiders claim that [gays] already are" included in the privileges of the straight world. But gay subjects are excluded from the privileges of procreation, of family, of the public fantasy that circulates through these institutions: indeed it seems that only the public discipline of gayness keeps civilization from "melt[ing] back into the primeval ooze."

In the face of an exile caused by this arrogant heterosexual presumption of domestic space and privilege, the speaker launches into a list of proclamations headed by "I hate straights": "I" hates straights on behalf of the gay people who have to emotionally "take care" of the straights who feel guilty for their privilege; "I" hates straights for requiring the sublimation of gay rage as the price of their beneficent tolerance. "You'll catch more flies with honey," the speaker hears;

"Now look who's generalizing," they say, as if the minoritized group itself had invented the "crude taxonomy" under which it labored.[14] In response, the flier argues, "BASH BACK.... LET YOURSELF BE ANGRY...THAT THERE IS NO PLACE IN THIS COUNTRY WHERE WE ARE SAFE."

The speaker's designation of "country" as the space of danger complexly marks the indices of social identity through which this invective circulates. "I" mentions two kinds of "we": gay and American subjects, all of whom have to "thank President Bush for planting a fucking tree" in public while thousands of PWAs die for lack of political visibility. The nation of the Bush and the tree here becomes a figure of nature that includes the malignant neglect of AIDS populations, including and especially (here) gay men. Straights ask the gay community to self-censor, because anger is not "productive": meanwhile, the administrators of straight America commit omissions of policy to assert that healthy heterosexual identity (the straight and undiseased body) is a prerequisite to citizenship of the United States. The treatise goes on to suggest that the national failure to secure justice for all citizens is experienced locally, in public spaces where physical gay-bashing takes place, and in even more intimate sites like the body: "Go tell [straights to] go away until they have spent a month walking hand in hand in public with someone of the same sex. After they survive that, then you'll hear what they have to say about queer anger. Otherwise, tell them to shut up and listen."

The distribution of this document to a predominantly gay population at gay pride parades underscores a fundamental Queer Nation policy. *Visibility* is critical if a safe public existence is to be forged for American gays, for whom the contemporary nation has no positive political value. The cities where Queer Nation lives already contain local gay communities, locales that secure spaces of safe embodiment for capital and sexual expenditures. For Queer Nation they also constitute sites within which political bases can be founded. This emphasis on safe spaces, secured for bodies by capital and everyday life practices, also, finally, constitutes a refusal of the terms national discourse uses to frame the issue of sexuality: "Being queer is not about a right to privacy: it is about the freedom to be public.... It's not about the mainstream, profit-margins, patriotism, patriarchy or being assimilated.... Being queer is 'grass roots' because we know that everyone of us, every body, every cunt, every heart and ass and dick is a world of pleasure waiting to be explored. Everyone of us is a world of infinite possibility." Localness, here transposed into the language of worldness, is dedicated to producing a new politics from the energy of a sentimentally and erotically excessive sexuality. The ambiguities of this sexual geography are fundamental to producing the new referent, a gay community whose erotics and politics are transubstantial. Meanwhile, in the hybrid Queer/American nation, orthodox forms of political agency linger, in modified form: for example, Queer Nation proclaims that "an army of lovers cannot lose!" But this military fantasy refers in its irony to a set of things: counterviolences in local places; 1960s movements to make love, not war; and also the invigorated persecution of queer subjects in the U.S. military during the Reagan/Bush years.

Thus too the self-proclaimed "queeritual" element in some Queer Nation productions exceeds secular American proprieties, as in broadsides that replace "I pledge allegiance to the flag" with "I praise life with my vulva" and "I praise God with my erection" (see figures 2 and 3).[15] Although we might say that this queerituality is reactionary, reflecting a suprapolitical move to spiritual identity, we might also say that this is literally conservative, an attempt to save space for hope, prayer, and simple human relations, a Queer Nation version of "Now I lay me down to sleep." These pieties assert the luck the praying subjects feel to be sleeping with someone of their own sex, thus promoting homosexuality in the way Queer Nation wants to do, as a mode of ordinary identification and pleasure. But these prayers also parody the narrative convention of normative prayer to find a safe space for eluding official and conventional censorship of public sexuality: *Thing* magazine reports, indeed, that the broadside has come under criticism for seeming to promote promiscuity.[16] In our view, the prayers counter the erotophobia of gay and straight publics who want to speak of "lifestyles" and not sex. Finally, just as the genre of the circulating broadside reveals how gay and straight populations topographically overlap, so does this use of prayer itself avow the futility of drawing comprehensive affective boundaries between gay and straight subjects. Queer Nation's emphasis on public language and media, its exploitation of the tension between local embodiment and mass abstraction, forfeits the possibility of such taxonomic clarity.

Figure 2

Figure 3

Outside: Politics in Your Face

On February 23, 1967, in a congressional hearing concerning the security clearance of gay men for service in the Defense Department, a psychiatrist named Dr. Charles Socarides testified that the homosexual "does not know the boundary of his own body. He does not know where his body ends and space begins."[17] Precisely: the spiritual and other moments of internal consolidation that we have described allow the individual bodies of Queer Nationals to act as visibly queer flash cards, in an ongoing project of cultural pedagogy aimed at exposing the range and variety of bounded spaces upon which heterosexual supremacy depends. Moving out from the psychological and physical "safe spaces" it creates, Queer Nation broadcasts the straightness of "public space," and hence its explicit or implicit danger to gays. The queer body — as an agent of publicity, as a unit of self-defense, and finally as a spectacle of ecstasy — becomes the locus where mainstream culture's discipline of gay citizens is written and where the pain caused by this discipline is transformed into rage and pleasure. Using alternating strategies of menace and merriment, agents of Queer Nation have come to see and conquer places that present the danger of *violence* to gays and lesbians, to reterritorialize them.

Twenty-three years after Dr. Socarides's mercifully brief moment of fame, New Yorkers began to display on their chests a graphic interpretation of his fear for the national defense. The T-shirt they wore portrays a silhouette of the United States, with the red tint of the East Coast and the blue tint of the West Coast fading and blending in the middle. Suddenly, the heartland of the country is a shocking new shade of queer: red, white, and blue make lavender. This, Queer Nation's first T-shirt, extends the project of an earlier graphic produced by Adam Rolston, which shows a placard that reads "I Am Out, Therefore I Am." But Queer Nation's shirt locates the public space in which the individual Cartesian subject must be out, transforming that space in order to survive. Queer Nation's design maps a psychic and bodily territory — lavender territory — that cannot be colonized and expands it to include, potentially, the entire nation. This lamination of the country to the body conjoins individual and national liberation: just as Dr. Socarides dreaded, the boundaries between what constitutes individual and what constitutes national space are explicitly blurred. "National Defense" and "Heterosexual Defense" become interdependent projects of boundary-maintenance that Queer Nation graphically undermines, showing that these colors *will* run.

While the Queer Nation shirt exploits heterosexist fears of the "spread of a lifestyle" through dirty laundry by publicizing its wearer as both a gay native and a missionary serving the spread of homosexuality, not all of its tactics are this benign. The optimistic assertion that an army of lovers cannot lose masks the seriousness with which Queer Nation has responded to the need for a pseudomilitia on the order of the Guardian Angels. The Pink Panthers, initially conceived of at a Queer Nation meeting but eventually splitting off into a separate organization, provided a searing response to the increased violence that has accompanied the general increase of gay visibility in America. The Panthers, a foot patrol that straddles the "safe spaces" described in the first section and the "unsafe spaces" of public life in America, not only defend other queer bodies but aim to be a continual reminder of them. Dressed in black T-shirts with pink triangles enclosing a black paw print, they move unarmed in groups, linked by walkie-talkies and whistles. In choosing a uniform that explicitly marks them as targets, as successors of the Black Power movement, and as seriocomic detectives, the Panthers bring together the abstract threat implicit in the map graphic described above, the embodied threat implicit in individual queers crossing their subcultural boundaries, and the absurdity that founds this condition of sexual violence.

Their slogan is "Bash Back." It announces that the locus of gay oppression has shifted from the legal to the extralegal arena, and from national-juridical to ordinary everyday forms.[18] The menace of "Bash Back" reciprocates the menace of physical violence that keeps gays and lesbians invisible and/or physically restricted to their mythically safe neighborhoods. But rather than targeting specific gay-bashers or lashing out at random heterosexuals, the Panthers train in self-defense techniques and travel unarmed: "Bash Back" simply intends to mobilize the threat gay-bashers use so effectively — strength not in numbers, but in the presence of a few bodies who represent the potential for widespread violence — against the bashers themselves. In this way, the slogan turns the bodies of the Pink Panthers into a psychic counterthreat, expanding their protective shield beyond the confines of their physical "beat." Perhaps the most assertive "bashing" that the uniformed bodies of the Pink Panthers deliver is mnemonic. Their spectacular presence counters heterosexual culture's will-to-not-recognize its own intense need to reign in a sexually pure environment. While the rage of "Bash Back" responds to embodied and overt violence, Queer Nation's "Queer Nights Out" redress the more diffuse and implicit violence of sexual conventionality by mimicking the hackneyed forms of straight social life. "Queer Nights Out" are moments of radical desegregation with roots in civil rights era lunch counter sit-ins; whereas the 1960s sit-ins addressed legal segregation, these queer sorties confront customary segregation. Invading straight bars, for example, queers stage a production of sentimentality and pleasure that broadcasts the ordinariness of the queer body. The banality of twenty-five same-sex couples making out in a bar and the silliness of a group of fags playing spin-the-bottle efface the distance crucial to the ordinary pleasures straight society takes in the gay world. Neither informational nor particularly spectacular, Queer Nights Out demonstrate two ominous truths to heterosexual culture: one, that gay sexual identity is no longer a reliable foil for straightness, and, two, that what looked like bounded gay subcultural activity has itself become restless and improvisatory, taking its pleasures in a theater near you.

Queer Nights Out have also appropriated the model of the surprise attack — which the police have traditionally used to show gays and lesbians that even the existence of their subcultural spaces is contingent upon the goodwill of straights. Demonstrating that the boundedness of heterosexual spaces is also contingent upon the (enforced) willingness of gays to remain invisible, queers are thus using exhibitionism to make public space psychically unsafe for unexamined heterosexuality. In one report from the field, two lesbians were sighted sending a straight woman an oyster, adding a Sapphic appetizer to the menu of happy hour delights. The straight woman was not amused.[19] Embarrassment was generated — the particular embarrassment liberals suffer when the sphere allotted to the tolerated exceeds the boundaries "we all agree upon." Maneuvers such as this reveal that straight mating techniques, supposed to be "Absolutly Het," are sexual lures available to any brand of pleasure: "Sorry, you looked like a dyke to me."[20] This political transgression of "personal space" can even be used to deflect the violence it provokes. Confronted by a defensive and hostile drunk, a Queer Nation gayboy addresses the room: "Yeah, I had him last night, and he was terrible."

In this place of erotic exchange, the army of lovers takes as its war strategies "some going down and butt-fucking and other theatricals."[21] The genitals become not just organs of erotic thanksgiving, but weapons of pleasure against their own oppression. These kinds of militant-erotic interventions take their most public form in the Queer Nation kiss-in, in which an official space such as a city plaza is transfused with the juices of unofficial enjoyment: embarrassment, pleasure, spectacle, longing, and accusation interarticulate to produce a public scandal that is, as the following section will reveal, Queer Nation's specialty.

Hyper-Space: "Try Me On, I'm Very You"

In its most postmodern moments, Queer Nation takes on a corporate strategy in order to exploit the psychic unboundedness of consumers who depend upon products to articulate, produce, and satisfy their desires.[22] Queer Nation tactically uses the hyper-spaces created by the corporeal trademark, the metropolitan parade, the shopping mall, print media, and finally advertising, to recognize and take advantage of the consumer's pleasure in vicarious identification. In this guise the group commandeers permeable sites, apparently apolitical spaces through which the public circulates in a pleasurable, consensual exchange of bodies, products, identities, and information. Yet it abandons the conciliatory mode of, for instance, Kirk and Madsen's plan to market "positive" (read "tolerable") gay images to straight culture.[23] Instead, it aims to produce a series of elaborate blue-light specials on the queer body. The Queer National corporate strategy — to reveal to the consumer desires he/she didn't know he/she had, to make his/her identification with the product "homosexuality" both an unsettling and a pleasurable experience — makes consumer pleasure central to the transformation of public culture, thus linking the utopian promises of the commodity with those of the nation.

One particular celebrity oscillates between local/embodied and corporate/abstract sexual identification: the bootleg "Queer Bart" T-shirt produced by Queer Nation in the summer of 1990. Queer Bart reconfigures Matt Groening's bratty, white, suburban anykid, Bart Simpson, into the New York gay clone: he wears an earring, his own Queer Nation T-shirt, and a pink triangle button. The balloon coming out of his mouth reads, "Get used to it, dude!" Like all bodies, Queer Bart's body is a product that serves a number of functions. In the first place, he provides a countertext to the apparent harmlessness of the suburban American generic body: Queer Nation's Bart implicitly points a finger at another bootleg T-shirt in which Bart snarls, "Back off, faggot!" and at the heterosexuality that Normal Bart's generic identity assumes. In the second place, the original Bart's "clone-ness," when inflected with an "exceptional" identity — Black Bart, Latino Bart, and so on — not only stages the ability of subcultures to fashion cultural insiderhood for their members, but also reinscribes subcultural identity into mainstream style. The exuberant inflection of Bart Simpson as queer speaks to the pleasures of assuming an official normative identity, signified on the body, for those whom dominant culture consistently represents as exceptional.

Queer Nation's reinflection of Bart's body, which, precisely because it *is* a body, readily lends itself to any number of polymorphously perverse identities, graphically demonstrates that the commodity is a central means by which individuals tap into the collective experience of public desire. Queer Bart, himself a trademark, is a generic body stamped with Queer Nation's own trademarked aesthetic, which then allows consumers to publicly identify themselves as members of a trademarked "nation."[24] Thus he embodies the nonspaces we will discuss in the following paragraphs: his own unboundedness as a commodity identity exploits the way that the fantasy of being something else merges with the stereotype to confer an endlessly shifting series of identities upon the consumer's body.[25]

The genealogy of the Queer Bart strategy extends from the gay pride parades of the 1970s, when for the first time gay bodies organized into a visible public ritual. In addition to offering gays and lesbians an opportunity to experience their private identities in an official spectacle, the parades also offered flamboyant and ordinary homosexuality as something the heterosexual spectator could encounter without having to go "underground" — to drag shows or gay bars, for voyeuristic pleasure or casual sex.[26] In the last twenty years, the representation of "gayness" in the gay pride parade has changed, for its marching population is no longer defined by sexual practice alone. Rather, the current politicization of gay issues in the metropolitan and civic public spheres has engendered broadly based alliances, such that progressive "straights" can pass as "queer" in their collective political struggles.[27] As a result, the gay pride parade no longer produces the ominous gust of an enormous closet door opening; its role in consolidating identity varies widely, depending on what kind of communication participants think the parade involves. While gay pride parades have not yet achieved the status in mainstream culture of, for instance, St. Patrick's Day parades (in which people "go Irish for a day" by dressing in green), they have thus become pluralistic and inclusive, involving approval-seeking, self-consolidating, saturnalian, and transgressive moments of spectacle.[28] Although Queer Nation marches in traditional gay pride parades, it has updated and complicated the strategy of the parade, recognizing that the planned, distanced, and ultimately contained nature of the form offers only momentary displacement of heterosexual norms: after all, one can choose not to go to a parade, or one can watch the scene go by without becoming even an imaginary participant.

In parades through urban American downtowns, Queer Nationals often chant, "We're here, we're queer, we're not going shopping." But shopping itself provides the form of a tactic when Queer Nation enters another context: the Queer Shopping Network of New York and the Suburban Homosexual Outreach Program (SHOP) of San Francisco have taken the relatively bounded spectacle of the urban pride parade to the ambient pleasures of the shopping mall. "Mall visibility actions" thus conjoin the spectacular lure of the parade with Hare Krishna–style conversion and proselytizing techniques. Stepping into malls in hair-gelled splendor, holding hands and handing out fliers, the queer auxiliaries produce an "invasion" that conveys a different message: "We're here, we're queer, *you're* going shopping."

These miniature parades transgress an erotically, socially, and economically complex space. Whereas patrons of the straight bar at least understand its function in terms of pleasure and desire, mall-goers invest in the shopping mall's credentials as a "family" environment, an environment that "creates a nostalgic image of [the] town center as a clean, safe, legible place."[29] In dressing up and stepping out queer, the network uses the bodies of its members as billboards to create what Mary Ann Doane calls "the desire to desire."[30] As queer shoppers stare back, kiss, and pose, they disrupt the antiseptic asexual surface of the malls, exposing them as sites of any number of explicitly sexualized exchanges — cruising, people watching, window-shopping, trying on outfits, purchasing of commodities, and having anonymous sex.[31]

The inscription of metropolitan sexuality in a safe space for suburban-style normative sexual repression is just one aspect of the network's critical pedagogy. In addition, mall actions exploit the utopian function of the mall, which connects information about commodities with sensual expressivity, and which predicts that new erotic identities can be sutured to spectacular consuming bodies. The Queer Shopping Network understands the most banal of advertising strategies: sex sells. In this case, though, sex sells not substitutions for bodily pleasures — a car, a luxury scarf — but the capacity of the body itself to experience unofficial pleasures. While the network appears to be merely handing out another commodity in the form of broadsides about homosexuality, its ironic awareness of itself as being on display links gay spectacle with the window displays that also entreat the buyers. Both say "buy me"; but the Queer Shopping Network tempts consumers with a commodity that, if they could recognize it, they already own: a sexually inflected and explicitly desiring body. Ultimately, the mall spectacle addresses the consumer's own "perverse" desire to experience a different body and offers *itself* as most stylish of the many attitudes on sale in the mall.

Queer Nation exploits the mall's coupling of things and bodies by transgressively disclosing that this bounded safe commercial space is also an information system where sexual norms and cultural identities are consolidated, thus linking it with Queer Nation's final frontier, the media. As it enters the urban media cacophony, Queer Nation scatters original propaganda in the form of graffiti, wheatpasted posters, and fliers into existing spaces of collective, anonymous discursive exchange. While the mall circulates and exchanges bodies, print media circulates and exchanges information in the most disembodied of spaces. Queer Nation capitalizes on the abstract/informational apparatus of the media in a few ways, refunctioning its spaces for an ongoing "urban redecoration project" on behalf of gay visibility.[32] First, it manipulates the power of modern media to create and disseminate cultural norms and other political propaganda: Queer Nation leeches, we might say, onto the media's socializing function. Second, Queer Nation's abundant interventions into sexual publicity playfully invoke and resist the lure of monumentality, frustrating the tendency of sexual subcultures to convert images of radical sexuality into new standards of transgression.

In addition to manufacturing its own information, Queer Nation's mass mediation takes on a more ironic Madison Avenue mode, "queering" advertisements so that they become vehicles of protest against and arrogations of a medium that renders queerness invisible, sanitary, or spectacularly fetishized. More ambiguous than the tradition of political defacement from which it descends — feminist spray-painting of billboards with phrases like "this offends women," for example[33] — Queer Nation's glossy pseudoadvertisements involve replication, exposure, and disruption of even the semiotic boundaries between gay and straight. The group's parodies and reconstructions of mainstream ads inflect products with a sexuality and promote homosexuality as a product: they lay bare the queerness of the commodities that straight culture makes and buys, either translating it from its hidden form in the original, or revealing and ameliorating its calculated erasure. In short, the most overtly commercial of Queer Nation's campaigns, true to the American way, makes queer good by making goods queer.

One form this project takes is an "outing" of corporate economic interest in "market segments" with which corporations refuse to identify explicitly. The New York Gap series changes the final p in the logo of stylish ads featuring gay, bisexual, and suspiciously-polymorphous celebrities to a y. For the insider, these acts "out" the closeted gay and bisexual semicelebrities the Gap often uses as models. But the reconstructed billboards also address the company's policy of using gay style to sell clothes without acknowledging debts to gay street style: style itself is "outed," as are the straight urban consumers who learn that the clothes they wear signify gay.

Whereas the Gap ads confront both the closetedness of a corporation and the semiotic incoherence of straight consumer culture, another series addresses the class implications of advertising's complicity in the national moral bankruptcy. A series of parody Lotto ads exposes the similarities and differences between the national betrayal of poor and of gay citizens. The "straight" versions of a series of advertisements for New York's Lotto depict generic citizens of various assimilated genders and ethnicities who voice their fantasies about sudden wealth underneath the caption: "All you need is a dollar bill and a dream." The ads conflate citizenship and purchase, suggesting that working-class or ethnic Americans can realize the American dream through spending money. One of Queer Nation's parody ads shows an "ordinary citizen" in one of the frank, casual, head and shoulders poses that characterize the real ads. The caption reads, "I'd start my own cigarette company and call it Fags." The Queer Nation logo appears, along with the slogan, "All you need is a three-dollar bill and a dream." Again, the ads link citizenship with capitalist gain, but the ironized American dream cliché also establishes the group's resistance to a liberal "gay business" approach to social liberation, in whose view capitalist legitimation neutralizes social marginality. Queer Nation recognizes that the three-dollar bill remains nonnegotiable tender. The transformed caption reveals that the lottery's fundamental promise does not hold true for the nation's gay citizens in terms of the freedom to pursue sexual pleasure, which costs more than any jackpot or bank account has ever amassed.

In posing as a countercorporation, a business with its own logo, corporate identity, and ubiquity, Queer Nation seizes and dismantles the privileges of corporate anonymity.[34] It steals the privilege that this anonymity protects, that of avoiding painful recrimination for corporate actions. As it peels away the facade of corporate neutrality, Queer Nation reveals that businesses are people with political agendas, and that consumers are citizens to whom businesses are accountable for more than the quality of their specific products: abstracting itself, Queer Nation embodies the corporation. The Lotto ad finally promises an alternative to the capitalist dream-machine: its Queer Nation logo, juxtaposed against the "All you need is a three-dollar bill and a dream" caption, appeals to the consumer to invest in its own "corporate" identity.

The Queer Nation logo itself, then, becomes a mock-twin to existing national corporate logos: just as red, white, and blue "Buy

USA" labels, yellow ribbons, and flag icons have, by commodifying patriotism, actually managed to strengthen it, so does the spread of Queer Nation's merchandise and advertising expand its own territory of promises.[35] Because Gap clothes and lottery fantasies confer identities as much as flag kitsch does, Queer Nation has the additional power to expose or transform the meaning of these and other commodities — not simply through the reappropriation that camp enacts on an individual level, but through collective mimicry, replication, invasion of the pseudoidentities generated by corporations, including the nation itself.

Queer Nation's infusion of consumer space with a queer sensibility, and its recognition of the potential for exploiting spaces of psychic and physical permeability, are fundamental to its radical reconstitution of citizenship. For in the end, an individual's understanding of her- or himself as "American" and/or as "straight" involves parallel problems of consent and local control: both identities demand psychic and bodily discipline in exchange for the protection, security, and power these identities confer. If the official nation extracts public libidinal pleasure as the cost of political identity, queer citizenship confers the right to one's own specific pleasures. In the final analysis, America, understood not as a geographic but as a symbolic locus in which individuals experience their fundamental link to 250,000,000 other individuals, is the most unbounded of the hyper-spaces we have been describing. The official transformation of national identity into style — of flag into transvestite "flagness" — offers Queer Nation a seamless means of transforming "queerness" into a camp counternationality, which makes good on the promise that the citizen will finally be allowed to own, in addition to all the other vicarious bodies Queer Nation has for sale, his or her mighty real, very own national body.

With *You* Out We're Nothing, and Beyond

We have territorialized Queer Nation and described the production of a queer counterpublic out of traditional national icons, the official and useful spaces of everyday life, the ritual places of typical public pleasure (parades, malls, bars, and bodies), and the collective identities consumers buy in the mode of mass culture. The effect of casting gay urban life and practices as ongoing and scandalously ordinary is simultaneously to consolidate a safe space for gay subjects and also to dislocate utterly the normative sexual referent. If nationality as a form of fantasy and practice provides a legal and customary account of why American citizens in the abstract are secure *as heterosexuals,* Queer Nation exploits the disembodied structure of nationality by asserting that xenophobia would be precisely an inappropriate response for a straight community to have toward gay Americans. By asserting that straight and gay publics are coextensive with Americans at large, Queer Nation shows that the boundaries that might secure distinctions between sexual populations are local (like neighborhoods), normative (like taxonomies), and elastic (like latex). But these distinctions, in any event, must not be considered national, and in this sense Queer Nation's relay between everyday life and citizens' rights seems fitting.

Yet if Queer Nation tactically engages the postmodernity of information cultures, cutting across local and disembodied spaces of social identity and expressivity to reveal the communication that already exists between apparently bounded sexual and textual spaces, the campaign has not yet, in our view, left behind the fantasies of glamour and of homogeneity that characterize American nationalism itself. We might comment on the masculine a priori that dominates even queer spectacle; we might further comment on the relative weakness with which economic, racial, ethnic, and non-American cultures have been enfolded into queer counterpublicity.[36] In short, insofar as it assumes that "queer" is the only insurgent "foreign" identity its citizens have, Queer Nation remains bound to the genericizing logic of American citizenship, and to the horizon of an official formalism — one that equates sexual object-choice with individual self-identity. We concede the need to acknowledge the names people use for themselves, even when they originate in the service of juridical and medical discipline. Popular forms of spectacle and self-understanding are crucial for building mass cultural struggle. But it is not enough to "include" women, lesbians, racial minorities, etc. in an ongoing machine of mass counternationality. Achieving the utopian promise of a queer symbolic will involve more than a story of a multicultural sewing circle sewing the scraps of a pink triangle onto the American flag, or turning that flag, with its fifty times five potential small pink triangles, into a new desecrated emblem; more than a spectacle of young hard girl/woman flesh outing the pseudoabstraction of masculine political fantasy. Queer culture's consent to national normativity must itself be made more provisional.

We have argued that America has already become marked by a camp aesthetic in the 1990s. Camp America enrages, embarrasses, and sometimes benignly amuses official national figures and gives pleasure to the gay, the African-American, and the feminist- and left-identified communities who understand that to operate a travesty on the national travesty is to dissolve the frame that separates national fantasy from ordinary bodies. But the verb "dissolve" is a temporal fantasy, of course: tactical interventions, such as that of Dred Scott's flag doormat in Chicago's Art Institute or of Kelly and Ronnie Cutrone's transformation of the flag into a sheet for polymorphous lovemaking in New York, have momentarily disintegrated national abstractness by turning bodies into national art, and actually making censorship law look silly. These gestures were potentially dangerous, legally scandalous: but contained in museums and galleries, they depended on the usual protections of free high "artistic" expression to purchase the right to scandalize national iconography. At a time when existing laws against public and private sex are being newly enforced, the class distinction between sexual art and sex practices must be replaced by an insurgent renaming of sexuality *beyond* spectacle.

In other words, the exhibition of scandalous, direct contact between oppositional stereotypes of iconic America and its internally constructed others — say, between the "body" and the "nation" — solves as spectacle a problem of representation and power that is conceptually much harder to solve. But the indeterminate "we" from which we are writing, comfortable on neither side of most taxonomies, seeks to occupy a space of a more complexly dimensional sexuality/political identity than these simple sutures suggest. This is, as Monique Wittig contends, not simply a question of "de-dramatiz[ing] these categories of language.... We must produce a political transformation of the key concepts, that is of the concepts which are strategic for us."[37] As a gesture toward mapping this unsanctioned terrain, let us return to the problem of Sandra Bernhard: her pasty body wrapped in the flag, her extremely (c)little "red corvette," and her desire to seduce cathartically an African-American woman through a lesbian erotics that manipulates sentimentality, national parody, and aesthetic distance. This final seductive moment, when Bernhard "accidentally" stutters, "Without me/you I'm nothing," is framed by the "you" she addresses to the audience in the film's opening monologue. There, Bernhard wishes the impossible — that "you," the disembodied, autoerotic spectator, would traverse the space of aesthetic and celluloid distance to kiss her right "here," on a facial place where she points her finger; no such audience contact happens in the frame of the film. But in the end, after the masquerade, the racial, regional, ethnic, and class drag, and during the American striptease, the film stages a response that goes beyond the star's original request: the generic black-woman-in-the-audience about whom the film has periodically fantasized in nonnarrative, naturalistic segments writes on the café table with a lipstick, "FUCK SANDRA BERNHARD." This syntactically complex statement — a request, a demand, and an expletive — situates the black woman as an object of desire, as an author of feminine discourse, and as an image of the film's hopelessly absent audience: her proximity to Bernhard's final lesbian-nationalist striptease thus suggests neither a purely sentimental "essentialist" lesbian spectacle; nor a postmodern, consumer, feminine autoerotics; nor a phallocentrically inspired lust for lesbian "experience"; rather it suggests all of these, and more.

In this encounter Bernhard tries to merge national camp with lesbian spectacle.[38] She produces scandalous erotic pleasure by undulating between the impossibility of laminating the flag onto her body and the equal impossibility of ever shedding the flag altogether: as she peels off her flag cape she reveals three more in the form of a red, white, and blue sequined G-string and patriotic pasties, leaving us no reason to think that this exponential multiplication of flags would ever reach its limits. This undulation of the body and the flag, which eroticizes the latter as it nationalizes the former, is coterminous with the tease and the denial of the cross-race, homoerotic address to her consumer, the black-woman-in-the-audience. That is to say, the political liberation the flag promises and the sexual liberation its slipping off suggests make a spectacle of the ambiguity with which these subjects live American sexuality.

Bernhard's refusal to resolve her feminine and sexual identities

into a lesbian love narrative also illustrates how the eroticization of female spectacle in American public culture frustrates the
political efficacy of transgressive representations for straight and
lesbian women. The film imagines a kind of liberal pluralistic
space for Bernhard's cross-margin, cross-fashion fantasy of women,
but shows how lesbophobic that fantasy can be, insofar as it requires aesthetic distance — the straightness of the generic white
woman-identified-woman — as a condition of national, racial, *and*
sexual filiation. Her desire for acceptance from the black-woman-
in-the-audience perpetuates the historic burden black women in
cinema have borne to represent embodiment, desire, and the
dignity of suffering on behalf of white women, who are too
frightened to strip themselves of the privileges of white hetero-
spectacle. Thus, in addition, the rejection Bernhard receives from
the black-woman-in-the-audience demonstrates the inability of cinematic public spectacle to make good on its teasing promise to
dignify feminine desire in any of its forms. Bernhard's inability to
bridge the negativity of anyone's desire focuses the lens on female
spectacle itself, staging it as a scene of negativity, complete with producer, consumer, and audience resistance, and the representation
of multiple and ambiguous identifications.

The failed attempt to represent and to achieve a lesbian-national
spectacle foregrounds the oxymoronic quality of these two models
of identification. In the remainder of this essay we mean to explain how this failure to conflate sexual and political spectacle can
provide material to transfigure Queer as well as American nationality — not to commandeer the national franchise for our particular
huddled masses, but instead to unsettle the conventions that name
identity, frame expressivity, and provide the taxonomic means by
which populations and practices are defined, regulated, protected,
and censored by national law and custom. Lesbian-national spectacle emerges here as the measure of a transitory space, a challenge to
revise radically the boundaries of the normative public sphere and
its historical modes of intelligibility, among which are male homosociality, a very narrowly defined set of public "political" interests,
and garbled relations between politics and affect.[39] We understand
that to define sexual expressivity as public political speech, and to
resist censorship by expanding the range of erotic description, is
simultaneously to exercise a fundamental privilege of American cit-

izenship and to risk forsaking the refuge of camp. But these are risks that queers/Americans cannot afford to pass on. Indeed, the question of whether female/lesbian sexuality can come into any productive contact with the political public sphere is a founding problem of lesbian political writing of the last fifteen years, and this problem is a problem for us all, by which we refer to "us" queers and "us" Americans.

Female subjects are always citizens in masquerade: the more sexual they appear, the less abstractable they are in a liberal corporeal schema. Lesbian theory's solution to this dilemma has been to construct *imaginable* communities, which is to say that America's strategies for self-promotion have not worked for lesbians, who have historically and aesthetically often embraced the "space-off" in expatriate expression of their alienation from America.[40] The female body has reemerged in the safe spaces of lesbian political theory outside of the political public sphere, in tribal structures that emphasize embodied ritual and intimate spectacle as a solution to the indignities women and especially lesbians have had to endure. The blinking question mark beside the word "nation" in Jill Johnston's separatist *Lesbian Nation;* the erotogenic metamorphoses of the body, sex, and knowledge on the island of Monique Wittig's *The Lesbian Body;* and even the gender performances central to Judith Butler's sexual self-fashioning in *Gender Trouble* all reveal a disavowal or elision of nationality as we know it.[41] But for what public?

Separatist withdrawal into safe territories free from the male gaze secures the possibility of nonpornotropic embodiment in everyday life and aesthetic performance by emphasizing intimacy, subjectivity, and the literally local frame.[42] We do not mean to diminish the benefits of separatist expatriation: in its great historical variety, it has expressed a condition of political contestation lesbians and gays already experience in America, and has used the erotics of community to create the foundation of a different franchise. However, by changing the locus of spectacle — transporting it over state lines, as it were — lesbian theory has neglected to engage the political problem of feminine spectacle in mass society. Butler's metropolitan polymorphous solution to the politics of spectacle recognizes local, urban, consumer-oriented spaces as crucial sites of political transformation; but her imagined "gender performances" never link the politics of repeated contact between individual and visible bodies to collective forms of political affect or agency — in part because, for Butler as for Wittig, the desire is to make gender and the body unintelligible in the conventional lexicons of personhood. Thus they do not imagine for *lesbians* points of access to social change in the public sphere specific to the positions that accrue to this particular subject identity: the elastic range of sexual practices, subcultural norms, taboos, laws, and class and racial positions that must be involved in reimagining the possibility of a nonhomophobic national life. This substitution of identity issues for attention to spaces of ideology, mediation, and the contingencies of self-enunciation limits the power of transgression to what restaging the body can do to the signs of gender in custom and law. Queer Nation has shown us that no insistence on "the local" can secure national intimacy and national justice, where spectacle is intimacy's vehicle, and the vehicle for control. If the radical spectacle of the body's rendezvous with the flag has seemed to yoke unlike things together, the distance between persons and collective identities might be read as a space to be filled up by fantasies of sexually unintelligible or hyper-intelligible citizens. Or it might be read as a negative space, a place where suddenly the various logics of identity that circulate through American culture come into vibrant contradiction.

Along this axis the negativity of national life for nonwhite and/or nonmale queers has reemerged in a more radical diacritic, the queer fanzine.[43] We move away from the word "lesbian" and toward these descriptions of negative identity because it is this space — the space of nonidentification with the national fantasy of the white male citizen — that is both the symptom of even "queered" enlightenment nationality and also the material for its refunctioning. As a rule, underground fanzines make explicit their refusal of a property relation to information and art, repudiating the class politics of mainstream gay for-profit journals like *The Advocate* and *Outweek,* and shunning the mock–Madison Avenue production values of Queer Nation, Gran Fury, and ACT UP.[44] The editors of *BIMBOX* write that the magazine is free because "[t]he truth is, you have already paid for *BIMBOX*. We have all paid for it — dearly. We have paid for it in blood and we have paid for it in tears. Unrelenting pain is our credit limit, and we are cursed with interminable overdraft protection."[45] Xerox collage, desktop publishing, and other phototechniques have combined in a medium of comic and political communication whose geographically isolated examples have converged into the infocultural version of the tribe, a network.[46] Thus the contest over the territory of the queer symbolic has resulted in what "Bitch Nation," a manifesto in the Toronto fanzine *BIMBOX*, calls a civil war.

The fanzines' only shared "identity" is in their *counterproductivity* — a multifold mission they share with other sexual radicalisms to counter American and Queer National cultures' ways of thinking about political tactics and sexual intelligibility.[47] In the first place, the zines show that "obscenity" itself is political speech, speech that deserves constitutional protection: transforming "the American flag into something pleasant," Sondra Golvin and Robin Podolsky's "Allegiance/Ecstasy" turns "i pledge allegiance" into an opportunity to add "my cunt helplessly going molten," "her clit swelling to meet my tongue," "my fist knocking gently at her cunt" to the national loyalty oath.[48] Additionally, the zines have widened the semantic field of sexual description, moving sexual identity itself beyond known practical and fantastic horizons — as when *BIMBOX* imagines "fags, dykes, and USO's (*U*nidentified *S*exual *O*bjects)." But they are also magazines in the military sense, storehouses for the explosives that will shatter the categories and the time-honored political strategies through which queers have protected themselves. Queer counterspectacle might well be read as a means for aggressively achieving dignity in the straight world; however, in the zine context these spectacles are also icons that require smashing. The suspicion of existing tactics and taxonomies runs deep: "Dykes against granola lesbians. Fags against sensitive gay men. And bitches against everyone else."[49]

Along with joining queer culture's ongoing politics of dirty words, then, some zines engage in what would seem to be a more perverse activity: the aggressive naming and negation of their own audience. If citizenship in the Queer Nation is voluntary and consensual, democratic and universalist in the way of many modern nationalisms, the application for citizenship in the Bitch Nation, for example, repudiates the promise of community in common readership, the privileges of a common language, and the safety of counteridentity. "And — don't even bother trying to assimilate any aspect of Bitch Nation in a futile attempt to make your paltry careers or lame causes appear more glamorous or exciting. We won't hesitate to prosecute — and the Bitch Nation court is now in session!!"[50] As "Bitch Nation" endangers the reader who merely quotes, abstracts, and appropriates zine culture, many zines engage in a consumer politics of sexual enunciation, forcing the reader to see where she is situated, or to resituate herself politically, culturally: thus when the cover of *Thing* magazine proclaims that "She Knows Who She Is," it mobilizes the common gay use of the feminine pronoun in the ventriloquized voice of the woman's magazine to categorize "insiders" by attitude rather than by gender or sexual identity, disarming many different kinds of essentialism through arch, indirect address.

This move to materialize the spectator as *different* from the spectacle with which she identifies has powerful political force for women, whose collective and individual self-representations are always available for embarrassment, and most particularly for lesbians, whose sexual iconography has been overdetermined by the straight porn industry. By reversing the direction of the embarrassment from the spectacle toward the spectator, the zines rotate the meaning of *consent*. In severing sexual identity from sexual expressivity, the spectacle talks dirty to *you,* as it were, and you no longer have the privilege to consume in silence, or in tacit unconsciousness of or unaccountability for your own fantasies. As *Negativa,* a Chicago lesbian fanzine, puts it, "What you looking at bitch?" (see figure 4).

Linked complexly to the enigma of consensual sex is that of consensual nationality, which similarly involves theories of self-identity, of intention, and of the urge to shed the personal body for the tease of safe mutual or collective unboundedness. American and Queer National spectacles depend upon the citizen's capacity to merge his/her private, fractured body with a collectively identified "whole" one. Uncle Sam points his finger and says he wants *you* to donate your whole body literally and figuratively to the nation, and Queer Nation uses the allure of commercial and collective embodied spectacle to beckon *you* toward a different sort of citizenship. But the fanzines' postnational spectacle disrupts this moment of convergence: just as *you,* the desiring citizen, enter the sphere of what appears to be mutual consent, an invisible finger points back at you. It unveils your desire to see the spectacle of homoculture

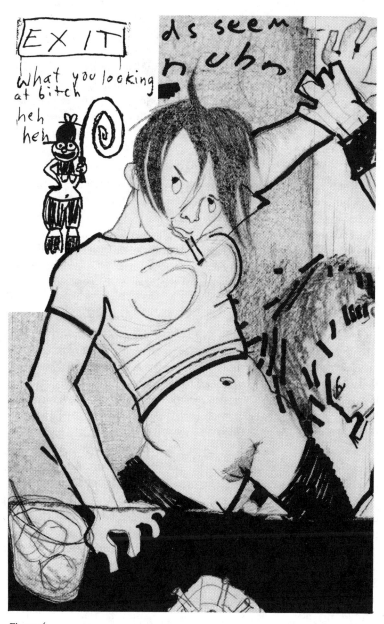

Figure 4

without being seen; it embarrasses you by making explicit your desire to "enter" and your need for "permission" to identify; it insists that you declare your body and your goods, and that you pay whatever political and erotic duty seems necessary.

Thus, like Queer Nation, the zines channel submission and bitterness into anger and parody. Queer Nation and allied groups struggle to reoccupy the space of national legitimation, to make the national world safe for just systems of resource distribution and communication, to make it safe for full expression of difference and rage and sexuality. Parody and camp thus become the measure of proximity to the national promise as well as distance from access to its fulfillment. Gestures of anger, parody, and camp in the zine network, by contrast, represent a disinvestment in authenticity discourse that moves beyond the intelligibility of gender, of sexual object-choice, and of national identity by cultivating a passionate investment in developing the negative for pleasure and politics. In their drive to embody *you*, the citizen/spectator/reader/lover, by negating your disembodiment, the zines represent the horizon of postpatriarchal and postnational fantasy.

Even in their most parodic manifestations, gestures of sexual and national intelligibility — both oppressive and emancipatory — are part of a process of making norms. The zines acknowledge the necessity and also the reality of stereotypical self-identity, and at the same time try to do violence to normative forms that circulate in America. In staging the process by which stereotypes become hybrid forms, exhausted of their clarifying function as sites of identity and oppression, the zines do more than deconstructively to put the icon "under erasure."[51] The negated stereotype remains available: mass politics requires a genuinely populist currency. But like all currency, the stereotype is expensive. The fanzines' gestures in countering national political sovereignty, then, lead us in another direction. They suggest a space of politics in which to be "out" in public would not be to consent parodically to the forms of the political public sphere, but rather to be *out beyond* the censoring imaginary of the state and the information culture that consolidates the rule of its names. We support Queer Nation and ACT UP's commitment to occupy as many hegemonic spaces as possible in their countering moves. But what we seek to describe in addition is the value in converting the space of negativity that distinguishes queer/

American identity into a discursive field so powerful that the United States will have to develop a new breed of lexical specialists to crack the code of collective life in a hot war of words about sex and America about which the nation already finds itself so miserably — and yet so spectacularly — archaic.

NOTES

We thank our collaboratrixes: Claudia L. Johnson, Tricia Loughran, Deborah N. Schwartz, Tom Stillinger, AK Summers, Michael Warner, the Gay and Lesbian Studies Workshop at the University of Chicago, and Cultural Forms/Public Spheres study group at the Center for Transcultural Studies.

1. There is yet no anthology or full history documenting Queer Nation, and its redefinitions in the print media are ongoing. For some contemporary accounts of Queer Nation, see the following articles: Allan Bérubé and Jeffrey Escoffier, "Queer/Nation," *Out/Look: National Lesbian and Gay Quarterly* 11 (winter 1991): 13–15; Alexander Chee, "A Queer Nationalism," *Out/Look: National Lesbian and Gay Quarterly* 11 (winter 1991): 15–19; Esther Kaplan, "A Queer Manifesto," quoted in Guy Trebay, "In Your Face," *Village Voice*, 14 August 1990, 36; Kay Longcope, "Boston Gay Groups Vow New Militancy against Hate Crimes," *Boston Globe*, 21 August 1990, 25, 31; Maria Maggenti, "Women as Queer Nationals," *Out/Look: National Lesbian and Gay Quarterly*, 11 (winter 1991): 20–23; Deborah Schwartz, " 'Queers Bash Back,' " *Gay Community News*, 24 June 1990, 14–15; Randy Shilts, "The Queering of America," *The Advocate* 567 (1 January 1991): 32–38; Guy Trebay, "In Your Face," *Village Voice*, 14 August 1990.

2. Bérubé and Escoffier, "Queer/Nation," 13–14.

3. These affinity groups include ASLUT (Artists Slaving under Tyranny); DORIS SQUASH (Defending Our Rights in the Streets, Super Queers United against Savage Heterosexuals); GHOST (Grand Homosexual Organization to Stop Televangelists); HI MOM (Homosexual Ideological Mobilization against the Military); LABIA (Lesbians and Bisexuals in Action); QUEER PLANET, an environmental group; QUEER STATE, which deals with state governments; QUEST (Queers Undertaking Exquisite and Symbolic Transformation); SHOP (Suburban Homosexual Outreach Program); and UNITED COLORS, which focuses on experiences of queers of color. For the extended list, see Bérubé and Escoffier, "Queer/Nation," 15.

4. Our construction of the manifold publics, polities, and symbolic cultures that traverse American life emanates from a number of sources: Benedict Anderson, *Imagined Communities* (London: Verso, 1983); Lauren Berlant, *The Anatomy of National Fantasy: Hawthorne, Utopia, and Everyday Life* (Chicago: University of Chicago Press, 1991); Alice Echols, *Daring to Be Bad: Radical Feminism in America, 1967–1975* (Minneapolis: University of Minnesota Press, 1989); Elizabeth Freeman, "Pitmarks on the History of the Country: the Epidemic of Nationalism in Hawthorne's 'Lady Eleanore's Mantle' " (unpublished MS); George Mosse, *Nationalism and Sexuality* (Madison: University of Wisconsin Press, 1986); Linda J. Nicholson, ed., *Feminism/Postmodernism* (New York: Routledge, 1990); Iris Marion Young, "Polity and Group Difference: A Critique of the Ideal of Universal Citizen-

226   Lauren Berlant and Elizabeth Freeman

ship," *Ethics* 9 (January 1989): 250–74; and idem, *Throwing Like a Girl and Other Essays in Feminist Philosophy and Social Theory* (Bloomington: Indiana University Press, 1989).

5. For the political need to postminoritize cultural experience through the manipulation of representational codes, see David Lloyd, "Genet's Genealogy: European Minorities and the Ends of the Canon," in Abdul R. JanMohamed and David Lloyd, eds., *The Nature and Context of Minority Discourse* (New York: Oxford University Press, 1990), 369–93.

6. Three works that argue for the need to retaxonomize sexual identity have inspired this essay: Esther Newton and Shirley Walton, "The Misunderstanding: Toward a More Precise Sexual Vocabulary," in Carole Vance, ed., *Pleasure and Danger* (Boston: Routledge, 1984), 242–50; Gayle Rubin, "Thinking Sex," in Vance, ed., *Pleasure and Danger,* 267–314; and Eve Kosofsky Sedgwick, *Epistemology of the Closet* (Berkeley: University of California Press, 1990), 1–63.

7. This death knell was sounded as early as June 1991, in Toronto, according to *Xtra!,* a Toronto publication. Cited in "Quotelines," *Outlines* 5, no. 1 (June 1991): 7. We have since heard that reports of its death have been greatly exaggerated.

8. See Andrew Ross, *No Respect: Intellectuals and Popular Culture* (New York: Routledge, 1989), 135–70.

9. Douglas Crimp and Adam Rolston, *AIDS DEMO GRAPHICS* (Seattle: Bay Press, 1990).

10. See Kaplan, "A Queer Manifesto," 36.

11. Nancy Fraser, "Rethinking the Public Sphere: A Contribution to the Critique of Actually Existing Democracy," *Social Text* 25, no. 6 (1990): 56–80.

12. Identity is linked to territorialization, both geographical and ideological: we mean to offer an account of a subcultural *topology,* a description of how modern space requires negotiating a complex relation between situated identities and mobilized *identifications.* The shifting terrain in the meaning of the phrase "gay community" symptomatized in Queer Nation's practices has been splendidly explicated by Richard Herrell, "The Symbolic Strategies of Chicago's Gay and Lesbian Pride Day Parade," in Gilbert Herdt, ed., *Gay Culture in America* (Boston: Beacon Press, 1993).

13. Gayatri Chakravorty Spivak, "In a Word: Interview," *Differences* 1 (summer 1989): 129.

14. See Sedgwick, *Epistemology,* 1–63.

15. We cite the texts in their entirety. "I praise life": "I praise life with my vulva. I thank the Gods for all the women who have kissed my lips. I praise life." "I Praise God": "I praise God with my erection. I thank God for all the men I've slept with. I praise God." They were created in 1990 by Joe Lindsay of Queer Nation Denver.

16. Robert Ford, "Sacred Sex: Art Erects Controversy," *Thing* 4 (spring 1991): 4.

17. John D'Emilio, *Sexual Politics, Sexual Communities* (Chicago: University of Chicago Press, 1983), 216.

18. John D'Emilio, "Capitalism and Gay Identity," in Ann Snitow, Christine Stansell, and Sharon Thompson, eds., *The Powers of Desire* (New York: Monthly Review Press, 1983), 108.

19. Trebay, "In Your Face," 36.

20. The "Absolutly Het" series, parodies of the ads for Absolut vodka, were produced by the anonymous group OUTPOST.

21. Trebay, "In Your Face," 39.

22. The quote in the title to this section is from Deee-Lite, "Try Me On, I'm Very You," *World Clique,* Elektra Entertainment, 1990.

23. Marshall Kirk and Hunter Madsen, *After the Ball: How America Will Conquer Its Fear and Hatred of Gays in the '90s* (New York: Doubleday, 1989). Kirk and Madsen advise the gay community to present nonthreatening images of homosexuality to straight culture, a "marketing campaign" designed to win mainstream approval for the bourgeois homosexual at the cost of eliminating drag queens, butch lesbians, transsexuals, and so on, from visibility.

24. For a discussion of the relationship between the trademark, commodity identification, and the colonized American body, see Lauren Berlant, "National Brands/ National Body: Imitation of Life," in Hortense J. Spillers, eds., *Comparative American Identities: Race, Sex, and Nationality in the Modern Text,* Selected Papers from the English Institute (Boston: Routledge, 1991), 110–40.

25. A powerful and extensive exploration of the role of this "stereotyped fantasy body" in the black gay voguing subculture is provided by Jenny Livingston's documentary *Paris Is Burning.* See also Berlant, "National Brands/National Body."

26. On the history of the gay pride parade, see D'Emilio, *Sexual Politics.*

27. See Ross, *No Respect.*

28. See Herrell, "Symbolic Strategies." Herrell discusses how Chicago politicians annually assume at the parade pseudo-Irish last names such as "Mayor Richard O'Daley." The stigma attached to certain cultural groups might well be discerned by such a litmus test: the unthinkable prospect of "Mayor Richard Gayley" suggests that there is as yet no such thing as "honorary" symbolic homosexuality in the realm of the civic.

29. See Anne Friedberg, "Flaneurs du Mal(l)," *PMLA* 106 (May 1991): 419–31. Whereas Friedberg analyzes the mall as a theater, an illusory and ultimately nonparticipatory realm, we would argue that "mall erotics" extend beyond the consumer/ commodity exchange she describes to include visual consumption of other people as products.

30. Mary Ann Doane, *The Desire to Desire* (Bloomington: Indiana University Press, 1987).

31. A letter in *Raunch* reveals that Southglenn Mall in Denver, Colorado, where guess-which-one-of-us hung out every Saturday for her entire adolescence, also used to contain one of the best arrays of glory holes in the country. Imagine my delight. Boyd McDonald, *Raunch* (Boston: Fidelity, 1990).

32. We first heard this phrase at Queer Nation Chicago, spring 1991.

33. See Jill Posener's photoessay on the British and Australian feminist billboard spray-painting movement, *Louder Than Words* (New York: Pandora, 1986).

34. Paradoxically, actual corporations have in turn exploited Queer Nation/Gran Fury's recognizable style to produce mock-gay ads such as the Kikit billboard that portrays two "lesbians" — actually an androgynous heterosexual couple — kissing.

35. *The New York Times* devoted a full section to paid advertisements supporting the Persian Gulf invasion and to commercial ads linking patriotism with purchase. Included were an ad for a Steuben glass flag paperweight, a Bloomingdale's spread saluting fathers' "devotion to family and country alike," and — in the most sinister pun of our times (apart from, perhaps, "Saddamize Hussein") — a Saks Fifth Avenue

ad captioned: "A woman's place is in the home of the brave and the land of the free" (*New York Times*, 9 June 1991).

36. Charles Fernandez, "Undocumented Aliens in the Queer Nation," *Out/Look* 12 (spring 1991): 20–23.

37. Monique Wittig, "The Straight Mind," in Russell Ferguson et al., eds., *Out There: Marginalization and Contemporary Cultures* (Cambridge: MIT Press, 1990), 51–57.

38. We have been orally instructed on the genealogy of camp counterpolitics and its intersection with radical sexuality by Richard Herrell and Pam Robertson. For textual support, see Esther Newton, *Mother Camp: Female Impersonators in America* (Chicago: University of Chicago Press, 1979); Ross, *No Respect;* and Pamela Robertson, "Guilty Pleasures: Camp and the Female Spectator" (unpublished MS, University of Chicago, 1990).

39. For an aligned project, see Scott Tucker, "Gender, Fucking, and Utopia," *Social Text* 27 (1991): 3–34.

40. See Teresa de Lauretis, *Technologies of Gender* (Bloomington: Indiana University Press, 1987), and Bertha Harris, "The More Profound Nationality of Their Lesbianism: Lesbian Society in the 1920's," in Phillis Birky et al., eds., *Amazon Expedition: A Lesbian Feminist Anthology* (New York: Times Change, 1973), 77–88.

41. We are indebted to Johnston, Wittig, and Butler for helping us refine and periodize our thinking about what a hybrid lesbian American would have to face and might come to mean. Butler, especially, has made possible and pleasurable a way of reading and imagining sexually motored social change in America. Judith Butler, *Gender Trouble* (New York: Routledge, 1990); Jill Johnston, *Lesbian Nation* (New York: Simon and Schuster, 1973); Monique Wittig, *The Lesbian Body,* trans. David Le Vay (Boston: Beacon, 1986).

42. Hortense J. Spillers, "Mama's Baby/Papa's Maybe: An American Grammar Book," *Diacritics* 17 (summer 1987): 65–81.

43. Citational proprieties in *The Chicago Manual of Style* are both inappropriate and virtually impossible with regard to the zines. Here is a selected list of those we consulted to makes these generic observations: *BIMBOX* 2 (summer 1990); *Don't Tell Jane and Frankie* (undated); *Dumb Bitch Deserves to Die* 2 (winter 1989); *The Gentlewomen of California* 6 (undated); *Holy Titclamps* 6 (fall 1990); *Homoture* 2 (undated); *Manhattan Review of Unnatural Acts* (undated); *Negativa* 1–3 (March–May 1991); *No World Order* (1990); *Screambox* 1 and 2 (November 1990; May 1991); *Sister/My Comrade* (winter 1991; *Taste of Latex* 4 (winter 1990–91); *Thing* 4 (spring 1991).

44. See Crimp and Rolston, *AIDS Demo Graphics.*

45. *BIMBOX* 2 (summer 1990).

46. In May of 1991 the Randolph Street Gallery of Chicago hosted the first international queer fanzine conference, called "SPEW: The Homographic Convergence."

47. Rubin, "Thinking Sex," and Lisa Duggan, "Sex Panics," in Brian Wallis, ed., *Democracy: A Project by Group Material* (Seattle: Bay Press, 1990), 209–12.

48. Sondra Golvin and Robin Podolsky, "Allegiance/Ecstasy," in *Screambox* 1 (November 1990): 20–21.

49. *Don't Tell Jane and Frankie,* no page number.

50. We understand the risk we take in citing *Bitch Nation* against its stated will:

we look forward to our punishment at the hands of editrix G. B. Jones, who "takes her girls like Tylenol — 2 at a time." See *Don't Tell Jane and Frankie.*
51. On the national stereotype and hybrid identities, see Homi K. Bhabha, "The Other Question: Difference, Discrimination and the Discourse of Colonialism," in Ferguson, ed., *Out There,* 71–87.

The Black Man's Burden
Henry Louis Gates, Jr.

The strictures of "representation" have had wide and varied permutations in the black community. For as we know, the history of African Americans is marked by its noble demands for political tolerance from the larger society, but also by its paradoxical tendency to censure its own. W. E. B. Du Bois was rebuked by the NAACP for his nationalism in the 1930s and then again for his socialism a decade or so later. James Baldwin and Ralph Ellison were victims of the Black Arts movement in the 1960s, the former for his sexuality, the latter for his insistence upon individualism. Martin Luther King, Jr., and Eartha Kitt, strange bedfellows at best, were roundly condemned for their early protests against the Vietnam War. Amiri Baraka repudiated a whole slew of writers in the 1960s for being too "assimilationist," then invented a whole new canon of black targets when he became a Marxist a few years later. Michele Wallace, Ntosake Shange, and Alice Walker have been accused of bashing black males and of calculated complicity with white racists. Not surprisingly, many black intellectuals are acutely aware of the hazards of falling out of favor with the thoughtpolice, whether in white face or black. In the case of artistic elites, the issues of representation arise with a vengeance. I want to discuss briefly a revisioning of the Harlem Renaissance in which such issues become particularly acute, the film *Looking for Langston,* which was directed by Isaac Julien and produced by the black British film collective Sankofa in 1989.

Distance and displacement have their benefits, as the literature of migrancy reminds us; so it isn't altogether surprising that one of the most provocative and insightful reflections on the Harlem Renaissance and the cultural politics of black America should come from across the Atlantic. I want to take a look at New York from the standpoint of black London; I want to examine the relationship between a New York–based cultural movement, such as it was, in the 1920s and one in London in the 1980s. Of course, the question of modernism has always also been one of a cultural vanguard or elite. And that means that the old "burden of representation" is always present. "The ordinary Negro never heard of the Harlem Renaissance," Langston Hughes remarked ruefully, "or if he did, it hadn't raised his wages any." Always, there is the question: What have you done for us?

But to see *Looking for Langston* as an act of historical reclamation, we might begin with the retheorizing of identity politics in black British cultural studies, among such critics and theorists as Stuart Hall, Paul Gilroy, Hazel Carby, and Kobena Mercer.

Hall insists, rightly, on distinguishing between a conception of identity founded in an archaeology — in the sense of *res gestae* — and one produced by a narrative, even if an archaeological narrative. For him, that "partnership of past and present" is always an "imaginary reunification." But he also insists — something forgotten too quickly in the postmodernist urge to exalt indeterminacy — that "cultural identities come from somewhere, have histories." In a rather nice formulation, he writes that "identities are the names we give to the different ways we are positioned by, and position ourselves in, the narratives of the past." There is a certain reciprocity here I want to hold on to. It says our social identities represent the way we participate in a historical narrative. Our histories may be irretrievable, but they invite imaginative reconstruction. In this spirit, diasporic feminist critics like Hazel Carby have made the call for a "usable past." This call for cultural retrieval — tempered with a sense of its lability, its contingency, its constructedness — has sponsored a remarkable time of black creativity, or as we are bidden to call it, "cultural production." I'm talking, of course, about the work of recent black British film collectives, which really can be seen to deepen and expand these arguments: this is not a relation of mirroring, however, but of productive dialogue.

To talk about the way *Looking for Langston* sets in play history, identity, and desire, we can start with the fact that *Looking for Lang-*

ston is avowedly a meditation on the Harlem Renaissance. And let me emphasize that historical particularity is an essential part of the film's texture, rather splendidly realized, I think, by Derek Brown, the film's art director. Throughout the film, archival footage, including film extracts from Oscar Michaux and period footage of Bessie Smith's "St. Louis Blues," is interspersed with Nina Kellgren's cinematography. What I want to argue is that its evocation of the historical Harlem Renaissance is, among other things, a self-reflective gesture: there is a relation, even a typology, established between black British cinema of the 1980s and the cultural movement of the 1930s that we call the Harlem Renaissance. By its choice of subject, the film brings out, in a very self-conscious way, the analogy between this contemporary ambit of black creativity and a historical precursor.

We look for Langston, but we discover Isaac.

It is an association that is represented quite literally in one of the opening images of the film, where the film's director makes his sole appearance in front of the camera. He is the corpse in the casket. With six mourners presiding, Hughes's wake is a black-tie affair. And of course the film is also an act of mourning, in memory of three men who died in 1987, Bruce Nugent, James Baldwin, and Joseph Beam. ("This nut might kill us," we hear Essex Hemphill say in one sequence, reflecting on the AIDS epidemic; "This kiss could turn to stone.")

Visually, as I mentioned, there is a circulation of images between the filmic present and the archival past. Textually, something of the same interplay is enacted, with poetry and prose from Bruce Nugent ("Smoke, Lilies and Jade," which receives perhaps the most elaborate and affecting *tableau vivant* in the film); Langston Hughes (including passages from "The Negro Artist and the Racial Mountain," *The Big Sea, Montage of a Dream Deferred,* and other works); James Baldwin's *The Price of the Ticket;* an essay by the critic and journalist Hilton Als; and six poems by Essex Hemphill. We hear an interchange of different voices, different inflections, different accents: including Stuart Hall reading expository prose of Hilton Als, Langston Hughes reading his own work, Toni Morrison reading Baldwin, and Erick Ray Evans reading Bruce Nugent. The credits identity Hall's as the "British voice," an interestingly ambiguous formulation. The result is an interlacement, an enmeshment of past and present, of the blues, jazz, motown, and contemporary dance music, of London and New York: a transtemporal dialogue on the nature of identity and desire and history.

But the typology to which the film is devoted also enables another critique of the identity politics that has been inherited from the black nationalisms of an earlier time, a critique that focuses on a malign sexual politics. Like the self-proclaimed "Aesthetic movement" of England's yellow 1890s — chronicled by Arthur Symons, parodied by Robert Hichens, promulgated by such "born antinomians" as Oscar Wilde, Alfred Douglas, and Lionel Johnson — the Harlem Renaissance was in fact a handful of people. The usual roll call would invoke figures like Langston Hughes, Claude McKay, Alain Locke, Countee Cullen, Wallace Thurman, and Bruce Nugent; which is to say that it was surely as gay as it was black, not that it was exclusively either of these. Yet this, in view of its emblematic importance to later movements of black creativity in this country, is what makes the powerful current of homophobia in black letters a matter of particular interest and concern. If *Looking for Langston* is a meditation on the Harlem Renaissance, it is equally an impassioned rebuttal to the virulent homophobia associated with the Black Power and Black Aesthetic movements. On this topic, the perfervid tone that Eldridge Cleaver adopts toward Baldwin — to whom *Looking for Langston* is dedicated — indicates only a sense of what was perceived to be at stake in policing black male sexuality. We see the same obsession running through the early works of Sonia Sanchez and, of course, Amiri Baraka. "Most American white men are trained to be fags," he writes in the essay collection *Home*. "For this reason it is no wonder their faces are weak and blank, left without the hurt that reality makes." Amid the racial battlefield, a line is drawn, but it is drawn on the shifting sands of sexuality. To cross that line, Baraka told us, would be an act of betrayal. And it is worth noting that, at least in a literal sense, the film opens in the year 1967, with the death of Langston Hughes and the playing of a Riverside radio program in memoriam.

It is difficult to read Baraka's words today: "without the hurt that reality makes." Baldwin once remarked that being attacked by white people only made him flare hotly into eloquence; being attacked by black people, he confessed, made him want to break down and cry. Baldwin hardly emerged from the efflorescence of black nationalism in the 1960s unscathed. Baldwin and Beam could both have told LeRoi Jones a great deal about the "hurt that reality makes," as could a lot of black gay men in Harlem today who are tired of being used for batting practice. And in the wake of a rising epidemic of physical violence against gays, violence of the sort that Melvin Dixon has affectingly depicted in his new novel, *Vanishing Rooms* — it is difficult to say that we have progressed since LeRoi Jones.

That is not to say that the ideologues of black nationalism in the United States have any unique claim on homophobia. But it is an almost obsessive motif that runs through the major authors of the Black Aesthetic and the Black Power movements. In short, national identity became sexualized in the 1960s, in such a way as to engender a curious subterraneous connection between homophobia and nationalism. It is important to confront this head-on to make sense of the ways *Looking for Langston* both fosters and transcends a kind of identity politics.

Surely one of the salient features of the work is its attitude toward the corporeal, the way in which the black body is sexualized. Gloria Watkins has noted that Nina Kellgren's camera presents the black male body as vulnerable, soft, even passive, in marked contrast to its usual representation in American film. It is a way of disrupting a visual order, a hardened convention of representation. There is a scene in which slides of Robert Mapplethorpe's photos are projected on a backdrop while a white man walks through them. And I think there is a tacit contrast between those images, with their marmoreal surfaces and primitivist evocations, and Kellgren's own vision of masculinity unmasked. Indeed, this may be the film's most powerful assault on the well-policed arena of black masculinity. "And soft," Nugent writes of his character, Beauty, "soft."

In short, by insistently foregrounding — and then refiguring — issues of gender and desire, filmmakers like Rhees August, Maureen Blackwood, Isaac Julien, and others are engaged in an act of both cultural retrieval and reconstruction. And the historicity of that act — the way it takes form as a search for a usable past — is, as Hazel Carby and Houston Baker show, entirely characteristic of diasporic culture.

So the dialogue with the past, even a past figured as nonrecuperable, turns out to be a salient feature of what might be called the Black London Renaissance. The "partnership of past and present" is recast across the distances of exile, through territories of the imagination and of space.

A film like *Looking for Langston* is able to respond to the hurt-fully exclusionary obsessions of the black nationalist moment, and our own cultural moment as well, by constructing a counterhistory in which desire and mourning and identity can interact in their full complexity, but in a way that registers the violence of history. There are two reductive ways of viewing the film, therefore. The first is preoccupied with fixing the historical question about Hughes's sex life. The second says that the film is an imaginative medita-tion, and "real" history is completely immaterial to it. On their own, both approaches are misguided. A more instructive approach is em-blematized nicely by the Akan figure of "sankofa" itself (the word literally means "go back and retrieve it"), which refers to the figure of a bird with its head turned backward: again, the "partnership of past and present." Obviously the film is not positivist history; and yet history and the status of history are its immediate concerns. So we need to take seriously what Kobena Mercer calls the "artis-tic commitment to archaeological inquiry"[1] that is at work and at play here; and of course Stuart Hall's insistence, cited above, that "cultural identities come from somewhere, have histories," is very much to the point. While the film is not a simple exercise in identity politics, it cannot dispense with the moment of narcissism, of self-recognition. Hence the use of the mirror tableaux that thematize the film critic's concern with the dialectic of identification and spectator-ship. A man in the club sees himself in the mirror and is caught up short. Water — ponds and puddles — is used as a reflecting surface. Indeed, toward the film's end, we are presented with a series of men who lie, Narcissus-like, with their faces to a reflective surface. A belated version of the Lacanian mirror stage? Self-recognition? Or something else entirely? In the prose poem "The Disciple," Oscar Wilde writes:

> When Narcissus died the pool of his pleasure changed from a cup of sweet waters into a cup of salt tears, and the Oreads came weeping through the woodland that they might sing to the pool and give it comfort....
>
> "We do not wonder that you should mourn in this manner for Narcissus, so beautiful was he."
>
> "But was Narcissus beautiful?" said the pool.... "I loved Narcissus

because, as he lay on my banks and looked down at me, in the mirror of his eyes I saw ever my own beauty mirrored."

The film, remember, is called *Looking for Langston;* it does not promise he will be found. In fact, I think that *Looking for Langston* leads us away from the ensolacement of identity politics, the simple exaltation of identity. We are to go behind the mirror, as Wilde urged. The film gives us angels — there are six of them, including the musician Jimmy Sommerville, with wings of netting and wire — but they are fallen angels, as Essex Hemphill tells us. There are moments of carnival — a club with spirited dancing amid the smashing of champagne glasses — but there are no utopias here. An angel holds a photograph of Langston Hughes, of James Baldwin, but history remains, in a phrase that Stuart Hall repeats, "the smiler with the knife." The carnival is disrupted by a group of men who are described indifferently by the credits as "thugs and police" and who represent both the authority of the state and the skinhead malevolence that is its fun-house reflection. In films like *Looking for Langston,* cultural studies becomes cultural work.

At the same time, the controversy that surrounds the productions of Sankofa and Black Audio, to mention the two most prominent collectives, leads to what has become *the* central problem for cultural criticism in our day. It is a theoretical terrain that can be taken either as a gold mine or a mine field, depending on your point of view. I speak of the "new politics of representation," and the way this impinges on the normative self-image of the so-called oppositional intellectual.

To the extent that black British cinema is represented as an act of cultural politics, it then becomes vulnerable to a political reproach as elitist, Europeanized, overly highbrow: as a black cultural product without a significant black audience, its very "blackness" becomes suspect.

This line of reproach ought to ring a bell: as I suggested at the start, it reprises one of the oldest debates in the history of African-American letters, a debate that is usually framed around the issue of "the responsibilities of the negro artist." But the populist critique always operates in tandem as a statement about artists and critics.

The centrality of the issue is shown in the fact that a synoptic manifesto on the "new politics of representation" has been issued jointly by Isaac Julien and Kobena Mercer. Their argument follows Paul Gilroy, Pierre Bourdieu, and Ernesto Laclau in linking the critique of essentialism to the critique of the paradigm of representation as delegation. That is, Julien and Mercer recast the ancient debate over "black representation" by focusing on the tension "between representation as a practice of depicting and representation as a practice of delegation. Representational democracy, like the classic realist text, is premised on an implicitly mimetic theory of representation as correspondence with the 'real.' "[2]

It has been argued that we should supplant the vangardist paradigm of "representation" with the "articulation of interests." In such a way, it is argued further, we can lighten the "burden of representation," even if we cannot dispense with it. But whose interest is being articulated?

Worrying that independent black British cinema has become too estranged from the black community, Paul Gilroy has recently proposed what he calls "populist modernism" — which some have decried as a highbrow version of the NAACP "Image Awards." There are worries that normative proposals such as "populist modernism" can become techniques for policing artistic boundaries, for separating the collaborationist sheep from the oppositional goats, or perhaps the other way around. Gilroy cites Richard Wright's *The Outsider* as a model for black art, but the poetic career of Langston Hughes might be an even more appropriate candidate for the category.

Perhaps more than any other African American this century, Langston Hughes was elected popularly to serve as our "representative negro," the poet of his race; as we know, the burden of representation bore heavily upon him, profoundly shaping his career and preoccupations, propelling and restraining his own involvement with literary modernism. Nor is it surprising that his image should be, even in our own day, subject to censorship and restriction; Julien's difficulties with appropriating Hughes's texts reflect, in an ironic way, the central argument of his film.

How "modernist" is Julien's own technique? Manthia Diawara, a leading intellectual champion of black British cinema, has observed that *Looking for Langston* has evident affinities with many avantgarde and experimental films of the 1970s. And yet, he argues, the

film "appropriates the forms of avant garde cinema not for mere
inclusion in the genre, but in order to redefine it by changing its
content, and re-ordering its formal disposition." In Julien's hands,
he suggests, the techniques of the avant-garde are made to "reveal
that which the genre itself represses." Nor is it an uncritical act of
reclamation. Diawara notes that "the dependency of artists and writers upon their white patrons, and the links between the movement
and Modernist Primitivism are revealed as moments of ambiguity
and ambivalence."

Indeed, the importance of open-textured films like *Looking for
Langston* is in presenting an aesthetics that can embrace ambiguity;
perhaps it is not without its reverential moments, but it is not a
work of naive celebration. It presents an identitarian history as a
locus of discontinuities and affinities, of shared pleasures and perils.
Perhaps the real achievement of this film is not simply that it rewrites
the history of African-American modernism, but that it compels its
audience to participate in this rewriting.

NOTES

1. Kobena Mercer, "Travelling Theory: The Cultural Politics of Race and Representation: An Interview with Kobena Mercer," *Afterimage* 18, no. 2: 9–90.

2. Isaac Julien and Kobena Mercer, "Introduction — De Margin and De Centre,"
Screen 29, no. 4 (autumn 1988): 4, 12.

Eloquence and Epitaph: Black Nationalism and the Homophobic Impulse in Responses to the Death of Max Robinson

Phillip Brian Harper

From June 1981 through February 1991, 167,803 people in the United States were diagnosed as having Acquired Immune Deficiency Syndrome. Of that number of total reported cases, 38,361 — or roughly 23 percent — occurred in males of African descent, although black males account for less than 6 percent of the total U.S. population.[1] It is common enough knowledge that black men constitute a disproportionate number of people with AIDS in the United States — common in the sense that, whenever the AIDS epidemic achieves a new statistical milestone (as it did in the winter of 1991, when the number of AIDS-related deaths in the United States reached one hundred thousand), the major media generally provide a demographic breakdown of the figures. And yet, somehow the enormity of the morbidity and mortality rates for black men (like that for gay men of whatever racial identity) doesn't seem to register in the national consciousness as a cause for great concern. This is, no doubt, largely due to a general sense that the trajectory of the average African-American man's life must "naturally" be rather short, routinely subject to violent termination. And this sense, in turn, helps account for the fact that there has never been a case of AIDS that riveted public attention on the vulnerability of black men the way, for instance, the death of Rock Hudson shattered the myth of the invincible white male cultural hero.[2] This is not to say that no nationally known black male figure has died of AIDS-related causes, but rather that numerous and complex cultural factors conspire to prevent such deaths from effectively galvanizing AIDS activism in

African-American communities. This essay represents an attempt to explicate several such factors that were operative in the case of one particular black man's bout with AIDS, and thus to indicate what further cultural intervention needs to take place if we hope to stem the ravages of AIDS among the African-American population.

The Sound of Silence

In December 1988, National Public Radio broadcast a report on the death of Max Robinson, who had been the first black newsanchor on U.S. network television, staffing the Chicago desk of ABC's *World News Tonight* from 1978 to 1983. Robinson was one of 4,123 African-American men to die in 1988 of AIDS-related causes (of a nationwide total of 17,119 AIDS-related deaths),[3] but rather than focus on the death itself at this point, I want to examine two passages from the broadcast that, taken together, describe an entire problematic that characterizes the existence of AIDS in many black communities in the United States. The first is a statement by a colleague of Robinson's both at ABC News and at WMAQ-TV in Chicago, where Robinson worked after leaving the network. Producer Bruce Rheins remembers being on assignment with Robinson on the streets of Chicago: "We would go out on the street a lot of times, doing a story . . . on the Southside or something, . . . and I remember one time, this mother leaned down to her children, pointed, and said, 'That's Max Robinson. You learn how to speak like him.'" Immediately after this statement from Rheins, the NPR correspondent reporting the piece, Cheryl Duvall, informs us that "Robinson had denied the nature of his illness for months, but after he died . . . his friend Roger Wilkins said Robinson wanted his death to emphasize the need for AIDS awareness among black people."[4] These are the concluding words of the report, and as such they reproduce the epitaphic structure of Robinson's deathbed request, raising the question of just how well any of us is addressing the educational needs of black communities with respect to AIDS.

That these two passages should be juxtaposed in the radio report is striking because they testify to the power of two different phenomena that appear to be in direct contradiction. Bruce Rheins's statement underscores the importance of Robinson's speech as an affirmation of black identity for the benefit of the community from which he sprang. Cheryl Duvall's remarks, on the other hand, implicate Robinson's denial that he had AIDS in a general silence regarding the effects of the epidemic among the African-American population. I would like, in this essay, to examine how speech and silence actually interrelate to produce a discursive matrix that governs the cultural significance of AIDS in black communities. Indeed, Max Robinson, newsanchor, inhabited a space defined by the overlapping of at least two distinct types of discourse that, though often in conflict, intersect in a way that makes discussion of Robinson's AIDS diagnosis — and of AIDS among blacks generally — a particularly difficult activity.

As it happens, the apparent conflict between vocal affirmation and the peculiar silence effected through denial is already implicated in the nature of speech itself, in the case of Max Robinson. There is a potential doubleness in the significance of Robinson's "speaking" that the mother cited above urges upon her child as an example to be emulated. It is clear, first of all, that the reference is to Robinson's exemplification of the articulate, authoritative presence that is ideally represented in the television newsanchor — an exemplification noteworthy because of the fact that Robinson was black. Bruce Rheins's comments illustrate this particularly well: "Max really was a symbol for a lot of people. . . . Here was a very good-looking, well-dressed, and very obviously intelligent black man giving the news in a straightforward fashion, and not on a black radio station or a black TV station or on the black segment of a news report — he was the anchorman." Rheins's statement indicates the power of Robinson's verbal performance before the camera, for it is through this performance that Robinson's "intelligence," which Rheins emphasizes, is made "obvious." Other accounts of Robinson's tenure as a television newsanchor recapitulate this reference. An article in the June 1989 issue of *Vanity Fair* remembers Robinson for "his steely, unadorned delivery, precise diction, and magical presence."[5] A *New York Times* obituary notes the "unforced, authoritative manner" that characterized Robinson's on-air persona, and backs its claim with testimony from current ABC newsanchor and Robinson's former colleague, Peter Jennings: "In terms of sheer performance, Max was a penetrating communicator. He had a natural gift to look in the camera and talk to people."[6] A 1980 *New York Times* reference asserts that Robinson was "blessed with a commanding voice and a handsome appearance."[7] A posthumous "appreciation" in the *Boston Globe* describes Robinson as "earnest and telegenic," noting that he "did some brilliant reporting... and was a consummate newscaster."[8] James Snyder, news director at WTOP-TV in Washington, D.C., where Robinson began his anchoring career, says that Robinson "had this terrific voice, great enunciation and phrasing. He was just a born speaker."[9] Elsewhere, Snyder succinctly summarizes Robinson's appeal, noting his "great presence on the air."[10]

All of these encomia embody allusions to Robinson's verbal facility that must be understood as praise for his ability to speak articulate Received Standard English, which linguist Geneva Smitherman has identified as the dialect upon which "White America has insisted... as the price of admission into its economic and social mainstream."[11] The emphasis that commentators place on Robinson's "precise diction" or on his "great enunciation and phrasing" is an index of the general surprise evoked by his facility with the white bourgeois idiom considered standard in "mainstream" U.S. life, and certainly in television news. The black mother cited above surely recognizes the opportunity for social advancement inherent in this facility with standard English, and this is no doubt the benefit she has in mind for her children when she urges them to "speak like" Max Robinson.

At the same time, however, that the mother's words can be interpreted as an injunction to speak "correctly," they might alternately be understood as a call for speech per se — as encouragement to *speak out* like Max Robinson, to stand up for one's interests as a black person as Robinson did throughout his career. In this case, the import of her command is traceable to a black cultural nationalism that has waxed and waned in the United States since the mid–nineteenth century, but which, in the context of the Black Power movement of the 1960s, underwent a revival that has continued to influence black cultural life in the United States.[12] Geneva Smitherman notes the way in which this cultural nationalism has been manifested in black language and discourse, citing the movement "among writers, artists, and black intellectuals of the 1960s who deliberately wrote and rapped in the Black Idiom and sought to preserve its distinctiveness in the literature of the period."[13] Obviously, Max Robinson did not participate in this nationalistic strategy in the context of his work as a network newsanchor. Success in television newscasting, insofar as it depends upon one's conformity to models of behavior deemed acceptable by white bourgeois culture, largely precludes the possibility of one's exercising the "Black Idiom" and thereby manifesting a strong black consciousness in the broadcast context. We might say, then, that black people's successful participation in modes of discourse validated in mainstream culture — their facility with Received Standard English, for instance — actually implicates them in a profound *silence* regarding their African-American identity.

It is arguable, however, that Max Robinson, like all blacks who have achieved a degree of recognition in mainstream U.S. culture, actually played both sides of the behavioral dichotomy that I have described — the dichotomy between articulate verbal performance in the accepted standard dialect of the English language and vocal affirmation of conscious black identity.[14] Although Robinson's performance before the cameras provided an impeccable image of bourgeois respectability that could easily be read as the erasure of consciousness of black identity, he was at the same time known for publicly affirming his interest in the various sociopolitical factors that affect blacks' existence in the United States, thus continually emphasizing his African-American identity. For example, in February 1981, Robinson became the center of controversy when he was reported as telling a college audience that the various network news agencies, including ABC, discriminated against their black journalists, and that the news media in general constitute "a crooked mirror" through which "white America views itself."[15] In this instance, not only does Robinson's statement manifest semantically his consciousness of his own black identity, but the very form of the entire incident can be said to embody an identifiably black cultural behavior. After being summoned to the offices of then–ABC News president Roone Arledge subsequent to making his allegations of network discrimination, Robinson said that "he had not meant to single out ABC for criticism,"[16] thus performing a type of rhetorical backstep by which his criticism, though retracted, was effectively lodged and registered both by the public and by the network. While this mode of protecting one's own interests is by no means unique to African-American culture, it does have a particular resonance within an African-American context. Specifically,

Robinson's backstepping strategy can be understood as a form of what is called "loud-talking" or "louding" — a verbal device, common within many black–English-speaking communities, in which a person "says something of someone just loud enough for that person to hear, but indirectly, so he cannot properly respond," or so that, when the object of the remark *does* respond, "the speaker can reply to the effect, 'Oh, I wasn't talking to you.'"[17] Robinson's insistence that his remarks did not refer specifically to ABC News can be interpreted as a form of the disingenuous reply characteristic of loud-talking, thus locating his rhetorical strategy within the cultural context of black communicative patterns and underscoring his African-American identification.

Roone Arledge, in summoning Robinson to his offices after the incident, made unusually explicit the suppression of African-American identity generally effected by the networks in their news productions; such dramatic measures are not usually necessary because potential manifestations of strong black cultural identification are normally subdued by blacks' very participation in the discursive conventions of the network newscast.[18] Thus, the more audible and insistent Max Robinson's televised performance in Received Standard English and in the white bourgeois idiom of the network newscast, the more secure the silence imposed upon the vocal black consciousness that he always threatened to display. Robinson's articulate speech before the cameras always implied a silencing of the African-American idiom.

Concomitant with the silencing in the network news context of black-affirmative discourse is the suppression of another aspect of black identity alluded to in the above-quoted references to Max Robinson's on-camera performance. The emphasis these commentaries place on Robinson's articulateness is coupled with their simultaneous insistence on his physical attractiveness: Bruce Rheins's remarks on Robinson's "obvious intelligence" are accompanied by a reference to his "good looks"; Tony Schwartz's inventory of Robinson's assets notes both his "commanding voice" and his "handsome appearance"; Joseph Kahn's "appreciation" of Robinson cites his "brilliant reporting" as well as his "telegenic" quality; it seems impossible to comment on Robinson's success as a newsanchor without noting simultaneously his verbal ability and his physical appeal.

Such commentary is not at all unusual in discussions of television newscasters, whose personal charms have taken on an increasing degree of importance since the early day of the medium. Indeed, Schwartz's 1980 *New York Times* article entitled "Are TV Anchormen Merely Performers?" — intended as a critique of the degree to which television news is conceived as entertainment — actually underscores the importance of a newscaster's physical attractiveness to a broadcast's success; and by the late 1980s that importance had become a truism of contemporary culture, assimilated into the popular consciousness, through the movie *Broadcast News*, for instance.[19] In the case of a black man, such as Max Robinson, however, discussions of a newsanchor's "star quality" become potentially problematic and, consequently, extremely complex, because such a quality is founded upon an implicitly acknowledged "sex appeal," the concept of which has always been highly charged with respect to black men in the United States.

In the classic text on the subject, Calvin C. Hernton has argued that the black man has historically been perceived as the bearer of a bestial sexuality, as the savage "walking phallus" that poses a constant threat to an idealized white womanhood and thus to the whole U.S. social order.[20] To the extent that this is true, then for white patriarchal institutions such as the mainstream media to note the physical attractiveness of any black man is for them potentially to unleash the very beast that threatens their power. Max Robinson's achievement of a professional, public position that mandates the deployment of a certain rhetoric — that of the newsanchor's attractive and telegenic persona — thus also raises the problem of taming the threatening black male sexuality that that rhetoric conjures up.

This taming, I think, is once again achieved through Robinson's articulate verbal performance, references to which routinely accompany acknowledgments of his physical attractiveness. In commentary on white newscasters, paired references to both their physical appeal and their rhetorical skill serve merely to defuse accusations that television journalism is superficial and "image-oriented." In Robinson's case, however, the acknowledgment of his articulateness also serves to absorb the threat of his sexuality that is raised in references to his physical attractiveness; in the same way that Robinson's conformity to the "rules" of standard–English-language performance suppresses the possibility of his articulating a radical identification with African-American culture, it also, in attesting to his refinement and civility, actually *domesticates* his threatening physicality that itself *must* be alluded to in conventional liberal accounts of his performance as a newsanchor. James Snyder's reference to Robinson's "great presence" is a most stunning example of such an account, for it neatly conflates and thus simultaneously acknowledges both Robinson's *physical* person (in the tradition of commentary on network news personalities) and his virtuosity in standard *verbal* performance in such a way that the latter mitigates the threat posed by the former. Max Robinson's standard-English speech, then, serves not only to suppress black cultural-linguistic forms that might disrupt the white bourgeois aspect of network news, but also to keep in check the black male sexuality that threatens the social order that the news media represent.[21] Ironically, in this latter function, white bourgeois discourse seems to share an objective with forms of black discourse, which themselves work to suppress certain threatening elements of black male sexuality, resulting in a strange reaction to Max Robinson's death in African-American communities.

Homophobia in African-American Discourse

Whether it is interpreted as a reference to his facility at Received Standard English, whereby he achieved a degree of success in the white-run world of broadcast media, or as a reference to his repeated attempts to vocalize, in the tradition of African-American discourse, the grievances of blacks with respect to their sociopolitical status in the United States, to "speak like Max Robinson" is simultaneously to silence discussion of the various possibilities of black male sexuality. We have seen how an emphasis on Robinson's facility at "white-oriented" discourse serves to defuse the "threat" of rampant black male sexuality that constitutes so much of the sexual-political structure of U.S. society. Indeed, some middle-class blacks have colluded in this defusing of black sexuality, attempting to explode whites' stereotypes of blacks as oversexed by stifling discussion of black sexuality generally.[22] At the same time, the other tradition from which Max Robinson's speech derives meaning also functions to suppress discussion about specific aspects of black male sexuality that are threatening to the black male image.

In her book on "the language of black America," Geneva Smitherman cites, rather unself-consciously, examples of black discourse that illustrate this point. For instance, in a discussion of black musicians' adaptation of themes from the African-American oral tradition, Smitherman mentions the popular early 1960s recording of "Stagger Lee," based on a traditional narrative folk poem. The hero for whom the narrative is named is, as Smitherman puts it, "a fearless, mean dude," so that "it became widely fashionable [in black communities] to refer to oneself as 'Stag,' as in..., 'Don't mess wif me, cause I ain't no fag, uhm Stag'" (52). What is notable here is not merely the homophobia manifested in the "rap" laid down by the black "brother" imagined to be speaking this line, but also that the rap itself, the very verbal performance, as Smitherman points out, serves as the evidence that the speaker is indeed *not* a "fag"; verbal facility becomes proof of one's conventional masculinity and thus silences discussion of one's possible homosexuality.[23] This point touches upon a truism in studies of black discourse. Smitherman herself implies the testament to masculine prowess embodied in the black "rap," explaining that, "While some raps convey social and cultural information, others are used for conquering foes and women" (82); and she further acknowledges the "power" with which the spoken word is imbued in the African-American tradition (as in others), especially insofar as it is employed in masculine "image-making," through braggadocio and other highly self-assertive strategies (83, 97).[24] Indeed, a whole array of these verbal strategies for establishing a strong masculine image can be identified in the contemporary phenomenon of "rap" music, a form indigenous to black male culture, though increasingly appropriated and transformed by members of other social groups, notably black women.[25]

If verbal facility is considered as an identifying mark of masculinity in certain African-American contexts, however, this is only when it is demonstrated specifically through use of the vernacular. Indeed, a too-evident facility in the standard white idiom can quickly identify one not as a strong black man, but rather as a white-identified Uncle Tom who must also, therefore, be weak, effeminate, and probably a "fag." To the extent that this process of homophobic identification reflects powerful cross-class hostilities, then it is certainly not unique to African-American culture. Its imbrication with questions of racial identity, however, compounds its potency in the African-American context. Simply put, within some African-American communities the "professional" or "intellectual" black male inevitably endangers his status both as black and as "male" whenever he evidences a facility with Received Standard English — a facility upon which his very identity as a professional or an intellectual in the larger society is founded in the first place. Max Robinson was not the first black man to face this dilemma;[26] a decade or so before he emerged on network television, a particularly influential group of black writers attempted to negotiate the problem by incorporating into their work the semantics of "street" discourse, thereby establishing an intellectual practice that was both "black" enough and virile enough to bear the weight of a stridently nationalist agenda. Thus, a strong Stagger Lee–type identification can be found in the poem "Don't Cry, Scream," by Haki Madhubuti (Don L. Lee):

> swung on a faggot who politely
> scratched his ass in my presence.
> he smiled broken teeth stained from
> his over-used tongue, fisted-face.
> teeth dropped in tune with ray
> charles singing 'yesterday.'[27]

Here the scornful language of the poem itself recapitulates the homophobic violence that it commemorates (or invites us to imagine as having occurred), the two together attesting to the speaker's aversion to homosexuality and, thus, to his own unquestionable masculinity. Although it is striking, the violent hostility evident in this piece is not at all unusual among the revolutionist poems of the Black Arts movement. Much of the work by the Black Arts poets is characterized by a violent language that seems wishfully conceived of as potent and performative — as capable, in itself, of wreaking destruction upon the white establishment to which the Black Power movement is opposed.[28] What is important to note, beyond the rhetoric of violence, is the way in which that rhetoric is conceived as part and parcel of a black nationalism to which all sufficiently proud African Americans must subscribe. Nikki Giovanni, for instance, urges, "Learn to kill niggers / Learn to be Black men," indicating the necessity of cathartic violence to the transformation of blacks from victims into active subjects, and illustrating the degree to which black masculinity functions as the rhetorical stake in much of the Black Arts poetry by both men *and* women.[29] To the extent that such rhetoric is considered an integral element in the cultural-nationalist strategy of Black Power politics, then a violent homophobia, too, is necessarily implicated in this particular nationalistic position, which since the late 1960s has filtered throughout black communities in the United States as a major influence in African-American culture.

Consequently, Max Robinson was put in a very difficult position with respect to talking about his AIDS diagnosis. Robinson's reputation was based on his articulate outspokenness; however, as we have seen, that very well-spokenness derived its power within two different modes of discourse that, though they are sometimes at odds, both work to suppress issues of sexuality that are implied in any discussion of AIDS.[30] The white bourgeois cultural context in which Robinson derived his status as an authoritative figure in the mainstream news media must always keep a vigilant check on black male sexuality, which is perceived to be threatening generally (and it is assisted in this task by a moralistic black middle class that seeks to explode notions of black hyper-sexuality). At the same time, the African-American cultural context to which Robinson appealed for his status as a paragon of black pride and self-determination embodies an ethic that precludes sympathetic discussion of black male homosexuality. However rapidly the demography of AIDS in this country may be shifting as more and more people who are not gay men become infected with HIV, the historical and cultural conditions surrounding the development of the epidemic ensure its ongoing association with male homosexuality, so it is not surprising that the latter should emerge as a topic of discussion in any consideration of Max Robinson's death. The apparent *inevitability* of that emergence (and the degree to which the association between AIDS and male homosexuality would become threatening to Robinson's reputation and discursively problematic, given the contexts in which his public persona was created) is dramatically illustrated in the 9 January 1989 issue of *Jet* magazine, the black-oriented weekly. That number of *Jet* contains an obituary of Max Robinson that is very similar to those issued by the *New York Times* and other nonblack media, noting Robinson's professional achievements and his controversial tenure at ABC News, alluding to the "tormented" nature of his life as a symbol of black success, and citing his secrecy surrounding his AIDS diagnosis and his wish that his death be used as the occasion to educate blacks about AIDS. The *Jet* obituary also notes that "the main victims [*sic*] of the disease [*sic*] have been intravenous drug users and homosexuals," leaving open the question of Robinson's relation to either of these categories.[31]

Printed right next to Robinson's obituary in the same issue of *Jet* is a notice of another AIDS-related death, that of the popular disco singer Sylvester. Sylvester's obituary, however, offers an interesting contrast to that of Robinson, for it identifies Sylvester, in its very first sentence, as "the flamboyant homosexual singer whose high-pitched voice and dramatic on-stage costumes propelled him to the height of stardom on the disco music scene during the late 1970s." The piece goes on to indicate the openness with which Sylvester lived as a gay man, noting that he "first publicly acknowledged he had AIDS at the San Francisco Gay Pride March last June [1988], which he attended in a wheelchair with the People With AIDS group," and quoting his recollection of his first sexual experience, at age seven, with an adult male evangelist: "You see, I was a queen even back then, so it didn't bother me. I rather liked it."[32]

Obviously, a whole array of issues is raised by Sylvester's obituary and its juxtaposition with that of Max Robinson (not the least of which has to do with the complicated phenomenon of sex between adults and children). What is most pertinent for discussion here, however, is the difference between *Jet*'s treatments of Sylvester's and Max Robinson's sexualities, and the factors that account for that difference. It is clear, I think, that Sylvester's public persona emerges from contexts that are different from those that produced Max Robinson's. If it is true that, as *Jet* puts it, "the church was . . . the setting for Sylvester's first homosexual experience" (18), it is also true that "Sylvester learned to sing in churches in South Los Angeles and went on to perform at gospel conventions around the state" (18). That is to say that the church-choir context in which Sylvester was groomed for a singing career has stereotypically served as a locus in which young black men both discover and sublimate their homosexuality, and also as a conduit to a world of professional entertainment generally conceived as "tolerant," if not downright encouraging, of diverse sexualities. In Sylvester's case, this was particularly true, since he was able to help create a disco culture characterized by a fusion of elements from black and gay communities and in which he and others could thrive as openly gay men. Thus, the black-church context, though ostensibly hostile to homosexuality and gay identity, nevertheless has traditionally provided a means by which black men can achieve a sense of themselves as homosexual and even, in cases such as Sylvester's, expand that sense into a gay-affirmative public persona.[33]

The public figure of Max Robinson, as we have seen, is cut from entirely different cloth, formed in the intersection of discursive contexts that do not allow for the expression of black male homosexuality in any recognizable form. The discursive bind constituted by Robinson's status both as a conventionally successful media personality and as exemplar of black male self-assertion and racial consciousness left him with no alternative to the manner in which he dealt with his diagnosis in the public forum — shrouding the nature of his illness in a secrecy that he was able to break only after his death, with the posthumous acknowledgment that he had AIDS. Consequently, obituarists and commentators on Robinson's death are faced with the "problem" of how to address issues relating to Robinson's sexuality — to his possible *homo*sexuality — the result being a large body of wrongminded commentary that actually hinders the educational efforts Max Robinson supposedly intended to endorse.

It is a mistake to think that, because most accounts of Robinson's death do not mention the possibility of his homosexuality, it is not conceived of as a problem to be reckoned with. On the contrary, since, as I have attempted to show, the discursive contexts in which Max Robinson derived his power as a public figure function to prevent discussion of black male homosexuality, the silence regarding the topic that characterizes most of the notices of Robinson's death actually marks the degree to which the possibility of black male homosexuality is worried over and considered problematic. The instances in which the possibility of Robinson's homosexuality *does* explicitly figure actually serve as proof of the anxiety that founds the more usual silence on the subject. A look at a few commentaries on Robinson's death will illustrate this well; examining these pieces in the chronological order of their appearance in the media will especially help us to see how, over time, the need to quell anxiety about the possibility of Robinson's homosexuality becomes increasingly desperate, thus increasingly undermining the educational efforts that his death was supposed to occasion.

In the two weeks after Robinson died, there appeared in *Newsweek* magazine an obituary that, once again, includes the obligatory references to Robinson's "commanding" on-air presence, to his attacks on racism in the media, and to the psychic "conflict" he suffered that led him to drink.[34] In addition to rehearsing this standard litany, however, the *Newsweek* obituary also emphasizes that "even [Robinson's] family . . . don't know how he contracted the disease." The reference to the general ignorance as to how Robinson became infected with HIV — the virus widely believed to cause the suppressed immunity that underlies AIDS — leaves open the possibility that Robinson engaged in "homosexual activity" that put him at risk for infection, just as the *Jet* notice leaves unresolved the possibility that he was a homosexual or an IV drug user. Yet, the invocation in the *Newsweek* piece of Robinson's "family," with all its conventional heterosexist associations, simultaneously indicates the anxiety that the possibility of Robinson's homosexuality generally produces, and constitutes an attempt to redeem Robinson from the unsavory implications of his AIDS diagnosis.

The subtlety of the *Newsweek* strategy for dealing with the possibility of Robinson's homosexuality gives way to a more direct approach by Jesse Jackson, in an interview broadcast on the NPR series on AIDS and blacks. Responding to charges by black AIDS activists that he missed a golden opportunity to educate blacks about AIDS by neglecting to speak out about modes of HIV transmission soon after Robinson's death, Jackson provided this statement:

> Max shared with my family and me that he had the AIDS virus [*sic*], but that it did not come from homosexuality, it came from promiscuity. . . . And now we know that the number one transmission [factor] for AIDS is not sexual contact, it's drugs, and so the crises of drugs and needles and AIDS are connected, as well as AIDS and promiscuity are connected. And all we can do is keep urging people not to isolate this crisis by race, or by class, or by sexual preference, but in fact to observe the precautionary measures that have been advised, on the one hand, and keep urging more money

for research immediately because it's an international health crisis and it's a killer disease.[35]

A number of things are notable about this statement. First of all, Jackson, like the *Newsweek* writer, is careful to reincorporate the discussion of Robinson's AIDS diagnosis into the nuclear family context, emphasizing that Robinson shared his secret with Jackson *and his family,* and thereby attempting to mitigate the effects of the association of AIDS with male homosexuality. Second, Jackson invokes the problematic and completely unhelpful concept of "promiscuity," wrongly opposing it to homosexuality (and thus implicitly equating it with heterosexuality) in such a way that he actually appears to be endorsing it over that less legitimate option, contrary to what he must intend to convey about the dangers of unprotected sex with multiple partners; and, of course, since he does not actually mention safer sex practices, he implies that it is "promiscuity," per se, that puts people at risk of contracting HIV, when it is, rather, unprotected sex with however few partners that constitutes risky behavior. Third, by identifying IV drug use over risky sexual behavior as the primary means of HIV transmission, Jackson manifests a blindness to his own insight about the interrelatedness of various factors in the phenomenon of AIDS, for unprotected sexual activity is often part and parcel of the drug culture (especially that of crack) in which transmission of HIV thrives, as sex is commonly exchanged for access to drugs in that context.[36] Finally, Jackson's sense of "all we can do" to prevent AIDS is woefully inadequate: "urging... people to observe the precautionary measures that have been advised" obviously presupposes that everyone is already aware of what those precautionary measures are, for Jackson himself does not outline them in his statement; to demand more money for research is crucial, but it does not go the slightest distance toward enabling people to protect themselves from HIV in the present; and to resist conceptualizing AIDS as endemic to one race, class, or sexual orientation is of extreme importance (though it is equally important to recognize the relative degrees of interest that different constituencies have in the epidemic), but in the context of Jackson's statement this strategy for preventing various social groups from being stigmatized through their association with AIDS is utilized merely to protect Max Robinson in particular from speculation that his bout with AIDS was related to homosexual sex. Indeed, Jackson's entire statement centers on the effort to clear Max Robinson from potential charges of homosexuality, and his intense focus on this homophobic endeavor works to the detriment of his attempts to make factual statements about the nature of HIV transmission.[37]

Jackson is implicated, as well, in the third media response to Robinson's death that I want to examine, a response that, like those discussed above, represents an effort to silence discussion of the possibility of Max Robinson's homosexuality. In his June 1989 *Vanity Fair* article, Peter J. Boyer reports on the eulogy Jackson delivered at the Washington, D.C., memorial service for Max Robinson. Boyer cites Jackson's quotation of Robinson's deathbed request: "He said, 'I'm not sure and know not where [*sic*], but even on my dying bed . . . let my predicament be a source of education to our people.'" Boyer then asserts that "two thousand people heard Jesse Jackson keep the promise he'd made to Robinson . . . : 'It was not homosexuality,' [Jackson] told them, 'but promiscuity,'" implicitly letting people know that Robinson "got AIDS from a woman" (84). Apparently, then, the only deathbed promise that Jackson kept was the one he made to ensure that people would not think that Robinson was gay; no information about how HIV is transmitted or about how such transmission can be prevented has escaped his lips in connection with the death of Max Robinson, though Peter Boyer, evidently, has been fooled into believing that Jackson's speech constituted just such substantive information. This is not surprising, since Boyer's article itself is nothing more than an anxious effort to convince us of Max Robinson's heterosexuality, as if that were the crucial issue. Boyer's piece mentions Robinson's three marriages (74); it comments extensively on his "well-earned" reputation as an "inveterate womanizer," and emphasizes his attractiveness to women, quoting one male friend as saying, "He could walk into a room and you could just hear the panties drop," and a woman acquaintance as once telling a reporter, "Don't forget to mention he has fine thighs" (74); it notes that "none of Robinson's friends believe that he was a homosexual" (84); and it cites Robinson's own desperate attempt "to compose a list of women whom he suspected as possible sources of his disease" (84), as though to provide written corroboration of his insistence to a friend, "But I'm not gay" (82).

From early claims, then, that "even Robinson's family" had no idea how he contracted HIV, there developed an authoritative scenario in which Robinson's extensive heterosexual affairs were common knowledge and which posits his contraction of HIV from a female sex partner as a near certainty. It seems that, subsequent to Robinson's death, a whole propaganda machine was put into operation to establish a suitable account of his contraction of HIV and of his bout with AIDS, the net result of which was to preclude the effective AIDS education that Robinson reputedly wanted his death to occasion, as the point he supposedly intended to make became lost in a homophobic shuffle to "fix" his sexual orientation and to construe his death in inoffensive terms.

In order to ensure that this essay not become absorbed in that project, then, which would deter us from the more crucial task of understanding how to combat the AIDS epidemic, it is important for me to state flat out that I have no idea whether Max Robinson's sex partners were male or female or both. I acknowledge explicitly my ignorance on this matter because to do so, I think, is to reopen sex in all its manifestations as a primary category for consideration as we review modes of HIV transmission in African-American communities. Such a move is crucial because the same homophobic impulse that informs efforts to establish Max Robinson's heterosexuality is also implicated in a general reluctance to provide detailed information about sexual transmission of HIV in black communities; indeed a deep silence regarding the details of such transmission has characterized almost all of what passes for government-sponsored AIDS education efforts throughout the United States.

Sins of Omission:
Inadequacy in AIDS-Education Programs

Even the slickest, most visible print and television ads promoting awareness about AIDS consistently thematize a silence that has been a major obstacle to effective AIDS education in communities of color. Notices distributed around the time of Max Robinson's death utilized an array of celebrities — from Rubèn Blades to Patti Labelle — who encouraged people to "get the facts" regarding AIDS, but didn't offer any, merely referring readers elsewhere for substantive information on the syndrome.[38] A bitter testimony to the

inefficacy of this ad campaign is offered by a thirty-one-year-old
black woman interviewed in the NPR series on AIDS and blacks.
"Sandra" contracted HIV through unprotected heterosexual sex; the
child conceived in that encounter died at ten months of age from
an AIDS-related illness. In her interview, "Sandra" reflects on her
lack of knowledge about AIDS at the time she became pregnant:

> I don't remember hearing anything about AIDS until either the year
> that I was pregnant, which would have been 1986, or the year after
> I had her; but I really believe it was when I was pregnant with her
> because I always remember saying, "I'm going to write and get that
> information," because the only thing that was on TV was to write or
> call the 1–800 number to get information, and I always wanted to call
> and get that pamphlet, not knowing that I was going to have firsthand
> information. I didn't know how it was transmitted. I didn't know that
> it was caused by a virus. I didn't know that [AIDS] stood for "Acquired
> Immune Deficiency Syndrome." I didn't know any of that.[39]

By 1986, when Sandra believes she first began even to hear about
AIDS, the epidemic was at least five years old.

If, even today, response to AIDS in black communities is characterized by a profound silence regarding actual sexual practices,
either heterosexual or homosexual, this is largely because of the
suppression of talk about sexuality generally and about male homosexuality in particular that is enacted in black communities through
the discourses that constitute them. Additionally, however, this continued silence is *enabled* by the ease with which the significance
of sexual transmission of HIV can be elided beneath the admittedly
massive (but also, to many minds, more "acceptable") problem of
IV drug-related HIV transmission that is endemic in some black
communities. George Bellinger, Jr., a "minority outreach" worker at
Gay Men's Health Crisis, the New York City AIDS service organization, recounted for the NPR series "the horrible joke that used to
go around [in black communities] when AIDS first started: 'There's
good news and bad news. The bad news is I have AIDS, the good
news is I'm an IV drug user' ";[40] this joke indicates the degree to
which IV drug use can serve as a shield against the implications of
male homosexuality that are always associated with AIDS and that
hover as a threat over any discussion of sexual transmission of HIV.
This phenomenon is at work even in the NPR series itself. For all its
emphasis on the need for black communities to "recognize homo-

sexuality and bisexuality" within them, and despite its inclusion of articulate black lesbians and gay men in its roster of interviewees, the radio series still elides sexual transmission of HIV beneath a focus on IV drug use. One segment in particular illustrates this point. In an interview broadcast on "Morning Edition," 4 April 1989, Harold Jaffe, from the federal Centers for Disease Control, makes a crucial point regarding gay male sexual behavior in the face of the AIDS epidemic: "The studies that have come out saying gay men have made substantial changes in their behavior are true, but they're true mainly for white, middle-class, exclusively gay men." As correspondent Richard Harris reports, however, Jaffe "doesn't see that trend among black gays." Harris notes that "Jaffe has been studying syphilis rates, which are a good measure of safe-sex practices." Jaffe himself proclaims his discoveries: "We find very major decreases [in the rate of syphilis] in white gay men, and either no change or even increases in Hispanic and black gay men, suggesting that they have not really gotten the same behavioral message." Harris continues: "White gay men have changed their behavior to such an extent that experts believe the disease has essentially peaked for them, so as those numbers gradually subside, minorities will make up a growing proportion of AIDS cases." Up to this point, Harris's report has focused on important differences between the rates of syphilis and HIV transmission among gay white men and among black and Latino gay men, suggesting the inadequacy of the educational resources made available to gay men of color. As his rhetoric shifts, however, to refer to the risk that *all* members of "minority" groups face, regardless of their sexual identification, the risky behaviors on which he focuses also change. After indicating the need for gay men of color to change their sexual behavior in the same way that white gay men have, and after a pause of a couple beats that would conventionally indicate the introduction of some narrative into the report to illustrate this point, Harris segues into a story about Rosina, a former IV drug user who has AIDS, and to a claim that "about the only way to stop AIDS from spreading in the inner city is to help addicts get off of drugs." Thus, Harris's early focus on AIDS among black and Latino gay men serves, in the end, merely as a bridge to discussion of IV drug use as the primary factor in the spread of AIDS in communities of color. Moreover, the diversity of those communities is effaced through the conventional euphemistic reference to the "inner city," which, because it disregards class differences among blacks and Latinos, falsely homogenizes the concerns of people of color and glosses over the complex nature of HIV transmission among them, which, just as with whites, implicates drug use *and* unprotected sexual activity as high-risk behaviors. The ease with which middle-class blacks can construe IV drug use as a problem of communities that are completely removed from their everyday lives (and as unrelated to high-risk sexual activity in which they may engage) makes an exclusive emphasis on IV, drug-related HIV transmission among blacks actually detrimental to efforts at effective AIDS education.

To the extent that Max Robinson hoped that his death would occasion efforts at *comprehensive* AIDS education in black communities, we must consider programs that utilize the logic manifested in Richard Harris's NPR report as inadequate to meet the challenge that Robinson posed. The inadequacy of such efforts is rooted, as I have suggested, in a reluctance to discuss issues of black sexuality that is based simultaneously on whites' stereotyped notions (often defensively adopted by blacks themselves) about the need to suppress black (male) sexuality generally, and on the strictness with which traditional forms of black discourse preclude the possibility of the discussion of black male homosexuality specifically. Indeed, these very factors necessitated the peculiar response to his own AIDS diagnosis that Max Robinson manifested — initial denial and posthumous acknowledgment. I suggested at the beginning of this essay that Robinson's final acknowledgment of his AIDS diagnosis — in the form of his injunction that we use his death as the occasion to increase blacks' awareness about AIDS — performs a sort of epitaphic function. As the final words of the deceased that constitute an implicit warning to others not to repeat his mistakes, Robinson's request has been promulgated through the media with such a repetitive insistence that it might as well have been literally etched in stone. The repetitive nature of the request ought itself to serve as a warning to us, however, since repetition can recapitulate the very silence that it is meant to overcome. As Debra Fried has said, regarding the epitaph, it is both

silent and . . . repetitious; [it] refuses to speak, and yet keeps on saying the same thing: refusal to say anything different is tantamount to a refusal to speak. Repetition thus becomes a form of silence. . . . According to the fiction of epitaphs, death imposes on its victims an endless verbal task: to repeat without deviation or difference the answer to a question that, no matter how many times it prompts the epitaph to the same silent utterance, is never satisfactorily answered.[41]

In the case of Max Robinson's death, the pertinent question is: How can transmission of HIV and thus AIDS-related death be prevented? The burden of response at this point is not on the deceased, however, but on us. We must formulate educational programs that offer comprehensive information on the prevention of HIV transmission. In order to do so, we must break the rules of the various discourses through which black life in the United States has traditionally been articulated. A less radical strategy cannot induce the widespread behavioral changes that are necessary in the face of AIDS, and our failure in this task would mean sacrificing black people to an epidemic that is enabled, paradoxically, by the very discourses that shape our lives.

NOTES

An earlier version of this essay was presented at the conference on Nationalisms and Sexualities, held at the Center for Literary and Cultural Studies, Harvard University, June 1989.

The following people have assisted me in the preparation of this article by providing statistical information, directing me to source materials, or commenting on early drafts of the essay: Harold Dufour-Anderson, David Halperin, Paul Morrison, Timothy Murphy, Suzanne Poirier, Julie Rioux, and Thom Whitaker.

1. Centers for Disease Control, *HIV/AIDS Surveillance Report* (March 1991), table 7, p. 2.

2. Or at least not until November 1991, after the body of this essay was written, when pro basketball player Earvin "Magic" Johnson announced his infection with the human immunodeficiency virus, believed to be the chief factor in the aetiology of AIDS. That announcement precipitated a public response unprecedented in the history of the epidemic. While I do not address directly the nature of that response in this essay, I do believe that it was shaped largely by the set of social phenomena that I have tried to describe here. Indeed, I would argue that the very status of the black basketball player as a sports superstar who thus warrants mass attention (in contrast, for example, to the relatively lower profile of black tennis champion Arthur Ashe, who in April 1992 announced that he himself had AIDS) derives in the main from the very intersection of racial, sexual, and class politics that comprises the primary subject matter of my essay. While the rapidly changing course of the epidemic will no doubt quickly render out-of-date the various topical observations that I make

here, I fear that much time will pass before the validity of my analysis, and of the general claims based on it, expires.

3. National Center for Health Statistics, *Health United States 1989* (Hyattsville, Md.: Public Health Service, 1990), table 3, p. 151.

4. From a broadcast on National Public Radio, "All Things Considered," 20 December 1988.

5. Peter J. Boyer, "The Light Goes Out," *Vanity Fair* (June 1989): 70.

6. Jeremy Gerard, "Max Robinson, 49, First Black to Anchor Network News, Dies," *New York Times,* 21 December 1988, sec. D, p. 19.

7. Tony Schwartz, "Are TV Anchormen Merely Performers?" *New York Times,* 27 July 1980, sec. 2, pp. 1, 27.

8. Joseph P. Kahn, "Max Robinson: Tormented Pioneer," *Boston Globe,* 21 December 1988, 67.

9. Cited in Boyer, "The Light Goes Out," 72.

10. "Max Robinson, 49, First Black Anchor for Networks; of AIDS Complications," obituary in the *Boston Globe,* 21 December 1988, 51.

11. Geneva Smitherman, *Talkin and Testifyin: The Language of Black America* (Boston: Houghton Mifflin, 1977), 12.

12. For an overview of the various black nationalist movements that have emerged in the United States since the late eighteenth century, see John H. Bracey, Jr., August Meier, and Elliott Rudwick, eds., *Black Nationalism in America* (Indianapolis and New York: Bobbs-Merrill, 1970). It should be noted here that the different nationalisms (cultural, revolutionary, and economic, for instance) are not always considered as sharing a common objective. See, for example, Linda Harrison's commentary on the inadequacy of cultural nationalism with respect to a black revolutionary agenda ("On Cultural Nationalism," in Philip S. Foner, ed., *The Black Panthers Speak* [New York: Lippincott, 1970], 151–53). Nevertheless, it seems to me that a generalized cultural nationalism, more than any other form, has been a pervasive influence in African-American life since the 1960s, and it is to this brand of nationalism that I allude repeatedly in this essay.

13. Smitherman, *Talkin,* 11.

14. This dichotomy corresponds, of course, to that described by W. E. B. Du Bois in his classic discussion of blacks' "double-consciousness" — the effect of their inability to reconcile their blackness and their "American" identity. See *The Souls of Black Folk* (1903), especially, chap. 1, "Of Our Spiritual Strivings."

15. Tony Schwartz, "Robinson of ABC News Quoted as Saying Network Discriminates," *New York Times,* 11 February 1981, sec. C, p. 21; see also "Gerard, "Max Robinson."

16. "Gerard, "Max Robinson."

17. Roger D. Abrahams, *Talking Black* (Rowley, Mass.: Newbury House, 1976), 19, 54; see also Claudia Mitchell-Kernan, "Signifying, Loud-talking and Marking," in Thomas Kochman, ed., *Rappin' and Stylin' Out: Communication in Urban Black America* (Urbana: University of Illinois Press, 1972), 315–35.

18. An additional example of the networks' explicit suppression of African-American identity involves black newsman Ed Bradley, a correspondent on the CBS News program "60 Minutes." Bradley sent "60 Minutes" producer Don Hewitt into a panic when he decided to change his name to Shaheeb Sha Hab, thereby reflecting his allegiance with Islamic black nationalism. Hewitt was able to convince Bradley

not to take this step, and thus to keep black nationalist politics out of the scope of the "60 Minutes" cameras. See Don Hewitt, *Minute by Minute* (New York: Random House, 1985), 170.

19. This development may indicate a perverse "feminization" of the television newsanchor insofar as an insistent emphasis on physical appearance to the neglect of professional accomplishment has historically characterized women's experience in the public sphere. An indication of the extent to which this tyranny of "beauty" can now shape mass cultural phenomena is provided in the field of contemporary pop music. Since the advent of music video in the 1980s, the importance of musical acts' eye appeal has increased to such a degree that models are sometimes hired to lip sync and otherwise "visualize" a song that is actually sung by someone else outside the audience's range of view. The most notorious such case involved the male duo Milli Vanilli, but the mere fact that men are increasingly subject to the imperative of "sex appeal" by no means implies that they now suffer from a social oppression parallel or equal to that borne by women.

20. Calvin C. Hernton, *Sex and Racism in America* (New York: Doubleday, 1965). As support for his argument, Hernton cites numerous instances of white-perpetrated violence against black men perceived to embody a threat to white femininity. Although such instances may be much less frequent now than in 1965, a structure of sociosexual relations that confers an inordinately threatening status upon black men remains very firmly in place in the United States. Consider, for instance, the intense response to the April 1989 attack by a group of black youths on a white woman jogger in Central Park. This response, like the incident itself, was highly overdetermined, and too complex to analyze here, but it culminated in a widely publicized call by real estate magnate Donald Trump for application of the death penalty. It was suggested by numerous people that the intensity of the response was a function of the racial and gender identities of the parties involved, and that a different configuration (white attackers or a black or male victim) would not have produced the same degree of outrage or media coverage. See Craig Wolff, "Youths Rape Jogger on Central Park Road," *New York Times,* 21 April 1989, sec. B, pp. 1, 3; and the full-page display ad paid for by Donald Trump, *New York Times,* 1 May 1989, sec. A, p. 13. See also the daily coverage provided by the *Times* during the period framed by these two editions of the paper.

21. I want to emphasize that I consider this management of sexuality to be an operation that the culture continually performs upon each individual black male. The very appearance of a black man on the network newscast may seem to indicate that *he,* at least, has been judged safe for exposure before the bourgeois white audience, and his use of articulate and "objective" journalistic language would then serve merely as a sort of seal of his innocuousness. This could only be true, though, if the recognizably "professional" black male were generally seen as distinct from the mass of black men whose presence on U.S. streets is routinely considered a threat to the well-being of the larger community. As any of us who have been detained and questioned by white urban police for no reason can attest, however, this is not the case. Just as every black man might suddenly manifest an ideological challenge that would certainly have to be kept in check (by a Roone Arledge or a Don Hewitt, for instance, in the broadcast news context), so too does every black man represent an ongoing threat of untamed sexuality that must continually be defused. Thus Max Robinson's expert use of Received Standard English is not merely a mark of his

already having been neutralized as a threat to white bourgeois interests; rather, it is itself the neutralization of the threat, continual proof against black male insurgency.

22. This phenomenon was noted in a report on the 5 April 1989 broadcast of National Public Radio's "Morning Edition." The report was part of the NPR series "AIDS and Blacks: Breaking the Silence," broadcast on "Morning Edition" and "All Things Considered" during the week of 3 April 1989.

23. Frequently in this essay I will use the term "homosexual" (and "homosexuality") rather than "gay" or the even more militant "queer" when talking about sexual identifications within an African-American context. I do this not because I prefer the clinical connotations of "homosexual" to what I, personally, experience as the infinitely more liberating resonances of "gay" or "queer," but because I want to point out the limited degree to which many men of color feel identified with these latter terms. Indeed, "gay," especially, conjures up in the minds of many who hear it images of a population that is characteristically white, male, and financially well-off; thus it can actually efface, rather than affirm, the experiences of women and of men of color. (This is why some groups of black men who might have identified as gay have chosen instead to designate themselves by terms they feel reflect a specifically Afrocentric experience. Consider the case of "Adodi," which has been used by black men in both Philadelphia and Boston; see Elizabeth Pincus, "Black Gay Men in Boston Organize," *Gay Community News* 15, no. 46 [12–18 June 1988]: 3, 9.) I use "homosexual," then, to signal the difficulty of fairly designating any "minority" group, due to the inevitably complex and multifaceted nature of minority identity.

24. Other researchers, too, have noted the peculiarly male-identified nature of the black "rap," among them Thomas Kochman (" 'Rapping' in the Black Ghetto," *Transaction* 6 [February 1969]: 26–34); Roger D. Abrahams ("Playing the Dozens," *Journal of American Folklore* 75 [July–September 1962]: 209–220); and Mitchell-Kernan, "Signifying."

25. See Lauren Berlant, "The Female Complaint," *Social Text* 19/20 (Fall 1988): 237–59.

26. Nor was he the last. My own performance in this essay (let alone in the other sites of my intellectual practice) sets me up to be targeted as too white-identified or too effete (or both) to be a "real" black man in certain contexts. The fact that I already identify *myself* as gay may mitigate my vulnerability on that score somewhat. At the same time, the fact that my work takes the form of scholarly writing that does not generally circulate outside the academy largely insulates me from charges that I am not sufficiently engaged with the day-to-day concerns of the black populace, even as it substantiates the claim. This latter paradox constitutes a dilemma not for black intellectuals alone, certainly; but the embattled position that blacks still occupy in this country — socially, politically, economically — makes the problem especially pressing for us.

27. Don L. Lee (Haki R. Madhubuti), *Don't Cry Scream* (Detroit: Broadside Press, 1969), 27–31.

28. An effective manifesto for such a poetic practice can be seen in Imamu Amiri Baraka's "Black Art," with its call for "poems that kill." See the *Selected Poetry of Amiri Baraka/LeRoi Jones* (New York: William Morrow, 1979), 106–7.

29. Nikki Giovanni, "The True Import of Present Dialogue: Black vs. Negro," in Dudley Randall, ed., *The Black Poets* (New York: Bantam, 1971), 318–19.

30. There is an evident irony here, in that the intense masculinism of black na-

tionalist discourse was developed as a reaction against the suppression of black manhood and black male sexuality (often taking the form of literal castration, and at any rate consistently rhetorically figured as such) enacted by the dominant white society. Of course, the emphasis on traditional masculinity is not unique to black nationalism, either in the United States or elsewhere. For an extensive discussion of the relation between European nationalist ideologies and the promulgation of a masculine ideal, see George Mosse, *Nationalism and Sexuality: Respectability and Abnormal Sexuality in Modern Europe* (Madison: University of Wisconsin Press, 1985).

31. The *Jet* obituary reflects a general journalistic ignorance of the appropriate terms to be used in reference to the AIDS epidemic. "AIDS victim," with its connotations of passivity, helplessness, and immutable doom, and its reduction of the person under discussion to a medical condition, should be rejected in favor of "person with AIDS" (PWA) or "person living with AIDS" (PLWA). Additionally, AIDS is not a "disease"; it is a "syndrome," a constellation of symptoms (and in the instance of AIDS many of the characteristic symptoms are themselves diseases) that indicates an underlying condition — in the case of AIDS, suppressed immunity likely caused by infection with the human immunodeficiency virus (HIV).

32. "Max Robinson, First Black National TV News Anchor, Succumbs to AIDS in D.C."; "Singer Sylvester, 42, Dies of AIDS in Oakland, CA," *Jet,* 9 January 1989, 14–15, 18.

33. For some commentary on this phenomenon, see Joseph Beam, ed., *In the Life: A Black Gay Anthology* (Boston: Alyson, 1986), particularly essays by James S. Tinney ("Why a Black Gay Church?" 70–86), Bernard Branner (an interview with Blackberri, "Singing for Our Lives," 170–84), and Max C. Smith ("By the Year 2000," 224–29).

34. "Max Robinson: Fighting the Demons," *Newsweek,* 2 January 1989, 65.

35. National Public Radio, "Morning Edition," 5 April 1989.

36. Noted in a report from the National Public Radio series "AIDS and Blacks," on "All Things Considered," 7 April 1989.

37. Among Jackson's misstatements is his reference to the "AIDS virus." There is no virus that "causes AIDS," only HIV, which produces the immunosuppression that allows the conditions that constitute AIDS to flourish. Moreover, neither HIV infection nor AIDS "comes from" either homosexuality or "promiscuity"; HIV is a virus extant in the biosphere that is merely *transmitted* through sexual contact.

It is particularly ironic, by the way, that the homophobia-informed task of legitimizing Robinson's AIDS diagnosis should be undertaken by Jackson, whose 1988 presidential campaign was characterized by support for a lesbian and gay political agenda.

38. For an extensive analysis of this characteristic of AIDS-education programs in the United States, see Douglas Crimp, "How to Have Promiscuity in an Epidemic," *AIDS: Cultural Analysis/Cultural Activism* 43 (winter 1987): 237–71.

39. National Public Radio, "AIDS and Blacks," on "All Things Considered," 4 April 1989.

40. Ibid., 3 April 1989.

41. Debra Fried, "Repetition, Refrain, and Epitaph," *ELH* 53, no. 3 (fall 1986): 620.

"Symbolic" Homosexuality, "False Feminine," and the Problematics of Identity in Québec

Robert Schwartzwald

> *Disputes over sexual behavior often become the vehicles for displacing social anxieties, and discharging their attendant emotional intensity. Consequently, sex should be treated with special respect in times of great social stress.*
>
> Gayle Rubin, "Thinking Sex"

In a gesture typical of the early years of the Quiet Revolution, the period in the 1960s and 1970s when Québec adopted the infrastructure of the modern state and its secularist, participatory ideological parameters with breathtaking speed, essayist and novelist Hubert Aquin retrospectively dismissed French-Canadian literature as "generally weak, without brilliance, and truly boring." What was new in this condemnation, however, was Aquin's attribution of this failure to the "overvaluing of all human situations that approach inversion." In fact, this "sexual deviationism" dissimulated itself behind "a proportional majority of stereotypes which present themselves precisely as cases of non-inversion."[1] For Aquin, the ease with which this ruse was performed was but a thundering proof of the identitary *under*development of the Québécois. He considered his compatriots to be inexperienced in "adult" love relationships, bereft of egos sufficiently coherent to enter into, and maintain, relations with the other. Their inability to distinguish between true and false *heterosexuality signified an easy acceptance of the inauthentic that would become the incontrovertible sign of ontological alienation in a discourse that increasingly refigured the Québécois as a colonized subject.[2]

At the same time, this discourse of decolonization gave new value to the metaphorical, sometimes allegorical, often sentimentalized conscription of homosexuality in Québec popular culture. Michel Tremblay's *Hosanna* (1972),[3] for example, was embraced as a powerful declaration of Québec's right to "be itself." When Hosanna (the character) removes her Elizabeth-Taylor-as-Cleopatra drag at the end of the play and, naked, receives her lover's embrace, we are meant to understand that she has really abandoned a masquerade in order to draw nearer to the essence of her homosexual "truth." Here, transvestism was legible as the "fantasy" of an alienated, oppressed national collectivity that needed proudly to acknowledge and assert its *spécificité* as a necessary prelude to taking its place among the universal community of nations. Nevertheless, the play's construction of homosexual and national identitary quests as adequate metaphorical substitutions for each other could not be unproblematic for nationalist intellectuals who largely adopted a developmental narrative in which Québec's independence would be the culmination of a process leading from "infancy" to "maturity." Even though Tremblay's attention to the topos of *authenticity* was typical of a discourse of national affirmation largely informed by the ontological and existential concerns of decolonization theory as elaborated in the francophone world, it could not resolve the worrisome paradox that Hosanna's rapprochement with his homosexual "essence" permanently *marginalized* him as a sexual minority even as it authenticated him.[4] Hosanna's reconciliation with the authenticity of his sexual desire seemed to promise no accompanying "normalcy"; on the contrary, did it not confirm that Québec's "specificity" was to be a permanently countercultural society, and consequently excluded from easy integration into the extended family of modern nations?

In the years since Hosanna's spectacular coming out, it has been easy to locate an astonishingly varied representation of homosexuality across all registers of cultural production in Québec, be they literary, cinematic, televisual, or in the theater. More recently, gays in Québec have also been encouraged to claim the status of a "cultural community," and it is worth recalling that it was the *nationalist* Parti Québécois government elected in 1976 that introduced amendments to the provincial Charter of Rights forbidding discrimination on the basis of sexual orientation. It should be clear, therefore, that my intention in this essay could not be to cast aspersions on the *tolerance* of homosexuality in Québec; instead, it is to better understand the particular resistances of learned discourse, and specifically how neither the outlawing of discrimination against homosexuals nor the relative violence in Québec is able in itself to obviate Québec's more equivocal inscriptions of homosexuality. One of the most salient features of modern intellectual (self-)representation in Québec turns out to be that the homophobic elements of its *learned* discourse on identity are largely inconsistent with both liberal legal discourse and popular attitudes. What provides the impetus for such a situation, and what can it elucidate about discursive engagements between subject positions articulated around nationhood, on the one hand, and sexualities, on the other?

Elsewhere, I have spoken of the desire of Québécois intellectuals to "give voice" to the people during the Quiet Revolution. This project sought to create new solidarities between popular classes and their "sons" who had gained access to the world of intellectual labor. To this end, it dictated a discursive production of difference from earlier intellectual generations, who were figured as politically compromised (*fédérastes* was a choice term of derision) and contemptuous of the oppressive situation of their compatriots. At the same time, the preoccupation with internal differentiation produced a supplemental requirement that "the people" conform to the image of the emerging subject-nation in which intellectuals sought to affirm themselves. This requirement led to a certain impatience with the articulation of other subject positions that were suspected of being "in conflict" with a recovery of national authenticity. It is in this sense that " '[t]o give voice to a people' may be understood not only causatively, but transitively.... Thus 'faire parler', 'donner la parole à', both suggest not only the crucially enabling potential of intellectually refracted discourse, but its disciplinary aspect, as well."[5]

The defeat of the 1980 referendum on sovereignty association[6] could not help but provoke a thorough "settling of accounts" around this implicit social contract. Québec intellectuals who massively campaigned for the "OUI" side found themselves under generalized assault not only by triumphant federalists eager to crow about how the people had not been "duped," but by a good number of their colleagues who chose to jump onto the anti-intellectual bandwagon in a desperate attempt to regain some measure of credibility.[7] One response to this onslaught was for more recalcitrant intellectuals to engage in their own reevaluation of "the people," who failed to provide the necessary mandate for independence. Sometimes, this took a brazenly *revanchard* form, as in Denys Arcand's film *Le Confort et l'indifférence* (1981) where the cynical manipulation of a people at once anesthetized by the bread and circuses of consumer culture and haunted by a fear of the unknown successfully dulls any popular will to self-determination.[8] More significantly, however, the diagnostic urge proved to be especially volatile around homosexually inflected articulations of identity, which are compulsively read for clues that might explicate the identitary impasse of the Québécois subject-nation. In learned discourse, intellectuals determined to bring Québec "into" the world as a modern national community have been more apt to adopt the homophobic assignation of homosexuality as *arrested* development, and to rely upon this diagnosis to buttress explanations of Québec's long, halting progress toward self-determination.

A recent special issue of the theater journal *Jeu* devoted to "Theater and Homosexuality in Québec" is particularly telling in this regard. Here, the psychologist Hélène Richard opines that "gay theater [in Québec] produces in its own way the universal problematic of filiation and its impact on narcissism, by which we mean self-esteem and the sentiment of having an identity."[9] In fact, *JEU*'s decision to invite Richard, a *clinician,* to preside over the opening "roundtable" discussion for an issue on gay *theatrical production* underscores how her remarks, as "neutral" as they may seem, cannot help but be coded within a critical lineage where the positing of a relation between homosexuality and the problematics of identity is typically couched in profound ambivalence, if not outright hostility. Indeed, the issue takes as its point of departure the "malaise" induced among many of the editors and collaborators by the "overrepresentation" of homosexuality on the Québec stage. In a tone typical of most of the issue, another contributor confesses that he finds the enthusiasm of the Québec public for homosexual theater to be "chilling." For Gilbert David, another contributor, it is the sure sign of the facile triumph of a festive postmodernism whose claim to accommodate all difference elides "the worrisome reality that a love relationship between a man and a woman can engender a be-

ing who is their living contradiction." The corollary that David poses
to this seemingly incontrovertible reality is in truth itself a performative: "Whether we like it or not, couples who decide to bring
a child into the world don't do so, it seems, dreaming that he will
become a homosexual . . . whence springs the inescapable question
of failure which haunts the homosexual conscience."[10]

There are a number of obvious objections one could raise to
David's assertion: Did these couples dream of engendering a *hetero*sexual? No, they simply "took it for granted," but instead of
recognizing that it is precisely this certainty that should be put
into question, David is satisfied to displace the responsibility for
the asymmetry onto the shoulders of the homosexual, who is to
feel haunted by his ontological "failure." Moreover, David never
explains in exactly which way homosexuals are the living contradiction of their parents. Such a statement depends upon a notion
of naturalized sexes that would predetermine any definitions of
gender and sexuality, not to mention prescribe their complete iso-
morphism. The reduction of the question of homosexuality in David
to a transgression of the "law of the species" (as if homosexual
acts prevented procreative ones) is *itself* the naturalization of a
concern profoundly rooted in the social and represented by the
question/accusation, "What share of responsibility do homosexuals
recognize for themselves in relation to future generations, especially children?"[11] This question supposes an irreducible opposition
between homosexuality and parenting that does not exist in "fact"
(there are many homosexual mothers and fathers), but that is instead
regulated by laws and social institutions that privilege a particular
form of family.[12]

Beyond these objections, however, David's remarks are significant because they are symptomatic of a series of basic assumptions that still govern most attempts to ascribe cultural meaning
to homosexuality. In Québec, the notion of "failure" so central
to David's thesis is particularly charged, since the burden of a
collective shortcoming haunts the colonized consciousness. In traditional, conservative nationalism, messianic ideology sought to turn
Québec's underdevelopment into a virtue; unlike Protestant, mate-
rialistic, English-speaking America, Québec was to witness in the
New World for its "spiritual, Latin" ancestors. Conversely, modern
nationalism sought to expose the compensatory self-deception be-

hind this acceptance of being "born for a small loaf" (*né pour un petit pain* — also a reference to the buns given out on the feast of Saint John the Baptist, the patron saint of French Canada). In this context, the heterosexual syntax in relation to which the homosexual is a failure is necessarily evocative of the Québécois' own failure to achieve national "maturity."[13]

To the extent that David's anxieties about the "irresponsibility" of homosexuals also serve as a "cardinal figure for the commodity world operating under the principle of generalized seduction,"[14] they are also reminiscent of elements in Denys Arcand's more recent films, *Le déclin de l'empire américain* (1986) and *Jésus de Montréal* (1989). In *Le déclin,* the fascination exercised by the homosexual over the other men preparing dinner for the women who will soon join them is symptomatic of a national "confusion" that portends an incapacity (impotence, as it were) to forge a destiny that would be something other than a benign simulacrum of American decadence. In *Jésus,* the cynicism characteristic of this "decline" animates the ambitious gay lawyer who is completely prepared to corrupt the disciples of the young actor/director Daniel, promising to convert them into a commercial success that would exploit the memory of the "Jesus" that had "saved" them from their mediocre careers. Moreover, this devalorization of the film's Jesus is foreshadowed in the lubricious gaze that the lawyer fixes upon his lacerated, suffering body....[15]

The reintroduction by Arcand of religious thematics into an excoriation of Québec's own experience of 1980s Yuppie-dom is particularly significant because it comes from a filmmaker whose documentaries and feature films throughout the Quiet Revolution sought to ground national self-determination in a struggle against class and colonialist exploitation.[16] Here, the national "family" was shown to be divided; the formation of a viable Québécois nation implicitly depended upon the forging of a new, emancipatory social contract. In fact, the propagation of a "contractual" model of nationhood for Québec had been one of the most powerful discursive ruptures initiated by the Quiet Revolution. One might assume that greater latitude could be potentially offered for articulations of identity with social heterogeneity — and for sexuality to enjoy a greater degree of definitional autonomy — in "contractual" notions of nationhood that rely upon secular, juridical, and jurisdictional paradigms for their legitimacy. But finally, the overarching persistence of a developmental model for nationhood within this contractual paradigm and its particular claims to modernity reveals an enduring reliance upon heterosexually ordered and ultimately archaicizing *familial* models when constructing the national "body" itself. Subjecting contractual models to pressures as great as the defeat of a popular referendum on sovereignty is perhaps a sad but effective way of demonstrating how the attendant figures of a familial model never entirely disappear, but are instead held "in reserve" until a disastrous conjuncture resuscitates them. Arcand's most recent films remind us that such discursive constructions of nationhood are not about to relinquish their appropriation of sex/gender models of identity, and that in specific circumstances they are in a position to naturalize a heterosexually hierarchalized and seemingly immutable regime of sexual practices.

The analyses of the three theorists we shall undertake in the second part of this essay are intended to demonstrate more closely the implications of deploying homosexuality as a way of "importing" familial models back into the civically inflected discourse characteristic of modern nationalism in Québec. On the one hand, these theorists reveal a dependency on a same/other binarism proposed by structural anthropology, where taboos against homosexuality and incest assure the passage from a regime of kinship to one of *exchange*.[17] On the other hand, what gives these interventions their particular contours is a recourse to psychoanalytically inflected models that, in the context of the Quiet Revolution, seem able to provide the most radically secular and disruptive response to earlier intellectual paradigms, including those of "enlightened" Christianity. The privileging of Symbolic/Imaginary relations and the preoccupation with origins reintroduce not only the primal scene as central to national self-definition, but render its (re)appearance legible as the trace of the homogeneous, "ethnic" national community.[18] Finally, the inscription of homosexuality in the work of these theorists is not a matter of mere representational exploitation, but involves instead the construction of a complex symbolic network where it becomes central to the identitary matrix of the subject-nation, becoming the repressed whose return portends only disruption and signifies failure.

Of the three theoretical contributions that we shall examine, Jacques Lavigne's is certainly the least known. This is certainly in part because his concepts of *symbolic homosexuality* and the *false feminine,* as well as his therapeutic practice of provoking a "homosexual crisis" in his patient, resulted in his being transferred, then dismissed from tenured positions at the Université de Montréal, after which he continued to teach for many years at the junior college level. Both Hubert Aquin and Jean Larose were at one time students of his. As for Jean Larose, it may safely be said that he is considered one of Québec's most acerbic social and cultural critics. When English-Canadian federalists became almost apoplectic over his receipt of the Governor General's Award (Canada's highest literary honor) for *La Petite noirceur* (1987), a collection of essays in which confederation and English Canada are both excoriated, they missed the truly subversive aspect of the volume: its elaboration of a proindependence position for Québec that vehemently took issue with contemporary nationalist ideology. In fact, Larose's work is at its best when it situates itself on the "cusp" of identity, negotiating its strategic stabilization with its necessary disruption. Gilles Thérien's semiotically informed cultural criticism is especially suited to examine how identities, be they homosexual or (as is more recently the case in his work) Amerindian, are conferred with meaning in Québec. Like Benedict Anderson,[19] he may be said to be interested in how a community comes to "imagine" itself, and has astutely assembled a filmic series from the last decade that addresses this question in an elliptical mode symptomatic of the repositioning incited by the defeat of the 1980 referendum.

Jacques Lavigne's *L'Objectivité*

Published in 1971, *L'Objectivité*[20] claims to be an investigation into the achievement of the objectivity of knowledge, or at least that knowledge that assures an adequate relationship to the Other. For Lavigne, there is no doubt that this knowledge is at once constituted and confirmed by "a definite heterosexual capacity" (61), but this in turn depends upon the integration of an earlier, homosexual erotic image and "its dissolution into its constituents: conjugal love, the paternal instinct, and filial love" (61).[21] Here, then, is the *symbolic* homosexuality of which Lavigne speaks, situated in a preoedipal zone and characterized by an eroticized relationship between two persons of the same sex of different generations.[22] The successful integration of this symbolic homosexuality renders possible the meaningful encounter of the self with the other, the whole envisaged through "those fundamental categories, the masculine and the feminine" (24). In this process, "the fundamental erotic images of homosexuality are symbolic because their mission is to transform a psychic state which is not the desire for the same sex into an expression of the life of the instincts."[23] This assurance with regard to the *translational* function of homosexual erotic images depends for its part on a physio-neurological demonstration in which the division between the feminine and masculine is itself founded upon "the hypothesis of a psychic location that we may call drive-oriented in Freudian language and, in ontological language, the suturing of the soul and the body, a location which represents the function of symbolization which supports language" (31).[24]

Nevertheless, "coding accidents" cannot be entirely avoided: "[A] signifier may, instead of bringing into consciousness the signified that it connotes, engender a biological mutation or even transmit its message to consciousness but at the price of disruptions in the biological and physiological order" (33). There would then exist "the possibility that the significatory energy of the term would be deviated" (34).[25] Through a curious detour (in French, the term for detour is appropriately enough *déviation*), Lavigne is led to anchor his symbolic in a prediscursive biological reality that is ultimately held responsible for the deviations that result from a "faulty" reading of symbolic language. The heterosexual model is posed here as the natural state of the self–other relation, and the very suggestiveness of an analysis that took the symbolic as its point of departure is summarily elided.[26]

The inability to achieve *real* heterosexuality, or more precisely the fall into real homosexuality, is for Lavigne the sign of a profound failure in the search for identity. In fact, "real" homosexuality represents the ambush of "symbolic" homosexuality by the principle of the *false feminine*. This occurs when the primary relationship of bodily intimacy that exists between the mother and child is transformed into a fantasmatic pact where "what the child asks from the mother is to be given the place of the father so that, in turn, he confers upon her the virile attributes and the prestige of the father. . . . [P]ower is sought to institute an order where one becomes similar to the father without having traversed the time he has spent in becoming who he is. It's a world of exalted false power and the annihilation of the true" (68–69).[27]

Lavigne insists on the crucial importance of the counter-transference operated by the adult for the ordering of the erotic images of the ephebe. A "real father" will know how properly to respond to the symbolic homosexuality of his son, while sexual inversion is reinforced or even caused by adults who fear their own homosexual images and project the crises that result from them onto their still fragile children (245–46). In order to avoid such "misunderstandings," the adult must "accept the possibility of an erotic component within this relationship in order to integrate it with paternal, maternal, and filial feelings" (247).[28]

In fact, Lavigne is particularly anxious to exculpate children for their neuroses. For him, these are the consequence of the injustices they have suffered at the hands of their elders. Unlike the Oedipus complex, which "culpabilizes childhood, adolescence, and neurosis," Lavigne claims his concept of the false feminine "allows [us] to distinguish a natural and real love from another that is false and, when all is said and done, contrary to the positive and creative forces of nature" (69–70).[29] Likewise, "the castration myth substitutes the victim for the guilty party by transforming an unjust act by the guilty party into a sexual offense on the part of the victim" (85).[30] Sublimation itself is reinterpreted in light of Lavigne's contention that "it is in greater conformance with reality that certain sentiments and activities which are not finally sexual borrow, in certain circumstances, the language of eroticism for their first stages of manifestation" (244–45).[31] The convention that holds the opposite to be true would represent yet another example of the *mauvaise foi* with which adults seek to dissimulate their own failures by reading them back into their defenseless children!

If there was a specific sector of society where this discourse would be certain to produce shock waves, it was in Québec's educational sector, which had only recently emerged from clerical control thanks to the reforms of the Quiet Revolution. By insisting on the inevitably eroticized nature of all pedagogical relations, Lavigne put clerics face-to-face with a reality they had always denied. The implications of Lavigne's theory are clear enough on this point: we would be within our rights to blame these clerics who took advantage of their position as "false fathers" to install a regime of the "false feminine"; the priest (*père*) would take the place of the real father who had already been reduced to the "passive, dominated, managed, subservient, mutilated being of whom the child was the image" (68).[32] The Catholic school system would produce complex-ridden children who, upon becoming adults incapable of dealing with their own homoerotic drives, would communicate their anxieties to their own children. If the children never had the opportunity to integrate their own symbolic homosexuality either at home or at school, it would be implicitly thanks to the authoritarian pedagogical regime that turned out such guilt-ridden souls.

Despite Lavigne's anticlericalism, important elements persist in his thought from a religious tradition anchored in certain temporal and sexual dualisms. Beyond the strong tendency toward *angélisme* where children are concerned, which we have already noted, it is useful to recall Gilles Thérien's observation that the epistemological point of departure of *L'Objectivité* is not in itself inconsistent with "Aristotelian-Thomist tradition, which until recently was still preponderant in Québec." This tradition privileged "the knowledge of the other as the Other, the perception of alterity as alterity, [and] the objective recognition of alterity that did not put into question the knowing subject."[33] Indeed, Lavigne's emphasis on the ubiquitousness of the symbolic is always counterbalanced by its being taken in charge by cognitive processes. The unconscious plays a disruptive role only so long as we *allow it* to do so; the theory of symbolism is designed to provide us with greater access to the unconscious in order better to master it.

It is true that Lavigne distinguished himself from Thomism and neo-Thomist circles in Québec, where references to the unconscious or the instability of meaning were greeted as highly suspect.[34] His determination to elaborate a theory of symbolism as the foundation of knowledge signaled an important rupture in the Québec context. Yet in the succession of social discourses, Lavigne's *ethical* condemnation of homosexuality within the secularizing dynamic of the Quiet Revolution turns out to be even more severe than those of his predecessors. In a paradigm governed by the obsession with overcoming "infantilism," homosexuality is a particular evil because it signifies "a dishonest moral, ontological, and instinctual compromise, ... an abdication of one's overall personality faced with the norms of natural affectivity and the laws of intelligence" (249).[35]

This is the spirit in which Lavigne speaks of the possibility (and the professional duty) of helping those men who "ask themselves all through life whether or not they carry unconsciously and deep within themselves the seed of that [homosexual] deviation" (57). The aim of his therapy will be to demonstrate that in the majority of cases (adolescent attractions, its appearance during an analytic transference, or even as a perpetual, nagging doubt), homosexuality "is not that at all. [It is] a phenomenon that effectively does find its language in homosexual imagery and sentimentality, but is nonetheless the exasperated manifestation of a constituent part of normal human dynamism that, reduced to its just proportions, is an essential factor in the vital contact with the real, the foundation of all authentic knowledge" (57).[36] If at first glance an unambiguous dividing line seems to separate the symbolization of "normal" homosexual desire from inadmissible homosexual acts in this theory, the problems begin to multiply upon closer scrutiny. For precisely when would homosexual imagery and sentimentality constitute a "real" desire to be counteracted, and when would they merely be symbolizations of other desires? In a theory of symbolism, the fact of not carrying through with the act is of little solace if the desire "wants" to be realized through an act; but how are we to evaluate the "symbolic" or "real" quality of a desire? If a therapist is able to proclaim that a homosexual desire in one patient is only symbolic, then by implication a similarly felt desire in another patient may well be real! Or conversely, the less than total hold of the "false feminine" principle over an individual may lead, if not to "real" homosexuality, then at least to a situation where the symbolization is perfectly heterosexual but the *heterosexuality "false."* In Lavigne, we find a range of symbolic intensities of which real homosexuality is but the most acute expression; even if one doesn't "end up" there, there is always the possibility of discovering oneself to be the object of a series of superficially heterosexual behaviors whose "authenticity" is finally questionable. Of course, the actual mapping of this range is justified in relation to coitus, "the erotic image ... which is, on the level of instinct, the terminal and fundamental one of the system" (77).[37] Ultimately, it is this hierarchization of sexual acts and the accompanying problematization of homosexual desire that are responsible for investing the stabilization of sexuality with such crucial identificatory significance. The erecting of such a jealously controlled, yet protean, frontier between desire and acts recalls the regulatory mechanism described by Eve Kosofsky Sedgwick as *homosexual panic*.[38] In according epistemological privilege to homosexuality while conferring hermeneutic authority onto practitioners of disciplines associated with social order and "hygiene" — medicine, psychotherapy, law enforcement, and criminology — this panic mechanism incites even the most "upright" of male citizens to fear that he may be that most ontologically compromised of creatures. It is no accident that it is within the reformist dynamic of Québec's Quiet Revolution, and especially its valorization of the "human sciences," that homosexual panic becomes deployed to an unprecedented degree, becoming the currency whereby circulate the charges of cowardice, complacency, and self-hatred leveled against the traditional elites. Through the displacement of interpretive authority to the professional disciplines of the social sciences, the earlier theological grids of interpretation and distinction between impure thoughts and deeds are recast as so much "hypocrisy" worthy of contempt and rejection. Under the clericalist regime of the "false feminine," the constituent parts of a society turned in upon itself had reinforced each other in the messianic lie of their "exceptional destiny." Here, men were deprived of authentic virility, women culpabilized but in reality unjustly accused, and children falsely blamed for their neuroses.[39]

Finally, Lavigne's analysis explicitly evokes the possibility that "instead of resisting a neurotic personality [and obliging it] to adapt to universally accepted norms or to receive appropriate care, a milieu adapts itself to this personality and in so doing progressively loses the sense of the normal, the natural, the real" (101).[40] Although Lavigne never goes on to *name* the Québécois as the focus of this concern, the observation certainly underlies the analyses performed by many of the theorists who advocated the "decolonization" of Québec. They sought not only to analyze the "personality" of the *colonisé* in Québec, but the entire society's complicity in his alienated fantasies. Even theorists who have been somewhat critical of the "primitivist" and idealist presuppositions of analysis performed from within this paradigm largely retain the notion of a social "personality" that reinforces, rather than reflects, aberrant individual behavior. In this regard, Lavigne's concepts of the *false feminine* and *symbolic homosexuality* will be crucial for the elaboration of the nationally oriented problematics of Gilles Thérien and Jean Larose.

Gilles Thérien: Cinema and Identity

In an article prepared for a special issue of the French journal *Littérature* devoted to contemporary Québec culture, Gilles Thérien embarks upon a reading of a series of films produced in the years following the defeat of the May 1980 referendum in order to examine "the semiogenesis of a process of self-definition in the absence of an identitary figure."[41] Thérien chooses his films[42] because they seem to demonstrate in diverse ways that in the absence of such an identitary figure the individual's necessary evolution from an identitary pole to a pole of alterity is blocked, and the subject delivered back to himself (105). The sign of this blockage would be a homoethical crisis, which most often connotes and sometimes even leads to "real" homosexuality. In Jacques Lavigne's terms, the failure to negotiate symbolic homosexuality through a truly identitary figure leads to the preeminence of the false feminine to varying degrees in these films.

For Thérien, cinema is both a "machine and machination" that depends less upon a spectator identifying with a particular filmic series than *including* himself or herself within it. Within this framework, "the film is an argument, a proposition, and the name of the game is to fabricate an object that will be validated by the spectator's reaction" (105).[43] Thérien therefore wonders what the significance of the homoethical crises in these films, and the homosexual relations they depict or suggest, would be for a Québécois spectator. In other words, what proposition is being made to such a spectator through these representations (105)?

From the outset, we should note how "spectator" and "homosexuality" are identified — or more precisely, constructed — as the two discrete and mutually exclusive terms of this analysis. Furthermore, this spectator is *nationally* inflected in Thérien: "[P]eople in

the same [movie theater] together generally belong to the same society, the same nation, the same 'idiolectal' culture; and perhaps
they go to the movies to see those characters that represent them
on the screen. . . . This aspect is fundamental to the survival of a
national cinema . . . as well as for the construction of the collective
imaginary in which each person is free to find himself" (102).[44]
Within this overarching imperative, "homosexual relations" become
condensed to "*this* relation" that will always exist "next to" or be
superimposed over the "collective." That these films may be making several propositions, notably about the articulation of several
sites of subjectivity without either privileging or abandoning the
national; that the films may privilege a subjectivity whose preferred
referential field would be a variegated, quotidian, "lived" homosexuality; that such a reference may not be immediately legible as
a "proposition" about the nation — these are possibilities that have
no relevance within the proposed analytical framework. Instead,
the homosexual is excluded from possible integration with the "series" when the time comes to consider what kind of proposition is
being made to the community. We shall see that this flows from the
logic of Thérien's argument, which situates the Québec spectator
in a relation to the collective imaginary so that cinematically represented homosexuality becomes assimilated as the sign of a national
deformation.

For Thérien, homosexuality serves as a heuristic device for taking
the measure of the cognitive and identitary progress of a community. This function tends to allow a symptomatic reading of
homosexuality to occult any recognition of it as a constituent part
of social construction. At the same time, it of course essentializes
it, as in Thérien's claim that each of his selected films connotes
homosexuality "to a greater or lesser extent." Such a homosexuality
is stabilized, monadic, and would reliably help us determine the
intensity of each of the "homoethical" situations represented in the
films. According to Thérien, the "absolute point of departure" of all
the films in his series is this homoethical relation, "[which] poses
the Same as the proper object" (111).[45] It is taken for granted that
this Same is adequately, even ideally, signified by the representation of a relation of two persons of the same sex, whether this
relation be sexual or not, for even those that aren't would be so
potentially. Finally, then, to say "homoethical" in this context only

serves to qualify or to relativize the dominant term, which would be "homosexuality." In this model, the "homoethical" becomes as atemporal, as ahistoric, and as removed from any concrete relation to the social as the essentialization of homosexuality itself.[46] And when homosexuality becomes here the "zero degree" for an analysis that aims to be "a reflection on relations to the Same," "Same" is inflected negatively, in order that another same — the nation — receive a conversely positive inflection, presumably because it represents a mature, purified Same prepared to enter into meaningful and viable relations of exchange!

In Thérien, the hegemony of the principle of the Same is related to a model of development that grounds itself in the exigencies of survival — "the sharing of a common territory, of a same topos (defined as kinship)... a common site from which it will be possible to go toward the territory of the other and discover whether the other is a proper object or may become one" (111).[47] This (re)construction of the classical narrative of structuralism recounts the passage from a kinship regime (the Same) to one of properly social relations. According to Thérien, what is normally at stake in deciding whether or not to undertake this passage is "the choice between the closing in on oneself which implies defeat and assuming the role of the dominated, or of combat in which victory isn't guaranteed" (113).[48] In Québec, however, an "in-between" situation is to be found: in the films' representations of this passage, "at the very moment when the structure of reproduction becomes blurred and the structure of domination emerges, the choice is so difficult to make that only death appears as a solution" (112).[49]

Here, the implication would be that the oedipal road (toward domination) is less accessible to the Québécois, at least according to the "normal" rules of the game. Thérien seems to believe that the Québécois will be too reticent to embark upon the path of revolt, at least partly because the possibility *already* exists of fixating upon an *absent* father whose domination is even more effective because of his extraterritorial — that is, colonial or imperialist — character. In other words, the absence of a "national" father causes a revolt to be deferred that an oedipal process would otherwise authorize by symbolically confusing father with the Father, a "luxury" not available to the nationally oppressed Québécois.[50] Thérien thus "nationalizes" Lavigne's analytical model, which had accorded no explicit status to Québec. In Lavigne's view, the child's success in passing from a regime of domination to dominating in his own right is initially marked by his negotiation of symbolic homosexuality, then of the oedipal complex that enables him to make the appropriate sexual choice and achieve real heterosexuality. For his part, Thérien contends that symbolic homosexuality is not merely a pivotal point between reproduction and domination; it may also allow "the realization of the social system *within* the framework of the kinship system," where it resolves the search for origins (and thus for "grounding" in preparation for the encounter with the Other) in its own way: "[T]he search for origins through homosexuality is an 'introspective,' 'gentle' form of quest; another variant would be the search for origins through the violent elimination of the Other, as with Oedipus" (114).[51]

The inscription of homosexuality within an intermediary site is *already* an effect of having created a gulf between kinship and the social, between "nature" and "culture," as if relations of reproduction (and the discursive constructions that privilege heterosexuality and its familial forms) were not part of these cultural relations of domination. In other words, the compelling, master term of Thérien's discourse remains the figure of the passage itself, in relation to which such an "introspective" mode can only appear as an *intermediary* moment that holds the entire process in suspense. To situate homosexuality at this intermediary site is already to encode it as an impediment, throwing the subject back onto a familial paradigm of nationhood that, however "gentle" and reassuring it may be in the short term, is fatal to the emergence of a subject-nation with agency in the larger world. In fact, Thérien confirms that he is hardly satisfied with his newly discovered *spécificité québécoise* when he observes that in his selected films, "the failure consists in being unable to accede to the other *as* an other or to alterity as a social, heterogeneous fact, and instead to go backward to once more take up the question of origins, the question of identity" (113–14).[52] In this sense, the homosexual relation that is meant to symbolize this crisis and its putatively novel resolution becomes not an alternative to death, but its structural substitution and moral equivalent.

In the final analysis, Thérien seems impelled to read his selected films as further, corroborating "proof" for what the defeat of the 1980 referendum had already suggested: that Québec was insufficiently anchored in viable identitary (self-)representations successfully to affirm itself before the world (to interpellate the other). Thus, "the pseudo recurrence of the theme of homosexuality appears rather as a variant of the question of identity, and the extent to which the problem appears despite the diversity of the films only emphasizes the continuing importance of this question in Québec, in spite of the political defeat" (114).[53]

In other words, homosexuality is "pseudo" because it is legible primarily as the trace of an unresolved identitary quest that needs to regroup on the political level. This raises some rather troubling questions: If the presence of homosexuality is only a "pseudo," and if homosexuality can encode only the single and specific problematic of the Same and the Other, what place could there be for it in a paradigm that looks forward to the emergence of an integral subject-nation? If the representation of homosexuality is merely the symptom of an identitary impasse, are we to conclude that it will "disappear" once the nationally inflected problem of the relation to the Other is "resolved"? The problem is that such a view of the national question itself suggests a homology between the crises of national and sexual identities that are to be "transcended" in the life of each nation as in the life of each person. This homology not only assures that the developmental trope remains intact, but its reliance upon the powerful, culturally sanctioned binary model for the construction of the subject-nation in turn subjects homosexuality to a discursive control that deprives it of both autonomy and the ground on which to elaborate its own identitary preoccupations. In short, it is an asymmetrical homology that seeks to constrain the epistemological status of homosexuality to a symptom of a more "urgent" ontological issue.

Jean Larose: The Fantasy of Introjection

Like Gilles Thérien, Jean Larose's analysis of Québec's identitary crisis proceeds from the consideration of key cultural artifacts, beginning with Québec's most celebrated *poète maudit,* Emile Nelligan. Born in Montréal in the late nineteenth century of a well-to-do Irish father and a French-Canadian mother, the young Emile produced an impressive oeuvre in the symbolist vein in adherence to the fashions of contemporary French poetry. The poems are redolent with nostalgia for a disappearing childhood and steeped in the ambiance of perfumed, lush gardens and Victorian parlors with mother sitting at the piano. This maternal poetic world is at odds with Nelligan's actual conflicts with his father, who disapproved of his artistic endeavors. In 1899, Nelligan *père* had his son interned. Emile would spend the forty-two remaining years of his life in various retreats and hospitals. During the Quiet Revolution, Nelligan became a symbol for the stifling of Québec's creative forces by reaction and fear. His portrait — a full mane of dark, wavy hair, sensuous lips, penetrating eyes — was reproduced and sold on posters and T-shirts, and his life has been chronicled in plays, operas, and song cycles. Literary prizes and university halls have been named for him, while scholars continue to publish biographies and complete editions of his work, which now include several poems that were "reworked" during his confinement, as well as new lyrics. Although official biographers refuse to acknowledge it, others have written with conviction about another aspect of Nelligan's tragedy — that the father's decision to send his son "away" was at least in part provoked by discovering Emile's sexual involvement with a working-class lad. In short, a myth has grown up around Nelligan, the "Rimbaud of Québec," and it is this myth that becomes the subject of Jean Larose's first major volume, *Le Mythe de Nelligan.*[54]

"In my text, 'nation' and 'poet' are interchangeable," Larose informs us. In fact, Larose's treatment of the myth of Nelligan is organized around the manner in which each of these figures "imagines" and is "imagined," in the Lacanian sense of the term. In order to explain how this is so, Larose (like Thérien) returns to the question of origins, but in this instance to contextualize its importance with regard to the precise historical drama of Québec. Like the theorists of decolonization, Larose is haunted by the search for origins, but he also demonstrates how for the Québécois colonial subjects the problem is aggravated by their ancestors' earlier status as *colonizers:* "Perhaps the particular vexatiousness of our servitude today comes from this unforeseen inversion" (27).[55] Traditionally, the repression of this "inversion" has enabled the search for delusional Québécois origins, but at the price of projecting upon France, the "real" mother, accusations of abandonment, if not outright betrayal. This *spécificité québécoise* is a supplement to the more general difficulty of negotiating the constitution of the ego in the colonial context, where the object that is normally figured as lost is recast as absent and therefore incapable of transmitting to the ego "all the desired enlargement." This explains why "for the colonized, the process of introjection always behaves like a fantasy, the fantasy of the process [of introjection] itself, and in this way already participated in a 'work of mourning'... resulting in the temptation of incorporation, the substitution of the fantasy for the thing itself" (38).[56]

In ceding to this "temptation of incorporation," what the myth of Nelligan obscures is at once the poet's true originality and the social roots of his profound failure. In the first instance, Larose reminds his reader that Nelligan actually belongs to "the line [of poets] who neither forget the Origin nor deny their desire for what is lacking; a tragic 'feminine' line of poets who treat France not as an effeminate father but as a phallic mother" (25).[57] And Nelligan's own failure? It is to be traced to his status as a colonized subject and his consequent inability to take the decisive step toward poetic modernism: "Nelligan could not help but be carried to the extreme point where the 'poet' encounters his aporia; but as an idealistic subject, as a colonized subject, he was unable to find matter to symbolize this extreme advance of the subject, the advance of the subject toward the extreme. In his case, there is no possibility of symbolizing the limits imposed upon symbolization, of reflecting the end of literature and the beginning of écriture" (105).[58]

The realm of pure presence that circumscribes Nelligan's poetry is complemented by the immediate gratification sought by readers anxious to participate in his mythologized "triumph." For Larose, both are finally evocative of the state of *childhood* Nelligan was so loathe to leave behind and symptomatic of a more pervasive "infantilism" in Québec culture. Quoting approvingly the historian Michel Brunet, who linked this infantilism to Québec's dependent condition within the Canadian confederation, Larose proceeds to remind his reader that a "purifying" decolonization has often taken as its heroic figure a "noble savage" who, restored to his precolonial authenticity, possesses all the simplicity... of a child! Far from sanctioning such notions, Larose contends that such a romanticization of origins only detracts from the actual identitary challenges that confront a nation intent upon exercising its right to self-determination in the (post)modern world. He ironizes with regard to the identitary pretensions of *pure laine* (dyed in the wool) nationalism, "Perhaps this ungainly, apparent adequation of an undivided culture to itself, or of a fully present Subject-Nation to its own unity, is the nerve-center of ideological colonialism?... Perhaps this is, culturally speaking, the impasse of any process of decolonization: to believe that the removal of alienation resolves the unity of the Subject-Nation with its 'roots' " (15, 18).[59]

For Larose, the ideal of a reconciliation with one's "roots" harbors an equally fantasmatic yearning for an unproblematic, "fusional" self-other relation. Nationalists may claim their objective is to bring Québec "into" the world as an autonomous interlocutor, but in his essay published one year after the referendum defeat, Larose reads the Parti Québécois's surfeit of symbolic productions designed to bolster a sense of collective, national identity as a substitute for a sufficient political will to achieve independence.[60] For him, these productions are symptomatic of the extent to which Québec is *already* integrated within the parameters of the advanced capitalist world. This "symbolic" sovereignty is the *à rebours* sign of Québec's capitulation before the siren song of immediate gratification: "A catastrophic effect of the cultural and ideological regression under the banner of 'full presence' or of 'collective identity' is the substitution of a fantasmatical mode of thought for a critical mode, [which is] condemned in the name of the pleasure principle as an abusive and devitalizing authority because it is too rationalist" (18).[61] Paradoxically (and perhaps fatally) the obsession for "presence" was most acutely manifested during the years of the Parti Québécois's first mandate and culminated in the 1980 referendum, when the governing and the governed contented themselves with "gloriously consuming the representation of a real that had not yet been created... For a Québécois, this could be a way of remaining more 'French-Canadian' than ever" (12).[62]

By "French-Canadian," Larose means the fearful, equivocating, *colonisé* only too eager to buy into a fantasy of "symbolic" victory rather than taking on the hard labor of emancipation. Reading backward, Larose sees a continuum between Nelligan's fate at the hands of his literary "protector," Louis Dantin, and the contemporary "consumption of representations" that leaves Québec a province rather than helping it become a state. Dantin's decision to propagate a myth of a fully realized oeuvre by Nelligan, while cloaking himself in the simulacrum of (literary) paternity, is seen as a gesture typical of the anti-intellectualism that consistently defers Québec's necessary encounter with the exigencies of symbolic inscription: "Better to mask the castration of the mother than to recognize virility in the son. Better to lie in order to mask the Church's idiocy than to recognize that one has a right to think critically" (123).[63]

"Critical thought" is linked here precisely to a "deangelized" reading of the poet's relation to the figure of the mother. In Nelligan, the latter "accumulates the functions of representing both the Origin and creative fullness. . . . [T]he subject will have first attributed to poetry — to Music — a power conceived through the 'imitation' of maternal power, which in turn is unconsciously represented as a full vulva, a true falsity, an authentic artifice" (47).[64] According to Larose, surrender before such "artifice" is rife in contemporary Québec, where the Québécois have accordingly become the passives of their own discourse, passionate in their passivity and hystericized to the point where critical reflection becomes impossible.[65]

This figure of the ruseful mother/flattered son recalls Jacques Lavigne's principle of the *false feminine*. Unlike Lavigne, Larose admits it is illusory to pursue any "true" power of the Father; in this, he conforms to Lacanian theory when it insists upon the instability of phallic power and its perpetual reconstitution as lack. Nevertheless, there is an undeniable conviction in Larose that it wouldn't be such a bad thing for Québec to participate in the illusion of such a "classical" phallocentrism, at least for a while! To take the side of the father and "real" virility, be it aggressive and interdictive, seems to Larose to constitute progress when the alternative is the continuing reign of the false feminine with its conformist untruths and intellectually narcoleptic comforts.

In fact, "virility" is worth pursuing at almost *any* price in this work saturated with the fear of the false feminine. This is contrary to Thérien, who regrets the absence of true revolt in Québec but speculates as to whether homosexuality couldn't provide a "gentle" way of negotiating questions of identity. In Larose, homosexuality signifies the absence of phallic maturity in a model where masculine sexual identity is predicated upon the interminable, futile, but ultimately formative (in the process rather than the result) desire to be the phallus. The homosexual, far from dedicating himself to this thankless but disciplining task, proceeds as if his partner's penis would suffice as a substitute for the phallus he is meant to "earn." The homosexual thus becomes a privileged figure for self-deception, for complacency before the falsehood of the simulacrum. In a particularly telling example, Larose muses upon the propensity for Québécois to mock the French for speaking with an "effeminate" accent. This "ethnocentric deafness in fact constitutes an excellent subject for North American ethnology, in this part of the world where virility is marked by the timbre of the voice and effeminacy gives itself away as the nonobliterated word." And he adds, "Especially since many Québécois speak with a 'homosexual accent' without being homosexuals" (25).[66] How are we to read this curious afterthought? Is Larose positing a generalized "false heterosexuality" along the lines suggested by Hubert Aquin, where situations signifying inversion present themselves as cases of noninversion? In any case, the self-deception is attributable to colonization, which has disrupted identitary processes in Québec so as to render it difficult, if not impossible, to know oneself, and therefore to know others. The terminal figure of this confusion is the "imaginary topos [of a] cone opened infinitely in the direction of the Origin, while the opposite should be the case: in the imaginary, the enlargement should proceed from the punctiformal Origin toward the present and the future. The inverted cone is the image of regression toward the missing marker" (26).[67] Indeed, Larose's "inverted" cone that aberrantly opens *toward* the nothingness of the past and the finality of death deploys the anal space and its sodomitical deviation as the site par excellence not only of deception, but of ontological perdition.

Conclusion: A Theory Made in Québec?

Gilles Thérien raises the possibility of a certain *québécité* to Jacques Lavigne's theory, but we may wonder whether the term can be applied to the ensemble of ideas examined in this essay. In the final analysis, both Thérien and Lavigne elaborate upon Lavigne's work to argue for a "nationally specific" problematics of identity in Québec.

In Thérien, where the concept of *symbolic homosexuality* is privileged, the identitary is referred back to a naturalized Same, the stable point from which one may begin to approach the Other.

Thérien proposes that the Same, even if frustrated in this outward movement due to the lack of a strong, oedipally constituted object, may nonetheless improvise another mode for identitary exploration under the obsessive sign of origins. The "real" homosexuality connoted by this alternative would be a "gentle" substitution for a failed self/other encounter, while the preponderance of homoethical situations would be ambivalent to the extent that they hold out at least the potential for an alternative resolution through a trajectory toward the Real, understood as a remobilization on the properly political front. The relevant consequence of this model for our argument is the hypostatization of homosexuality, and especially of the homosexual, who by always signifying *something else* must always bear the weight of representing and filling a social lack. What is finally a reductive appropriation of homosexuality for analytical ends flows from a performative that seeks to ensconce the primacy of the subject-nation at the expense of a heterogeneously articulated national subject. In fact, for all practical purposes the term "heterogeneous" appears in Thérien *in apposition* to alterity, and is bereft of the leverage with which it might ordinarily destabilize a binary model.

In Larose, the search for full presence is rejected as an identitary ideal. Moreover, a nationalist discourse that seeks to establish its "own" origins must necessarily at once deform and repress the true Origin, which in the case of Québec can never be the putative purity of a precolonized epoch, but rather a filiation with the colonizing gesture itself. Of course, Larose's point here is not to dispute the deformed character of Québec society through its subordinate structural location in the Canadian confederation. Rather, he is in search of a process of liberatory symbolization that will enable a frank recognition of the tasks of the Real as well as its transformation. To refuse this task is precisely to be complicit in a charade of personal and national autonomy figured in terms of Lavigne's concept of the *false feminine*. Characterized by self-castration and a fantasmatic, mimetic existence, the false feminine accommodates a kind of lethargic complacency (a "perpetual vacation," to use another one of Larose's characterizations of homosexuality) while the "national question" rolls headlong into disaster. In his most recent book, Larose in fact has one of his personae pose a question with tongue — barely — in cheek: "After all, isn't Québec already a kind of gay country, where not only are the boundaries between people poorly marked, nor difficult to cross, but are even considered to be reprehensible in and of themselves? Yes, among us it is practically considered inappropriate to define limits between oneself and others! And we speak of independence!"[68] The contrast is offered by way of France, the Origin itself, where the young Québécois intellectual is afforded the opportunity to establish his autonomy through discipline and productive intellectual confrontation. This properly modernist agenda is a necessary corrective to Québec's comforting but superficial postmodernity: "We are the modern clowns of the subversion of the subject, the contortionists of speech.... Our original sin is to have sawed off the tree of knowledge!" (218); it also has its rewards: "Upon his arrival in Paris, the Québécois man experiences a significant growth of his virile member" (231–32)![69]

Even if one accepts these utterances in all the outrageous, deliberately provocational spirit in which they are intended, it is difficult to ignore how they point to their own, more ominous, opposites. In this case, the conviction that a "phallic deficiency" impedes the satisfactory resolution of the national question may dissimulate another, preconscious desire that the national question be resolved as a precondition to the "disappearance" of the problem of deviant sexualities, as if these would no longer have any social "basis" in a country whose citizens' psychosexual health had finally been certified by their demonstrated ability to achieve independence. After all, more than one "postcolonial" society has claimed this much!

There is a final irony in Larose's rhetorical strategy, which consists of dismantling the figures of national "full presence" and insisting on the dynamism of symbolization that will be required to legitimate a viable subject-nation. In his theory, homosexuality itself becomes the new "presence," which is at once "full" (unitary and adequate unto itself) and metonymic (as the à rebours, inverted "full presence" of false feminine complacency in immediate gratification). Larose has done a fine and important job by deconstructing nationalist rhetoric, knowing that, in the words of Doris Sommer, "[to ignore] the fictionality of this rhetoric lets the tropes harden into unassailable truths.... Instead of distinguishing one cause from another, rhetoric often constitutes the common [battle]ground for competing ideologies that vie for the authority to establish the referents for shared signifiers."[70] Why not extend this lesson to the signifying field of homosexuality? Instead, when it comes to homosexuality, Larose seems all too content to "let the tropes harden."

Of course, the anxieties attached to the instability of sexual identities are hardly unique to Québec. In their contemporary manifestations, they derive from a mutation in social discourse that posits the abandonment of the naturalist paradigm in which "sex" has been contained and calls forth new readings of the body. Yet, there seems to be a particular relevance in examining how the naturalization of sexual difference and its conscription as a metafigure of identitary stability continue to weigh heavily on the subject-nation. The inscription of homosexuality as the *Same,* or as the retreat before the encounter with the Other, underwrites a model that foresees a nation's singular presence (as a state) as the evidence of its universal validity (as a state among states). This is a model whose binary interdependency of Same and Other does not spontaneously accommodate representations of heterogeneity, particularly insofar as it is invoked by an oppressed national group that sees itself as involved in a process of self-determination.

The problematic reminds me of Rosa Braidotti's interrogation of *feminism:* "If the minimal feminist position consists in bringing the asymmetry between the sexes to the forefront of the debate on the postmodern condition, the question remains: How far can we push the sexualization of the debate while remaining in tune with the insight of modernity about the fundamental failure of identity? How can we affirm the positivity of female difference while resisting the reduction of subjectivity to consciousness, of self to willful rationality?"[71] This kind of interrogation may be very suggestive when dealing with the crisis of the subject-nation. I am not talking about mechanically substituting "nation" for "sex," "Québécois" for "female," but rather about underscoring how identitary preoccupations always have a *strategic* basis. The "dissolution of difference" can never be realized through the voluntarism of an oppressed group, precisely because this difference is constructed in the first place in relation to another master term that will not be "transcended" through either the absence or the refusal of its object. We can therefore understand Braidotti's resistance to the invitation to situate herself "beyond" sexual difference: "In a cultural order that, for centuries, has been governed by the male homosocial bond, the elimination of sexual difference can only be a one-way street towards the appropriation, elimination, or homologizing of the feminine in/of women."[72] This kind of resistance is well-known in the context of nationalism where an "indigenist" thought disputes the claim that the problematic of identity has been surpassed in the postmodern context, and sees in it the specter of a definitive assimilation into the culture of the colonizer or dominant power. But at the same time, such an indigenist temptation may lead the intellectual or cultural producer charged with "imagining" the nation to demand an "all or nothing" position of the emerging subject-nation, willing all other subject positions to silence. Which leads to a final pair of proposals: First, to theorists of the subject-nation: Why not see homosexuality as a range of practices inscribed within a complex discursive construction suited to protect a national identitary against its naturalization into the Same? This would open up the space of the political so that it could be invested with broader strategies than those embodied in positions preoccupied by the exclusivity of nationhood. The variegated subject-nation that results may finally be less impatient of the identitary claims of a contemporary social heterogeneity from which it stands to gain resilience and strength. Second, to sex/gender theorists: Why not acknowledge that the capacity of conceptions of nationhood to disrupt and tie knots around sexually defined affirmations of identity demonstrates precisely why it is deleterious for those articulating sex/gender and "queer" theory to persist in the undertheorization of the national? What seems to be on the agenda is no longer a dismissal of the national as antinomous with the sexual (ironically, much as "orthodox" Marxists had long dismissed the national as antinomous with concerns of social class), but a recognition of the resilience of variegated national claims that an antiessentializing theory ought to accommodate. In this essay, our concern has been to demonstrate how such theory might productively illuminate a situation where contemporary nationalism has taken largely progressive forms while revealing profound discrepancies between its popular, legal, and learned inscriptions of homosexuality. Offered in closure, these proposals obviously can only look forward to future constructive engagements between theorists of the national and the sexual on the unavoidably common terrain of identity.

NOTES

This essay is a substantially revised version of "(Homo)sexualité et problématique identitaire," which appeared in Sherry Simon et al., eds., *Fictions de l'identitaire au Québec* (Montréal: XYZ éditeur, 1991), 117–50. The original essay was written in 1990 during my participation in a research project on "L'Identitaire et l'Hétérogène dans la prose romanesque québécoise de 1940 jusqu'à nos jours" at Concordia University, Montréal. This participation was made possible with a fellowship from the Social Sciences and Humanities Research Council of Canada. I am grateful to the other members of the research group (the aforementioned editors, plus our research assistant, David Leahy) for their interest in my work and their valuable insights and suggestions. Andy Parker, Michael Warner, and Sean Holland have all been very helpful in guiding me through the process of revising this text for appearance in English.

1. Hubert Aquin, "Commentaire I," in Fernand Dumont and Jean-Charles Falardeau, eds., *Littérature et Société canadiennes-françaises* (Québec: Les Presses de l 'Université Laval, 1964). The French original states that French-Canadian literature is "globalement faible, sans éclat ... et vraiment ennuyeuse, principalement à cause de sa sur-valorisation de toutes les situations humaines qui se rapprochent de l'inversion. Pourtant, ce déviationisme sexuel se dissimulait derrière une proportion majoritaire de stéréotypes qui, précisément, s'annoncent comme des cas de non-inversion" (191–92). All translations from French to English in the body of the text are my own.

2. For discussions of the "discourse of decolonization," see my "Literature and Intellectual Realignments in Québec," *Québec Studies* 3 (1985): 32–56. Also, Simon Harel's *Le Voleur de parcours: Identité et cosmopolitisme dans la littérature québécoise contemporaine* (Montréal: Le Préambule, 1991), esp. chaps. 2 and 3.

3. Michel Tremblay, *"Hosanna" suivie de "La Duchesse de Langeais"* (Montréal: Leméac, 1973).

4. In fact, Tremblay's deployments of sex and gender in *Hosanna* are wonderfully rich and authorize the complication and destabilization of the dialectic of "*universalité/spécificité*" in which homosexuality is legible as a precise identity of a minority group. In 1991, a new production gives an interrogative, rather than a declamatory tenor to Hosanna's closing "I am a man," underscoring the play's interrogation throughout of identities based on assumed symmetries between gender and sexuality. See my "From Authenticity to Ambivalence: Michel Tremblay's *Hosanna*," *American Review of Canadian Studies* 22, no. 4 (1992): 499–510, and Robert K. Martin, "Gender, Race, and the Colonial Body: Carson McCullers's Filipino Boy and Daven Henry Hwang's Chinese Woman," *Canadian Review of American Studies* 23, no. 1 (1992): 95–106.

5. Robert Schwartzwald, "Fear of Federasty: Québec's Inverted Fictions," in Hortense Spillers, ed., *Comparative American Identities: Race, Sex, and Nationality in the Modern Text* (New York and London: Routledge, 1991), 189.

6. In the May 20, 1980, referendum, the independentist Parti Québécois government sought a "mandate to negotiate" sovereignty association with the Canadian

government in Ottawa. Approximately 60 percent of voters responded "no" and 40 percent "yes" to this question that foresaw political independence for Québec combined with an economic common market with the rest of Canada.

7. During the referendum campaign, supporters of the "no" side ran on the slogan that "NO means YES"... to immediate federal constitutional reform. In fact, the Canadian constitution was subsequently repatriated (the original British North America Act of 1867 creating the Canadian confederation was adopted as an act of the British parliament) in 1982 *without* Québec's approval, since the amended version did not include provisions that sufficiently recognized what would come to be known as Québec's status as a "distinct society." In 1990, new negotiations that produced the "Meech Lake accords" meant to bring Québec into the constitutional fold also collapsed when two provinces refused to ratify them, once again largely due to objections over recognizing Québec's cultural and national specificity. As this essay is being completed, so are another round of constitutional negotiations.... In the meantime, Canada functions under a constitution that has not been accepted by a legislative assembly representing almost one-quarter of the federation's population.

8. Arcand went on to excoriate intellectuals, as well, in *Le Déclin de l'empire américain* (film script) (Montreal: Boréal, 1986), discussed below.

9. Hélène Richard, "Le théâtre gai québécois: conjoncture sociale et sentiment de filiation," *Jeu* 54 (1990): 16. "Le théâtre gai met en scène, à sa façon, une problématique universelle qui est celle de la filiation et de son impact sur le narcissisme défini ici comme l'estime de soi et le sentiment d'avoir une identité."

10. Gilbert David, "Ce qui est resté dans le placard," *Jeu* 54 (1990): 119, 119 n. 3. "[L]'inquiétante réalité qui fait qu'une relation amoureuse entre un homme et une femme puisse engendrer un être qui en est la contradiction vivante." "[Q]u'on le veuille ou non, les couples qui prennent la décision de mettre au monde un enfant ne le font pas, à ce qu'il semble, en rêvant qu'il devienne homosexuel... d'où l'incontournable question de l'échec qui hante la conscience homosexuelle."

11. Ibid. "Quelle part de responsabilité les homosexuels se reconaissent-ils en regard des générations futures, notamment face aux enfants?"

12. These project onto the homosexual the opprobrium of a society that often creates insurmountable obstacles for lesbians and gay men who, if they have not parented a child, would like to adopt one or work in a child-care related occupation.

13. Indeed, since Québec is begotten by France, itself the very model of modern national sovereignty, it is easy to see how this model would view Québec's failure to achieve independence as the proof of its being the "living contradiction" of its parent!

14. David, "Ce qui est resté," 120. "[L]a figure cardinale d'un univers de la marchandise sous l'emprise de la séduction généralisée."

15. Arcand's tendency to exploit homosexuality as a symbol for the falseness of the "postmodern festival" is articulated within a more pervasive tendency to identify sexuality with the privilege of knowledge, especially self-knowledge. For a convincing discussion of this, see Jean Larose's "Savoir et Sexe," in *La Petite noirceur* (Montréal: Boréal, 1987), 9–17.

16. Arcand's documentary *On est au coton,* which is a shocking exposé of working conditions in Québec's garment and textile industries, was only recently reintroduced for distribution by the National Film Board of Canada. In an act of unofficial censorship, it was removed from the NFB's catalog shortly after its release; Arcand's

feature film *Réjeanne Padovani* is a biting satire and a thinly veiled treatment of alleged collusion between the first Québec Liberal Party government of Premier Robert Bourassa (1970–76), the Montréal municipal administration under Mayor Jean Drapeau, construction contractors, and the Mafia.

17. Gayle Rubin's well-known radicalization of this model ("The Traffic in Women: Notes toward a Political Economy of Sex," in Rayna Reiter, ed., *Toward an Anthropology of Women* [New York: Monthly Review Press, 1975], 157–210) identifies the traffic in women as the basis for exchange through the production of sex/gender systems that rely upon compulsory heterosexuality. More recently, she has modified her theory by suggesting that the gender identities thus established need not have a determining impact upon sexuality. Especially in "postindustrial" societies, she argues, contemporary systems of sexual identity are marked by a significant degree of autonomy ("Thinking Sex: Notes for a Radical Theory of the Politics of Sexuality," in Carole S. Vance, ed., *Pleasure and Danger: Exploring Female Sexuality* [Boston: Routledge and Kegan Paul, 1984], 307).

18. Two other important articles characteristic of the "psychoanalysis of decolonization" in Québec are Paul Chamberland's "De la damnation à la liberté," *Parti pris* 9–10–11 (summer 1964): 53–89; and Pierre Maheu's "L'Œdipe colonial," in the same issue, pp. 19–29. Both appear in a special issue entitled *Portrait du colonisé québécois,* after the well-known volume by Albert Memmi.

19. Benedict Anderson, *Imagined Communities: Reflections on the Origin and Spread of Nationalism,* rev. ed. (London and New York: Verso, 1991).

20. Jacques Lavigne, *L'Objectivité: Ses conditions instinctuelles et affectives* (Montréal: Leméac, 1971).

21. "Une capacité hétérosexuelle certaine ... "; "sa dissolution en ses constituants: la conjugalité, l'instinct paternel et l'amour filial."

22. Lavigne specifies: "By eroticism, we always mean a way of perceiving the other by utilizing the dynamism of the sex derive, that is, to perceive the other as apt for sexual love, as an image that evokes sexuality. This is a form of experience, rather than of comprehension. This perception does not mean that the other is an object for the sex drive." ("Par érotisme nous entendons toujours un mode de percevoir l'autre utilisant le dynamisme de la pulsion sexuelle. Ainsi percevoir l'autre comme apte à l'amour sexuel, comme image qui évoque la sexualité. C'est une façon d'éprouver et non une compréhension. Cette perception ne signifie pas que l'autre est un objet pour la pulsion sexuelle") (in *L'Objectivité,* 244 n.).

23. "[L]es images érotiques fondamentales de l'homosexualité sont symboliques parce qu'elles ont pour mission de traduire un état de psychisme qui n'est pas le désir du même sexe comme expression de la vie des instincts." Even if Lavigne proposes a symbolic rather than a literal way of reading these images, this in no way alters the "logic" for decoding them according to a preexisting heterosexual exigency. In this sense, Lavigne is only proposing a more sophisticated reading, as the following example illustrates: "It has been noted, for example, that the intromission of the penis into the mouth was the imitation of sucking on the breast, ... an explanation that doesn't explain much since it is too limited, because its symbolism is entirely external and too close to appearances" (ibid., 60) ("On a noté, par exemple, que l'intromission du pénis dans la bouche était l'imitation de la succion du sein ... une explication qui n'explique pas grand-chose parce qu'elle est trop limitée, parce que son symbolisme est tout extérieur et trop proche aux apparences.") It is clear that

an "internal" symbolic reading of this act would not make it less reprehensible to Lavigne, even if his analysis has the merit of rejecting the topos of homosexual *imitation*.

24. "[L]'hypothèse d'un lieu psychique que l'on peut appeler pulsionnel dans le langage freudien et, dans un langage ontologique, la soudure de l'âme et du corps, lieu qui est le principe de la fonction de la symbolisation qui soutient le langage."

25. "[Un] signifiant peut, au lieu de conduire à la conscience le signifié qu'il connote, engendrer une mutation biologique ou encore transmettre à la conscience son message mais au prix des perturbations dans l'ordre biologique et physiologique. ... [Existe alors] la possibilité de cette déviation significative du vocable."

26. In its own way, this analysis depends on what Gayle Rubin calls "the hierarchy of sexual acts," where "marital, reproductive heterosexuals are alone at the top of the erotic pyramid. ... Hierarchies of sexual value ... rationalize the well-being of the sexually privileged and the adversity of the sexual rabble" ("Thinking Sex," 279–80).

27. "Ce que l'enfant demande à la mère c'est de lui donner la place du père, afin que, à son tour, il lui confère le prestige et les attributs du père. ... Ce qui est recherché, c'est le pouvoir, afin d'instituer un ordre où l'on obtient d'être devenu semblable au père sans avoir à traverser le temps qu'il a parcouru pour devenir ce qu'il est. C'est le monde de l'exaltation de la fausse puissance et de l'annihilation de la vraie."

28. "[A]ccepter la possibilité d'une composante érotique à l'intérieur de cette relation pour l'intégrer au sentiment paternel, maternel et filial."

29. "Il existe une différence considérable entre le concept du faux-féminin et celui du complexe d'Oedipe. Ce dernier culpabilise l'enfance, l'adolescence et la névrose alors que le premier permet de distinguer un amour naturel et vrai d'un autre qui est faux et, somme toute, contre les forces positives et créatrices de la nature."

30. "[L]e mythe de la castration substitue la victime au coupable en transformant un acte d'injustice chez le coupable en un délit sexuel chez la victime."

31. "[N]ous croyons plus conforme à la réalité de penser que certains sentiments et activités qui ne sont pas, à la fin, sexuels, empruntent, en certaines circonstances, comme première étape de leur manifestation, le langage de l'érotisme."

32. "[R]éduit à cet être passif, dominé, entretenu, asservi, mutilé dont l'enfant était l'image. ... "

33. Gilles Thérien, "Cinema québécois: La difficile conquête de l 'altérité," *Littérature* 66 (May 1987): 105. "[L]a connaissance de l'autre en tant que l'autre, la perception de l'altérité en tant qu'altérité, la reconnaissance objective de l'altérite qui ne met pas en question le sujet connaissant."

34. This partly explains the hostile reception accorded the "automatist" manifesto *Refus global* ("Total Rejection") when it appeared in 1948. The manifesto bitterly denounced clericalism in Québec, particularly the fear and conformism it had instilled in the population, and was condemned from several different perspectives. Noteworthy for our purposes here is the opposition expressed to its valorization of the unconscious, as in Père Hyancinthe Robillard's "L'Automatisme surrationnel et la nostalgie du Jardin d'Eden," *Amérique française* 8, no. 4 (1949–50): 44–73.

35. "[L]a compromission morale, ontologique et instinctuelle ... une démission de la personnalité globale en face des normes de l'affectivité naturelle et des lois de l'esprit."

36. "[C]es hommes qui s'interrogent toute leur vie afin de savoir s'ils porteraient

pas au fond d'eux-mêmes et inconsciemment le germe de cette déviation." . . .
"[L'homosexualité] n'en est pas, mais que nous sommes en face plutôt d'un phénomène qui, s'il découvre, effectivement et réellement, son langage dans l'imagerie et la sentimentalité homosexuelles, n'en est pas moins la manifestation exaspérée d'un constituant qui appartient au dynamisme humain normal et qui, réduit à ses justes proportions, est un facteur essentiel à ce contact vital avec le réel, fondement de toute connaissance authentique."

Lavigne's theory conforms here to what Eve Kosofsky Sedgwick identifies as a tendency in Freudian revisionism to offer a rather repressive interpretation of Freud's observation that the sexual instinct does not in the first instance serve the needs of reproduction, but rather of the realization of certain forms of pleasure: "Freud's study of Dr. Schreber shows clearly that *the repression of homosexual desire* in a man who by any commonsense standard was heterosexual, occasioned paranoid psychosis; the prophylactic use that has been made of this perception, however, has not been against *homophobia,* but against *homosexuality*" (*Between Men: English Literature and Male Homosocial Desire* [New York: Columbia University Press, 1985], 20).

37. "[L]'image érotique . . . qui est, au niveau de l'instinct, l'image terminale et fondamentale de ce système."

38. Sedgwick, *Between Men.*

39. In fact, Lavigne's social critique extends to the status of women. He explains that in his theory of symbolism, the "feminine" does not designate "what belongs to women — femininity — and it is therefore not a question of what is woman's alone and exclusive to her sex" (*L'Objectivité,* 66). ("[C]e qui appartient à la femme, la féminité, et il n'est pas question, par conséquent, de ce qui est propre à la femme et ce qui est exclusif à son sexe.") To condemn a culture because it has been elaborated under the sign of the mother, if understood as designating the real mother, "seems quite unjust to us with regard to women and without any serious basis" (ibid., 67). ("[N]ous paraît fort injuste à l'endroit de la femme et sans aucun fondement sérieux.") Beyond good intentions, however, this formulation begs the question of what would be "woman's alone" and "exclusive to her sex."

40. "[L]a possibilité qu'un milieu, au lieu de résister à une personnalité névrotique, au lieu de la forcer à s'adapter à des normes objectives et acceptées universellement, ou à se faire soigner, s'adapte lui-même à cette personnalité et perde, peu à peu, pour la suivre, le sens du normal, du naturel et du réel."

41. Thérien, "Cinema québécois," 101. "[L]a sémiogenèse d'un processus de définition de soi faute d'une figure identitaire."

42. The films discussed by Thérien are *La Bête lumineuse* (Pierre Perrault), *Au clair de la lune* (André Forcier), *Sonatine* (Micheline Lanctôt), *Mario* (Jean Beaudin), *Visage pâle* (Claude Gagnon), *Anne Trister* (Léa Pool), and *Pouvoir intime* (Yves Simoneau). "The selected films are all recent, produced since 1980, i.e., since the failure of the referendum on the independence of Québec, the repatriation from England [*sic*] of the Canadian constitution, the change in [federal] governments, and the departure of the protagonists of the debate over Québec's autonomy from the political scene. They are all works of well-known filmmakers. All have had a measure of success. None is the director's first feature-length film" (Thérien, "Cinema québécois," 102). ("Les films choisis sont tous récents, produits depuis 1980, c'est-à-dire depuis l'échec du référendum sur l'indépendance du Québec, le repatriement de la constitution canadienne d'Angleterre, le changement de gouvernements et le

départ de la scène politique des protagonistes du débat sur l'autonomie du Québec. Ils sont tous l'oeuvre d'un cinéaste connu. Ils ont tous connu une forme de succès. Il ne s'agit jamais d'un premier long métrage.") For critical readings of individual films that amplify arguments advanced in this essay, see my "(Homo)sexualité et problématique identitaire," in Sherry Simon et al., eds., *Fictions de l'identitaire au Québec* (Montréal: XYZ éditeur, 1991), 135–37.

43. "[L]e film est un argument, une proposition. L'enjeu est donc de fabriquer le bon objet qui restera bon grace à la reaction du spectateur."

44. "Ces gens dans une même salle font généralement partie d'une même société, d'une même nation, d'une même culture 'idéolectale' et ils viennent peut-être voir sur l'écran les personnages qui les représentent. . . . Cet aspect est fondamental pour la survie du cinéma national . . . mais aussi pour la constitution de l'imaginaire collectif dans lequel chacun sera libre de se retrouver."

45. "[C]ette relation homoéthique, une relation qui pose comme bon objet le même."

46. For speaking about relations among men that are not necessarily genital, but where questions of power, privilege, and desire enter into the picture, I prefer the term "homosocial" as used by Sedgwick (*Between Men*). It reintroduces historicity into relations between men, and is thus more amenable to variable and shifting inscriptions. On the other hand, the homoethical presents itself as a system of thought and behavior to be privileged or restrained.

47. "[L]e partage d'un même territoire, d'un même topos . . . un lieu à partir duquel il sera possible d'aller vers le territoire de l'autre et de découvrir si l'autre est un bon objet ou s'il peut le devenir."

48. "[L]'enjeu, c'est le choix entre l'enfermement sur soi qui implique la défaite et le rôle du dominé ou le combat qui ne garantit pas la victoire."

49. "[A]u moment où s'estompe la structure de reproduction et où se profile la structure de domination, [le] choix est si difficile à faire que seule la mort apparaît comme solution."

50. For an interesting discussion of the role oedipal logic plays in another longstanding national scenario, see Stephen Tift's "The Parricidal Phantasm: Irish Nationalism and the *Playboy* Riots," in Andrew Parker et al., eds., *Nationalisms and Sexualities* (New York and London: Routledge, 1992), 313–32.

51. "[L]a realisation du système social dans le cadre du système de parenté." . . . "[L]a recherche de l'origine par le biais de l'homosexualité est une recherche en douceur, 'introspective': une autre variante pourrait être la recherche de l'origine par l'élimination violente de l'autre, comme Oedipe."

52. "[Cela] consiste à être incapable d'accéder à l'autre en tant qu'autre, à l'altérité comme donnée sociale, hétérogène, et a retourner en arrière pour reprendre la question des origines, la question de l'identité."

53. "[L]a pseudo-recurrence du thème de l'homosexualité apparaît plutôt comme une variante de la question de l'identité et l'étendue du problème à travers la diversité des films ne fait que dire plus fort l'importance de cette question dans le contexte québécois malgré la défaite au plan politique."

54. "C'est à cette inversion imprévue que notre asservissement doit, peut-être, nous travailler aujourd'hui."

55. Jean Larose, *Le Mythe de Nelligan* (Montréal: Boréal, 1981).

56. "[L]e processus d'introjection agit toujours, pour un colonisé, comme un

fantasme, fantasme du processus, et participe déjà à ce titre d'une 'maladie de deuil' ... débouchant sur la tentation de l'incorporation, de la substitution du fantasme à la chose."

57. Nelligan "appartient à la lignée de ceux qui n'oublient pas l'Origine, qui ne nient pas leur désir de ce qui y manque, tragique lignée 'féminine' des poètes qui traitent la France non comme un père efféminé mais comme une mère phallique."

58. "Pleinement 'poète', Nelligan ne pouvait que se trouver entraîné vers l'extrême, là où le 'poète' rencontre son aporie; mais en tant que sujet idéaliste, en tant que colonisé, il ne pouvait pas trouver matière à symboliser cette avancée extrême du sujet, l'avancée du sujet vers l'extrême. Dans son cas, nulle possibilité de symboliser la limite imposée à la symbolisation, de réfléchir la fin de la littérature et le début de l'écriture."

59. "Peut-être cette dégaine, l'apparente adéquation à elle-même d'une culture non-divisée, ou d'un sujet-nation pleinement présent à sa propre unité, est-elle le nerf de la colonisation idéologique? ... Telle est, peut-être, culturellement, l'impasse de toute décolonisation: croire que la levée de l'aliénation résoud l'unité du sujet-nation avec ses 'racines.' "

60. Examples of such productions range from lavish festivities to celebrate the national holiday to engineering diplomatic events at home and abroad that would implicitly bestow upon Québec the status of a sovereign state. Profederalists often charged, for example, that Québec "government offices" abroad often behaved more like embassies while Québec's Ministry of International Affairs conducted itself like a full-fledged foreign ministry. A whole series of organisms and structures emphasized Québec's national status, sometimes by fulfilling parallel functions to federal institutions, sometimes simply by boasting the epithet *nationale*. In any case, it was always the federal, Canadian institution or organism that was made to appear redundant or unnecessarily intrusive. One of the main graphics for the "yes" side in the referendum depicted a balanced scale that represented Canada and Québec negotiating *D'égal à égal* (between equals), a claim that accurately reflects the "two nations" view of the Canadian confederation held even by many federalists in Québec, but that proclaimed an equality between states that, far from existing, was the very objective of the referendum and the campaign for independence. This is the kind of image that inspires Larose's denunciation of "symbolic sovereignty."

61. "Un effet catastrophique de la régression culturelle et idéologique sous l'étendard de la 'présence pleine' ou de 'l'identité collective' est la substitution du mode fantasmatique de la pensée à son mode critique, condamné au nom du principe de plaisir comme autorité abusive et dévitalisante, parce que trop rationnaliste."

There are certainly affinities between Larose's thought and positions advanced in texts such as Alain Finkielkraut's *La défaite de la pensée* (Paris: Gallimard, 1987) and Christopher Lasch's *The Culture of Narcissism* (New York: Norton, 1979). On the latter, as well as an extended treatment of relations between homosexuality and narcissism as read through Freud and Lacan, see Michael Warner's "Homo-Narcissism; or, Heterosexuality" in Joseph A. Boone and Michael Cadden, eds., *Engendering Men* (New York and London: Routledge, 1990), 190–206.

62. "[À] consommer glorieusement la représentation d'un réel qu'on n'a pas encore produit ... Cela pourrait être, pour le Québécois, une manière de demeurer plus que jamais 'Canadien français.' "

The reelection of the Parti Québécois to a second term in 1991, *after* the defeat of the referendum, could only amplify the sense of Larose's critique: it was as if the society wanted to live in this collective illusion for another five years and deny the gesture it had just made.

63. "Plutôt masquer la castration de la mère que de reconnaître au fils de la virilité. Plutôt mentir pour voiler la connerie de l'Eglise que de reconnaître le droit à une pensée critique." Following the logic of this analysis, Larose claims that at the time of the "Yvette" affair during the referendum campaign, the castrated (profederalist) fathers appealed to the mother (traditionalist women offended by the PQ's Minister for the Status of Women's remark that women supporting the "no" reminded her of Yvette, the docile, happy homemaker in textbooks once used in Québec schools) against the rebellious (proindependence) sons, but that the sons had already castrated themselves through an ineffectual, suicidal campaign even before her intervention!

64. "La Mère cumule les fonctions de la représentante de l'Origine et celle de la plénitude créatrice. . . . [L]e sujet aurait déjà reconnu à la poésie — à la Musique — un pouvoir conçu par 'imitation' du pouvoir maternel, lequel à son tour se représente inconsciemment comme une vulve pleine, fausseté vraie, un artifice authentique."

65. In *La Petite noirceur,* Larose "homosexualizes" this "feminine" figure of paralysis: he interprets the public's enthusiasm for a homosexual hairdresser in one of Québec's more popular TV sitcoms as a form of abjection, in which the vulvic horror is masked by the comedic anus: "Between the false and the true, the vulvic cave agape, but to laugh, for the anus is a vulva for laughs, not for real" (92–93). ("Entre faux et vrai, l'antre vulvaire ouvert, mais pour rire, l'anus est une vulve pour rire, pas pour vrai.")

66. "[Cette] surdité ethnocentrique constituerait un excellent sujet en ethnologie nord-américaine, au lieu où la virilité se prouve au timbre, et l'efféminité se dénonce comme parole non-oblitérée. D'autant plus que beaucoup de Québécois parlent avec 'l'accent homosexuel' sans être homosexuels."

There is a play on words in the French, where *timbre* means both timbre (of the voice) and a postage stamp, and *oblitérée* refers both to the sonority of the spoken word and a canceled stamp.

67. "Topique imaginaire: je me représente un cône ouvert infiniment en direction de l'Origine, alors que cela devrait être le contraire; dans l'imaginaire, l'élargissement devrait se faire depuis l'Origine punctiforme vers le présent et l'avenir. Le cône inversé est l'image de la régression vers la marque manquante."

68. Jean Larose, *L'Amour du pauvre* (Montréal: Boréal, 1991). "Après tout, le Québec n'est-il déjà une sorte de pays 'gay,' où non seulement les limites entre les gens ne sont pas bien marquées, et pas bien difficiles à sauter, mais sont même une chose presque répréhensible en soi? Oui, chez nous, il est mal vu de marquer la limite entre soi-même et les autres! Parlons-en, de l'indépendance!"

69. "Nous sommes les clowns modernes de la subversion du sujet, les contortionnistes de la parole. . . . Notre péché originel, c'est d'avoir scié l'Arbre de la Connaissance!" "[L]es hommes québécois, dès leur arrivée à Paris, connaissent un important accroissement du membre viril."

70. Doris Sommer, "National Romances and Populist Rhetoric in Spanish America," in Francis Barker, ed., *Europe and Its Others* (Colchester: University of Essex, 1985), 2:35.

71. Rosa Braidotti, "Organs without Bodies," *Differences* 1, no. 1 (1989): 159.

72. Ibid., 157. This is not the place to take up the summary usage Braidotti makes of "the homosocial bond" in her argument. Nevertheless, it is important to remember that this bond is almost always homophobically disrupted, with male entitlement proceeding through relations that at once include and deploy profound regulations of homosexuality.

Right On, Girlfriend!
Douglas Crimp

At Vito Russo's memorial service in December of 1990, the first speaker was New York's mayor David Dinkins. It had been reported in the gay press that Dinkins paid a hospital visit a few days before Vito died, and that Vito had mustered the strength to sit up and say, "In 1776, Edmund Burke of the British Parliament said about the slavery clause, 'A politician owes the people not only his industry but his judgment, and if he sacrifices his judgment to their opinions, he betrays them.'"[1] Those of us who are queer and/or AIDS activists knew very well what Vito was alluding to, because Mayor Dinkins had by then already sacrificed what we took to be his judgment when we voted for him. He failed to make a public issue of the rising tide of violence against gays and lesbians, refusing to march with us in Staten Island to protest the homophobically motivated murder of a disabled gay man, and unwilling to press for labeling as bias-related the murder of a gay Latino in a Jackson Heights cruising area.[2] He appointed Woodrow Myers health commissioner over the vehement objections of AIDS activists; he canceled New York's pilot needle-exchange program, initiated by Myers's predecessor but opposed by the city's conservative black leadership; he allowed thousands of homeless people with HIV infection to remain in warehouse shelters, where they are vulnerable to opportunistic diseases, especially to the terrifying new epidemic of multi–drug-resistant strains of tuberculosis; and he drastically cut funding for health services even as the city's health-care system faced collapse from underfinancing. Still, when Dinkins eulogized

Vito Russo, he quoted what Vito had said to him in the hospital and, with no apparent sense of irony, professed that he would always remember it.

As soon as he had delivered his short speech, the mayor and his entourage left the memorial service, accompanied by a small chorus of boos. The next speaker was Vito's old friend Arnie Kantrowitz, who began by saying that, just in case we thought we had learned something new about Vito — that he was a student of American history — we should know that the lines he'd quoted to Dinkins came from the movie version of the Broadway musical *1776*. Our laughter at Arnie's remark brought back the Vito we knew and loved, the fierce activist who was very funny and very queer, a very funny queer who knew and loved movies, who knew better than anybody how badly the movies treated queers, but still loved them. Those qualities were captured yet again in another of Arnie's remarks. Reminiscing about Vito's pleasure in showing movies at home to his friends and about his unashamed worship of Judy Garland, Arnie summed up Vito's brand of gay militancy (or perhaps I should say, his gay brand of militancy): "In Vito's house," Arnie quipped, "either you respected Judy . . . or you left."

A very different chord was struck later in the service by Larry Kramer. "The Vito who was my friend was different from the one I've heard about today," the Hollywood screenwriter said. "Since I hate old movies, I wasn't in his home-screening crowd." Kramer went on to ask, rhetorically, "Who killed Vito?" And his answer? "As sure as any virus killed him, we killed him. Everyone in this room killed him. Twenty-five million people outside this room killed him. Vito was killed by 25 million gay men and lesbians who for ten long years of this plague have refused to get our act together. Can't you see that?"

The "can't you see that?" was the refrain of Kramer's speech, which went on to name names — mostly those of closeted gay men and lesbians in the entertainment industry. The last names mentioned were those associated with an AIDS fundraiser:

> There's going to be a benefit screening of a movie called *Silence of the Lambs*. The villain is a gay man who mass-murders people. AmFAR is holding the benefit. Thanks a lot, Mathilde Krim [Mathilde Krim is, as is well known, the chairperson of the American Foundation for AIDS Research]. Thanks a lot, Arthur Krim, for financing the film

[Arthur Krim, Mathilde's husband, is the founder of Orion Pictures]. Thanks a lot, Jodie Foster, for starring in it [Jodie Foster is ... well, we know who Jodie Foster is ...].[3]

Some other people at the memorial service disagreed with Larry about who killed Vito. As several hundred of Vito's friends and admirers arrived at the service, we were handed a xeroxed flier signed "Three Anonymous Queers." "On the same night last month," it began,

> Vito Russo died from AIDS and Jesse Helms was reelected to another six years of power. ... I believe with all my heart that Jesse Helms killed Vito Russo. And I believe without question that when I was queer-bashed, Helms was as responsible for my injuries as if he had inflicted the wounds with his own hands. I fully imagine in a meeting with Helms, he would have the blood and flesh of dead dykes and fags dripping from his hands and mouth. And I hate him and I believe he is a threat to my very existence and I have every right to defend myself against him with any amount of force I choose.

The flier closed with two questions: "If I am ever brave enough to murder Jesse Helms, will you hand me the gun to carry out the deed? Will you hide me from the law once it is done?"

Most queers will recognize, in these two rhetorical answers to the question, Who killed Vito?, positions taken on debates in contemporary queer politics, debates about "outing" and "bashing back." My interest here is not so much to take sides in these debates as to describe both the political conjuncture within which they take place and some of the cultural interventions within them. I also want to attend to their relevance for AIDS activism, the movement that to some degree brought them to the fore and in which they are sometimes played out. It is not coincidental that they surfaced at Vito Russo's memorial service, for in many ways Vito was the quintessential gay activist turned AIDS activist.

Vito's death was more than a personal loss to his friends and admirers. It was also a great symbolic loss to ACT UP. The Three Anonymous Queers put it this way: "Vito is dead and everything remains the same. I thought I might go to sleep the night after his death and wake up to find the city burned to the ground." Such a fantasy, which recalls spontaneous riots in the wake of murdered civil rights leaders of the 1960s, arises, I think, not only because

Vito was a cherished leader, but because he held out hope in a very particular way, hope that he voiced in his famous Albany speech from ACT NOW's Nine Days of Protest in the spring of 1988.[4] The speech began:

> A friend of mine has a half-fare transit card which he uses on busses and subways. The other day when he showed his card, the token attendant asked what his disability was. He said, "I have AIDS," and the attendant said, "No you don't. If you had AIDS, you'd be home, dying." I'm here to speak out today as a PWA [Person with AIDS] who is not dying from, but for the last three years quite successfully living with, AIDS.

Vito ended the speech by saying, "After we kick the shit out of this disease, I intend to be alive to kick the shit out of this system, so that this will never happen again."

Vito's death painfully demonstrated to many AIDS activists that the rhetoric of hope we invented and depended upon — a rhetoric of "living with AIDS," in which "AIDS is not a death sentence," but rather "a chronic manageable illness" — was becoming difficult to sustain. I don't want to minimize the possibility that anyone's death might result in such a loss of hope for someone, and, moreover, within a two-week period of Vito's death, four other highly visible members of ACT UP New York also died, a cumulative loss for us that was all but unbearable. But I think many of us had a special investment in Vito's survival, not only because he was so beloved, but because, as a long-term survivor, as a resolute believer in his own survival, and as a highly visible and articulate fighter for his and others' survival, he fully embodied that hope.

Vito's death coincided with the waning not only of our optimism but also of a period of limited but concrete successes for the AIDS activist movement. During that period — roughly, the first two and one-half years after the founding of ACT UP in the spring of 1987 — we had succeeded in focusing greater public attention on AIDS, in shifting the discussion of AIDS from one dominated by a punitive moralism to one directed toward combating a public health emergency, and in affecting policy in concrete ways, particularly drug development policy.

During the past two years, however, we have experienced only disappointments and setbacks. We have seen almost no new drugs to combat AIDS, whether antivirals or treatments for, or prophy-laxes against, opportunistic infections (OIs). The results of ddI and ddC studies have been less than encouraging, and the few poten-tially effective treatments for OIs are either held up in the FDA's approval process or, when granted marketing approval, subject to record-breaking price gouging. We have had to return to other bat-tles we had thought were behind us, such as the call for mandatory testing of health-care professionals in the wake of hysteria caused by the possible transmission of HIV from a dentist to his patients; after having worked tirelessly to get the voices of people with AIDS heard, the media and Congress finally listened sympathetically to one, that of Kimberly Bergalis, who in fact spoke not as a person with AIDS ("I didn't do anything wrong," she protested), but as the "victim" of people with AIDS ("My life has been taken away").[5] We have seen the leveling off or shrinking of spending on AIDS at local, state, and federal levels, a particularly disheartening ex-ample of which was the passage, with great fanfare, of the Ryan White Emergency CARE bill providing disaster relief to the hardest hit cities, and then, at budget time, the failure to provide most of the funding for it. At the same time, case loads continue to spiral upwards, new HIV infections continue to multiply, and the epi-demic becomes more entrenched in populations already burdened with other poverty-related problems, populations with no primary health care, no health insurance, often no housing.

Perhaps even more demoralizing than the cumulative effects of these setbacks, we are faced with a new kind of indifference, an indifference that has been called the "normalization of AIDS." If, for the first eight years of the epidemic — the term of Ronald Reagan's presidency — indifference took the form of callously ignoring the crisis, under George Bush, AIDS was "normalized" as just one item on a long list of supposedly intractable social problems. How often do we hear the list recited? — poverty, crime, drugs, homelessness, and AIDS. AIDS is no longer an emergency. It's merely a permanent disaster. One effect of this normalization process is the growing cre-dence granted the claim that AIDS has received a disproportionate amount of federal funding for medical research. This claim over-looks the fact that AIDS is a new disease syndrome, that it primarily threatens the lives of the young, that it is not merely an illness but a bewildering array of illnesses, and, most importantly, that it is an epidemic still out of control. The saddest irony is that, now that our optimism has turned to grim realism, our old rhetoric is appropriated to abet the process of normalization and defunding. Hence our ambivalence at Magic Johnson's powerful example of "living with HIV," since we now know that, particularly among people of color, Johnson's ability to "fight the virus," as he puts it, will be exceptional, and that the sense that AIDS is already manageable will only relax efforts to make it so.

This is a very sketchy background against which new tactics have been embraced by queers. More importantly, it is the background against which AIDS activism is being painfully transformed. The interrelation between the two — queer activism and AIDS activism — is complex, shifting, sometimes divisive. As a means of analyzing the transformations and the divisions, I want to return to Larry Kramer's finger-pointing at Vito Russo's memorial service.

Before coming to Jodie Foster and *The Silence of the Lambs,* a short archaeology of "outing."[6] All queers have extensive experience with the closet, no matter how much of a sissy or tomboy we were as children, no matter how early we declared our sexual preferences, no matter how determined we are to be openly gay or lesbian. The closet is not a function of homosexuality in our culture, but of compulsory and presumptive heterosexuality. I may be publicly identified as gay, but in order for that identity to be acknowledged, I have to declare it on each new occasion. By "occasion," I mean something as simple as asking a cab driver to take me to a bar like the Spike, or kissing my friend Jeff good-bye on a crowded subway when he gets off two stops before me on our way home from the gym. Fearing for my safety, I might choose not to kiss Jeff, thereby hiding behind our fellow riders' presumption that we're straight.[7]

As part of our experience with the closet, which was for most of us the only safe place to be as adolescents, we also know what it's like to keep the closet door firmly shut by pretending not only to be heterosexual but also to be homophobic — since in many circumstances the mark of one's heterosexuality is the open expression of hatred toward queers. Thus most of us have the experience, usually from our youth, of oppressing other queers in order to elude that same oppression. Eve Sedgwick writes in *Epistemology of the Closet* that "it is entirely within the experience of gay people to find that a homophobic figure in power has . . . a disproportionate likelihood of being gay and closeted."[8] I'm not so sure. I don't think there is much likelihood at all that Jesse Helms or Cardinal O'Connor or Patrick Buchanan, for example, are gay and closeted. We do have experience with homophobia dictated by the closet, but that experience is as much of ourselves as of others. And it is often the projection of that experience that makes us suspicious of the homophobic figure in power.

Such suspicions, enhanced by rumors, have sometimes lead us to impugn the heterosexuality of our oppressors. A celebrated case is that of former New York City mayor Ed Koch. A confirmed bachelor, Koch required a former beauty queen for a "beard" to win his first mayoral primary, since the opposition's slogan was "Vote for Cuomo, not the homo." The "homo" won the election, and thereby gained control of the city that would soon have the highest number of AIDS cases of any city in the world. During the time when attention to AIDS implied attention to a gay disease, Koch paid no attention, and many interpreted his need to dissociate himself as a form of self-defense, the defense of his closet. The spectacular conclusion, some years later, was Koch's open admission on a radio talk show of his *hetero*sexuality, which, after many years of insisting that his sexuality was nobody's business, made the front page of *New York Newsday*. For ACT UP's Target City Hall demonstration in March 1989, an affinity group pasted that *Newsday* cover to placards. Its banner headline — "KOCH: I'M HETEROSEXUAL" — answered with "Yeah, and I'm Carmen Miranda." The *Newsday* headline also inspired a tongue-twister chant for the day: "Why's New York AIDS care ineffectual? Ask Ed Koch, the heterosexual." Target City Hall was an outing with a queer sense of humor.

The tendency to suspect a closeted homosexual behind a lack of commitment to fighting AIDS migrated, in the figure of Michelangelo Signorile, from ACT UP to *Outweek*, New York's short-lived gay and lesbian weekly. In charge of ACT UP's media committee during Target City Hall and later *Outweek*'s features editor, Signorile also wrote a column called "Gossip Watch," a queer variation on media watches that restricted its purview to gossip columns. Using the blunt instruments of all-caps, four-letter-word invective and the AIDS crisis as an excuse for righteous indignation, "Gossip Watch" chastised gossip columnists — often themselves closeted

homosexuals — for, among other things, inventing beards for closeted celebrities who had done nothing publicly about the AIDS
crisis.

This circumscribed context of what came to be called outing has
important bearing on the ensuing debate. Signorile appeared initially to want to say something about the privileged position of
gossip in our culture's management of *the* open secret. Outing
is not (at least not at first) the revelation of that secret, but the
revelation that the secret was no secret at all. That was the scandal of *Outweek*'s Malcolm Forbes cover story, for which *Time* and
Newsweek — not *Outweek* — invented the term "outing."[9] The dominant media heaped fear and loathing upon Signorile, *Outweek,* and
queers generally, not because Forbes's homosexuality had been revealed, but because their own complicity in concealing it had been
revealed. Forbes was not "outed," the media's homophobia was.

From the moment "outing" was named, however, the straight media set the terms of debate, and we queers foolishly accepted those
terms by seeking to justify an act of which we had not been guilty.
We resorted then to our two, mutually contradictory excuses: that
our oppressors are disproportionately likely to be gay and closeted
and that we need them as role models. In adopting our paradoxical
defense, we ignored the ways in which both of these positions are
turned against us, especially in the context of AIDS.

AIDS has often resulted in a peculiarly public and unarguable
means of outing. Day after day, as we read the obituary section of
the *New York Times,* we are faced with incontrovertible proof —
in their survival by "long-time companions" (a term invented by
the *Times*) — of the homosexuality of artists, actors, and dancers;
of fashion designers, models, and interior decorators; of doctors,
lawyers, and stockbrokers. The tragic irony is that it has taken AIDS
to prove our Stonewall slogan: "We are everywhere."[10]

But the two most notorious outings by AIDS should give us pause
about the benefits of such revelations. Responses to the deaths of
Rock Hudson and Roy Cohn have a perverse symmetry. Hudson
was locked in Hollywood's 1950s closet, hiding from, among other
things, a McCarthyism that equated commies and queers. Cohn was
the closeted McCarthyite. Hudson personified decency to a majority
of Americans, and his homosexuality was seen as a betrayal. He
became "the hunk who lived a lie."[11] Roy Cohn came belatedly

to represent indecency to most Americans; *his* homosexuality was seen as fidelity to his very being. He was the McCarthyite queer, the evil homosexual who lied about everything.[12] The revelation of the secret — the secret that was, of course, no secret in either case — became in both cases the revelation that homosexuals are liars and traitors. Nothing new about that.

In this scenario, who is the oppressor and who the role model? As I read the homophobic press accounts, Hudson is the oppressor (guilty of oppressing himself and all the innocent fans who believed him) and Cohn the role model (absolutely faithful to the truth of homosexuality in his duplicity and cowardice). Our outing fantasy — that the revelation of homosexuality would have a transformative effect on homophobic discourse — was only a fantasy after all, and a dangerous one at that. As Sedgwick counsels in *Epistemology of the Closet:*

> We have too much cause to know how limited a leverage any individual revelation can exercise over collectively scaled and institutionally embodied oppressions. Acknowledgment of this disproportion does not mean that the consequences of such acts as coming out can be circumscribed within *predetermined* boundaries, as if between "personal" and "political" realms, nor does it require us to deny how disproportionately powerful and disruptive such acts can be. But the brute incommensurability has nonetheless to be acknowledged. In the theatrical display of an *already institutionalized* ignorance no transformative potential is to be looked for.[13]

Signorile's initial impulse was perhaps, then, more productive: not to "out" supposedly closeted gay men and lesbians, but to "out" enforcers of the closet, not to reveal the "secret" of homosexuality, but to reveal the "secret" of homophobia. For it is only the latter that is truly a secret, and a truly *dirty* secret. As for the former, the speculation about the sexuality of celebrities, gossip is a privileged activity for queers, too.

Which brings us to Jodie Foster... and *The Silence of the Lambs.* Larry Kramer, who claimed in his speech that Vito Russo "was the only person who agreed with me unequivocally on everything I said and did," added, after his thank you to Jodie Foster for starring in *Silence:* "Vito would really have screamed about that one." But Vito can speak for himself. In his introduction to *The Celluloid Closet*, entitled "On the Closet Mentality," Vito wrote:

> The public should...be aware of the sexuality of gay actors just as it is aware of the heterosexuality of the majority. I do not believe that such a discussion is nobody's business, nor do I believe that it is one of a sexual and therefore private nature. Discussing such things in a book without the knowledge or consent of the people in question is, alas, immoral and libelous. It is immoral because unless people by their own choice come out of the closet, the announcement is valueless; it is libelous because such information has been known to destroy people's lives. Some of us will change that in time.[14]

The last sentence is characteristic of Vito, of his fighting spirit, his optimism, and his understanding of what needed changing. Among the things we need to change is the fact that calling someone homosexual is, to this day, considered by our legal system to be libelous per se. Malicious intent does *not* have to be proved.

One thing Vito would surely have disagreed with Larry about is whom to blame for his own death. Vito pointed his finger at queers only to tell us how much he loved us and to praise our courage. As for *The Silence of the Lambs,* Vito would have been the best equipped among us to show just how careless Jonathan Demme was in his characterization of serial killer Buffalo Bill, aka Jame Gumb, with his miniature poodle named Precious, his chiffon scarves, his made-up face, his nipple ring, and his murdered boyfriend. Maybe these features don't have to add up to a homophobic stereotype within the complex alignments of sexuality and pathology represented in *The Silence of the Lambs,* but they most certainly do within the history of their deployment by Hollywood, the history Vito Russo wrote.

Up to a point, Demme was careful about his portrayals in *Silence* — of both Clarice Starling and the men around her. Feminist approval of the film derives, I think, not only from the strength and intelligence of Foster's character, Clarice, but also from her independence from an array of alternately annoying or sinister patriarchal figures, although just *how* independent is a matter of contention. But Clarice does reject every attempt to put the make on her; her commitment is to the captured woman. Demme ultimately failed, though, to follow through on his film's antipatriarchal logic. He let patriarchy off the hook by homosexualizing the psychopaths — Buffalo Bill, obviously, but Hannibal Lecter as well, whose disturbing appeal can hardly be divorced from his camp, effete intelligence. What straight man would get off a line like, "Oh, Senator, . . . love your suit!"? Demme's homophobia is thus a matter not only of underwriting the tradition of Hollywood's stereotyping of gay men as psychopathic killers, but also of his displacement of the most horrifying consequences of patriarchy onto men who are far from straight.

In Thomas Harris's novel, Jame Gumb is not homosexual — the boyfriend he murdered was not his, but Hannibal Lecter's patient's. On the contrary, Gumb is explicitly referred to in the book as a fag-basher.[15] He was refused the sex-change operation he applied for at Johns Hopkins not only because he failed the requisite psychological tests, but also because he had a police record for two assaults on gay men. One has to wonder why Demme decided to leave out this information in a film that otherwise follows the novel very precisely. Would the fact that the killer was a homophobe have brought yet another murderous consequence of patriarchy too close to home?

The displacement of patriarchy's most serious consequences can also be seen in the film's illustration of another mode of feminist analysis, one that moves beyond positive-versus-negative images to the enforcement of sexual difference through psychic processes provoked in the spectator by cinematic codes. Laura Mulvey might well have written the climactic scene.[16] Deprived of agency by being the object rather than the subject of vision, Clarice Starling is stalked by the voyeuristic gaze of the spectator, who, unseen in the darkness, just like the serial killer, sees her through infrared glasses worn by Jame Gumb. There is no question where spectatorial identification ought to lie, and how it ought to be gendered: what the killer male's gaze sees is all the camera shows, and the image of the woman is trapped by the cinematic apparatus, represented in the prosthetic device the killer wears. But something unexpected happens. The tension of the scene is broken not by Clarice's gunshots, but by an often-remarked male spectator's shout in the dark: "Shoot the fucking faggot!" Homophobia breaks the power of cinema, "proper" interpellation fails, and only then is Clarice restored to agency.

The film is thus perhaps feminist, though insufficiently, and certainly homophobic, quite sufficiently. Acknowledging these two different positions should not be impossible; although they are interdependent in the film's mapping of them, they do not have to be mutually exclusive in our reading of the film. What makes the debate about *The Silence of the Lambs* troubling, however, is its polarization along gender lines. Women, including lesbians, have tended to defend the film, while gay men usually decry it. And Jodie Foster gets caught in the middle. As B. Ruby Rich, an "out" lesbian, put it in the *Village Voice,* "Male and female desires, fears, and pleasures in the cinema have rarely coincided, so it should come as no surprise that dyke and faggot reactions to this movie are likely to diverge as well."[17] For gay men, Foster lends her prestige to the film's homophobic portrayal; for women, including lesbians, she lends her skill to a feminist one. For gay men, Foster is a closeted oppressor; for lesbians, she's a role model.

The division is a double one, for it entails, on the one hand, the identity of Foster and, on the other, the conception of identity itself. Castigating Foster as oppressor both presumes her (closeted) lesbian identity and presumes that identity precedes and determines political enactment. Praising Foster as role model, by contrast, accepts her feminism as itself constitutive of her identity. Rich insists, "I'm not willing to give up the immense satisfactions of a heroine with whom women can identify. Not willing to reduce all the intricate components of this movie down to the pass/fail score of one character. Please excuse me if my attention is focused not on the killer, but on the women he kills." And her defense concludes, "Guess I'm just a girl." Which is to say that in this debate, Rich's identification, her politics, emphasizes gender identity over sexual identity. As we know from her writing, in debates *within* feminism, Rich is perfectly capable of reversing the emphasis. Rich's identity is not fixed, does not determine her political identifications; rather her political identification momentarily fixes her identity: "Guess I'm just a girl." But where is the lesbian in this picture? Hasn't she again been rendered invisible? And what, if not outing, will make her visible?

Videomaker Jean Carlomusto's video *L Is for the Way You Look* provides one answer. In the central section of the tape, nine women, speaking singly or in groups, tell the story of an evening at the Lower East Side performance space PS 122 when lesbian comedian Reno was performing. What made the occasion worth talking about was that someone special was in the audience. First Zoe tells us that halfway through Reno's performance, Nancy leaned over to say, "Fran Liebowitz is over there"; Zoe adds, "We're both, you know, we both kinda have a thing for Fran." Nancy then says she had more fun watching Fran laughing at Reno than she did laughing at Reno herself, after which Cynthia, sitting with her friend Bea, describes a commotion on the stairway as the audience was leaving. "Finally," Cynthia says, "the crowd parted a little bit and...," cut back to Nancy in midsentence, "...and all I see is this giant hair. It's almost like it could've been hair on a stick passing by, this platinum huge thing on this little black spandex." In case we haven't yet figured out what the commotion is about, Zoe adds another clue: "I turned around, and I saw her breasts, I saw this cleavage, I saw this endowment, and, oh my God, I saw the hair, and it was...Dolly Parton." It turns out that Hilery was there, too, and though Emily, Polly, and Gerri weren't, the news has traveled, and, after joking around about it, they decide to say they *were* there, and that Dolly had a crew cut like Nancy's, and that she was making out with Fran.

This sequence of *L Is for the Way You Look* (which was initially titled *The Invisible Woman*) is, as Carlomusto told me, not really about Dolly Parton; it's about gossip. Dolly Parton may be the subject of the gossip, but the subjectivity represented in the video is that of the lesbians who gossip among themselves about Dolly. What matters is *their* visibility. Dolly is the absence around which a representation of lesbianism is constituted. But this is no simple structuralist lesson about representation founded on absence; rather it is meant to tell us something about the identifications we make and the communities we form through these identifications.

I don't mean to suggest that the focus of gossip on Dolly Parton doesn't matter at all. Of course it matters that Dolly's lesbianism has long been rumored and that her attendance at a lesbian perform-ance in the company of another well-known closeted lesbian seems to confirm the rumors. But the emphasis on signifiers of Dolly's feminine masquerade — huge hair, huge cleavage, tiny spandex miniskirt — by a group of women whose masquerade differs so significantly from hers implicates their identifications and their de-sire in difference. None of the lesbians visible in *L Is for the Way You Look* looks femme like Dolly; compared with her absent image, they are in fact a pretty butch bunch.

Identification is, of course, identification with an other, which means that identity is never identical to itself. This alienation of identity from the self it constructs, which is a constant replay of a primary psychic self-alienation, does not mean simply that any proclamation of identity will be only partial, that it will be exceeded by other *aspects* of identity, but rather that identity is always a relation, never simply a positivity. As Teresa de Lauretis put it so concisely in her essay on lesbian spectatorship in Sheila McLaughlin's *She Must Be Seeing Things*, "It takes two women, not one, to make a lesbian."[18] And if identity is relational, then perhaps we can begin to rethink identity politics as a politics of relational identities, of identities formed through political identifications that constantly remake those identities. As Zoe says in *L Is for the Way You Look*, "We decided to milk this for all it was worth, in terms of a female bonding experience."

Again in *Epistemology of the Closet*, Sedgwick writes:

> I take the precious, devalued arts of gossip, immemorially associated in European thought with servants, with effeminate and gay men, with all women, to have to do not even so much with the transmission of necessary news as with the refinement of necessary skills for making, testing, and using unrationalized and provisional hypotheses about what *kinds of people* there are to be found in one's world. . . . I don't assume that all gay men or all women are very skilled at the nonce-taxonomic work represented by gossip, but it does make sense to suppose that our distinctive needs are peculiarly disserved by its devaluation.[19]

The most fundamental need gossip has served for queers is that of the construction — and reconstruction — of our identities. Most of us can remember the first time we heard someone called a queer or a fag or a dyke, and — that someone *not* being ourselves — nevertheless responding, within, "So that's what I am." Because the name-calling is most often a derogation, our identifications are also self-derogations. We painstakingly emerge from these self-derogations through new identifications, a process that often depends on gossip among ourselves: "Really, *he's* gay? *She's* a dyke? Jodie's a dyke? Then maybe I'm fabulous, too." From this, we go on to deduce the role-model defense. "If little tomboys growing up today knew about Jodie, they'd be spared the self-derogation." But the deduction misses two crucial points: first, what Sedgwick means by "an already institutionalized ignorance," and second, our conception of identity.

Little tomboys won't be told about an openly lesbian actress, whose career will in any case probably be cut short the moment she comes out. As Vito Russo famously quipped about coming out, "The truth will set you free . . . but first it will make you miserable." The eradication of the homophobia that constructs the celebrity's closet does not depend on the individual celebrity's avowal, the limitations of which we have seen again and again: Did the exemplary midshipman's confession of his homosexuality change the rules at Annapolis or the Pentagon? Did the Olympic medal winner's founding of the Gay Olympics persuade the U.S. Olympics committee or the Supreme Court to let us use that rubric? No, the eradication of homophobia — of this already institutionalized ignorance — depends on our collective political struggle, on our identity politics.

Identity politics has most often been understood, and is now denigrated, as essentialist (denigrated in certain quarters, in fact, as *essentially* essentialist; this is what Diana Fuss recognizes as the essentialism of antiessentialism).[20] We were gay, and upon our gayness, we built a political movement. But is this really what happened? Wasn't it an emerging political movement that enabled the enunciation of a gay — rather than homosexual or homophile — identity? And wasn't that political movement formed through identifications with other political movements — Black Power and feminism, most particularly? Remember, the Gay Liberation Front, named in identification with third-world liberation struggles, came apart over two issues: whether to support the Black Panthers and whether women would have an equal voice. It was our inability to form alliances with those movements identifications with which secured our own identities, as well as our inability to acknowledge those very same differences of race and gender within our own ranks, that caused the gay and lesbian movements to shift, on the one hand, to an essentialist separatism and, on the other, to a liberal politics of minority rights. The AIDS crisis brought us face-to-face with the consequences of both our separatism and our liberalism. And it is in this new political conjuncture that the word "queer" has been reclaimed to designate new political identities.

The setbacks for the AIDS activist movement that I mentioned above avoided one of the most difficult of them: troubles within the movement itself. Our political unity has been badly shaken by our constantly increasing knowledge of both the breadth and depth of the crisis — breadth, in the sense of the many different kinds of people affected by HIV disease; depth, in the sense of the extent of social change that will be required to improve all these different people's chances of survival. It is impossible here to describe fully either the scope of the crisis or the factionalism it has caused. But consider just this: whereas at first the structure of ACT UP in New York consisted of six committees — Actions, Coordinating, Fundraising, Issues, Media, and Outreach — by 1991, when our internal difficulties emerged most damagingly, we had fourteen committees, twenty-one working groups, and ten caucuses: forty-five different subgroups in all. Apart from a few remaining committees that are still essentially organizational and several working groups centered on actions-in-progress, these various committees, working groups, and caucuses are mostly oriented either toward specific issues (Addicts' Rights, Alternative and Holistic Treatment, Insurance and Access, Health-care Action, Medicaid Task Force, Needle Exchange, Pediatric Caucus, Police Violence, Prison Issues, PWA Housing, Treatment and Data, YELL [Youth Education Life Line]) or toward identities (Asian and Pacific Islanders, Black AIDS Mobilization, Foreign Nationals, Latina/o AIDS Activists, Lesbian Caucus, PISD [People with Immune System Disorders], and Women's Action). This level of specialization does not, in and of itself, necessarily result in factionalism; it merely suggests something of the complexity of issues raised by the epidemic and of the make-up of the AIDS activist movement. But conflict does exist, and much of it concerns competing identities and contradictory identifications *across* identities. There are conflicts between men and women, between lesbians and straight women, between white people and people of color, between those who are HIV-positive or have AIDS and those who are HIV-negative. There are also conflicts between those who think we should devote all our energies to militant direct action and those who favor meeting with government officials and pharmaceutical company executives as well; between those who want to concentrate on a narrowly defined AIDS agenda and those who feel we must confront the wider systemic ills that AIDS exacerbates; between those who see ACT UP as the vanguard in the struggle against AIDS and those who see direct action as only one of many forms of AIDS activism, which also includes advocacy, fundraising, legal action, and providing services. Negotiating these conflicts is painful and perilous; it has even resulted in splits or dissolutions of ACT UP chapters in some cities. These conflicts are not new to ACT UP, but their intensity is. Earlier in our history, they were mitigated by a queer hegemony. Most of us were gay and lesbian, and ACT UP meant for us not only fighting AIDS, but fighting AIDS as queers, fighting homophobia, and rejuvenating a moribund queer activism. In New York, we met at the Lesbian and Gay Community Services Center; you had to confront your homophobia just to cross the threshold. Our meetings and actions, our fact sheets and chants, our T-shirts and placards, our videos and even our acronyms — everything about us was queer. We camped a lot, laughed a lot, kissed each other, partied together. ACT UP fundraisers at nightclubs were the hot ticket in queer social life.

But that hegemony didn't last. Attacks on queers escalated, both officially, with the congressional assault on government support of our culture, and unofficially, on the streets. As queers became more and more visible, more and more of us were getting bashed. Overburdened by the battles AIDS required us to take on, ACT UP couldn't fight the homophobia anymore. That, too, was a full-time struggle, a struggle taken on by the newly formed Queer Nation. I don't want to oversimplify this capsule history. Queer Nation didn't take either the queers or the queerness out of ACT UP. But it made possible, at least symbolically, a shift of our attention to the nonqueer, or the more-than-queer, problems of AIDS.

It was then that new political identifications began to be made, as I said, across identities. I have already mentioned a number of identities-in-conflict in ACT UP: men and women, whites and people of color, and so forth. In spite of the linguistic necessity of specifying identities with positive terms, I want to make clear that I am not speaking of identity as nonrelational. Because of the complexities of the movement, there is no predicting what identifications will be made and which side of an argument anyone might take. A white, middle-class, HIV-negative lesbian might form an identification with a poor, black mother with AIDS, and through that identification might be inclined to work on pediatric health-care issues; or, outraged by attention to the needs of babies at the expense of the needs of the women who bear them, she might decide to fight against clinical trials whose sole purpose is to examine the effects of an antiviral drug on perinatal transmission and thus ignores effects on the mother's body. She might form an identification with a gay male friend with AIDS and work for faster testing of new treatments for opportunistic infections, but then, through her understanding that her friend would be able to afford such treatments while others would not, she might shift her attention to health-care access issues. An HIV-positive, gay Latino might fight homophobia in the Latin community and racism in ACT UP; he might speak Spanish at Latina/o AIDS Activist meetings and English everywhere else.

Political identifications remaking identities are, of course, productive of collective political struggle, but only if they result in a broadening of alliances rather than an exacerbation of antagonisms. And the latter seems often to result when, from within a development toward a politics of alliance based on relational identities, old antagonisms based on fixed identities reemerge. Activist politics then faces the impasse of ranking oppressions, moralism, and self-righteousness. This is the current plight of AIDS activism, but it is not the whole story.

During the very time that ACT UP's internal antagonisms began to tear us apart, we won a crucial victory. Arrested for taking to the streets of New York to distribute — openly and illegally — clean IV needles to injecting drug users, a group of ACT UP queers stood trial, eloquently argued a necessity defense, and won a landmark ruling that called into question the state's laws against possession of hypodermic needles and eventually forced Mayor Dinkins to relent on his opposition to needle exchange. AIDS activists are still — I'm sorry and angry to have to say — mostly a bunch of queers. But what does *queer* mean now? Who, for example, were those queers in the courtroom, on trial for attempting to save the lives of drug addicts? They were perhaps queers whose sexual practices resulted in HIV infection, or placed them at high risk of infection, or made them members of gay communities devastated by the epidemic, and for any of these reasons brought them to AIDS activism. But once engaged in the struggle to end the crisis, these queers' identities were no longer the same. It's not that "queer" doesn't any longer encompass their sexual practices; it does, but it also entails a *re-*

lation between those practices and other circumstances that make very different people vulnerable both to HIV infection and to the stigma, discrimination, and neglect that have characterized the societal and governmental response to the constituencies most affected by the AIDS epidemic.

ABSOLUTELY QUEER: that was the anonymous group OUTpost's headline claim about Jodie Foster on the poster that appeared around New York about the time *The Silence of the Lambs* was released. "Jodie Foster," the caption beneath her photograph read, "Oscar winner. Yale graduate. Ex-Disney Moppet. Dyke." Well yes, . . . but queer? Absolutely queer? Through what identification? Interviewed about queer protests at the 1992 Academy Awards ceremony, where she won her second best-actress Oscar for her performance in *The Silence of the Lambs,* Foster declared, "Protesting is constitutional. You can learn from it. Anything beyond that falls into the category of being undignified."[21] Confronted with such a statement, I'm forced to agree with Larry Kramer: "Vito would really have screamed about that one." For Vito's was a feistier kind of dignity, not Jodie's idea of dignity but Judy's, a survivor's dignity. If we really want to honor Vito's memory — as a film scholar and movie buff, as a queer, an activist, and a friend — we shouldn't forget that he loved Judy, and that his identification with her made *him* queer, not her.

NOTES

1. Arnie Kantrowitz, "Milestones: Vito Russo," *Outweek* 73, 21 November 1990, 37.

2. Several months later, however, Dinkins took a courageous stand against antigay and antilesbian prejudice by marching with the Irish Gay and Lesbian Organization (IGLO) in New York's St. Patrick's Day parade. He did this in order to broker a compromise between IGLO and the Ancient Order of Hibernians, the parade organizers who had refused IGLO's application to participate. The result was that Dinkins was subjected to torrents of abuse from the crowd and a cold shoulder from Cardinal O'Connor, which led the mayor to compare his experience to civil rights marches in the South in the 1960s. See Duncan Osborne, "The Cardinal, the Mayor and the Balance of Power," *Outweek* 92, 3 April 1990, 30–37.

3. Larry Kramer, "Who Killed Vito Russo?" *Outweek* 86, 20 February 1990, 26.

4. See Douglas Crimp, with Adam Rolston, *AIDS Demo Graphics* (Seattle: Bay Press, 1990), 53–69.

5. Quoted in *The New York Times,* 27 September 1991, sec. A, p. 12.

6. For a detailed account of outing, including historical background and analysis of the contemporary debates as well as an appendix of essential articles from

the media, see Larry Gross, *The Contested Closet: The Politics and Ethics of Outing* (Minneapolis: University of Minnesota Press, 1993).

7. It's not that Jeff and I are so butch as to be unreadable as gay; indeed many people might presume that we *are* gay, but our not behaving "overtly" allows them to act precisely as if the operative presumption is that everyone is straight unless openly declaring themselves not to be.

8. Eve Kosofsky Sedgwick, *Epistemology of the Closet* (Berkeley and Los Angeles: University of California Press, 1990), 81.

9. William Henry III, "Forcing Gays Out of the Closet," *Time,* 29 January 1990, 67; David Gelman, " 'Outing': An Unexpected Assault on Sexual Privacy," *Newsweek,* 30 April 1990, 66. See also Michelangelo Signorile, *Queer in America* (New York: Random House, 1993).

10. This was not always the case. It took intense pressure from queers and AIDS activists to force the *Times* to list surviving lovers of gay men. Even now, the *Times* only mentions a "companion" in the course of an obituary story, not as one of the survivors, who are still limited to blood relatives and legal spouses.

11. See Richard Meyer, "Rock Hudson's Body," in Diana Fuss, ed., *Inside/Out: Lesbian Theories, Gay Theories* (New York and London: Routledge, 1991), 259–88.

12. See, for example, Robert Sherrill, "King Cohn," *The Nation,* 21 May 1988, 719–25. Beginning with the sentence, "Cohn was a particularly nasty homosexual," Sherrill recounts stories of Cohn's extreme promiscuity and his supposed relations with other duplicitous right-wing homosexuals, then ends his account with the following paragraph: "Typically disloyal, Cohn gave no support to homosexuals who were trying to win public acceptance. He called them 'fags,' did all he could to make their lives miserable, lectured against them, berated politicians for any display of tolerance toward homosexuals and urged laws to restrict their freedom. To his death he denied that he was homosexual, but the Dorian Gray scene of his dying of AIDS said it all: 'Roy . . . lay in bed, unheeding, his flesh cracking open, sores on his body, his faculties waning' and with a one-inch 'slit-like wound above [his] anus.' " The final quotations, indicative for Sherrill not of disease but of homosexuality (or perhaps the two are not to be differentiated), are uncredited, but are taken from one of the two books under review in the article, *Citizen Cohn* by Nicholas von Hoffman.

13. Sedgwick, *Epistemology,* 78.

14. Vito Russo, *The Celluloid Closet: Homosexuality in the Movies* (New York: Harper & Row, 1987), xi.

15. In the novel, Dr. Danielson of Johns Hopkins reports to Jack Crawford: "The Harrisburg police were after [Gumb] for two assaults on homosexual men. The last one nearly died" (Thomas Harris, *The Silence of the Lambs* [New York: St. Martin's, 1989], 312). And Crawford reports to Clarice Starling about Gumb: "He's a fag-basher" (322). This is not to say that Harris's portrayal of Gumb is free of homophobic stereotyping. Most of the details of Gumb's characterization in the film are taken directly from the novel. Demme added one (the nipple ring) and omitted one (Gumb's obsession with his mother). But it is important to add that stereotyping functions differently in the two media and that their respective histories of homophobic portrayals differ even more significantly.

16. I have in mind, of course, Mulvey's classic and often-reprinted essay "Visual Pleasure and Narrative Cinema" (1975), now in her collected essays, *Visual and Other Pleasures* (Bloomington and Indianapolis: Indiana University Press, 1989), 14–26.

17. B. Ruby Rich, contribution to "Writers on the *Lamb:* Sorting Out the Sexual Politics of a Controversial Film," *Village Voice,* 5 March 1991, 59. This series of short pieces on the film was partially in response to questions raised about the film's homophobic stereotyping and the threat of "outing" Jodie Foster by Michelangelo Signorile in *Outweek.*

18. Teresa de Lauretis, "Film and the Visible," in Bad Object Choices, ed., *How Do I Look? Queer Film and Video* (Seattle: Bay Press, 1991), 232.

19. Sedgwick, *Epistemology,* 23.

20. See Diana Fuss, *Essentially Speaking: Feminism, Nature, and Difference* (New York: Routledge, 1989).

21. See John Gallagher, "Protest Threats Raise Visibility at Academy Awards," *The Advocate,* 5 May 1992, 15. In this same issue of *The Advocate,* the "etcetera" column contains a photo of Jodie Foster whose caption reads, "A first-rate actress with a third-rate consciousness we hope is straight" (88).

Contributors

Lauren Berlant teaches English at the University of Chicago. She is the author of *The Anatomy of National Fantasy: Hawthorne, Utopia, and Everyday Life* (Chicago, 1991), and several essays on gender, sexuality, race, capitalism, and the public sphere during the nineteenth and twentieth centuries in the United States. This essay will be a chapter in the forthcoming *The Queen of America Goes to Washington City.*

Douglas Crimp is Visiting Professor of Visual and Cultural Studies at the University of Rochester and also teaches lesbian and gay studies at Sarah Lawrence College. He is the author of *On the Museum's Ruins* and *AIDS Demo Graphics* (with Adam Rolston), and the editor of *AIDS: Cultural Analysis/Cultural Activism.*

Elizabeth Freeman is a graduate student in English literature and queer/feminist theory at the University of Chicago. She is also a member of Chicago's Coalition for Positive Sexuality, an activist group dedicated to guerrilla safe sex education in the public schools.

Diana Fuss is assistant professor of English at Princeton University. She is the author of *Essentially Speaking: Feminism, Nature and Difference* (Routledge, 1989) and editor of *Inside/Out: Lesbian Theories, Gay Theories* (Routledge, 1991).

Henry Louis Gates, Jr., teaches English at Harvard University, where he is W. E. B. Du Bois Professor of the humanities, chairman of the Afro-American studies department, and head of the Du Bois Institute.

Jonathan Goldberg is the Sir William Osler Professor of English Literature at The Johns Hopkins University. His most recent book is *Sodometries: Renaissance Texts, Modern Sexualities*, and he is editor of *Queering the Renaissance* and *The Sodomy Reader.*

Cathy Griggers is assistant professor in the department of English's Literary and Cultural Theory Program at Carnegie Mellon University, where she teaches feminist cultural studies, gender studies, and media theory. She has published articles on the cinema, popular culture, film theory, and gay and lesbian studies in journals such as *Differences, Semiotica,* and *Postmodern Culture* and in anthologies such as *Theory Goes to the Movies* and *The Lesbian Postmodern.* She is coproducer of two pedagogical videos, *Discourse/ Intercourse* and *Hirohito's Funeral.*

Janet E. Halley is associate professor of law at Stanford Law School. She is hard at work on sodomy, particularly as it has been represented by the Supreme Court in *Hardwick v. Bowers,* and this year will publish essays on that topic in Jonathan Goldberg's volume *Queering the Renaissance* (Duke University Press, 1993) and in the *Virginia Law Review.* She is on the editorial advisory board of *GLO: A Quarterly of Gay and Lesbian Studies.*

Phillip Brian Harper is assistant professor of English and of Afro-American studies at Harvard University. He is the author of *Framing the Margins: The Social Logic of Postmodern Culture* (Oxford, 1993). His essay in this volume is part of a book in progress titled *The Same Difference: Social Division in African-American Culture.*

Andrew Parker is associate professor of English and women's and gender studies at Amherst College. He is, most recently, coeditor of *Nationalisms and Sexualities* (Routledge, 1992).

Cindy Patton is assistant professor of rhetoric and communication at Temple University in Philadelphia. A long-time activist and critic, she is author of several books on AIDS and representation, including *Inventing AIDS* (1990) and forthcoming volumes on sex and representation and on gender and the HIV pandemic.

Eve Kosofsky Sedgwick is the Newman Ivey White Professor of English at Duke University. Her books include *Between Men: English Literature and Male Homosocial Desire; Epistemology of the Closet;* and *Tendencies.*

Robert Schwartzwald is associate professor of French at the University of Massachusetts at Amherst and Director of the Canadian Studies program of the Five Colleges consortium. He has published numerous articles and essays on Québec literature and culture, with recent emphasis on the figuration of homosexuality in nationalist discourse. He is the editor of *an/other Canada,* a special issue of *The Massachusetts Review* (1990), and coeditor of *Fictions de L'Identitaire au Québec* (1991).

Steven Seidman is the author of *Romantic Longings: Love in America, 1830–1980* and *Embattled Eros: Sexual Ethics and Politics in Contemporary America.* He coedits Cultural Social Studies, a series for Cambridge University Press.

Michael Warner teaches English at Rutgers University. He is the author of *The Letters of the Republic: Publication and the Public Sphere in Eighteenth-Century America* (Harvard, 1990), and, editor, with Gerald Graff, of *The Origins of Literary Studies in America* (Routledge, 1988).

Index

334   Index